THE SPANISH INSTITUTE, INC.

684 Park Avenue, New York, New York 10021
Telephone: (212) 628-0420

You are cordially invited to attend

a talk in English by

BRIAN JEFFERY

"FERNANDO SOR, SPAIN'S GREATEST CLASSICAL COMPOSER"

Friday, October 20, 1978
at 8:00 P.M.
684 Park Avenue (at 68th Street)

Brian Jeffery took his degrees in musicology and French at Oxford and has taught at St. Andrew's University in Scotland and the University of California at Berkeley. He has specialized in studies on plucked instruments and their literature, and has edited a five-volume series of facsimiles of Sor's complete guitar works. Recently he published **Fernando Sor: Composer and Guitarist** (Miami Beach: Tecla Ediciones, 1977), commemorating the Spanish musician's bicentenary.

. . . .

Please fill in below if you plan to attend.

. . . . will attend the talk by
Brian Jeffery on Friday,
October 20, 1978 at 8:00 P.M.

FERNANDO SOR, COMPOSER AND GUITARIST
by Brian Jeffery

This book provides more information about Sor than has ever been available before. This major Romantic figure in the history of the classic guitar was born in Spain, fought in the Napoleonic Wars, then travelled throughout Europe. The book is the result of extensive research on Sor and contains many new facts and documents as well as a discussion of all of Sor's music: his songs, ballet music, piano music, and of course, the guitar compositions for which he is famous. The book includes illustrations, musical examples, and a complete catalogue of all of Sor's works.

"No music library, public or private, could be complete without it . . . It sets a new standard of scholarship by which similar books of the future are sure to be ultimately judged" (Richard Pinnell in *Soundboard*).

Cloth $16.95 / TE051.   Paper $10.95 / TE052.

FREE CATALOGUE AVAILABLE

UPON REQUEST

FERNANDO SOR: COMPLETE WORKS FOR GUITAR
Editor: Brian Jeffery

First modern edition, commemorating the bicentennial of the composer's birth.

A complete facsimile of all the known works for guitar of the most celebrated composer for the instrument. This edition includes all of his well-known studies, sonatas, etc., as well as many fine and hitherto unpublished pieces. No changes have been made, so that all fingering, phrasing, etc., are those of the original editions and may be assumed to be Sor's own.

The set of five volumes: $50.00 / CGF11.

Volume I: guitar solos, op. nos. 1-15 and works without opus number. $10.95 / CGF04.

Volume II: guitar solos, op. nos. 16-30. $10.95 / CGF05.

Volume III: guitar solos, op. nos. 31-45. $10.95 / CGF06.

Volume IV: guitar solos, op. nos. 46-60. $10.95 / CGF07.

Volume V: guitar duets. $11.95 / CGF08.

SEPARATELY PRINTED EXCERPTS FROM THE ABOVE:

The Complete Studies for guitar, $7.95 / CGF10.

Variations on a Theme of Mozart, op. 9, $3.50 / CGF09.

The Bold Strummer
156 Fifth Avenue
Suite 733
New York, N.Y. 10010
Telephone:
(212) 242-6780

"BRIAN JEFFERY PRESENTS FERNANDO SOR"

A long-playing record, being a spoken presentation with musical examples. $5.95 / MM122.

POSTER

This poster (17" x 22") reproduces the well-known lithograph of Sor by Bordes of Paris. $1.95 / G120.

FERNANDO SOR: SEGUIDILLAS
Edited by Brian Jeffery

Twelve Spanish songs for voice and guitar or piano. This is the first modern edition of these newly discovered and beautiful songs, which were called "veritable jewels" by those who heard them. Complete edition, with introduction, notes, facsimiles, and English translation of the Spanish texts. 64pp. Cloth $11.95 / TE001. Paper $6.95 / TE002.

A selection of six of the songs is available as **Six Seguidillas Boleras.** For voice and guitar only. No introduction or notes. 16pp. $3.50 / TE003.

FERNANDO SOR: "O CRUX, AVE SPES UNICA"

The composer's only known sacred piece, for unaccompanied four-part chorus. A deeply felt and impassioned composition in honour of the Holy Cross.
$1.25 / TE124.

FERNANDO SOR
INTRODUCTORY OFFER

For a limited time only, we are offering a package at a special introductory price.

Brian Jeffery's book **Fernando Sor, Composer and Guitarist.** The new and unique biography.

PLUS Sor's **Complete Studies** for guitar. A standard work for students of the instrument.

PLUS Sor's **Variations on a Theme of Mozart,** op. 9. His most famous work, in a facsimile of the first edition.

. . . All packaged in an elegant double-sided white box. **$17.95 / CGF12**

The above package is available for a limited time only, and orders for it can be accepted only on this form.

ORDER FORM

Return this order form to

The Bold Strummer

156 FIFTH AVENUE, SUITE 733
NEW YORK, NEW YORK 10010

Please send me the items checked above in the quantity indicated. My check is enclosed.

NAME _____

STREET _____

CITY / STATE _____ ZIP_____

_____

please add 15% of the total amount shipping and handling.

N.Y.Res. please add tax

FERNANDO SOR
COMPOSER AND GUITARIST

For Eugene Bergmann

with all good wishes

Brian Jeffery

New York, 20 October 1978

FERNANDO SOR
COMPOSER AND GUITARIST

BRIAN JEFFERY

TECLA EDITIONS, PREACHERS' COURT, CHARTERHOUSE, LONDON EC1M 6AS, ENGLAND

Printed in the U.S.A. by Hansen Publications, Inc., Miami Beach

Distributed in the U.S.A. by Charles Hansen, Inc., Educational Sheet Music & Books
1860 Broadway, New York, N.Y. 10023

Typography by Jim Fragos
Graphics by Jim Shaffer

TE051 (Cloth)
TE052 (Paper)

ISBN: 0 9502241 4 6 (Cloth)
ISBN: 0 9502241 5 4 (Paper)

Contents

Illustrations

My warm thanks are due to the Anglo-Spanish Cultural Foundation for a Vicente Cañada Blanch Senior Research Fellowship at the University of London which enabled me to carry out research on Sor.

Also to the staff of very many libraries who have been most helpful, but especially at the Instituto Municipal de Historia de la Ciudad in Barcelona; the Staatsbibliothek Preussischer Kulturbesitz in Berlin; the Royal Library in Copenhagen; and the Monastery of Montserrat.

Also to many friends, colleagues and collectors, for their suggestions and assistance, especially Roger Boase; Vladimir Bobri; Maria Condeminas; Federico Cook; Ivor Guest; Thomas F. Heck; Martha Nelson; Ingolf Olsen; Ana Maria Pecanins; Professor Józef Powrózniak; Maestro Emilio Pujol; Hans Radke; John Roberts; Manuel Rocamora; Robert Spencer; José Subirá; Stefan Themerson; J. Edward Thomas; Mme André Verdier; and John and Anne Willett.

For permission to reproduce material, I am grateful to the Instituto Municipal de Historia de la Ciudad, Barcelona; *Guitar Review;* the British Library, London; the Guildhall School of Music and Drama, London; the Victoria and Albert Museum, London; the Bodleian Library, Oxford; the Bibliothèque Nationale, Paris; Robert Spencer; and Mary Belle Swingle.

CHAPTER 1

SPAIN
1778-1813

Fernando Sor spent the first thirty-five years of his life in Spain. In that country he received his musical education, established a career and a reputation, and composed many works. It was a significant period in his life for its length, for his musical formation, and for his material and artistic achievement.

From this period, we have an opera, a cantata, a motet, Spanish patriotic songs, and pieces for solo guitar, as well as a number of Spanish seguidillas for voice and guitar or piano which have only recently come to light. The symphonies and string quartets which we know he composed at this time have unfortunately disappeared. Those works which survive show a man who was well aware of the Spanish native tradition and contributed to it above all in his seguidillas, but who also looked outwards, to Italian opera, to Mozart and to Haydn. They are confident and talented works, and they show a character of their own when compared with Sor's later music composed outside Spain. The early guitar pieces have vigour, the later ones delicacy; the early seguidillas clearly stand within a living tradition, while the later boleros show the disintegration of exile. I shall return later to the music which Sor composed in Spain; first, however, some biographical facts.

Baptism and family

Sor was baptized in Barcelona Cathedral on 14 February 1778, the son of a bourgeois Catalan family of some education, prosperity and musicality. Many years later, he himself said that he was born on 17 February 1780, but it has been possible to establish that 1778 is indeed the true date. The reasons for the mis-statement remain obscure, but may have had something to do with claiming a war pension in Paris in the latter part of his life, or something of this nature.[1]

The record of his baptism may be found in the baptism registers of Barcelona Cathedral. It was discovered by Baltasar Saldoni, who pointed it out, together with the discrepancy, in his *Diccionario de Efemérides de Músicos Españoles,* I (Madrid, 1868), pp. 261-2. I had thought that the entry might perhaps refer to some other person of the name of Sors, but this is not so. For the baptism registers of Barcelona Cathedral also contain an entry recording the baptism on 5 August 1785 of 'Carlos Maria Caetano Ignaci Sors', son of the same parents and godson of Caetano Gispert, director of the Barcelona Opera. We know that the composer had a younger brother named Carlos; we know, too, that Gispert was later a friend of the composer. It would be too much of a coincidence to suppose that there were in Barcelona at the same period two sets of brothers called Fernando and Carlos Sors and that Gispert was a friend of both sets. It seems, therefore, that Sor's own statement must be dismissed and that his true baptism date was 14 February 1778.

He was baptized with the names 'Joseph Fernando Macari Sors': Joseph probably for his grandmother and godmother Josepha Bargibant, and Fernando probably for the kings of Spain. His date of birth, as opposed to baptism, is unknown. His brother Carlos appears to have been born and baptized on the same day, and so this may well also have been the case with the composer.[2]

Here are the entries for the composer and his brother in the baptism registers of Barcelona Cathedral:

> Als catorze de dit mes, y any [February 1778], en la mateixa Iglesia [Barcelona Cathedral]. Per mi lo sobredit Domer. Fonch batejat Joseph, Fernando, Macari fill llegitim, y natural de Joan Sors Comerciant, y de Isabel Sors y Montadas Conjuges. Fou Padrina Josepha Sors Viuda del Dr. Joan Sors tots en Barcelona habitants.

> (*Baptismes de 1776 a 1780,* f. 111)

---

[1] Sor's statement is found in the article 'Sor' in the *Encyclopédie Pittoresque de la Musique* of A. Ledhuy and H. Bertini (Paris, 1835), an article which, as we shall see, Sor almost certainly wrote himself. It is even possible that the composer himself did not know the exact date, or did not consider it important. A century later, this was the case, for example, with Villa-Lobos: see Lisa Peppercorn, 'History of Villa-Lobos' Birthday Date', *Monthly Musical Record,* July-August 1948, pp. 153-6.

[2] 5 August 1785 is the date of birth given for Carlos Sors in the records of the French Army (communication from General Marsauche, Château de Vincennes, 1974). And it is also the date of baptism given in the baptism registers of Barcelona Cathedral. On Carlos Sors, see chapters 2 and 5 below.

('On the fourteenth of the said month and year [February 1778], in the same church [Barcelona Cathedral], by me the said priest, was baptized Joseph Fernando Macari, legitimate and natural son of Joan Sors merchant and of Isabel Sors y Montadas his wife. The godmother was Josepha Sors, widow of Dr. Joan Sors. All living in Barcelona.')

Dit die mes y any [5 August 1785] en dita Iglesia [Barcelona Cathedral] ab llicencia del sobradit Domer per mi Joseph Forn prebere fonch Batejat Carlos Maria Caetano Ignaci fill llegitim y natural de Dn. Joan Sors oficial de la superintendencia de Camins y de Isabel Sors y Muntadas Conjuges. Fou padri Dn. Caetano Gispert Regidor perpetuo de Barcelona tots habitans en Barcelona.

(Baptismes de 1783 a 1786, f. 165)

('On the said day, month and year [5 August 1785] in the said church [Barcelona Cathedral], by license from the said priest, was baptized Carlos Maria Caetano Ignaci, legitimate and natural son of Joan Sors, official in the administration of roads, and of Isabel Sors y Muntadas his wife. The godfather was Caetano Gispert, administrator in perpetuity in Barcelona. All living in Barcelona.')

And from the register of marriage licences of the Cathedral, here is the marriage licence of his parents:

[18 October 1776] Joan Sor Escrivent en el Monte de Piedad fill del Dr en Medicina Joan Baptista y Josepha Bargibant conjuges ab Isabel Muntada Donzella filla del Dr en Drets Cadalt, i Isabel conjuges Parroquia del Pi 12 sueldos.

(Libre de Licencias de Esposalles 1776-78, f. 41 verso)

('[18 October 1776] Joan Sor, clerk in the Monte de Piedad, son of Joan Baptista Sor, Doctor of Medicine, and of Josepha Bargibant his wife; with Isabel Muntada, spinster, daughter of Cadalt Muntada, Doctor of Laws, and of Isabel his wife. Parish of Santa María del Pino. 12 sueldos.')

The marriage probably took place in the bride's parish church, Santa María del Pino, Barcelona.

From these three entries, the composer's family tree can be deduced as follows:

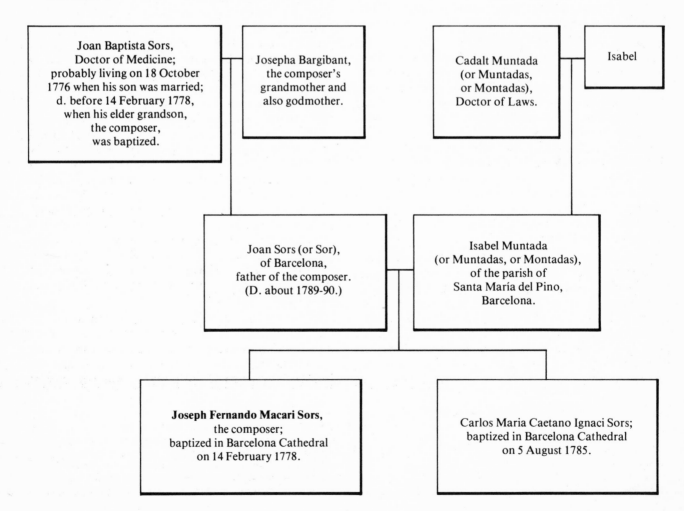

The composer's father, Joan Sors, appears in the registers in 1776 as 'Escrivent en el Monte de Piedad' (clerk in the municipal pawn establishment); in 1778 he is 'Comerciant' (merchant), and in 1785 'Oficial de la superintendencia de Camins' (official in the administration of roads). For his marriage licence he paid a fee on a sliding scale, at a point corresponding to 'Tots los Artistes Joves', a term indicating that he was young at that time. From the article in Ledhuy's *Encyclopédie* we know quite a lot about him: that he was a man of some musical accomplishment himself, who sang, played the guitar, and — though somewhat reluctantly — allowed the musical education of his son, and that he died in about 1789-90.

Forms of the name 'Fernando Sor'

The composer was baptized 'Fernando', like the kings of Spain both past and future. Later in England and in France he used the form 'Ferdinand': this is the form that appears, for example, on the title-page of his *Méthode pour la Guitare* in 1830 and in a letter to the Queen of France in 1839. 'Ferdinando' is a rare variant of 'Fernando'. 'Ferran' is a Catalan form without any contemporary documentary authority.

The family name appears in the official records just quoted six times as 'Sors' and once as 'Sor'. There is no doubt that 'Sors' was and is the more common Catalan form. Even today, numbers of people with this form of the name may be found listed in the Barcelona telephone directory. In Spain outside Catalonia it seems that the forms 'Sors' and 'Sor' were used indifferently: thus, for example, in the MSS London, British Library, Egerton 3288 and 3289, which originate from Spain and contain seguidillas by the composer, the name appears sometimes as 'Sors' and sometimes as 'Sor'. Outside Spain the composer himself used only the form 'Sor' and signed himself thus.

So we have a choice between 'Fernando' (Catalonia, and Spain outside Catalonia) and 'Ferdinand' (the rest of Europe); and between 'Sors' (Catalonia and sometimes the rest of Spain) and 'Sor' (sometimes in Spain, and in the rest of Europe). In fact, it seems that the orthography was no more important to the composer than it was to Shakespeare; and accordingly, in this book established usage is followed which calls him 'Fernando Sor'.

Early education

Ledhuy[3] tells us that the social standing of his family was such that he would normally have been expected to follow a military or administrative career: and indeed, as well as following music, he did both of these things. This means that his family was respected and prosperous; yet the family's prosperity was probably not enormous, for when his father died a few years later there was not enough money for his mother to continue the child's musical education. Yet we may suppose that their social standing was high rather than low: there seems to have been no problem in bringing the boy's gifts to the notice of musical people in the city; when he arrived at Montserrat we hear that the other boys came from lower milieux; when he left there was no difficulty in obtaining a commission in the army straight away; and when he eventually went to Madrid, it was friends of his family who were able to have him presented in the proper circles.

Since the boy was destined for a military or administrative career, music was regarded as something of a trap. His father sang and took his son to the Italian opera, but did not have him trained in music because it would interfere with his Latin: Sor therefore composed songs to words from his Latin grammar, and so obtained approval. A suggestion that he be trained in music came from a musical friend of the family, the 'chevalier de Sabatea' (Ledhuy), but was rejected. ('Sabatea' is probably a misprint for 'Sabater', a common Catalan name; perhaps this was the Marquis de Capmany, on whom see later in this chapter.) Meanwhile he had begun to play the guitar, to sing, to play the violin, and to write down music by a system which he invented, having had as yet no training. From the opera *Giulio Sabino* by Sarti he set a trio for his father, his mother and himself, with guitar accompaniment. This trio, as we know today, was but the first of a series of arrangements from operas which he was to make throughout his life; and in Barcelona at that time it brought him to the attention of musicians. The leader of the orchestra of Barcelona Cathedral heard of him and began to teach him music.

So it seems that his father was prepared to encourage music so long as it did not get in the way of other more important things necessary for the boy's career; and thus things might have continued if his father had not died. His mother could not afford to continue musical

---

[3] Most of the facts in the next few pages come from the article already cited in the *Encyclopédie Pittoresque de la Musique* of A. Ledhuy and H. Bertini (Paris, 1835), which is very detailed on Sor's early years. The whole of the article is reprinted in facsimile at the end of the present book. For convenience I refer to it hereafter simply as 'Ledhuy'. For more on the circumstances of its writing, see chapter 5.

instruction. But meanwhile, Ledhuy tells us that the new Abbot of Montserrat, Josef Arredondo, heard of Sor and offered to take him into the Escolanía or choir school of the famous monastery; and his mother accepted. She took him to Montserrat, and it was she who took him away again some years later; but after that we hear no more of her. Since Sor remained in Spain for another twenty years, often indeed in Barcelona, we may suppose that they remained in contact, but no more is known for certain.

Josef Arredondo became Abbot of Montserrat in 1789, so we may date Sor's arrival there at 1789 or 1790, when he was eleven or twelve years old. The actual words in Ledhuy are: 'Le père D. Josef Arredondo, bénédictin, venait d'être élu abbé de Montserrat' ('Father Josef Arredondo, a Benedictine, had just been elected Abbot of Montserrat').[4]

By the time Sor went to Montserrat, his musical knowledge may be summarized as follows. At the age of five, he tells us, he was already singing arias from Italian operas: and this influence was to be an abiding one, for later he adapted arias from *Don Giovanni* for voice and guitar, taught singing in London, and composed the series of Italian Arietts in London which are in pure operatic style. Above all, this vocal influence is seen in the style, the lyrical nature, of most of his guitar music. He was already playing his father's guitar — again an influence which he did not shed. He was also playing a violin and receiving instruction from a violinist; and so most of his early training was in the field of secular music. Indeed, despite the training in religious music which he was to receive at Montserrat, for the rest of his life his activity was nearly all in secular music and not sacred.

Montserrat

The monastery of Montserrat today is still a monastery, still has a famous choir school, still enjoys a most marvellous site; but many of the buildings that Sor knew have disappeared, and the place has lost its isolation and has become something of a tourist attraction. When I first visited it on 12 October 1972, it was the double festivity of the discovery of America and of Nuestra Señora del Pilar, and despite the rain the place was overflowing with day-excursionists from Barcelona.

Beautiful it remains, however, and it certainly made a very great impression on Sor. His memories of Montserrat, published *verbatim* by Ledhuy, are so long and detailed that they constitute a major source not only on Montserrat but also on musical practice and education in eighteenth-century Spain. They describe, for instance, how the introduction and allegro of a Haydn symphony were played at the offertory of a mass, the andante at the communion, and the final allegro at the gospel. They mention the Spanish *villancicos* (carols) and *gozos* (songs of praise). They say much about Sor's principal teacher, the monk Father Viola. And they describe an early contact of Sor with French music, when French clergy, refugees from the French Revolution, came over the Pyreneees to Montserrat. Exiled from Spain at that time for over twenty years, Sor looked back nostalgically on his childhood there, and wrote most eloquently about it. Here, for instance, is a description, from Ledhuy, of a scene when Sor first arrived at Montserrat as a boy:

> Le lendemain le père abbé nous conduisit dans la sacristie pour admirer toutes les richesses qu'elle contient. L'église, vue au grand jour, me frappa d'admiration: ce pavé en mosaïque, ces murs sans ornemens ni tableaux qui tranchent l'harmonie ni les proportions de l'édifice; ce fond blanc, qui paraît brodé d'or avec les nuances du mat et du brillant, relevé par quelques contours noirs; tout cet ensemble, qui rappelle la destination de l'édifice, produisit un effet que je n'oublierai jamais.

> ('The next day the father Abbot took us to the sacristy to admire all the riches which it contains. The church, seen in full daylight, struck me with admiration: that mosaic floor, those walls without ornaments or pictures to disturb the harmony or proportions of the edifice; that white background with its nuances of plain and glittering, emphasized by black contours; the whole ensemble, which recalls the purpose of the building, produced an effect which I shall never forget.')

The whole description, together with a number of pictures, will be found in facsimile at the end of this book.

A military career

Sor's musical studies at Montserrat, however, were not destined to lead directly to a professional musical career. His mother, who as a widow must have considered her son's choice of career particularly important, found him the possibility of a commission in the army, and following the advice of family friends, took

[4] I am indebted to the Abbot of Montserrat, the Reverend Father Cassià M. Just, for the information that Arredondo became Abbot in 1789. Because of the wording in Ledhuy, Saldoni is probably wrong in stating that Sor was at Montserrat from 1791 to 1795 (*Reseña histórica de la Escolanía o Colegio de Música de la Virgen de Montserrat*, Madrid, 1856, p. 59).

him away from Montserrat. He returned to Barcelona, and was commissioned as sub-lieutenant in the 'corps de Villa franca', by General Vives. This regiment was probably the 'corregiment de Vilafranca' from Vilafranca del Penedès, thirty miles west of Barcelona, which was formed in 1714 (*Salvat Català, diccionari enciclopèdic*). Sor must have been about seventeen or eighteen years old.

Now, this appointment must be seen in proper perspective. A career as a paid musician was something which the monastery of Montserrat could certainly have arranged for him; but this would not have been normal for the son of a bourgeois family. Nor, at that time, had the opposition between artist and bourgeois reached the pitch which it was to reach with Romanticism a few years later; the two were still compatible. Furthermore, a commission obtained by family influence, or an administrative post such as Sor held a few years later, did not very much impede the practice of music; without necessarily being entirely sinecures, it is true to say that such posts were not full-time occupations as they might be today. As far as the Spanish army was concerned, music was an honourable occupation — and indeed, it was largely for his performance on the piano and guitar that Sor soon found himself promoted to the rank of full lieutenant.

And so Sor spent four years at the military school; and since it left time for the composition of guitar music and an opera, it can scarcely have been very irksome. His regiment was a Catalan one based near Barcelona, and it seems therefore fairly certain that these four years were spent in or near that city. The four years are not specified, but must have been about 1796-1800.

The guitar

As a child Sor played on his father's guitar, and to some extent continued with the instrument at Montserrat. Baltasar Saldoni tells us:

> Estando ya en dicho colegio, hacía con la guitarra cosas tan prodigiosas, que admirában á sus condiscípulos y á cuantos la oían, lo cual nos lo ha referido á nosotros varias veces el presbítero Martí, que le tuvo de condiscípulo en Montserrat.
>
> (*Diccionario*, I, 1868, p. 264)

> ('When he was at that school, he performed such prodigious things on the guitar that all his co-pupils and everyone who heard it were amazed. This was told to me on several occasions by the priest Martí, who was a co-pupil of his at Montserrat.')

The guitar as a classical instrument has for centuries been associated with Catalonia. Joan Carles y Amat, who published his *Guitarra Española* in 1596, was a

Catalan; and more recently there have been Miguel Llobet, Emilio Pujol, and many others. The instrument was in Sor's time, and is still, native to that country.

On his return to Barcelona he took it up again seriously, heard the music of Federico Moretti, began composing in a new style, and soon his compositions for the instrument were in demand:

> A cette époque il entendit le frère du général *Solano* jouer sur cet instrument un morceau dans lequel on distinguait un chant et un accompagnement. L'auteur du morceau était Moretti, officier des gardes wallonnes, qui fut le premier à comprendre le véritable caractère de la guitare.
>
> La musique de Moretti donna à Sor une route nouvelle, et avec un peu de travail et l'application de ses connaissances en harmonie, il parvint promptement à écrire et à exécuter la musique à plusieurs parties réelles.
>
> Les guitaristes lui demandaient ses compositions, puis ils changeaient les valeurs des notes pour écrire, disaient-ils, dans le vrai genre de la guitare.
>
> (Ledhuy)

> ('At that time he heard the brother of General Solano playing on the guitar a piece in which one could distinguish a melody and an accompaniment. The composer of the piece was Moretti, an officer in the Walloon Guards, who was the first to understand the true nature of the guitar.
>
> Moretti's music gave Sor a new direction, and with a little work and by applying his knowledge of harmony, he soon came to compose and perform music in several real parts.
>
> Guitarists asked him for his compositions, but then they changed the note-values, in order to write — so they said — according to the true nature of the guitar.')

Moretti was, then, an important influence on Sor at this time. In his *Méthode pour la Guitare* (Paris, 1830), p. 3, after dismissing the ideas of those who considered the guitar as merely a subordinate instrument, Sor writes of Moretti:

> J'entendis un de ses accompagnements exécuté par un de ses amis; et la marche de la basse, ainsi que les parties d'harmonie que j'y distinguai, me donnèrent une haute idée de son mérite; je le regardai comme le flambeau qui devait servir à éclairer la marche égarée des guitaristes.

> ('I heard one of his accompaniments played by one of his friends; and the shape of the bass line, as well as the harmony which I could distinguish, gave me a high regard for his merit; I regarded him as the torch which should serve to illuminate the faltering steps of guitarists.')

A word or two, then, about Moretti and the state of the guitar in Spain before Sor. In the late eighteenth century, the guitar's official prestige in that country was not high; the court musicians in Madrid spoke of 'les *frons frons* ordinaires' (Ledhuy). But its association

with the seguidillas and other songs of the time shows
that it was very important in the upsurge of popular
culture in that age. After the somewhat mysterious
Padre Basilio, a monk who taught the guitar in Madrid,
Federico Moretti was certainly the most important
figure in the history of the guitar in Spain.[5] An Italian
who became an officer in the Spanish army, he composed solos for the guitar and songs: and he dedicated a
collection of *Doce Canciones* to the Englishman Lord
Fife, the man who, after fighting in the Spanish army,
brought back to England with him the celebrated dancer
Maria Mercandotti. Moretti's music inspired Sor to
compose in several real parts or voices, something which
he continued to do for the rest of his life: many years
later, his concerts in Paris were reviewed in the *Revue
Musicale,* and the reviewer', F.J. Fétis, praised him
continually for doing just that.

What kind of guitar did Sor play at this time? At
home in the 1780s, his father's guitar would almost certainly have had five courses rather than six, and double
rather than single strings. The sixth course was added
towards the end of the eighteenth century in Italy and
France, and was probably not common in Spain until
around 1800 and after. A publication called *Etrennes de
Polymnie* (Paris, 1785), p. 148, shows a low G and
speaks of a 'Guitarre portant une Corde de plus': probably an open G but possibly a low E string stopped at
the third fret. A low E is shown in P. Delicati's *Sei Can-
zoncini* (Rome, 1797) and in Fernando Ferandiere's
Arte de tocar la guitarra española (Madrid, 1799). In
some cases, the addition of a sixth course was made easy
by the fact that some eighteenth century guitars had
triple stringing on their fourth and fifth courses: such a
guitar is shown, for example, in Manoel da Paixão
Ribeiro's *Nova arte de viola* (Coimbra, 1789), Estampa
I. Such guitars already had twelve pegs, and it would be
easy to reduce the stringing on the fourth and fifth
courses to double and add a sixth course instead.

An early reference to single stringing rather than
double is in A. Le Moine's *Nouvelle Methode Courte et
facile pour la guithare* (Paris, 1794 or before), which
while speaking of guitars with only five courses and not

six, mentions single or double stringing as alternatives.
There seems to be no evidence, however, for the use of
single strings rather than double in Spain before 1800.[6]

'Telemaco'

It is no exaggeration to say that musical life in
Barcelona at this time, in the late eighteenth century,
was dominated by Italian opera. Throughout Europe,
indeed, its influence was enormous, to an extent which
is still sometimes not fully recognized today. Sor had
heard Italian operas such as Sarti's *Giulio Sabino* as a
child in the 1780s, and now, back in Barcelona in the
1790s, this influence continued. The city had a new
opera house, built in 1788 after a fire in 1787; and in the
late 1790s an Italian troupe was in residence there,
directed by the Italian composer Tozzi (J. Subirá, *La
Opera en los Teatros de Barcelona,* I, Barcelona, 1946,
pp. 42-3). The 'censeur' or administrator of the theatre
was Caetano Gispert, a friend of Sor's family and godfather of his younger brother Carlos. Saldoni calls
Gispert a 'buen profesor de música en Barcelona en
1793, capitan de voluntarios' (*Diccionario,* IV, 125); ('a
good teacher of music in Barcelona in 1793, and a captain of [military] volunteers'). And Sor, not content
with watching and hearing, tried his hand at composing.
Here is Ledhuy's account of what happened:

> En parcourant la bibliothèque musicale de M. de
> Gispert, censeur du théâtre de Barcelonne, Sor trouva un
> vieux libretto: *Telemaco, opera in due atti,* musica *del
> Maestro Cipolla.* L'idée lui vint de s'essayer sur cet
> ouvrage inconnu à Barcelonne, et qui se composait de
> quatre personnages et des choeurs de nymphes. Il avait
> déjà fait la moitié de l'opéra, lorsque la réouverture de
> l'école militaire vint l'arrêter dans son essor. Néanmoins
> au bout de trois mois tout était achevé. Il montra quel-
> ques fragmens à M. de Gispert qui voulut le faire enten-
> dre à l'entrepreneur du théâtre, Tozzi. Celui-ci en-
> couragea le jeune Sor en lui distant: "A votre âge je
> n'étais point capable d'en faire autant."
>
> Il voulut faire jouer l'ouvrage, et dit au jeune artiste
> d'écrire l'ouverture. — Celui-ci se trouva embarrassé. Le
> père Viola qui l'avait si bien instruit de la contexture, de
> la marche et de la conduite des morceaux classiques de
> musique vocale, ne pouvait porter le même esprit
> d'analyse sur les compositions instrumentales; celles
> qu'on trouvait à Montserrat n'étaient point en partitions.
> Les oeuvres seules du savant moine eussent pu servir de
> modèle, mais son extrême modestie l'empêchait de les

---

[5] 'Padre Basilio', or Miguel Garcia, and his manner of playing, are
described in the article 'Aguado' in Ledhuy's *Encyclopédie.* He is
also the subject of an article by Franco Poselli, 'L'enigmatica figura di
Padre Basilio', *Il Fronimo,* I, 3 (1973), 27-29. On Moretti, see Thomas
F. Heck, 'The role of Italy in the early history of the classic guitar',
Guitar Review, 34 (1971), 1-6; Franco Poselli, 'Federico Moretti e il
suo ruolo nella storia della chitarra', *Il Fronimo,* I, 4 (1973), 11-19;
and J. Subirá, *Historia de la Música Española e Hispanoamericana*
(Barcelona, 1953), p. 625.

---

[6] I am indebted to Robert Spencer for his suggestions and for the
above references. See also Thomas F. Heck, 'The role . . .', and
Harvey Turnbull, *The Guitar from the Renaissance to the Present Day*
(London, 1974), pp. 62-70.

proposer comme des sujets d'étude. Sor n'osait se proposer de faire un *allegro* dans le genre d'Haydn; il prit
une autre route, et tant bien que mal il écrivit son ouverture. Cependant, en faveur de ses dix-sept ans et de son
titre de compatriote, l'opéra de *Télémaque* eut du succès.
Il est vrai de dire que n'ayant eu en vue que le sens des
paroles, et ne pouvant songer à vendre sa partition, il
n'avait point été forcé, comme de nos jours, d'y
intercaler des contre-danses, et malgré les défauts du
compositeur imberbe, on rendait justice à la vérité de son
chant.

Son opéra fut joué, pendant toute l'année, avec les
meilleures pièces du répertoire.

('Browsing through the musical library of M. de
Gispert, administrator of the Barcelona theatre, Sor
found an old libretto: *Telemaco, opera in due atti,* music
del Maestro Cipolla. It occurred to him to try his hand at
composing an opera on this libretto, which was unknown
in Barcelona and which consisted of four characters and
choruses of nymphs. He had already finished half the
opera, when the re-opening of the military school stopped him in mid-stream. Nevertheless, after three months
all was ready. He showed some fragments to M. de
Gispert, who wanted Tozzi, the head of the troupe in
residence, to hear the opera. Tozzi encouraged the young
Sor, saying: "At your age I couldn't do that."

He wanted to perform the work, and told the young
composer to write the overture. Sor was in a quandary.
Father Viola, who had instructed him so well in the
texture, construction and voice-writing of classical vocal
music, had not brought the same analytical spirit to bear
on instrumental compositions; those at Montserrat were
not in score. The works of the learned monk himself
could have served as models, but his extreme modesty
prevented him from proposing them as subjects for
study. Sor did not dare try to write an allegro in the style
of Haydn; he took another route, and in one way or
another he composed the overture. And, partly because
he was only seventeen and from the city, the opera
Telemaco was a success. It is true that since he had
thought only of the sense of the words, and not of selling
the score, he had not been obliged, as he would today, to
insert contredanses; and despite the faults of the inex-
perienced composer, people praised the true nature of his
vocal writing.

His opera was performed all year, together with the
best pieces of the repertory.')

Sor's opera, *Il Telemaco nell'Isola di Calipso,* was
first performed at the Barcelona Opera on 25 August
1797. According to Subirá it had fifteen performances
in the 1797-8 season (*Historia de la Música teatral en
España,* Barcelona, 1945, p. 123). On 25 August 1797
the *Diario de Barcelona* announced it at length, including the fact of the composer's youth, and on 26 August
and 5 September published poems dedicated to Sor on
his opera.[7]

An orchestral score of *Telemaco* is in the Arxiú de
Música at Montserrat, MSS 659-60, and some extracts
are known in other sources.[8] The style is completely
Italian. Its importance in Sor's career lies in its part in
his formation as a composer for the voice, and in the
encouragement which so early a success gave him.

Other compositions

In Barcelona at this time Sor also composed other
works, of which today no trace remains. The *Diario de
Barcelona* on 10 December 1798 announced a benefit
performance for Luis Bianchi, to include 'una pequeña
pieza entre la Señora Agata Bevilaqua y el Señor
Próspero Pedrazzi, que consiste en una Cabatina, una
Aria, unos Boleros, un Recitativo instrumental, con-
cluyendo con un Duo, todo composición del célebre
Autor del *Telemaco*' ('a small item by Mrs. Agata
Bevilaqua and Mr. Próspero Pedrazzi, consisting of a
cavatina, an aria, some boleros, and an instrumental
recitative, ending with a duet, all composed by the
famous composer of *Telemaco*'). Again on 2 February
1799 the *Diario de Barcelona* announced a tonadilla by
Sor entitled *Las Preguntas de la Morante:* 'tonadilla
nueva que cantará la Graciosa, titulada las preguntas de
la Morante, compuesta por el conocido y acreditado
autor del Telemaco' ('a new tonadilla which will be sung
by La Graciosa, called *Las Preguntas de la Morante,*
composed by the well-known and accredited composer
of *Telemaco*').[9] The 'boleros' in the first item may have
been either instrumental pieces or songs in the form of
seguidillas boleras, which will be discussed below. In
either case, the fact that he composed them and also a
tonadilla shows that he was already composing not only
in the Italian style but also within the native Spanish
tradition.

The first Madrid visit

At the end of these years in Barcelona, the young Sor,
now in his early twenties, set out for the capital,
Madrid. There, people who had known his father were
able to give him introductions; and he found, too, that
his reputation as a guitarist had preceded him. A royal
introduction and consequent success would have been
most useful. The story of the attempt is told in Ledhuy:

---

[7] The three texts are published in M. Rocamora's *Fernando Sor
(1778-1839), Ensayo Biográfico* (Barcelona, 1957), pp. 37-41.

[8] Overture in piano reduction: Montserrat, Arxiú de Música, MS
1562, pp. 36-40. Sinfonia in piano reduction: Barcelona, Biblioteca
Central, M 791/19. Recitative and Aria: Barcelona, Orfeó Catalá, MS
II/305.

[9] These references were discovered by José Subirá and published in
his article 'La Música en el Teatro Barcelonés', in *Música* [a short-
lived Barcelona periodical], April 1938, pp. 9-32.

Quelques amis voulaient lui préparer les voies pour qu'il jouât à la cour; mais Charles IV n'écoutait d'autre avis sur la musique que celle des musiciens de sa chambre, et ceux-ci, bien loin d'encourager et d'applaudir au talent de leur compatriote, voyaient de mauvais oeil qu'un amateur eût acquis des connaissances positives dans leur art. Le roi avait entendu parler de Sor, il demanda au chef de sa musique ce qu'il en pensait. ''C'est, dit celui-ci, quelque chose de mieux que les *frons frons* ordinaires, mais le talent de Sor est celui de tant d'amateurs, qui jouent par instinct et d'oreille, mais sans connaître une note de musique.'' Cette réponse chagrina Sor; mais plus désireux d'obtenir de l'avancement par ses services que par la guitare, il se résigna.

('Some friends wanted to make it possible for him to play at court; but King Charles IV did not listen to any opinons on music except those of his household musicians; and these, far from encouraging and applauding the talent of their compatriot, looked with disapproval on the acquisition by an amateur of any positive knowledge of their art. The king had heard people speak of Sor, and he asked the head of his music what he thought of him. ''It's something better than the usual *frons-frons*'', he said, ''but Sor's talent is that of so many amateurs, who play by instinct and by ear without knowing a note of music.'' This reply annoyed Sor; but preferring to obtain promotion by his services rather than by the guitar, he resigned himself.')

The king in question was Charles IV, who even though he played the violin, 'mehr Kenntnisse von der Jagd, als von der Musik hat' ('knows more than hunting than about music') *(Allgemeine musikalische Zeitung,* I, 1798, p. 401). The 'chef de sa musique', whose opinion the king sought, seems to have been a Frenchman, Alexandre Boucher (M. Soriano Fuertes, *Historia de la Música Española,* IV, Madrid, 1859, p. 239). The most curious words are the last ones: 'plus désireux d'obtenir de l'avancement par ses services que par la guitare'. Once again, Sor appears as something other than a professional musician: at that time he was a commissioned officer in the army, and he was soon to become an administrator.

What kind of place was Madrid around 1800? For a young man with introductions to good society, it must have been magnificent. The shadows of war were as yet still on the horizon. Goya was painting court pictures and not yet grim political subjects. Boccherini was at the court composing above all chamber music. The Italian opera flourished and was considered of great importance; yet at the same time the native dramatic forms, the zarzuela and the tonadilla, were being highly developed. In 1768 Antonio Rodríguez de Hita composed the zarzuela in popular style *Las Segadoras de Vallecas* to words by Ramón de la Cruz, and since then many zarzuelas of similar nature had been produced. Opinion may have been divided about which was better, Italian opera or Spanish native forms; but at least both

flourished and were produced in large quantities. It was 'the age of the growth of the bullfight, of the flowering of the minor arts and handicrafts, and above all of popular music and dance' (Gerald Brenan, *The Literature of the Spanish People,* London, 1963, p. 302). Madrid around 1800 was perhaps frivolous, perhaps decadent, but above all vigorous.[10]

Sor's first patron was the famous Duchess of Alba, she who was also the patroness of Goya.

A cette époque la duchesse d'Alba le prit sous sa protection et lui montra toute l'affection d'une mère. Elle ne voulait pas qu'il fît le métier de musicien, ou qu'il restât militaire en activité. Pour faciliter ses études, elle lui avait fait préparer dans son hôtel une chambre de travail, où il pouvait aller consulter des partitions italiennes et s'exercer sur le piano. Sous les prétextes les plus délicats, la duchesse trouvait moyen d'améliorer la position du jeune officier qui pouvait se livrer avec sécurité à son goût pour la musique. Il composa quelques morceaux d'un libretto *Don Trastullo.* Quelque temps après, la duchesse, qui était malade, quitta tout à coup Madrid, et laissa à son protégé une somme assez forte pour se soutenir avec honneur pendant son absence. Sor fut affligé de cette séparation, qui devait être éternelle, car la duchesse mourut presque subitement.

(Ledhuy)

('At this time the Duchess of Alba took him under her protection and showed him all the affection of a mother. She did not wish him to become a professional musician, nor to remain an active soldier. To assist his studies, she prepared for him a room in her house, where he could consult Italian scores and practise the piano. On the most delicate pretexts, the duchess found ways of improving the position of the young officer who could thus dedicate himself confidently to his taste for music. He composed some fragments of a libretto, *Don Trastullo.* Some time later, the duchess, who was ill, suddenly left Madrid, and left her protégé a considerable sum with which to sustain himself during her absence. Sor grieved at this separation, which was to be eternal, for the duchess died almost at once.')

It was on 23 July 1802 that she died.

At some time between his arrival in Madrid and 1808 (see below), Sor probably composed (in some form or other) his sonata now known as op. 22, and dedicated it to Manuel Godoy, at that time at the height of his political power in Spain, under his title 'Prince of the Peace'. Whatever his faults, Godoy was 'an intelligent and generous patron of the arts' (Brenan, op. cit., p. 295), encouraging the dramatist Moratín and many other writers and artists. It is not at all surprising that Sor should have dedicated this work to him.

---

[10] See Gilbert Chase, *The Music of Spain* (New York, 1959); Gerald Brenan, op. cit.; and C.E. Kany, *Life and Manners in Madrid 1750-1800* (Berkeley, 1932).

Ledhuy tells us that while Sor was in Madrid he heard the singer Crescentini and knew Mlle Colbran (Rossini's first wife). This must have been at this time, for Crescentini was based on Lisbon, coming from time to time to Madrid, from 1798 to 1802.

Back to Barcelona

After the Duchess of Alba's death, the Duke of Medinaceli offered Sor a post in the administration of his estates in Catalonia. This was accepted: by this time, as a trained officer, his military duties seem to have been few and to have allowed the acceptance of such posts as this. He returned to Barcelona.

Le duc de Medina-Coeli voulut lui être utile; il lui donna une commission dans l'administration générale de ses domaines, en Catalogne. L'espoir de retourner à Barcelonne le fit accepter. Sa place était une sinécure, et il continua son opéra, mais avec moins de rapidité. L'expérience l'avait rendu plus difficile. M. Quéralt, maître de chapelle de la cathédrale, ne dédaignait point de le consulter sur ses ouvrages; et celui de Sainte-Marie-del-Mar, M. Cau, le chargea de l'instrumentation de quelques morceaux de ses oratorios. Il composa alors deux symphonies, trois quatuors, un salve, cinq ou six *rosarios,* et beaucoup d'airs espagnols.

(Ledhuy)

('The Duke of Medinaceli wanted to help him, and gave him a post in the general administration of his property in Catalonia. The prospect of returning to Barcelona made him accept. The post was a sinecure, and he continued his opera, but less rapidly. Experience had made him more demanding. M. Queralt, chapel master of the cathedral, did not disdain to consult him on his compositions; and the chapel master of Santa Maria del Mar, M. Cau, entrusted to him the instrumentation of some parts of his oratorios. At that time he composed two symphonies, three quartets, a salve, five or six rosarios, and many Spanish airs.')

There is no trace of any of these works, unless some of his seguidillas are among the 'airs espagnols'. But there is one other work which, if it is indeed by Sor, probably dates from this period: the four-part composition on Catalan street-cries 'Draps i Ferro Vell' ('Rags and Old Iron'). Although the style is unlike Sor's, this is perhaps not surprising in a work based on these fascinating and extraordinary street-cries. It exists in four manuscript versions: one for four voices and piano and one for three voices and small orchestra are both in the Arxiú de Música at Montserrat, while another for four voices and piano and one for four voices and string quartet are in the library of the Orfeó Catalá,

Barcelona.[11] The version for three voices and orchestra is an arrangement by Blanch, director of the Escolanía (choir school) at Montserrat; it names Sor and is dated 1861; and this early date rather suggests that the attribution is to be believed and that the original work was indeed by Sor. This work, which takes its place in a long European tradition including Gibbons' 'The Cries of London' and Janequin's 'Les Cris de Paris', is all in Catalan except for the words of the night watchman, which are in Castilian. In 1924 it was performed by the Orfeó Catalá in Barcelona with the greatest success.

Francesc Queralt and Josep Cau, mentioned in Ledhuy, were major figures in the Barcelona musical world. Works by them both are in manuscript in the Biblioteca Central in Barcelona, and articles on them are in the *Gran Enciclopèdia Catalana.*

The second Madrid visit

Ayant obtenu un congé du duc de Medina-Coeli, Sor revint à Madrid, où il composa la musique d'un mélodrame, *La Elvira Portuguesa,* un motet à quatre voix, avec orchestre, pour l'église de la *Merced,* et plusieurs boleros. A cette époque on vendait déjà les copies de sa musique, qu'il donnait aux personnes pour lesquelles elle avait été faite. On tirait ainsi des fragmens de ses symphonies, des airs de *Télémaque,* et surtout de ses boleros.

(Ledhuy)

('Having obtained leave from the Duke of Medinaceli, Sor returned to Madrid, where he composed the music for a melodrama, *La Elvira Portuguesa,* a motet for four voices and orchestra for the church of La Merced, and several boleros. Already at this time copies were being sold of music which he had given to the people for whom he had composed it. Thus, copies were being made of parts of his symphonies, of airs from *Telemaco,* and above all of his boleros.')

This second visit to Madrid must have taken place about 1804. Of the works mentioned, the 'boleros' may perhaps be identical with some of Sor's surviving seguidillas. No trace has been found of *La Elvira Portuguesa.* The 'motet à quatre voix, avec orchestre' may very well be the same as his motet 'O crux, ave spes unica', which does survive, printed in Ledhuy's *Encyclopédie, a 4* but a cappella. It is a deeply felt work with some chromaticisms, and is reproduced in facsimile at the end of the present book. Sor refers to what is again probably the same motet in a letter to King Fernando VII of Spain (see chapter 5), in which he says

[11] A work called 'Serrafoll de Barcelona' formed part of the library of J. Carreras y Dágas in the last century (*Catálogo de la Biblioteca . . . de D. Juan Carreras y Dágas,* Barcelona, 1870). As 'serrafoll' means 'noise' in Catalan, this is probably the same work.

that the Pope, to whom he had presented a 'hymn' in honour of the Holy Cross, had bestowed on him a decoration.

Málaga

During the four years that preceded the Napoleonic invasion of Spain, that is to say 1804-8, Sor was 'chef d'une petite administration royale' in Andalusia. Here is Ledhuy:

> Après un séjour assez long à Madrid, il fut nommé chef d'une petite administration royale, en Andalousie. Les devoirs de son emploi ne l'empêchèrent point de passer une grande partie de son temps à Málaga, où il s'occupa de musique avec succès. Il dirigeait là les concerts du consul américain, M. Kirkpatrik. Sa liaison avec l'organiste de la cathédrale lui fut utile. Ainsi s'écoulèrent quatre années qui précédèrent l'arrivée de Napoléon en Espagne.

> ('After quite a long stay in Madrid, he was named head of a small royal administration in Andalusia. The duties of the post did not prevent him from spending much of his time in Málaga, where he occupied himself successfully with music. He directed there the concerts of the American Consul, Mr. Kirkpatrick. His connection with the organist of the cathedral was useful to him. Thus the four years went by that preceded the arrival of Napoleon in Spain.')

Málaga at that time was much smaller and doubtless much more pleasant than it is today. A small port with a certain pride in its liberalism, it was there for instance that Torrijos in 1831 tried, though unsuccessfully, to begin his liberal revolution (V. Llorens, *Liberales y Románticos,* 2nd edn., Madrid, 1968, pp. 138-42). The organist of the cathedral, whom Ledhuy mentions as a friend of Sor, was Joaquín Murguía. Málaga guitar-makers whom Sor praises in his *Méthode pour la Guitare* (p. 10) are Joseph and Manuel Martinez, and the latter's successor Rada. The American Consul whose concerts Sor directed was William Kirkpatrick, and Saldoni adds some details at this point. He describes one of Kirkpatrick's concerts, and although he gets the consul's name and country wrong, and Sor's employment, and probably the year as well, nevertheless his account is so explicit that the concert probably did in fact take place. He writes *(Diccionario,* I, p. 264):

> Por los años de 1802 y 1803 [sic], en que Sors era oficial del ejército, hallándose de guarnición en Málaga, ó muy cerca de esta ciudad, dió el cónsul de Austria [sic], Sr. Quipatri [sic], un gran concierto, en que reunió todo lo más elegante y notable que encerraba Málaga, en el cual tocó Sors un *solo* de contrabajo con variaciones, que dejó admirados y sorprendidos á cuantos le oyeron, incluso á los músicos que estaban presentes, entre los que se hallaba D. Vicente Ribera, maestro de trompa y músico

mayor que había sido durante muchos años, y que en aquella noche tocaba el serpentón en la orquesta, siendo dicho Sr. Ribera quien contó el asombro que había causado Sors, al que nos lo ha escrito á nosotros, y cuyo documento conservamos. El primer violín en este concierto lo fue D. Francisco Ibarra, que lo era asimismo de la catedral del citado Málaga; el primero de segundos, D. José Colocós; primer trompa, D. Vicente Leza, músico mayor, al parecer, del regimiento de Aragón.

('About the year 1802 or 1803 [sic], when Sor was an officer in the army and in garrison in Málaga or very near that city, the Austrian [sic] Consul, Mr. Quipatri [sic], gave a grand concert, to which came all the most elegant people in Málaga and all around. In this concert Sor played a solo on the double bass, with variations, which left everyone who heard him admiring and astounded, including the professional musicians who were present. This was told to me in a letter (which I still have) by D. Vicente Ribera, a fine trumpet player of much experience, who on that occasion was playing the serpent in the orchestra. The leader in that concert was D. Francisco Ibarra, who was also leader of the Málaga cathedral orchestra; the leader of the second violins was D. José Colocós; and the first trumpet was D. Vicente Leza, principal musician, it seems, of the Aragonese Regiment.')

In Saldoni's account, the year should probably be somewhere between 1804 and 1808, if we are to believe Ledhuy; Sor was not in the army but in a civil administrative post; and the consul in question was not the Austrian but the American Consul, Mr. Kirkpatrick.[12] However these details may be, the astonishing thing is that he appears to have played in this concert, not the guitar but the double bass! Certainly he composed for many instruments, and we know that he sang and played the piano as well as the guitar, but there is no other record of his playing the double bass.

These extracts from Ledhuy and Saldoni give us a picture of Sor established in a quiet country, in an administrative sinecure, with time for music, playing and composing and appearing in elegant concerts. The four years in Málaga seem to have been prosperous and peaceful ones.

One of his songs, the *Impromtu dans le genre du Boléro,* 'No tocarán campanas', is specifically dated at Málaga, 1 November 1809. However, if this dating is to be believed, it refers not to this stay in Málaga but to a subsequent visit to the town, for in 1808 he left for Madrid.

---

[12] William Kirkpatrick was appointed U.S. Consul in Málaga in 1800 and served in that capacity until 1818. His despatches to the American Government survive (National Archives and Records Office, Washington, T 217); I have examined them, but they are exclusively political and commercial and give no clue about the concerts.

Napoleon

The arrival of Napoleon's troops in Spain changed Sor's peaceful way of life. So far, he seems to have taken little part in politics. But now, no Spaniard could stand aside, and soon we find him composing martial and patriotic songs against the French. Invasion, bitter war, starvation, sieges, and the most outrageous horrors were the order of the day for six years, from 1808 to 1813, as we may judge from some of Goya's finest and most harrowing works, especially the *Desastres de la Guerra*. One of the best descriptions of the whole period is F.D. Klingender's *Goya in the Democratic Tradition* (London, 1948; reprinted New York, 1968), in which Klingender first describes the political and social events of the time and then relates Goya's work to them. Sor, who was a contemporary of Goya, composed some of the most famous political songs of the time, and so, although his work is certainly not so involved in these events as is Goya's, nevertheless we must still look in some detail at those events.

First we must go back on our tracks. In 1788 the Bourbon King Charles IV succeeded to the Spanish throne. Almost immediately, news of the French Revolution caused alarm; exiles began to arrive in Spain (some of whom Sor knew at Montserrat); and repressive measures were taken to prevent anything similar from happening in Spain. In 1793 Spain joined the interventionist coalition against France, but her armies were routed in the following year. Under these circumstances, there was rejoicing when in 1795 peace was signed between France and Spain under terms not unfavourable to Spain. This was the Peace of Basle. It was the work of Manuel Godoy, at one and the same time the king's favourite and the queen's lover, Prime Minister of Spain, who because of this treaty became known as the 'Prince of the Peace'. It was to him, under that name, that Sor's Sonata op. 22 was dedicated.

What was the reaction of Spaniards to these events? Certainly, there is no doubt that the Spanish establishment feared revolution: they had nothing to gain and everything to lose. But many men of good will admired the ideals of the French Revolution and indeed hoped that something similar might happen in their own country. Their admiration was certainly tempered with disgust at the excesses of that same Revolution; what is more, the ideals faded and gave way once more to the ascendancy of a single individual, Napoleon; yet given the unprogressive state of Spain, a desire for change could not but exist.

The situation crystallized in 1808. In March of that year a mob of Madrileños besieged the royal palace at Aranjuez and forced the dismissal of Godoy. The favourite escaped them only by hiding under carpets in the attic of the palace. Already Napoleon's troops were in the north of Spain, ostensibly on their way to Portugal and also to help, should they (in theory) be invited, to depose Godoy and establish Ferdinand, Charles IV's son, on the throne of Spain. They needed no further encouragement. Later in that same month, Ferdinand was installed as King and Murat entered Madrid at the head of a French army. By promises, Napoleon lured Ferdinand to Bayonne, where he abdicated in favour of his father, and the father abdicated in favour of Napoleon's brother, Joseph Bonaparte. Charles IV never returned to Spain, but with his queen spent the rest of his life in exile, and died in Rome in 1819. Godoy died in Paris in 1851.

When the French entered Madrid, Sor went there from Andalusia:

> Sor demanda la permission de retourner à Madrid, où il se lia avec plusieurs Français, excellens musiciens, notamment M. d'Auberlin et M. Le Barbier de Tinand.[13]
>
> (Ledhuy)
>
> ('Sor asked permission to return to Madrid, where he met a number of Frenchmen, excellent musicians, notably M. d'Auberlin and M. Le Barbier de Tinand.')

Foreign occupation of Madrid, and the news of the treachery at Bayonne, led to one of the most famous insurrections of all time: that of 2 May 1808, the 'Dos de Mayo'. It seems likely that Sor was there at the time. The Madrid people, apparently spontaneously and without need for incitement by agitators, rose against the French. The insurrection was put down, and executions followed, which were later commemorated in the famous painting by Goya. But although it was put down, the insurrection roused the rest of Spain. On 24 July 1808 a French army under Dupont, having taken and ravaged Córdoba, surrendered to the Spanish at the Battle of Bailén, and Valencia succeeded in resisting a siege by a French army under Moncey. Joseph Bonaparte was obliged to flee from Madrid only eleven day after arriving there, on 31 July 1808, and the Spanish army entered Madrid triumphantly on 23 August. Sor composed patriotic songs against the French, of which one of the most famous, 'Venid, vencedores', was sung at that triumphant entry. And he left Madrid at this time to fight against the French.

---

[13] I have not been able to trace any reference to these two. Doubtless the latter was related to the later French admiral Marie-Charles Adalbert Le Barbier de Tinand (1803-76).

Captain Sor of the Cordovan Volunteers

In 1808 Sor continued his military career, first in an unidentified regiment and then in the Cordovan Volunteers. He joined the first — which may have been either a new regiment or else his old one from Vilafranca — after the French were expelled from Madrid (31 July 1808) until they reoccupied it (5 December 1808). After that, he left for Andalusia and joined the Cordovan Volunteers with the rank of captain. Here is Ledhuy:

> Après la bataille de Bailen, Madrid fut évacué par les Français, on leva des troupes pour leur résister, et ceux qui avaient été liés avec des Français étaient signalés à la fureur populaire. Sor reprit du service; son régiment, à peine formé, prit part à la résistance, et ne se dispersa qu'après l'entrée des Français à Madrid. Sor partit alors pour l'Andalousie, où il fut nommé capitaine au régiment des volontaires de Cordoue.
>
> Mais les efforts des Espagnols n'empêchèrent point les mouvemens progressifs de l'armée ennemie, et le général Sébastiani arriva en Andalousie avant que les volontaires cordouans fussent réunis.

> ('After the Battle of Bailén, Madrid was evacuated by the French; troops were levied to fight them, and those who had been connected with the French were exposed to the popular fury. Sor joined up; his regiment, scarcely formed, took part in the resistance, and was disbanded only after the French re-entered Madrid. Sor then left for Andalusia, where he joined the regiment of volunteers at Córdoba with the rank of captain.
>
> But the Spanish efforts did not prevent the gradual advance of the enemy army, and General Sebastiani arrived in Andalusia before the Cordovan Volunteers were fully organized.')

The Cordovan Volunteers are described in M.A. Orti Belmonti's book *Córdoba durante la Guerra de la Independencia* (Córdoba, 1930). Their recruitment began on 15 August 1808. Not only did they have their own musicians, but they even gave concerts. Here is a description, from a contemporary letter, of their march through Córdoba under their colonel, Francisco Carvajal, on 19 October 1808:

> Entraron formando un lúcido cuerpo a cuyo frente iba el Coronel del Regimiento don Francisco Carvajal al son de la música y cantando las tonadas populares. Durante el tiempo que permanecieron en Córdova estuvo toda la Ciudad llena de alegría, concurriendo todo el pueblo a la retrata y a los conciertos de las bandas militares, que se celebraron en la calle de Santa Victoria, donde vivía el Coronel.
>
> (Orti Belmonti, p. 55)

> ('They went in glittering formation, at their head the Colonel of the Regiment, Francisco Carvajal, to the sound of music and singing popular tunes. During the

time that they were in Córdoba, the whole city was full of joy, with all the populace rushing to hear the retreat and the concerts of the military bands which were held in the street of Santa Victoria, where the Colonel lived.')

According to the *Correo Político y Militar de Córdoba,* the Volunteers fought against the French in La Mancha in April 1809 and at Aranjuez in August 1809 (Orti Belmonti, pp. 64-5). It may be that Sor fought with them in that year. On 1 November 1809, as we saw, it is possible that Sor was in Málaga. But then, as Ledhuy says, the French arrived in Andalusia; and in January 1810 Córdoba itself was occupied.

Political decisions

There followed a difficult choice. The whole of Spain except Cádiz was occupied by the French. Should Spaniards fight on in the name of blind patriotism, or should they accept the occupation? After all, the French were not mere foreign conquerors, but also to some extent representatives of the ideals of the French Revolution; in these ideals might perhaps lie the means of a reformed Spain. Many, looking at their own inept and corrupt government, chose to accept the occupation. They came to be known as *afrancesados,* and because they put liberal ideals before blind patriotism and because in the event they proved to have chosen the losing side, they were often attacked in later years. Sor was one of them. In 1974, more than a century and a half later, an archivist in Spain even put obstacles in my way because Sor had been an *afrancesado.* In general, however, justice is done today to their liberal and progressive ideas and it is recognized that they were not collaborators in the odious sense that that word has acquired since the Second World War but in fact patriots of a more sensible kind than the supporters of Fernando, whose government later turned out to be the worst fate that Spain could undergo. Llorens calls them 'notables escritores, profesionales y hombres de ciencia, los funcionarios más aptos e inteligentes con que contaba el país' (*Liberales y Románticos,* p. 10) ('notable writers, professional men and men of science, the most able and intelligent administrators that the country possessed'). Raymond Carr puts it thus: 'they [the *afrancesados*] were often the progressive elements in Spanish society, liberal-minded civil servants who saw in Joseph's monarchy the hope of a reformed Spain' *(The New Cambridge Modern History,* IX, Cambridge, 1965, p. 447).

> Sor suivit l'exemple de tant d'autres; il crut le pouvoir de Joseph affermi et il prêta serment. Il occupa l'emploi de commissaire principal de police de la province de Xérez, jusqu'à la retraite des armées françaises.
>
> (Ledhuy)

('Sor followed the example of so many others; he believed Joseph's power to be established and he took the oath. He occupied the position of principal commissary of police of the province of Jerez, until the French armies retreated.')

Jerez

Jerez de la Frontera was then, as it still is, a town mainly occupied with producing sherry. In 1838 Captain C. Rochfort Scott, a British officer stationed at Gibraltar, wrote: 'The inhabitants are all, more or less, connected with the wine trade — which is the only thing thought of or talked of in the place!' *(Excursions in the Mountains of Ronda and Granada,* London, 1838, II, 80). It is very near Cádiz. This was the only part of Spain not in French hands, and there the Cortes met in 1810, the first freely elected assembly in Spain for three hundred years. There they hammered out a Constitution for Spain and proclaimed it in 1812. As Karl Marx said: 'At the Isla de León [Cádiz], ideas without action — in the rest of Spain, action without ideas' (quoted from Klingender, *Goya,* p. 127). Sor's post in Jerez as commissary of police may have been merely an administrative one — indeed, given the fact that he knew musicians in the French army, perhaps it was another administrative sinecure like his earlier posts. We do not know, and no musical composition of his can be specifically dated within this period. He was at Jerez presumably from about early 1810 until the French left Andalusia, which took place in the summer of 1812. The 'province of Jerez' disappeared in administrative changes made in 1833 (Gilbert Chase, *The Music of Spain,* New York, 1959, p. 223).[14]

Valencia

A Valence, le général Mazzuchelli, homme fort instruit et passionné pour la musique, le présenta à la duchesse d'Albuféra qui chantait fort bien. A sa fête, Sor composa une cantate à trois voix avec des choeurs et des accompagnemens, qui furent exécutés par les musiciens de l'orchestre du théâtre.

(Ledhuy)

('At Valencia, General Mazzuchelli, a man of learning and enthusiastic about music, presented him to the Duchess of Albufera, who sang very well. For her birthday, Sor composed a cantata for three voices with choruses and accompaniments which were performed by the musicians of the Valencia theatre orchestra.')

The background to this is political. Sor had spent probably two years in French service in Jerez. But in the summer of 1812 the French were obliged to evacuate Andalusia, and Sor certainly left with them. Wellington occupied Madrid and Joseph Bonaparte retired to Valencia. It was doubtless at this point that Sor came also to Valencia.

Count Louis Mazzuchelli (b. 1772) was a general in Napoleon's service and at this time governor of Valencia.[15] The Duchess of Albufera, daughter of the mayor of Marseilles, was the wife of Marshal Suchet, on whom Napoleon conferred the title of Duke of Albufera in January 1813.[16] The cantata that Sor wrote for her survives in manuscript in the collection of Manuel Rocamora, Barcelona. It is scored for soloists, four-part chorus, strings, and wind.[17]

But it was now only a question of time for the French. Wellington retired to Portugal for the winter of 1812, but in June 1813 won the Battle of Vitoria; and then Joseph Bonaparte and the French armies let Spain. The *afrancesados* were obliged to leave too. Whatever liberal ideals they may have had were already compromised by service with the hated invader, and they rightly feared what the new regime might bring them. Even the attitude of the British showed little hope for any liberals who might choose to remain, let alone *afrancesados*. Klingender quotes an exchange of letters between Lord Wellington and the British Secretary for War, Lord Bathurst. Wellington wrote to London on 5 September 1813: 'I wish you would let me know whether, if I should find a fair opportunity of striking at the democracy, the Government would approve of my doing it'; and Bathurst replied on 25 September: 'You may be assured that it you can strike a blow at the democracy in Spain, your conduct will be much approved here' *(Goya,* p. 130).

Sor's own position by now was untenable: his connections with the French were far too strong. And so, when Napoleon's star faded and Joseph Bonaparte left Spain forever in 1813, Sor left too. 'Lorsque les josephinos quittèrent l'Espagne, Sor les suivit en France' (Ledhuy) ('When the supporters of Joseph left Spain, Sor followed them to France'). He described his own attitude towards these political events in a poem

---

[14] When I was in Jerez in 1974, I was told that the archives there contained the lease of a house in Jerez taken by Sor. However, repeated correspondence has failed to produce documentary evidence of this.

[15] *Biographie Nouvelle des Contemporains* (Paris, 1824).

[16] *Nouvelle Biographie Générale* (Paris, 1865). Albufera is a marshy district to the south of Valencia.

[17] The only evidence that this is in fact the same cantata is the inscription 'Cantata de Sor' on the spine, in lettering apparently of the nineteenth century. The front cover bears the words 'Cantata à S.E. la Signora Duchessa ———— [here a word has been physically cut out of the cover]'.

which we will come to soon. But it is certain that he was right to leave: the new monarch, Fernando VII, who has been called the worst monarch that Spain has ever had and whose character may be judged from the portrait of him by Goya now in the Prado, immediately began reprisals against the ex-supporters of the French and suppressed any sign of liberalism. Within a few months the Constitution of 1812 had been abolished, all leading liberals arrested, and the Inquisition restored.

Patriotic songs

'El liberalismo español fue muy musical en su origen' ('Spanish liberalism was originally very musical'), writes Llorens *(Liberales y Románticos,* p. 71); and the battles against Napoleon produced patriotic music in large quantities. Sor took his part in this. Altogether we know four, possibly five, patriotic songs by him:

> *Himno de la Victoria,* 'Venid, vencedores'
> *Canción Cívica: Los Defensores de la Patria,*
>   'Vivir en cadenas'
> *Marche Patriotique Espagnole,*
>   'Marchemos, marchemos'
> *Chanson relative aux Evénements d'Espagne,*
>   'Adonde vas, Fernando incauto'
> 'Fuentes son de llanto'

The first two, to words by J.B. Arriaza, were the most famous and exist in many versions. The first, the *Himno de la Victoria,* celebrates the victorious entry of the Spanish troops into Madrid on 23 August 1808, after the Battle of Bailén. It has fifteen eight-line stanzas and a refrain that comes sixteen times. The style is hyperbolical to a degree. Here is the beginning:

> *Venid, vencedores,*
> *Columnas de honor,*
> *La Patria os dé el premio*
> *De tanto valor.*[18]
>
> Tomad los laureles
> Que habéis merecido,
> Los que os han rendido
> Moncey y Dupont.
>   Vosotros, que fieles
> Habéis acudido
> Al primer gemido
> De nuestra opresión,
>
> *Venid, vencedores, &c.*

('Come, victors, pillars of honour, let your country give you the reward of such valour. Take the laurels which you have deserved, those which were yielded to you by Moncey and Dupont. You, who faithfully responded to the first cry of our oppression, Come, victors, &c.')

Arriaza, the author of the words, was born in 1790 and so his ideals in these poems of 1808 and 1809 are those of a very young man. Later he became a court poet of the tamest kind; but for the moment his poems showed a fiery if naive patriotism.

Sor's music, in 6/8 time and in vigorous style, consists of a 'Coro' for the refrain and a 'Solo' for the verses. It exists in many sources. The most important is the *Poesías Patrióticas* of Arriaza printed in London in 1810, which includes three musical settings with piano accompaniment, two of them by Sor. This edition was textually reprinted in Mexico about 1812. The song also exists in a number of manuscripts in different versions, some of which put it into duple time (see the Catalogue below). According to one source, the hymn is not only about the victorious entry of the Spanish troops into Madrid, but was actually sung at that entry.[19] Here is the version from the *Poesías Patrióticas:*

---

[18] This is the refrain set by Sor, as published in the musical supplement to the 1810 edition of Arriaza's *Poesías Patrióticas.* In the purely literary version of the poem printed in the same edition, these words conclude the poem and the refrain proper reads:

> *Venid, vencedores,*
> *De la Patria honor,*
> *Recibid el premio*
> *De tanto valor.*

---

[19] This is a printed leaflet dated by the British Library *Catalogue of Printed Books* 'Mexico, 1815?'. This leaflet adds an extra stanza naming the heroes Palafox and Castaños, and a note wishing that yet more extra stanzas could be added naming all the provinces and all the victorious generals! — just in Mario Vargas Llosa's *Pantaleón y las Visitadoras* the Peruvian Navy has to be placated when it discovers that it has not been named in the 'Himno de las Visitadoras'. It also lists another possible musical setting: 'Se acomoda á la misma música en que se canta la letrilla de Melendez: *Bebamos, bebamos;* y puede servir entonces para renovar, al fin de nuestros convites la memoria de tan gloriosas hazañas'.

Los Defensores de la Patria, 'Vivir en cadenas', resembles the *Himno de la Victoria.* Again the conventional and highly patriotic words are by Arriaza. The song calls on Spaniards to fight the invader, to conquer or else to die for Spain and Fernando. According to Arriaza's *Poesías Patrióticas* it is an attempt to rouse the spirit of Spain after the disappointment of the Battle of Medellin (28 March 1809). Here is the beginning:

Vivir en cadenas,
Quan triste vivir!
Morir por la Patria,
Qué bello morir!

Partámos al campo,
Que es gloria el partir;
La trompa guerrera
Nos llama a la lid;
    La Patria oprimida,
Con ayes sin fin,
Convoca á sus hijos,
Sus ecos oid.

Vivir en cadenas, &c.

('To live in chains, what a sad way to live! To die for one's country, what a beautiful way to die! Let us leave for the battlefield; what a glorious departure! The warlike trumpet summons us to battle. The oppressed Fatherland, with endless sighs, calls her sons; listen to the echoes. To live in chains, &c.')

Sor's music is again in 6/8 time and again divides into 'Coro' and 'Solo'. It was printed in the musical section of Arriaza's *Poesías Patrióticas* of 1810 and again appears in many manuscripts, sometimes in duple time (see the Catalogue below). In about 1835 Johanning in London published a version with guitar accompaniment, called *Spanish Song of the Defenders of their Fatherland,* and another was published in Vienna; these arrangements are almost certainly not by Sor himself. Nor is another setting for voice and guitar in Madrid, Biblioteca Nacional, MS 5307, no. 17. Here is the version from the *Poesías Patrióticas:*

There exists also an entirely different anonymous setting of the same words for tenor, chorus, and wind band, in Madrid, Biblioteca Nacional, MS 5307, no. 1. The song was evidently famous, even famous enough for an ironic parody of it to be current in Spain about 1814, under the repression of Fernando VII:

> Vivan las cadenas,
> Viva la opresión;
> Viva el rey Fernando,
> Muera la Nación!
>
> (Klingender, *Goya,* p. 155)
>
> ('Long live chains; long live oppression; long live King Fernando, and let the nation die!')

This parody — for that, surely, is what it is — itself became famous in Spanish history. It even figures prominently in Luis Buñuel's film *Le Fantôme de la Liberté* (1975).

The next song dates from 1809: the *Marche Patriotique Espagnole,* 'Marchemos, marchemos', with words by 'M.N.'. Again this has a four-line refrain, and there are three eight-line stanzas. Again it calls on Spaniards to fight the hated invader, who has treacherously lured Fernando into captivity in Bayonne. But this time there is no musical distinction between a chorus and a solo: two tenors sing with piano accompaniment throughout. The music is military and rousing. It was published in Paris by Mme Benoist, with a French translation, and was listed in the *Bibliographie de la France* on 20 August 1814. An entirely different setting of the same words, for voices and piano, is in the collection of Robert Spencer, London, 'Clive' MS, pp. 295-8, called 'Marcha Nacional'.

Sor himself wrote the words, as well as the music, of a song about the political events in Spain up to the end of 1811: 'Adonde vas, Fernando incauto'. In his twelve-stanza poem, he tells how Fernando the Adored was treacherously captured by Napoleon. The Spaniards vowed vengeance, took up arms, and were victorious at Bailén. But because he who could save them was in captivity, one by one Spanish towns were forced to yield to the inhuman invader. Devastation and death followed. Some Spaniards judged that further resistance could lead only to complete destruction; others fought on, abandoning even their families to do so; and so Spain was bitterly divided. May this division, says Sor, one day be healed.

This is Sor's most personal song: not only is it the only one to which he is known to have written the words, but it explains his own political stance, his reasons for accepting the French rule in Spain. It is reproduced below, in a facsimile of Mme Benoist's

Paris edition probably of 1814. Sor provides an alternative guitar accompaniment; if it is used, the voice should sing a minor third lower, in A minor instead of C minor. Here is a translation of the words (the French version in the original edition is rather a paraphrase than a translation).

('Where are you going, unwary Fernando? Do not leave your country. See how your people, who adore you, know who Napoleon is; flee from the trap which he has laid for you, and foil his scheme and his intention. — But he won, and they captured Fernando of the House of Bourbon.

But as a good man judges others according to his own noble heart, Fernando judged treachery to be incompatible with a crown. He who had no experience of deceit, could not doubt the truth of this friendship; he imposed silence on his servants and followed his own path.

The innocent one arrived at Bayonne; and instead of the reward which he had expected for his excessive trust, he found humiliation; he who had called himself his friend and offered him his protection, robbed him of his crown and imprisoned him in a castle.

The Spaniards, angry at such atrocious perfidy, swore to avenge their monarch and to honour the name of Spain. All at once the cry of vengeance resounded throughout Spain, and everyone took for his device his King, his country and his religion.

The young, brave and strong, set out to face the champion, who had already arrived as far as Córdoba with his sacrilegious army. At the first encounter, victory crowned such a noble endeavour, and every Frenchman who did not die at Bailén was taken prisoner.

The people of Saragossa and of Valencia defended themselves valiantly; but their valour and fortitude in the end yielded to misfortune. Tarragona resisted attacks tenaciously but in vain, because he who could save her was a mere spectator.

The armies of the ambitious one overrun Spanish soil, and their inhuman commanders lend their consent to crimes; every soldier is a tyrant to property and to honour, and repays with desolation the hospitality which he receives.

Wicked men, a blotch upon the name of Spain, give themselves over to assassination, theft and devastation. They commit as many crimes as the imagination can conceive, and the name of Fernando serves for impunity from aggression.

Spaniards are divided in their opinion on this matter. Those who want to avoid ruin, are in favour of submission; they judge so obstinate a resistance to be useless, even disastrous, and that to continue the fight will complete the destruction of Spain.

Those who believe that the country can find its salvation in other ways, go off to its remotest parts. One abandons his father, another his wife and his house, another perhaps some innocent, the unhappy fruit of a marriage.

Sad Spain has become the scene of the most atrocious unhappiness; behold her sons, divided! Oh how great a misfortune! One calls another a fool, and in his turn he is called a traitor; may a bad end come to the ambitious one who caused this division.

O immense God, who reading in the hearts of men, knows what are my own feelings and desires, unite the prayers of Spain; bring to an end this wild dissension; let us all live together as brothers, that the nation may prosper thus.')

A fifth patriotic song has been attributed to Sor, but it is possibly spurious: 'Fuentes son de llanto'. It was printed in Eduardo Ocón's *Cantos Españoles* (Málaga, 1874), pp. 54-5, and again by Rafael Mitjana in A. Lavignac's *Encyclopédie de la Musique et Dictionnaire du Conservatoire* (Paris, n.d. [1917?]), pp. 2347-8. Ocón calls it 'Canción que sirve de introducción á un himno patriótico, escrito en 1820 probablemente y dedicado á la Señorita Doña Maria Setta, por Dn. Fernando Sors' ('Song which forms the introduction to a patriotic hymn, probably written in 1820 and dedicated to Maria Setta by Fernando Sor'). But Ocón was not a reliable editor, as he showed in his editing of seguidillas by Sor, and 'Fuentes son de llanto' contains harmonies which appear to be posterior to Sor's time. Nor was Sor in Spain in 1820. So I am inclined to think that if 'Fuentes son de llanto' is by Sor at all, then what we have is merely an arrangement, perhaps by Ocón, of Sor's original, which as Ocón says may have been an introduction to a patriotic hymn.

Seguidillas

As well as these patriotic songs, Sor also composed other songs in Spanish, nearly all in the form of *seguidillas boleras.* They are mentioned in Ledhuy's *Encylopédie,* where they are called 'boleros'; and in the late nineteenth century the Catalan singer Lorenzo Pagans used to sing them. In 1881 Antonio Peña y Goni wrote:

Por mi parte, he oído varias canciones españolas, originales de Sors, cantadas por Pagans en Paris y puedo asegurar que la originalidad y frescura de la melodía, el interés armónico y la viveza del ritmo aventajan con mucho á las de Manual García e Iradier. Débense sobre todo á Sors algunos boleros que son verdaderas joyas.[20]

('For my part, I have heard several Spanish songs by Sor sung by Pagans in Paris, and I can vouch for it that the originality and freshness of the melodies, the harmonic interest and the vivacity of the rhythms are much superior to those of Manual García or Iradier. Above all we owe to Sor some boleros which are veritable jewels.')

But these 'veritable jewels' remained lost until in the course of my research I found eleven of them — not in Spain or in Paris, but in London. They are in manuscripts that were collected in Spain in the earliest years of the nineteenth century, two in the British Library (MSS Egerton 3288 and 3289) and one in a private collection ((that of Robert Spencer). There is in addition one more in a printed source published in Paris in 1814. Despite extensive research, none has been found in Spain.

This is a major new aspect of Sor's achievement, representing the contribution of a gifted composer to a living and popular tradition. Nine of the twelve have guitar accompaniment, two have piano, and one has alternative guitar and piano accompaniments. A complete edition of them is now available: Fernando Sor, *Seguidillas,* edited by Brian Jeffery (London, Tecla Editions, 1976). One of them is reproduced below. It is called 'El que quisiera amando', and here are its words and a translation:

El que quisiera amando
   Vivir sin pena,
Ha de tomar el tiempo
   Conforme venga.

   Quiera querido;
Y si te aborrecieren
   Haga lo mismo.

('He who wants to love and yet live without problems, must just take time as it comes. Take someone to love; and then, even if they hate you for it — just take time as it comes.')

What exactly are seguidillas (or boleros)? One of our most important sources of information is an article by Sor himself, called 'Le Bolero', which he wrote for Ledhuy's *Encyclopédie.* It is reproduced in facsimile in the edition just mentioned. In it, Sor begins by explaining how seguidillas are related to the bolero. A seguidilla is a type of poem, which may be set to music. If it is set in such a way as to suit the dance known as the bolero, it is called a *seguidilla bolera* or *seguidillas boleras* (or simply, in the musical sources, *boleras* or *voleras*). This is the terminology used in Spain before the French invasion of 1808. However, outside Spain after the invasion, the one word that everybody knew was 'bolero', and this is why Sor called his article 'Le Bolero', why elsewhere he called his own songs boleros

---

[20] *La Opera Española y la Música Dramática en España en el Siglo XIX* (Madrid, 1881), pp. 131-2. Two pictures by Degas showing Pagans singing and accompanying himself on the guitar are reproduced in F.V. Grunfeld's *The Art and Times of the Guitar* (London, 1969), pp. 244-5.

CHANSON

Relative aux événements d'Espagne depuis le départ du Roi Ferdinand 7. jusqu'à la fin de l'an 1811

Paroles et Musique de Mr. Ferd. SOR l'an 1812.

Imitation Française par Made. × × ×

Prix 1.f 50.c

A PARIS A la Lyre Moderne Chez Mme BENOIST Editeur Mde. de Musique et d'Instrumens Rue de Richelieu No. 20.

A don de vas Fer_nan_do incau_to no salgas no de tu na_cion mira que un
Las ou vas tu, cré_du_le Ferdi_nand? chez les francais vois tu quel sort t'attend! leur chef in_

pueblo que te a_do_ra sabe quienes Na_po_le_on huye del la_zo que te
_grat qu'ils surnomment le grand, pour eux pour toi n'est déjà qu'un ty_ran. l'Es_pagne ain_si par_lait courant aux

tiende bur_la su ardid y su in_ten_cion. as_sien vi_to_ria de_te_ni_an a don Fer_
armes; de tou_tes parts formant ses es_ca_drons prête à venger son af_front ou ses larmes sur l'en_ne_

-nan-do de Bor - bon.
mi du ciel et des Bourbons

poco f   cres.   p

Accompagnement de Guitarre un ton et demi plus bas.

2

Mas como el bueno à todos juzga
Segun su noble corazon ,
Juzgó Fernando incompatible
Con la diadema la traycion ;
De la amistad dudar no supo
Aquel que engaños no estudió ,
Silencio inpuso à sus vasallos
Y su camino prosiguió .

3

Llego a Bayona el inocente ;
Y en vez del premio que esperó
De su excesiva confianza ,
Humillaciones encontró ;
El que su amigo sellamava ,
Que le ofreció su proteccion ,
Le despojó de su corona
Y en un castillo le encerró .

4

Los Españoles irritados
Contra pérfidia tan atroz ,
Juran vengar a su monarca
Y honrar el nombre de Español :
A un tiempo el grito de venganza
Por toda España resonó ,
Y todos toman por divisa
Su Rey , su Patria., y religion .

5

La juventud briosa y fuerte ,
Parte al encuentro del campeon
Que ya hasta Cordova llegava
Con su sacrilega legion ;
Al primer choque , la victoria
Tan noble esfuerzo coronó ,
Y el que en Baylen no hallo su tumba
Aprisionado se quedó .

6

En Zaragoza y en Valencia
Se defendieron con ardor ,
Mas el valor y la constancia
A la desgracia al fin cedió ;
Resiste en vano Tarragoña
De los ataques al teson ,
Porque el que puede socorrerla
Solo sirvio de expectador .

7

Del ambicioso las legiones
El suelo inundan Español ,
Y los caudillos inhumanos
Al crimen prestan su sancion ;
Cada soldado es un tirano
De las haciendas y el honor ,
Y el hospedage que recive
Paga con la desolacion

8

Por otra parte , los malvados
Que de la España son borron ,
Se entregan al asesinato ,
Al robo y la devastacion ;
Cometen quantos atentados
Caben en la imaginacion
Y sirve el nombre de Fernando
De inpunidad a la agresion .

9

Los Españoles dividieron
En este caso la opinion ;
Los que evitar quieren estragos ,
Recurren a la sumision ;
Juzgan inutil y ahun funesta
Tan pertinaz obstinacion ,
Y que la lucha proseguida
Completará su destruccion

Los que imaginan que la Patria
Puede encontrar su salvacion
Por ótros medios diferentes ,
Huyen al ultimo rincon ;
Abandonando aquel su Padre ,
Aquel su Esposa y su mansion ,
Y aquel tal vez a un inocente
Fruto infeliz de bendicion .

11

La triste España hecha el teatro
De la desgracia mas atroz ,
Mira a sus hijos divididos ;
Oh desventura la mayor ! . . .
Este a aquel trata de insensato ,
Y aquel a aqueste de traydor , ...
Mal haya amen el ambicioso
Que ocasionó tal division .

12

O Dios inmenso , que leyendo
En el humano corazon
Ves quales son mis sentimientos
Y mis deseos quales son ,
Une los votos españoles ;
Cese la fiera disencion ;
Vivamos todos como hermanos ,
Que asi prospéra una nacion .

2

Mais Ferdinand pouvait - il dans son cœur
Loger soupçon de cet art destructeur
Qui l'amenait à son persécuteur ,
Qui préparait tant de jours de douleur !
On vit , enfin , un roi trainer sa chaine ,
Dans nos chateaux , transformés en prisons ;
Puis , à son nom , la ligue européenne
Fille du ciel , protéger les Bourbons .

3

Toujours guidé par ses dieux infernaux ,
Sans amitié , sans crainte , sans repos ,
Malgré l'avis des sages , des héros ,
Napoléon poursuivait ses travaux ,
De Valencey le seigneur respectable
Pour prix secret d'une ferme raison ,
Se vit nommer , ô contrainte effroyable ! .
Premier geolier des Princes de Bourbon ,

4

Tandis qu'au loin par de trompeurs succès ,
Napoléon couronnait ses excès ,
Toujours luttant , Espagnols et français
Perdaient l'espoir de triomphe ou de paix :
De l'espagnol l'invincible constance ,
Et du français l'impétueux renom ,
Ressuscitaient les braves de Numance ,
Et les exploits des héros de Bourbon .

5

Le doigt divin ayant marqué le jour
De la vengeance , et du royal retour ,
Napoléon va connaitre à son tour
Combien vaut mieux de régner par amour :
Pour dissiper le fantôme de gloire
Il a suffi du souffle des saisons ,
Il est tombé ; . . . tombe aussi sa mémoire :
Gloire au très haut , et vivent les Bourbons ! .

Seguidillas boleras by Sor:
"El que quisiera amando",
for voice and guitar.

rather than seguidillas, and why Peña y Goni in 1881 also called them boleros. It is principally a later usage rather than the original one.

Sor sets out the history of the dance, the bolero. The first seguidillas that were danced to, he says, were *Seguidillas Manchegas* (i.e., from La Mancha), 'à cause de leur mouvement plus vite que celui des *Murcianas,* et surtout des *Sevillanas'* ('because of their tempo, which was quicker than that of seguidillas from Murcia or, especially, from Seville'). This dance was adopted by the 'bas peuple'. Then a young man nicknamed *bolero,* 'the flyer', because of his agility, added faster steps and in order to fit them in used the slower music of the *Seguidillas Murcianas,* while still (says Sor) beginning his dance with eight bars of the *Manchegas.* The dance was named, after him, the bolero.[21] This form of the dance became very popular, especially in theatres, where it was danced during the entr'actes, as Sor says he witnessed in Barcelona in 1797.[22] But it soon became very complex, grotesque, even lascivious, and fell out of fashion; yet at the same time the songs that were associated with it became more favoured:

> Au fur et au mesure que cette danse perdait de sa vogue, les *Seguidillas* que l'on y chantait furent généralement adoptées, et elles sont encore aujourd'hui à la mode, sous le nom de *Boleros* ou *Seguidillas Boleras.*

> ('At the same time as this dance lost its popularity, the *Seguidillas* that were sung to it came to be generally adopted, and they are still fashionable today, under the name of *Boleros* or *Seguidillas Boleras.*')

This passage is important because this is the stage to which most of Sor's seguidillas probably belong.

The next step (says Sor) was the rehabilitation of the dance, in about 1801, by a dancer named Requejo. He is said to have come from Murcia.[23] He made it slower, more dignified and graceful, and replaced the guitar with a small orchestra. This was the form of the bolero that was in vogue when the French invaded in 1808. But the professional dancers had fled, and those who remained and danced for the invader added gypsy steps to it. The French added some of their own; and the bolero that conquered Europe was unrecognizable.

---

[21] Estébanez Calderón (El Solitario), in his *Escenas andaluzas* (1847), pp. 21-32, agrees with this and says that the dancer's name was either Sebastián Cerezo from La Mancha or Anton Boliche from Seville. But other theories about the origin of the name *bolero* have been advanced; see, for example, the article 'Bolero' in the *Enciclopedia Universal Europeo-Americans.*

[22] Sor himself composed 'boleros' in Barcelona in 1798, as we saw; but whether they were songs or instrumental music is not clear.

[23] Estébanez Calderón, op. cit., p. 29.

M. Coulon a éprouvé plus de difficulté à instruire mademoiselle Mercandotti, Espagnole [the famous dancer], qui dansait déjà le *Bolero* dans le véritable genre caractéristique, que si elle n'eût jamais rien appris.

('M. Coulon had more difficulty in teaching Mlle Mercandotti, who as a Spaniard already danced the bolero in the characteristic style, than if she had never learned anything at all.')

We saw that Sor composed 'boleros' in Barcelona in 1798 and about 1802-3, and in Madrid in about 1803-4, and that they were much in demand. This coincides exactly with the statement above, that after about 1797 *seguidillas boleras* became very popular in Spain while at the same time becoming dissociated from the dance, and very probably this is the stage to which most of Sor's seguidillas belong. They are related to the dance yet independent of it. They can hardly date from before about 1797, when Sor as a young man of nineteen was just beginning his career in Barcelona; and (except for one published in 1814) they certainly date from before his exile in 1813. Therefore they are products of the late Spanish baroque, a period of which Manfred Bukofzer wrote: 'Here [in Spanish secular music of the seventeenth and eighteenth centuries] we have one of the very few examples in baroque music in which the influence of folk music on art music is more than wishful thinking' (*Music in the Baroque Era,* London, 1948, p. 175). Sor's seguidillas reflect just such an influence: they are the contribution of the greatest guitarist of his age to a popular tradition which is still alive today.

The text of a seguidilla usually had seven lines, and sometimes only four. The first four were called the *copla,* and the last three the *estribillo.* A strict metrical form was observed in which the lines always had alternately seven and five syllables. The rhyme-scheme, however, was looser than the metre: the second and fourth lines had to rhyme together, and the fifth and seventh, but either rhyme or assonance would do, and the other lines might or might not rhyme together. Here is an example:

> Las mujeres y cuerdas
>   De la guitarra,
> Es menester talento
>   Para templarlas.
>
> Flojas no suenan,
> Y suelen saltar muchas
>   Si las aprietan.

('Women and guitar strings: you need talent to tune them. If they're slack they don't sound; and lots of them, if you tighten them too much, break.')

So short a poem, like the limerick in English or the *haiku* in Japanese, must make its effect in a small space. It often does so by playing on words. In the above example, *templar* refers both to women and to guitar strings. The subject-matter is nearly always amorous. Either a mood is set, generally a sad one, or a humorous point is made. Sor says of the poems: 'En effet, les paroles en sont généralement très spirituelles' ('Indeed, the words [of seguidillas] are generally very witty').

Such brevity has a long tradition behind it, going back to the court lyrics of the Spanish Renaissance, to certain medieval poems throughout Europe, even perhaps to the very oldest of all Romance love poems, the tiny *kharjas* of Moslem Spain (see, for instance, Peter Dronke's *The Medieval Lyric,* London, 1968, pp. 86-91); and similar *coplas* are still being written, composed, sung, and collected today. The imagery is traditional too. One of Sor's songs, 'Si dices que mis ojos', is a love lyric but uses religious terminology, just as did the Spanish Renaissance court lyric: the woman says 'If you say that my eyes kill you, then you'd better make confession, take the sacrament; for I'm on my way . . '

The music of seguidillas, like the text, is short. But repetition is used, according to certain fixed permutations of words and musical sections, just as it had been centuries before in the Spanish villancico, the French rondeau, or the Italian ballata. In Sor's seguidillas, the repetition scheme is nearly always the same. And the rhythm is always triple. Other musical features are characteristic but not invariable. Thus, within the basic triple rhythm, triplets are common. A favourite melodic interval is the descending augmented second: for instance, C sharp to B flat, or D sharp to C natural. An instrumental introduction is frequent. And the accompanying instrument most favoured is the guitar, though the piano is also found. In seguidillas of this period, a solo voice is usual, though there are some duets and trios.

These features are found again and again in seguidillas composed in Spain at this time. They occur in seguidillas by Moretti; in anonymous songs of a simpler and more primitive type than Sor's; and in more advanced anonymous ones (examples of all of these are in the British Library, MSS Egerton 3288 and 3289). But the situation changed. The bolero caught the imagination of Europe and became part of the Spanish aura of Romanticism, an aura that produced such works as Hugo's *Hernani* or Bizet's *Carmen*. It was danced and sung everywhere in Europe, and examples were composed and published outside Spain by Sor and many others. Its popularity culminated in the most famous bolero of all, Ravel's *Boléro* for orchestra (1928). And in the boleros published outside Spain in the nineteenth century, the style changed. The guitar yielded to the piano as the favourite accompanying instrument; duets and trios with piano accompaniment became more frequent; the characteristic repetitions were abandoned;

and more and more the songs betray that they are no longer the genuine product of a culture on its own ground. Sor played his part in this later diffusion, by composing and publishing both arrangements of his old seguidillas and what appear to be new ones, under the name of boleros.

The early songs were distributed not in printed editions but in manuscripts. In Spain at that time it was customary to have music copied by a scribe, in an establishment called a *copistería,* and the three manuscripts in which Sor's seguidillas are found show every sign of having been copied in this way. Though they are all three now in London, they certainly originated in Spain, in one case about 1813 and in the others by 1819 at latest.

Sor's sophisticated yet simple accompaniments respect and delicately support the texts. They show an awareness and appreciation of these elegant, brief, and witty poems. The running triplets in his 'Las mujeres y cuerdas' gradually rise to suggest the idea of tuning a guitar (or, in this poem, a woman).

How far are Sor's seguidillas original compositions, and how far arrangements of popular songs? We cannot know the full answer without much more research on this neglected period, but the evidence suggests that the concept of originality is not relevant to this still pre-Romantic period. Sor took his place *within* a tradition, rather than using its materials to make entirely new compositions. The various different versions that are known of his songs demonstrate this fact. Sometimes versions are known in which the words are the same but the music different; sometimes versions in which the music is the same but the words different; and sometimes both words and music are similar but changes have been made (one of Sor's songs exists in a version for two voices instead of one and with piano accompaniment instead of guitar). It seems that interchanges were made readily; that there was little attempt to preserve existent material intact; and that this rich tradition allowed for continual new creation and adaptation. Sor's seguidillas spring directly from that rich tradition.

'Las quejas de Maruja'

One other Spanish song by Sor is known, 'Las quejas de Maruja' ('Maruja's complaints'). An early manuscript of it is in the Royal Library, Copenhagen, and the first page of a printed edition is reproduced in J. Subirá's *Historia de la Música Española e Hispanoamericana* (Barcelona, 1953), p. 670.[24] It is a love song

---

[24] The manuscript is undated but is probably Spanish, early nineteenth century; its shelf-mark is C.I.529. The song was published in Spain, both by itself and also as one of a collection of six Spanish songs entitled *La Sal de España.*

with alternative guitar or piano accompaniment, in which a girl called Maruja complains of her lover's indifference. Short and rapid musical phrases with a deliberately monotonous bass give the impression of a comic patter song.

Piano music

A manuscript containing minuets for piano by Sor was in the Arxiú de Música at Montserrat, but now appears to be missing. Parts of *Telemaco* exist in piano arrangements which may or may not be by Sor. There is no other evidence that Sor composed music for piano during his Spanish period.

Solo guitar music from Sor's Spanish period: dating

Ledhuy mentions that while in Spain Sor composed music for solo guitar, even that his compositions were in demand by other guitarists. On bibliographical grounds, it is now possible to establish that certain major works by Sor for solo guitar were composed before he left Spain (or in some cases, just possibly slightly later, within a year of leaving it). These works therefore stand not merely within the general European tradition, but can now be placed specifically within the history of music in the Spanish peninsula, having been composed by a Catalan in Spain. This important fact has not before been realized, for lack of evidence. The works in question are as follows.

> Minuet [a version of op. 11, no. 5]
> Minuet and Allegretto [= op. 23, nos. 4 and 2]
> Four minuets [the second = op. 11, no. 6]
> *Air Varié* [opp. 3 and 12 are later versions of this work]
> *Air Varié* (on a chromatic theme)
> *Sonata Prima* [= *Grand Solo*, op. 14]
> *Sonata Seconda* [= Sonata, op. 15]
> *Thema varié* [op. 20 is on the same theme]
> *Fantasia* [later called op. 4]
> *Six Petites Pièces* [later called op. 5]
> *Fantaisie* [later called op. 7]
> Sonata, op. 22
> Minuet, op. 11 no. 3; and possibly the rest of op. 11
> Possibly *Folies d'Espagne*

No guitar music by Sor — indeed, no music by him of any kind — is known to have been printed in Spain before his exile in 1813. We have only manuscripts, and for Sor's solo guitar music I have found only one relevant manuscript of this period. It is a graded instruction book for guitar called 'Música para Guitarra' in the collection of Robert Spencer, London, and it includes a minuet which is a version of op. 11 no. 5. The manuscript bears the signature 'R.H. Clive' and so was

presumably collected in Spain at the same time as Clive collected his other manuscripts, that is to say in about 1813 (for details on Clive and his travels in Spain, see my edition of Sor's *Seguidillas*).

The earliest known editions of Sor's guitar music were not Spanish, but French, and they appeared probably about 1810; the latest possible date is 1814. They consist of seven works for solo guitar published in Paris by Salvador Castro de Gistau in his *Journal de Musique Etrangère pour la Guitare ou Lyre*.[25] The works are the third to ninth items in the list above. There is a long and flattering article on Castro, quite possibly written by Castro himself, in the *Dictionnaire Historique des Musiciens* of A. Choron and F. Fayolle (Paris, December 1810). He was born in Madrid in 1770, and came to France, where he taught the guitar and published his *Journal*. He chose his pieces well: he includes a 'Sonata' which is the earliest known version of the work later known as *Grand Solo* (op. 14); another sonata which is that now known as op. 15; several small pieces, and a set of variations on a chromatic theme. They have every appearance of being good authentic texts, and are the earliest known versions of all these works.

In Paris again, this time in 1814 after Sor had arrived there, two more works for solo guitar were published: the six short pieces now known as op. 5, and the Fantasia now known as op. 7. These were listed in the *Bibliographie de l'Empire Français*[26] on 4 February and 3 September 1814, respectively. Opus numbers do not appear on these editions. The six short pieces were published by Mme Benoist, who also published two patriotic songs which we know were composed before Sor left Spain: this suggests that these pieces too may have been older works, not newly composed ones. The Fantasia, technically much more difficult, was dedicated to and published by Ignace Pleyel, the founder of the piano firm. There is no way of telling whether it was an older work or newly composed in 1814.

---

[25] The *Journal,* of which copies are in the Bibliothèque Nationale, Paris, and elsewhere, is undated. Choron and Fayolle mention it, so it must have been begun by December 1810. All numbers bear on the title-page the words 'Déposé à la Bibliothèque Impériale', which means that they must date either from before the fall of Napoleon in March 1814, when the word 'Impériale' ceased to be used, or else from the Hundred Days (March-July 1815). It may very well be that the *Journal* dates from the very earliest years of the century; that is the opinion of the *Catalogue Collectif des Périodiques* (Paris, Bibliothèque Nationale, 1969), which dates it 'entre 1802 et 1810' but without giving reasons.

---

[26] Called the *Bibliographie de la France* at the time of the second entry.

In London, Lewis Lavenu published a '2nd Fantasia' (now known as op. 4) whose exact date is a mystery. Lavenu was the same man who had printed two patriotic songs by Sor in the *Poesías Patrióticas* of Arriaza in London in 1810. On the '2nd Fantasia' his address is given as '26 New Bond Street' — which, however, he left about 1811, according to Charles Humphries & William C. Smith (*Music Publishing in the British Isles,* 2nd edn., Oxford, 1970, p. 206); whereas the words 'Printed & Sold for the Author' at the head of the music strongly suggest that Sor was by then in London, in which case it did not appear before 1815. In any case it dates from before 1818 when Lavenu died. I am inclined to think that the address '26 New Bond Street' is an error for Lavenu's new address 28 New Bond Street and that this Fantasia appeared in London in about 1815-18. If this was the second Fantasia, the first was doubtless that now known as op. 7.

Besides the two sonatas published by Castro, one later known as *Grand Solo* and the other as op. 15, a third must also be early, at least in some form: the sonata op. 22. Although not published until 1825 (Paris, Meissonnier), it bears the inscription 'Grand [sic] Sonate de Sor, qui fut dédiée au prince de la PAIX'. The 'prince de la PAIX' was Manuel Godoy, who as we saw fell from power in 1808, and the use of his title, together with the words 'qui *fut* dédiée', strongly indicate that the work in some form or another dates from before that.

Another work for which there is some evidence of an early date is the minuet op. 11 no. 3. In an edition of op. 11 belonging to Robert Spencer, London, is a manuscript note against this minuet, possibly in the hand of José de Lira (on whom see below), reading: 'En mai 1823 j'ai été logé à Girone chez M. le Marquis de Capmany dont le fils, D. Francisco Maria de Sabater y Camps, m'a assuré avoir composé le menuet suivant à Saragosse en 1803' ('In May 1823 I stayed at Gerona with the Marquis of Capmany whose son, Francisco Maria de Sabater y Camps, assured me that he had composed this minuet at Saragossa in 1803'). According to Ledhuy, Sor's father had a composer friend called 'le chevalier de Sabatea', which may be simply a misprint for 'Sabater'. Whoever composed the piece, the note does suggest an early date. Indeed, op. 11 seems to contain a number of old pieces. Op. 11 no. 5 is in an early manuscript belonging to Robert Spencer (see above), while no. 6 was published by Castro. In addition, the theme used at the beginning of op. 11 is the same as that used for the *Thème Varié,* a work published by Meissonnier without opus number; it was obviously a favourite theme.

The opus numbering of Sor's solo guitar music up to op. 23 is not in chronological order. Therefore it may

well be that a number of Sor's works bearing opus numbers up to that point are in fact works composed in his Spanish period, but the only evidence other than that already discussed would be the style, a notoriously unreliable criterion. At least, it seems to me very likely that *Folies d'Espagne* (op. 15) is one of his Spanish works: the very title suggests it, the style seems early, while it was actually the first work of Sor published by Meissonnier.

The first edition of op. 7 is written on two staves. This shows an ambitious attitude towards the guitar, and indeed the music of op. 7 is sometimes so rich harmonically that it needs two staves in order not to be too crowded. This original edition includes an *Avertissement* pointing out that to write guitar music in the G clef is to write it an octave away from its true pitch, and that the two-stave method obviates this disadvantage. However, the two-stave method did not catch on. Mme Benoist's edition of op. 5 specifically bears on the title-page the words 'écrites selon la méthode ordinaire' ('written in the ordinary manner'), meaning that the music was written, as usual, on one G clef.[27]

Solo guitar music from Sor's Spanish period: the music

The major pieces from this period are unquestionably the sonatas later known as op. 15, op. 22, and *Grand Solo.* For convenience I shall use these names, although it must be clearly understood that they are later names and not the original ones.

Grand Solo was first published by Castro as 'Sonata Prima'. It is a free fantasy in which themes recur, rather than a work in strict sonata form. A grandiose and large-scale piece in a single movement, it uses the range of the guitar to the full. The scordatura (sixth string to D) adds to its sonorousness. It starts and ends in D, but moves imaginatively among the keys, at one point to D flat major.[28]

The sonata in C now known as op. 15 was also first published by Castro. Again it consists of a single long movement, an allegretto. It is an uncompromising work, developing its ideas to the full and concentrating on musical values rather than on what the guitar can easily do.

---

[27] On early guitar notation, see Thomas F. Heck, 'The role of Italy in the early history of the classic guitar', *Guitar Review,* 34 (1971), pp. 1-6.

---

[28] I am referring to the Castro version. The later Meissonnier version of c. 1822 is a scandalously watered-down version of far less musical value, probably simplified by the publisher for commercial reasons. A third version is in Isaias Savio's edition of *19 Composiciones* by Sor (Buenos Aires, n.d.); Mr. Savio does not give its source. In addition, Aguado made an arrangement which is still in print. As far as I know, Castro's is the earliest surviving version.

The sonata now known as op. 22 has four movements: allegro, adagio, minuet, and rondo. Like op. 15, it is in C. As in *Grand Solo,* the first movement moves freely from key to key; on the first page we move suddenly from C to E flat major. This is a kind of change not characteristic of Sor's later works, and supports the idea derived from the dedication to Godoy that this is in fact an early work. Soriano Fuertes wrote of Sor's early style, in relation to this sonata: 'En un principio su gusto fué tan enérgico, que se le puede llamar soberbio, como se ve en la obra que dedicó al príncipe de la Paz' (*Historia de la Música Española,* IV, 1859, p. 211) ('At first his style was so energetic that one can call it magnificent, as can be seen in the work which he dedicated to the Prince of the Peace').

Sor wrote one other sonata, op. 25. It was first published in Paris in 1827 on his return from Russia, and while of course it, too, may have been composed earlier there is no evidence to suggest that idea. Again it is in C, again it has four movements: andante largo, allegro non troppo, andantino grazioso (theme and variations), and minuet. But the muscular style of the earlier sonatas is missing, and instead we have much attention given to precise and complex harmonics in the second movement, and a rather weak ending with a minuet. This work, surely, is a late one.

All these four sonatas or sonata-like works are uncommonly long for guitar music. In the whole of Europe at this time, Sor seems to have been the only composer to have attempted such a thing: not until Giuliani did any comparable work appear for guitar. How strange that such ambitious and large-scale pieces were not followed up until much later. They are completely unique in their time.

W.S. Newman has complimentary things to say about Sor's sonatas. He writes:

> The creative worth of Sor's guitar sonatas is high. The ideas, which grow out of the instrument yet stand up well enough apart from it, are fresh and distinctive. The harmony is skillful and surprisingly varied, with bold key changes and with rich modulations in the development sections. The texture is naturally of interest, too, with the melody shifted from top, to bottom, to middle, and frequent contrapuntal bits added. Among the extended forms, the first allegro movements still show considerable flexibility in the application of "sonata form," especially in the larger number of ideas introduced and recalled. For that matter, the style still goes back to that of Haydn and Boccherini, especially in Op. 22/i, which has all the neatness of syntax and accompaniment to be found in a Classic symphony, and Op. 22/iii and iv, which could nicely pass as a minuet and rondo by Haydn. Op. 15 is in one movement, with a development section that is short but effective, both tonally and thematically. Op. 22 is in 4 movements, F-S-M-F, the second being a

> warmly expressive "Adagio." Op. 25 is in 3 movements — a rather free, pathetic "Andante" in the tonic minor, a gay "Allegro" in 6/8 meter, and a theme-and-variations that recalls the problems publishers were supposed to have had in selling Sor's guitar music to amateurs, so much of it being scored in difficult 4-part textures.

> (*The Sonata in the Classic Era,* Chapel Hill, 1963, p. 664)

The two fantasias from Sor's early period, those now known as op. 4 and op. 7, are very different from each other. Op. 4 is a delightful work consisting of an introduction, rondo, and coda. Technical demands are not great. The harmonization is simple, and single melodic lines are preferred to complex chords. Op. 7 is far more ambitious, exploiting the possibilities of the guitar fully and uncompromisingly. It has an introduction, theme and variations, and coda, and is a major work on a level with *Grand Solo* or the sonata op. 22. A correspondent of the *Giulianiad* wrote in 1833:

> . . . I trust it will not be considered as prejudice on my part when I say, that the beautiful compositions of Sor have touched and inspired my soul above all others. What wonder then that such became the chosen objects of my particular study; and if it is said of Giuliani, that "he must be considered as the inventor of a new method of *playing*" — perhaps I may be permitted to say, that we ought to consider Sor as the inventor of a new method of *composing*. Let me point out to you, as a specimen, his delightful fantasia opera 7; the introductory largo, in C minor, with its heart-thrilling combinations of chords, (although rather spun out too long) which abounds with elegance and beauty from beginning to end, leading to the tender floating theme in C major, and its variations; all these beauties must be highly relished by the proficient, as they must likewise fascinate every sincere admirer of the guitar! Allow me, especially, to draw your attention to the variations, Nos. 1, 4, and 7, and say, whether music like that is not worthy of study?

Castro published three sets of themes and variations by Sor. One is a work which Meissonnier later provided with a minuet and issued as op. 3, and still later was revised, provided with an introduction and coda, and issued as op. 12. The theme of another is the same as that of op. 20, but the variations are different with only occasional resemblances. Finally, a piece called *Air Varié* is a completely unknown work, with a chromatic theme and six variations. Here it is in facsimile.

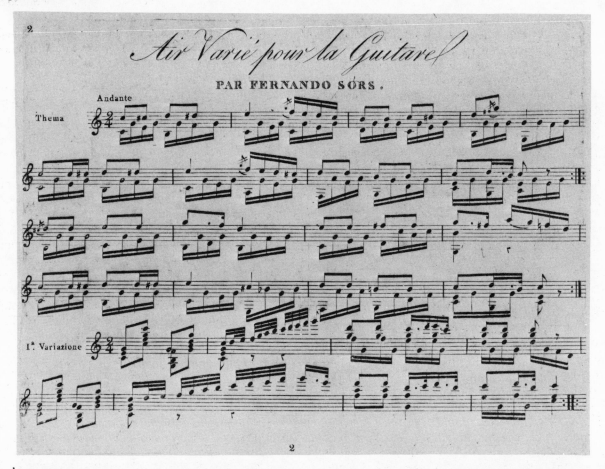

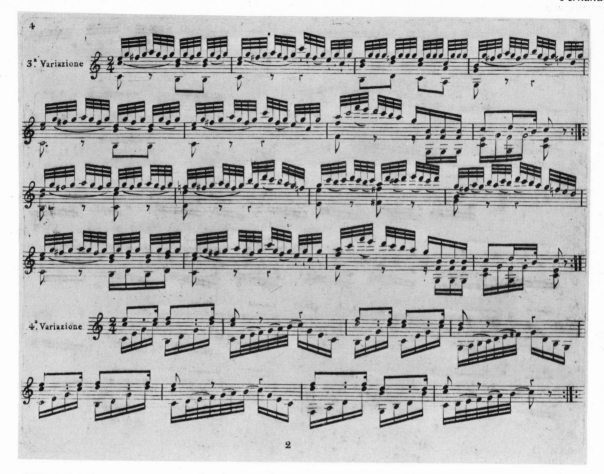

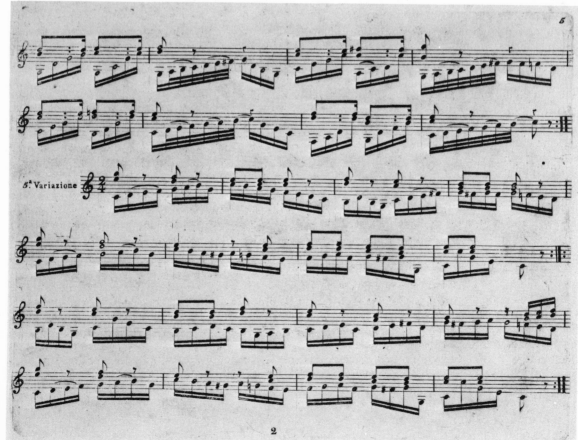

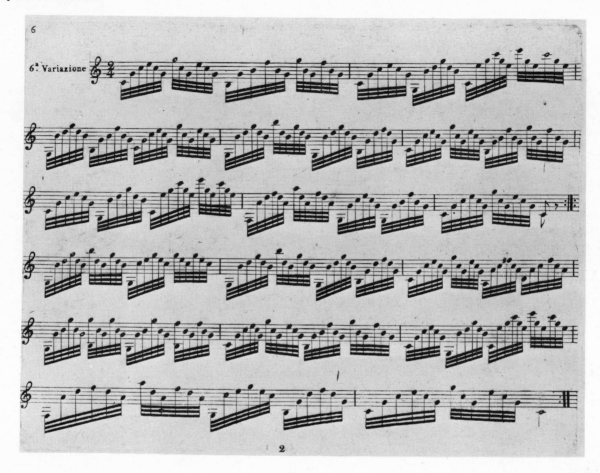

These sets of variations all have in common a sense of firmness and concision which is not evident, for example, in the nine variations of the later op. 16 on Paisiello's 'Nel cor piu non mi sento'. In the three early sets, as also in the variations of op. 7, the *Folies d'Espagne* or the famous Mozart variations op. 9, no space is wasted and the music devotes itself not to 'guitaristic' effects but only to itself. The models, plain to hear, are Haydn and Mozart.

Finally, the small pieces. Six minuets and an allegretto are definitely early: one minuet in an early manuscript and the rest in Castro. These are miniatures sometimes with interesting harmonic touches, especially in the set of four published by Castro. Some of them, as explained above, are also in op. 11, and it may well be that the whole of op. 11 is early. It was first published in Paris in 1822 or shortly before by Meissonnier, as *Deux Thêmes Variés et Douze Menuets*. The twelve minuets contain some splendid and original music. The opening of no. 5, which is one of the definitely early pieces, resembles a part of *Grand Solo*. — Op. 5, *Six Petites Pièces,* dedicated to Sor's wife, foreshadows the later

sets of divertimenti, groups of small-scale pieces. This set is noteworthy for the famous Andante largo which is today played in so many concerts.

A special word about *Folies d'Espagne,* later published as one of two works forming op. 15, and very probably an early work. This is one of my favourite pieces by Sor. A theme and four variations in E minor, it is followed in the first editions by a minuet which may or may not itself be early. It shows a natural musical gift, lyricism, and strength: surely one of the most attractive guitar pieces of this period.[29]

Sor's early guitar music, then, that which can be said to be truly from his Spanish period, consists of three sonatas, three sets of variations, a fantasia which is in fact another set of variations (Op. 7), a rondo (op. 4), and various small pieces. The sheer scale of the largest of these pieces is astonishing for the period; while their adventurous key changes and musical cohesion show a composer of considerable stature.

---

[29] On the history of the *Folies d'Espagne,* see Richard Hudson, 'The Folia Melodies', *Acta Musicologica,* XLV (1973), 98-119.

CHAPTER 2

PARIS
1813-1815

In 1813 Sor arrived in France with the retreating French armies, and went to Paris. There he was already known as a composer through the publications of Castro, and he could count on many friends among the French. For the time being, Napoleon was still in power.

Ledhuy speaks of praise by Cherubini, Méhul, and Berton: in other words, by the musical establishment that Berlioz, somewhat later, was to ridicule. According to Peña y Goni (*La Opera Española*, p. 131) and an anonymous reviewer in the *Allgemeine musikalische Zeitung* in September 1823, Sor is supposed to have arranged for the guitar the overture to *La Chasse du jeune Henri* by Méhul. This was one of Méhul's most successful operas, first produced in 1797, and its overture is still sometimes played today. Sor's arrangement for guitar is not known to survive.

Cherubini was a man with power; Méhul was more important than his reputation today suggests; and it is clear that in mentioning these names in the Ledhuy article Sor is expressing a wish to be accepted. Spain was, after all, outside the musical mainstream of Europe, and though Sor had already created highly original music for the guitar, that instrument was still thought of as exclusively Spanish and there was no guarantee that Europe would think highly of it. Sor had other strings to his bow, having composed successfully in the Italian style, having studied the style of Mozart and Haydn, and having written symphonies, quartets, and many other works.

One way in which he wished to achieve success was in composing operas. Ledhuy tells us of his first brush with the realities of the 'trade' in the Paris operatic world:

> Lorsque Sor eut entendu quelques opéras du théâtre Feydeau, il sentit qu'il pourrait bien écrire dans un genre qui lui permettait de s'éloigner des formes adoptées pour le grand opéra, qui ne l'avait point séduit. Il chercha un poëme; mais on lui fit observer que les poëtes de renom gardaient des positions tout-à-fait différentes avec les compositeurs. Ils sont peu traitables avec le musicien qui n'a pas encore débuté à Paris, tandis qu'ils s'offrent de grand coeur au compositeur à la mode. Cela s'explique. Le poëte Marsollier entendit quelques fragmens du *Télémaque*, et il dit à Sor que sa musique était tout-à-fait italienne, qu'elle ne pouvait convenir à la scène française; il lui conseillait d'attendre, et de se mettre sous la direction de quelque homme habile, qu'alors il deviendrait peut-être en état d'écrire pour le théâtre. A cette sortie, Sor ne put contenir sa colère, et après avoir longuement énuméré toutes les platises, les fautes de prosodie et les contre-sens de certains ouvrages qu'on portait aux nues, il blâma hautement les soi-disant connaisseurs, qui entendent avec indifférence de véritables beautés musicales. Tout fut dit, et Marsollier ferma son portefeuille.

('When Sor had heard some operas at the Théâtre Feydeau, he felt that he could well compose in this genre which would allow him to get away from the forms that grand opera had taken and which he did not like. He looked for a libretto; but people told him that famous poets took up very different positions towards composers. They are scarcely approachable by the composer who has not yet made his debut in Paris, while they willingly offer themselves to a fashionable composer. That is understandable. The poet Marsollier heard some fragments of *Telemaco*, and he said to Sor that his music was completely Italian and did not suit the French theatre; he advised him to wait, and to study with some expert, when he might perhaps become able to compose for the theatre. At that, Sor was unable to contain his anger, and after he had enumerated at length all the commonplaces, the faults of prosody and the contradictions of certain works which were being extravagantly praised, he vehemently attacked the so-called connaisseurs, who can listen with indifference to true musical beauty. That was that, and Marsollier closed his portfolio.')

On 16-19 October 1813 Napoleon fought and lost the Battle of Leipzig. By April 1814 the Allies were in Paris. Napoleon abdicated and left for Elba, and Louis XVIII came from London to Paris. From a letter which Sor wrote to the Duc de Fleury (for which see below), it seems that Sor took part in the concert music of the new regime.

From entries in the *Bibliographie de l'Empire Français,*[1] it is possible to establish that certain works by Sor were published in Paris at this time rather than during his later Paris period. The entries are as follows:

4 February 1814	*Six Petites Pièces* [op. 5]
4 February 1814	*Boléro de Société,* 'Mis descuidados ojos'
20 August 1814	*Marche Patriotique Espagnole*
3 September 1814	*Fantaisie* [op. 7]

In addition, the *Chanson Relative aux Evénements d'Espagne,* 'Adonde vas, Fernando incauto', was also published by one of the same publishers and has every appearance of having been published at the same time, making a total of five works. Of these, the two patriotic songs had certainly been composed earlier (they are specifically dated 1809 and 1812), and I suspect that the other three works had also, though there is no proof of this. Sor came to France with much music, either in score or in his memory. The publishers of the above works were Ignace Pleyel (the Fantasia) and Mme Benoist (all the rest).

The *Six Petites Pièces* are dedicated 'à son épouse' ('to his wife'). But despite considerable research, the identity of Sor's wife remains an impenetrable mystery. His daughter, as we shall see, was born between 1814 and 1817, which suggests that Sor's wife accompanied her husband out of Spain; but not even her name is known to us. Font y Moresco, writing about a visit to the composer in 1839 (see chapter 5), says that his wife had died many years before. About 1820, in London, Sor became involved with the ballerina Félicité Hullin. A mere theory: was his wife perhaps a Catalan or a Spaniard, who accompanied her husband when he left Spain in 1813, and did she perhaps die in childbirth when their daughter was born about 1815? In any case, we know that Sor's daughter survived, travelled to Russia with him, and later lived with him in Paris (see chapters 4 and 5). And so we may suppose that during these years in Paris, and during his later stay in London, Sor was not alone but was accompanied by a very young child, his daughter.

In 1815 or before, Sor's portrait was painted by Innocent-Louis Goubaud, a well-known artist who painted a portrait of, among others, Napoleon. It must have been made before Goubaud left France for America in 1815.[2] Although no trace has been found of the original painting, there survive two lithographs derived from it: one made by Gottfried Engelmann and Joseph Bordes in Paris and the other by M.N. Bate in London. They show Sor as a dashing young man, with his guitar, and together with the drawing by Adam in Ledhuy's *Encyclopédie* they are the only known portraits of Sor. They are reproduced below.

Engelmann was a celebrated lithographer of the time, Bordes and Bate minor ones. The French lithograph was in existence by about 1825, when Meissonnier published a so-called *Collection Complète* of Sor's works 'orné de son portrait' (see chapter 5 below); the English one presumably dates from Sor's London period, 1815-23.

On 14 January 1815 Sor wrote to the Duc de Fleury asking for a post which had recently become vacant in the royal musical establishment. According to W. Sasser, 'The Guitar Works of Fernando Sor' (Ph. D. thesis, University of North Carolina, 1960), p. 52, the letter was 'one of the autograph letters owned by the Bibliothèque du Conservatoire in Paris'. It is translated into Spanish by Manuel Rocamora in his *Fernando Sor (1779-1839), Ensayo Biográfico* (Barcelona, 1957), pp. 61-2. However, the letter seems to have disappeared: it is not to be found in the Bibliothèque Nationale in Paris, whither all such papers of the Bibliothèque du Conservatoire have been transferred. No reply is known to the letter. As it has not been possible to trace the original French text, here is Sr. Rocamora's translation into Spanish, by kind permission.

Monseñor —

Habiendo sabido que el empleo que tenía el Sr. Gebauer en la Capilla de Música del Rey quedaba vacante, tengo el honor de pedíroslo.

Además de poseer todos los conocimientos que el cargo requiere, mis talentos como Guitarrista y como Compositor no os son desconocidos Monseñor, pues los he consagrado contribuyendo a dar más brillantez a las fiestas organizadas por la Corte, que habéis honrado constantemente con vuestra presencia. Y podéis estar convencido que no será del todo indiferente que me aceptéis al Servicio de Su Majestad como músico que siente todavía más deseos de contribuir al Esplendor de la Música de la Capilla de la Corte.

Tengo el honor de ser, con el mayor respeto, Monseñor, de V. Excelencia, el más humilde Servidor. — Fernando Sor — Paris 14 enero 1815.

---

[1] Called the *Bibliographie de la France* at the time of the last two entries.

[2] U. Thieme & F.C. Willis, *Allgemeines Lexikon der bildenden Künstler,* 14 (Leipzig, 1921). The portrait of Napoleon is in the Musée de Versailles (E. Bénézit, *Dictionnaire . . . des Peintres,* IV, 1966).

('Sir,

Having heard that the post which M. Gebauer held in the Royal Chapel is vacant, I have the honour of asking you for it.

As well as possessing all the knowledge which the post requires, my talents as guitarist and composer are not unknown to you, Sir, since I have devoted them to adding more brilliance to the festivities organized by the Court, which you have yourself constantly honoured with your presence. And you may be assured that I shall not be indifferent to your accepting me for the service of His Majesty, since I feel continually more desire to contribute to the splendour of the chapel music of the Court.

I have the honour to be, Sir, with the greatest respect, the most humble servant of Your Excellency, —

Fernando Sor —

Paris, 14 January 1815.')

During this time we can catch occasional glimpses of Sor. His address in 1814, as given on the title-page of the Fantasia [op. 7], was 27 rue du Helder. The rue du Helder is still there but the house has been demolished. From plans in the Bibliothèque Historique de la Ville de Paris it is possible to establish that it stood just north of the present Boulevard Haussmann in the present Place Adrien Oudin. In 1814 the Boulevard Haussmann had not yet been built, and the rue du Helder joined directly the rue Taitbout; no. 27 was the last odd-numbered house in the street. In October 1974 the site was occupied by the left-hand half (looking from the street) of the Polish arts and crafts shop 'Cepelia'.

In London in about 1816 Sor was to dedicate his *Six Divertimentos* for guitar (later known as op. 2) 'to his friend Emanuel Palacio Faxardo'. This man was living in Paris in 1814, and it may have been there that Sor met him. Palacio Fajardo (to use a more modern spelling) was a revolutionary, born in what is now Venezuela, a friend of the Libertador Simon Bolívar, and had been sent on a mission to try to raise arms and money for the South American movement for independence from Spain. He had arrived in France in February 1813. Napoleon received him favourably, but then fell from power. Palacio Fajardo stayed in Paris, hoping to persuade the new powers to support the independence movement, but he soon saw that this was impossible under the new reactionary regime. He was arrested by the French police in October 1814. Released, he went to London, where he published his book *Outline of the Revolution in South America, by a South-American* (London, 1817); and he sailed for Venezuela with a shipload of British guns in 1818. It was to this man, whom he doubtless also knew in London, that Sor

dedicated his *Six Divertimentos*. This friendship, and the publication of his patriotic songs in Paris, show that Sor was to some extent involved at this time in politics and moved in Spanish-speaking circles.[3]

With the composer in Paris at this time was his brother Carlos Sor. Carlos was born, as we saw in chapter 1, on 5 August 1785. In Spain, like his brother, he had served as 'commissaire des guerres' for the French, in his case from 1811 to 1813[4], and doubtless had to leave Spain for the same reasons. Like his brother, he was a composer and guitarist, and Fernando Sor's famous Mozart variations, op. 9, are dedicated to him. Castro published a minuet and a 'Moderato' by Carlos Sors in his *Journal de Musique Etrangère;* and on 2 August 1817 the *Bibliographie de la France* listed two arrangements from Cimarosa, *Air del Matrimonio segreto: Udite, tutti, udite, etc., arrangé pour la guitare, par C. Sor,* and *Air del Matrimonio segreto: O povereto, me, etc., id.*[5]

In the Archives Nationales, Paris, is some correspondence concerning police surveillance (file F7 12000). On 30 October 1816 and again on 27 December 1816 the Minister of War informed the police that 'le Sr. Sor, ex-commissaire des guerres, espagnol' had permission to live in Paris and to draw a pension as a refugee, and invited them to keep surveillance on him. On 18 January 1817 the police reported that he was living quietly at rue de la Michaudière, no. 7, apparently as a musician. The Christian name is not given, but that address is the address of Carlos Sor as given in the *Bibliographie de la France.* It seems that when Fernando Sor left Paris, Carlos Sor stayed on. In 1829 the *Revue Musicale* reported a concert in which it seems that he played (see chapter 5 below). And many years later, when Fernando Sor died in Paris in 1839, it was Carlos Sor, together with José de Lira, who sent out the invitations to the funeral.

In 1815, Napoleon returned from Elba; after the Hundred Days, he was once again defeated on 18 June 1815 at the Battle of Waterloo. Once again, Paris was full of the British. J.B. Priestley writes: 'When Louis [XVIII] left London for Paris, half the rank and fashion of Britain followed him. Once the British have been denied Paris for a few years, they cannot wait to return there as soon as the way is open. Even by the end of April [1814] it was reported that Paris had twelve thousand British visitors' (*The Prince of Pleasure,* London, 1971, pp. 115-6). They looked on Paris as a source of culture. The ballet, above all, came from Paris. During

---

[3] C. Parra Pérez, *Una Misión Diplomática Venezolana ante Napoleon en 1813* (Caracas, 1953); and the *Enciclopedia Universal Europeo-Americana.*

[4] Communication from General Marsauche, Château de Vincennes, 1974.

[5] A copy of the second, autographed 'C. Sor', is in London, collection of Robert Spencer.

the Napoleonic Wars, it had suffered badly, but after them, when ballet dancers might again be enticed to cross the Channel, things looked up. By the end of the 1816 season, the *Times* wrote that the ballet in London had reached 'an extraordinary pitch of elegance and maturity for the meridian of London'.[6] Concerts thrived also: the Philharmonic Society was founded in 1813 and thereafter went from strength to strength. Spanish things were more and more in favour in London. Lord Fife (to whom Moretti had dedicated his *Doce Canciones*) brought back from Spain the child dancer Maria Mercandotti, and even in 1814, at the age of thirteen, she danced to 'unbounded applause'.[7] And the political climate for Spanish exiles was fair. It is not surprising that Sor should have been tempted to come to London; and towards the end of 1815, that is what he did.

---

[6] 12 August 1816. Quoted from Ivor Guest's *The Romantic Ballet in England,* 2nd edn. (London, 1972), p. 30.

---

[7] John Ebers, quoted in Guest, op. cit., p. 40.

Corbeau pinxit *Litho. par Berdes*

Lith. de Engelmann

Drawn by J. Goubaud.

Engraved by M. N. Bate.

F. Sor.

CHAPTER 3

LONDON
1815-1823

> Mr. Sor's vocal compositions have gained such favour among the higher order of musical dilettanti, that a new set of arietts from his pen causes almost as much sensation as the publication of a new novel by the author of *Waverley*.
>
> (Ackermann's *Repository of Arts,* London, March 1820)

Such words may surprise those who are used to thinking of Sor only as a guitar composer. But during the seven years that he spent in London, he was known as much for his Italian arietts as for his guitar music. He produced eleven sets of three arietts each, in the purest tradition of bel canto, some of them very beautiful. As well as this, he performed in many concerts; taught singing; published many works for piano; composed his first set of studies [op. 6] for the guitar; fell in love with a ballerina; and wrote ballet music. It was one of the most eventful and successful periods of his life.

He came to London from Paris 'quelque temps après l'arrivée des alliés en France' (Ledhuy) ('some time after the Allies arrived in France'). The Allies arrived in France twice: once after the Battle of Leipzig, on 31 March 1814, and once after the Battle of Waterloo, on 7 July 1815. Since we know from the letter to the Duc de Fleury that Sor was still in Paris in January 1815, Ledhuy presumably refers to the second arrival, and it was probably late in 1815 that he made the journey. He was certainly here by January 1816, for in that month his name appears in a list of Associates of the Philharmonic Society (British Library, K.6.d.3).

Spanish exiles

England had not so far been very favourable to Spanish liberals, as we saw from the exchange of letters between Lord Wellington and Lord Bathurst in chapter 1. But nevertheless, it is true that England did provide a haven for many refugees from Fernando VII's oppressive government in Spain, and even paid pensions to many of them. Sor was only one of many; so many, in fact, that a very detailed and informative book has been devoted to their life in London: Vicente Llorens' *Liberales y Románticos* (2nd edn., Madrid, 1968). Some came in 1813, when the *afrancesados* left Spain. Others

came the next year, in 1814, when Fernando VII clamped down so heavily on the very liberals to whom he owed his throne that they were obliged to leave in large numbers. But most came in 1823, after a French army under the Duc d'Angoulême crushed all liberal ambitions in Spain. In 1824 Fernando VII declared an amnesty, but on such terms that many more people left Spain, and this is when the Spanish population in England reached its height. It diminished again in 1830, when the success of the July Revolution in Paris led many to leave England for France. So the largest number of Spaniards was here between 1823 and 1830, that is after Sor's departure; but even during his stay here, Llorens estimates that more than a thousand Spanish families lived in exile in London.

Most of them lived in the quarter of London called Somers Town; it became so Spanish that at one time the English night watchman used to call out the time in Spanish (Llorens, p. 43). Today this quarter is occupied mainly by taxi-drivers and Euston Station, and little has survived London property developers of various epochs.

We may suppose that Sor was in touch with these exiles. For example, many years later (in about 1837) he dedicated a *Marche Composée pour la Musique Militaire* to General Antonio Quiroga. By then, Quiroga had received an amnesty; but in 1823, he was living in exile in London, where he engaged in commerce and even invented a new kind of tooth-powder (Llorens, p. 63). Sor could have known him then, or earlier during the fighting against Napoleon in Spain. Again, among the emigrés were the ex-minister Canga Argüelles and his daughter Paulina. This daughter married the ex-general Pedro Méndez de Vigo, and became celebrated in her own right as the singer Madame Vigo. Llorens (p. 71) tells us that she gave a Spanish character to at least one of her London concerts by singing songs by García and by Sor. Moreover, Sor already had political connections with England, for it was here in 1810 that his *Himno de la Victoria* and *Los Defensores de la Patria* had been published by anonymous Spanish patriots. Indeed, it was in this political context that his music first came to be known in England.

We know one London address of Sor: no. 26 Charlotte Street, from where he wrote a letter on 13 February 1822.[1] Charlotte Street is half-way between the Spanish emigrés in Somers Town and the music publishers in Bond Street. No. 26 no longer exists. It was demolished to make way for the Scala Theatre, itself now demolished in its turn to make way for a tower block. The site of the old no. 26 is now occupied by the present no. 60 Charlotte Street.[2]

Concerts

It was, perhaps, as a concert performer on the guitar that Sor made most impression in London; yet the concerts that I have been able to trace all took place only during the first part of his stay here, in the years 1816-19. In those years I have found references to seven concerts in which he appeared. The problem is largely one of source material: concerts were by no means automatically reported in newspapers or other periodicals, and one may hope to find reports only by reading through a great many papers. I would think it most likely that Sor played in many more concerts than these seven; but they do nevertheless give a general picture which is probably a faithful one.

On 28 May 1816 Sor played in London in a benefit concert given by the French violinist Pierre Baillot. Baillot, whom Sor may have met in Paris, was the last great player of the French classical school of violin playing before the changes which Paganini introduced. The *Morning Chronicle* reported the concert as follows: 'M. Baillot, the celebrated violin player from Paris, had his benefit concert last night at the house of Lady Saltoun. It was a fine combination of talents, vocal and instrumental, and the house was crowded at a guinea per ticket.' We know that Sor took part from a copy of the printed programme which survives in the Appleby Collection of the Guildhall School of Music and Drama, London: he played an unspecified guitar solo of his own composition. Among the other performers were the famous pianist Kalkbrenner (to whom Sor later dedicated his Fantasia op. 12) and the flautist Drouet, both of whom, as well as Baillot, played works of their own composition. The programme is reproduced below.

Now, this is clearly not a concert of the modern sort at all. Today benefit concerts are rare; you do not usually buy tickets for concerts when they are held at private houses; the performers are not generally also the composers; and it is unusual today for so many performers to present so many separate items in a mixed programme.

The next concert was also held in a private house, although again it was reported in the press: it was given on 20 July 1816 by the famous singer Mrs. Billington, to whom later Sor was to dedicate his *Three Canons for Three Voices*. The *Morning Chronicle* wrote: 'Mrs. Billington, on Saturday evening last, gratified a numerous party of her friends with a charming musical treat, in her villa at Fulham. The Concert was chiefly vocal. Sir George Smart [the fashionable conductor of the day] presided . . . Signor Sorr [sic], besides giving a solo on the Spanish guitar, indulged the company with a specimen of the style of Crescentini, a singer of the highest repute on the Continent, who has never visited this country. Mrs. Billington herself was finely in voice. The whole concluded with a cold supper of the best kind.'

So, in Mrs. Billington's villa at Fulham — now demolished and replaced by squalid shops in the Fulham Palace Road — we find Sor not only playing the guitar in public but also singing. We should remember that this had always been one of his main musical interests. His first successful composition, in Barcelona, had been the opera *Telemaco;* here in London he published much more vocal music than guitar music; and he even taught singing in London. So the imitation of Crescentini is not surprising, and is confirmed by Ledhuy, who says that Sor demonstrated the style of the famous singer not merely to Mrs. Billington's guests, but to the Duke of Sussex, one of the brothers of the Prince Regent.

This meeting with the Duke of Sussex may have taken place either at Mrs. Billington's house, or else on the very next day, 21 July 1816. On that evening he played at a grand entertainment given by the Duke and Duchess of Cumberland for the Duke of Cambridge. The *Morning Chronicle* reported that 'the splendid entertainment given to the Duke of Cambridge on Sunday was one of the most magnificent that has been given this season'. The Prince Regent (afterwards King George IV) was there. Now, the Duke of Cumberland and the Duke of Cambridge were *also* brothers of the Prince Regent; so although the *Chronicle* does not say so, it may very well have been that the Duke of Sussex, a fourth brother, was there too and that Sor repeated the imitation of Crescentini that he had given the night before. Here is Ledhuy:

Invité dans une soirée où se trouvait le duc de Sussex,

---

[1] The letter, to which we shall return, is in the collection of Mary Belle Swingle, Laguna Beach, California.

---

[2] R. Horwood's map of London, 4th edn., 1819, shows the street numbers. Only if the numbers were changed between 1819 and 1822 (which is very difficult to check but I think unlikely) would the above details be incorrect. Later in the century the numbers were changed, and the modern no. 26 has nothing to do with the old numbering.

MR. BAILLOT'S
CONCERT,
Tuesday, May 28, 1816.

Leader, Mr SPAGNOLETTI.
At the Piano Forte, SIR GEORGE SMART.

ACT I.

SINFONIA........................*Haydn.*

ARIA, Mr. BEGRI " Alma clementi Dei ".....*Mayer.*

SOLO. Guitar, Mr. SOR......*Sor.*

CONCERTANTE, for two Violins, Obligati.......*Baillot,*

Messieurs BAILLOT and FEMY.

Duetto, Mlles. DE LIHU, " Al Campo andiamo ".....*Portogallo*

ANDANTE, with Variations for the PIANO FORTE,

Mr. KALKBRENNER,......*Kalkbrenner·*

ACT II.

CONCERTO, Flute. Mr, DROUET .....*Drouet.*

ARIA, Mlle. DE LIHU·······*Martini.*

CONCERTO, and Variations for the Violin, Mr. BAILLOT....*Baillot.*

ARIA, Mr. LEVASSEUR, " Sei morelli "....*Cimarosa.*

DUETTINO, Mlles. DE LIHU, "O Pescator dell' onda

C. Lowndes, Printer, Marquis Court, Drury Lane.

frère du prince régent, celui-ci lui parla de son séjour en Italie et de la prédilection pour Crescentini, que Sor avait connu à Madrid lorsqu'il donnait des leçons à mademoiselle Colbran (madame Rossini). Le duc commença à fredonner un des airs de ce célèbre chanteur, et Sor offrit à le chanter dans le genre de l'auteur. Il réussit si complètement, que les journaux anglais qui rendirent compte de cette soirée disaient: "Si le jeu de Sor sur la guitare annonce un grand compositeur, sa manière d'imiter Crescentini annonce un grand maître de chant." Dès ce moment on vint à lui pour avoir des leçons de chant.

('He was invited to a soirée, where the Duke of Sussex, brother of the Prince Regent, spoke to him about his stay in Italy and the popularity there of Crescentini, whom Sor had known in Madrid when he was giving lessons to Mlle Colbran (Mme Rossini). The duke began to hum one of the pieces of this famous singer, and Sor offered to sing it in the style of the composer. He succeeded so well that the English newspapers which reported the soirée said: "If Sor's guitar-playing reveals a great composer, his manner of imitating Crescentini reveals a great singing-master." From then on people came to him to take singing lessons.')

Girolamo Crescentini (1766-1846) was the last great castrato, and a mezzo-soprano. Fétis wrote of him: 'Rien ne peut être comparé à la suavité de ses accents, à la force de son expression, au goût parfait de ses *fioritures,* à la largeur de son phrasé' (*Biographie Universelle des Musiciens*). As for the Duke of Sussex, J.B. Priestley writes of him: 'There is one innocently approving sentence in the *Dictionary of National Biography* that seems to tell us a great deal about him: "In his later years he was in great request as chairman at anniversary dinners" ' (*The Prince of Pleasure,* London, 1971, p. 18).[3] At the Duke of Cumberland's entertainment, the *Morning Chronicle* tells us that the famous singer García was there and performed; and that 'Mr. Sorr [sic] delighted the company with his wonderful performance on the guitar'. It does not say what he played.

In London at this time was the violinist Francesco Vaccari, a notable figure in London musical life. Sor dedicated his sixth Fantasia, 'Les Adieux', op. 21, to him. An edition of this work in the collection of Robert Spencer, London, bears a puzzling manuscript note: 'A Dios. F. Sor a su amigo F. Vaccari. Londres 28 de Julio de 1816'. The note seems not to be in Sor's hand, and the edition is a French one which cannot have been printed before 1825. It seems probable that the inscription refers to some occasion involving the two men, perhaps a concert, which took place in London on 28 July 1816.[4]

On 24 March 1817, having made his mark at these (and probably other) private concerts, Sor appeared in what was to be the most celebrated concert of his lifetime, mentioned today in all his biographies and most dictionary articles on him: the Third Concert of the 1817 season of the Philharmonic Society. This Society was without any doubt the principal concert-giving organization in London at this period, even commissioning works from Beethoven. Its declared aim was 'to promote the performance, in the most perfect manner possible, of the best and most approved instrumental music' (J.B. Priestley, *The Prince of Pleasure,* p. 109). Its concerts at the Argyll Rooms in Regent Street were major events in London musical life. Sor was elected an Associate of the Society almost immediately on his arrival in London, and remained one during the whole of his stay. By the Society's Constitution, there were not only Members but also Associates from whom alone vacancies among Members might be filled as and when they occurred. Both Members and Associates were elected from among the most distinguished members of the musical profession.

At this concert he played a Concertante for guitar and strings, of his own composition. The other players in the piece were the famous Spagnoletti (violin), Challoner (viola) and Lindley (cello). The newspapers praised both the work and its performance at length, though the *Morning Chronicle* had doubts about its suitability for a large hall. A correspondent of the periodical *The Giulianiad* wrote many years later, in 1833 (p. 27): 'The impression he then made on his first performance at the Argyll Rooms, which I attended, was of a nature which will never be erased from my memory; it was at once magical and surprising'. George Hogarth wrote of the same concert: 'In a concertante for the Spanish guitar, composed and performed by M. Sor, a guitarist in great vogue at that time, he astonished the audience by his unrivalled execution' (*The Philharmonic Society of London,* London, 1862, p. 17). The Concertante itself, which probably existed only in manuscript, does not seem to have survived.

Six weeks after the Philharmonic Society's concert, on 7 and 8 May 1817, Sor again played in two concerts on two successive days, and again at the Argyll Rooms. These were a benefit concert for the flautist Drouet, and a benefit concert for the singer Miss Frith. They are both reported briefly in the *Morning Post,* but without details other than that he played solos.

Two years later still, on 30 June 1819, Sor appeared in yet another concert at the Argyll Rooms, this time 'Mr. and Mrs. Ashe's Annual Concert'. Andrew Ashe was a well-known flautist in London who taught at the Royal Academy of Music when that institution was founded some years later, his wife sang, and his daughters had various musical talents. In this same year, 1819, Sor published in London one of his boleros, 'No tocarán campanas', under the title *Impromtu . . . as sung by the Misses Ashe:* perhaps it was at this same concert that they sang it. The *Morning Chronicle,* which reported this concert, did not give many details; but it is clear that Sor did not play the guitar, but appeared as one of the vocal performers.

But with that, the list of known London concerts in which Sor appeared comes to an end. If one were to hunt further through periodicals of the time, and perhaps also diaries, one might well find more. But I doubt if the basic pattern would change: that is, a pattern of private concerts in the houses of the gentry, and public benefit concerts for professional musicians, in which Sor usually plays (unspecified) guitar solos but

---

[3] Let me dispose here of a legend which has gained too much ground: that the Duke of Sussex was actually a patron of Sor. There is no evidence for this other than the occasion just described and Sor's dedication to the Duke of his *Three Italian Arietts,* 2nd Set.

---

[4] The note could well be a copy, perhaps by José de Lira, from an original inscription by Sor on some other copy which has now disappeared.

sometimes demonstrates vocal talents as well. There are always a large number of other musicians involved.

Sor's best-known work today, the variations on a theme of Mozart, op. 9, for guitar, was performed by him in London. The first edition was published in London in 1821, and on the title-page is printed: 'As Performed by the Author, at the Nobilities' Concerts'. So this work, which today is played in so many concerts, has many London associations: it seems that it was first composed here, first published here, and certainly performed here by Sor, at a musical party or parties at the house of some member or members of the nobility.

Why, though, does Sor appear to fade from the London concert scene by 1819? Is it merely a coincidence of source material? Or is it fact? I am inclined to think that it is fact. He stayed in London until 1822 or 1823, but we know from other sources that he became increasingly busy in other ways. At the same time as he began to fade from the concert scene, he began to compose ballet music, while his compositions poured from the London music presses with ever-increasing momentum: guitar music, Italian arietts with piano accompaniment, piano solos and duets, and it may well be that he came to prefer these evidently highly successful activities to performance.

Singing, singing teaching, and Italian songs

Soon after his arrival in London, then, Sor sang an imitation of Crescentini; and in 1819 he appeared as a singer in a public concert. It seems that singing and in particular singing teaching occupied him very much, and may very well have been a part of his livelihood at this time. In 1823, the *Allgemeine musikalische Zeitung* of Leipzig, reviewing Sor's ballet *Cendrillon,* wrote that 'Sor lebt gewöhnlich in London und ist dort sehr mit Sing-Unterricht beschäftigt' (No. 39, September 1823, 636) ('Sor generally lives in London and is very much occupied there in teaching singing'). Already, according to Ledhuy, he was considering pedagogical ideas: he studied the action of the vocal organs, began to form a teaching method, ideas which were to come to fruition later, not so much in singing teaching, but rather in the *Méthode pour la Guitare* of 1830. Philip J. Bone writes that a manuscript treatise by Sor on singing, in French, was in the possession of Madame Sidney Pratten (*The Guitar and Mandolin,* London, 1954, repr. 1972, p. 342), and though Bone can be unreliable, the story is plausible. The manuscript, if it existed, seems to have disappeared.

But though he may have sung in public, though he may have taught singing, the most important result of his interest in singing at this time was that he composed and published no less than eleven sets of three Italian

arietts for voice and piano, two sets of duets, and a set of canons, in the purest tradition of bel canto. None of them has been republished in this century; to rediscover them is to be reminded of Rossini's early operas, or Donizetti, or even early Verdi. The *Repository of Arts* is quite ecstatic about them, and in fact, some of them are among his finest works.

The first set, called *Three Italian Ariets,* was brought out by the very minor publisher William Milhouse, 'Military Instrument Maker to their Royal Highnesses the Dukes of Kent and Cumberland'. Clarinets by Milhouse are still well known today (Lyndesay G. Langwill, *An Index of Musical Wind-instrument Makers,* 3rd end., Edinburgh, 1972, p. 107), but as a publisher he was distinctly a minor figure. The title-page says clearly that the work was printed 'for the Author', which means that Sor engaged Milhouse to have the work printed, presumably taking the financial risk himself. It is a comparatively early work, dating from before the end of 1817, when the second and third sets are known to have been already published; doubtless at the time of the first set Sor was not well enough known in London for publishing houses to take the risk themselves. He was not to have to wait for long.

The choice of Milhouse may perhaps have had something to do with military connections: Sor was, after all, a commissioned officer, late Captain in the Cordovan Volunteers, and it was perhaps his aristocratic friends in London who suggested as publisher this maker of military instruments.

This first set shows the lyric and dramatic qualities which can be seen throughout the eleven sets. The first ariett, 'Dormia sul margine d'un ruscelletto', is marked Andante cantabile and contrasts with the third, 'O cara da quel giorno primier', which is much more dramatic. But it must be said that though this first set is confident enough, it is in the later sets that the best arietts are to be found.

The second and third sets were no longer printed 'for the Author', but taken on commercially by the firm of Chappell. Their plate numbers suggest late 1817.[5] The second set is dedicated to the Duke of Sussex, which fits in well with the date of the concert at which Sor is known to have met the Duke. Both sets were reviewed at length and favourably in Ackermann's *The Repository of Arts, Literature, Fashions, Manufactures, &c.* The anonymous reviewer wrote of the second set:

> If we were to allot to these arietts the space which we would fain wish to devote to their consideration, they would form the only article in our review. During the three weeks since we first opened them, they nearly

---

5 O.W. Neighbour and Alan Tyson, *English Music Publishers' Plate Numbers in the First Half of the nineteenth Century* (London, 1965).

caused us to neglect the rest of our critical calendar; they haunted us on our pillow, in our walks: we in return haunted our musical friends with them; we caught them even intruding on our more serious occupations of dry matter-of-fact business; in short, we absolutely pronounced them troublesome companions. In impressions so forcible and permanent, a great deal perhaps may be ascribed to a happy mood at the first meeting, or to a peculiar sympathy of taste; but the concurrence of other competent judges afforded us good reason to consider our own opinion as substantially correct.

(*Repository*, 1 January 1819)

And of the third set:

In the composition of these three ariettas, Mr. Sor has exhibited a combination of taste, feeling, and science, which cannot fail endearing his labour to the true vocal amateur . . . This is classic music.

(*Repository*, 1 September 1818)

On Monday 11 May 1818, at a concert of the Philharmonic Society in London, the famous singer Mrs. Salmon sang an aria by Sor. Mrs. Salmon was very celebrated in her own day. J.R. Planché recalls how he went to Paris in about 1826, where she was living 'in a charming house in the Allée des Veuves, Champs Elysées', to try to persuade her to come out of retirement to sing at Vauxhall — without success. He writes: 'for luscious sweetness of tone, purity of style, and power of expression, Mrs. Salmon was and remains unrivalled amongst English sopranos' (*Recollections and Reflections,* vol. I, London, 1872, pp. 88-9). The aria by Sor which she sang was not named in the programme, being called merely 'Aria, MS. (never performed)', but it is possible to hazard a guess as to which one it was. The *Morning Chronicle* reported on 18 May: 'Mrs. Salmon also sang an *Aria* by Sor, newly composed for the present occasion. This is a very original and beautiful composition, the words admirably expressed, and abounding in marks of genius'. Now, Sor's fourth set of arietts is dedicated to Mrs. Salmon and appeared later in the same year, so it may be that the aria which she performed was in fact one of the three in this fourth set. On examination, it turns out that the first and third arietts of the set, though good, are very short, and the second, 'Fra un dolce deliro', is a work of large proportions, with many ornaments and with every appearance of having been designed for professional performance. Accordingly, it may very well be that the aria which Mrs. Salmon sang on 11 May 1818 was in fact this one, 'Fra un dolce deliro'. It appears also in MS Add. 48,348 of the British Library, ff. 35-40 verso, with an added recitative beginning 'Oh stella'; perhaps it was this fuller version which Mrs. Salmon sang.

The second to the seventh sets inclusive were all reviewed in the *Repository of Arts*. The reviewer can scarcely contain his enthusiasm. He gives strong reasons for his delight in Sor's music, above all the careful marrying of the music to the words. He even compares the appearance of a new set of arietts by Sor to the appearance of a new novel by Sir Walter Scott.

The fifth set of arietts is one of the finest, and was the one which became best known abroad: Pacini in Paris published it in the 1820s, along with sets 1-4, and Peters in Leipzig published it in 1823, along with the second set of duets. Here is the first of the three songs which it contains, 'Ch'io mai vi posso lasciar d'amare', together with the beginning of the lengthy review which the *Repository of Arts* devoted to the fifth set in general and to this first song in particular.

THREE ITALIAN ARIETTS, with an Accompaniment for the Pianoforte, composed and dedicated to his friend J. B. Cramer, by F. Sor. Set V. Pr. 5s.

Mr. Sor's vocal compositions have gained such favour among the higher order of musical dilettanti, that a new set of arietts, from his pen, causes almost as much sensation, as the publication of a new novel by the author of Waverley. As for ourselves, we greet the appearance of Mr. Sor's productions with the delight with which we hail a mild sunny day at this season of dreary frosts and fogs. They warm and cherish our musical spirits amidst the numerous and dense clouds which so often overhang our critical labours. It does our heart good to pick his works into minute pieces (in a friendly way of course); they not only can stand the microscope, but, like the works of nature, present unexpected beauties, the closer they are analyzed. The more we examine them, the more we recognize a correspondence, a sympathy between the feelings which gave birth to such strains, and our own; we behold, as in a mirror, our musical self. We say to ourselves, ''Thus should we have sung, had nature granted us the talents, and education the cultivation of them, to give musical utterance to our sentiments.''

As it is, we are but a critic (and to that office chance led us): but if we cannot create, we can deeply feel what is great and good in the art; we can drop an involuntary tear at the thrilling harmonies of Mozart's *Requiem,* and laugh heartily at Cimarosa's humor in the *Matrimonio Segreto* — But we are getting astray: — to our subject!

Among the many important requisites and obligations of a lyric composer, the most essential, although the most neglected, is that of *just declamation*. Nature, the surest guide in the arts, demands that a melody should rise or fall, the measure quicken or slacken, according to the rules of perfect elocution: melody should be a mode of musical parlance. Sing as you would speak! The observance of this fundamental principle is sure to keep the composer in the right course; it is from this principle, that some few general rules have been deduced, which a sensible musical writer will seldom infringe. According to those, the most expressive word in a phrase receives a higher note; a question is melodized in ascent; low

Arietta Primo.

ne men per gioc_co.... v'in_ganne_ro   no

no   vo_i foste e sie__te le mie fa_vil__le.

e voi sa_re__te care pu_pil__le   il mio bel fo_co fin_

.... che vi_vró   il mio bel fo___co fin che vi_vró..

il .... mio bel fo _ _ _ _ co   fin   che vi _ vro

ch'io mai vi pos _ _ sa las _ ciar   d'a _ ma _ _ _ re.   non   lo cre_

_ de _ _ te . . . . .   pu _ pil _ le ca _ re   no no no non lo cre_

_dete pu _ pille ca _ re   ne   men pergioc _ co   v'in _ gan _ ne _ rò

ne men per gioco per gioco v'ingan_ne_ro... ne men per gioco per gioco v'in_

gan _ _ne_ro   voi foste e sie_te   le mie fa_vil_le

le mi_e fa_ _ville e voi   sa_re_te   ca_re pu_pil_le

ca_re pupil_le   il mio bel fo_co... fin che vivró   il mio bel

fo _ _ _ _ _ co fin che vi _ vro ch'io mai vi possa lasciar d'a _ mare non lo cre _

_ dete pupil _ le ca _ _ _ re . . . . ne men per gio _ _ _ _ _ _ co v'inganne _

_ ro ne men pergioco v'inganne _ ro ne men per gioco v'ingan _ ne _ ro.

sounds agree best with the sedate, the tranquil, the awful, &c.; while high notes are chosen for the gay, for violent emotions, &c. That this general principle is to be put in practice with discriminating judgement, that its application is to be tempered by good taste, is a matter of course. Poetry is not read exactly like homely prose, and melody does not declaim exactly like poetry, although the latter furnishes the guide, the hint to musical declamation.

This principle established, and it will follow that, other essential requisites not being wanting, a melody which enables us to guess the general purport of the test, comes near to perfection. We say the general purport, for it will hardly be expected, that mere sounds should become the unerring interpreters of every kind of sentiment and idea which language has it in its power to convey. Musical diction will ever be limited to impressions of a general nature: it has its uncertainties and imperfections; and these probably add to its advantages, perhaps to its beauties.

Just declamation forms so striking a feature in Mr. Sor's compositions, that in this respect they stand perhaps unrivalled. This secret charm constitutes one of the principal attractions in his arietts.

Mr. Sor feels what he has to say, and that feeling is not merely true, it is deep and intense, and thus again forms a second distinctive feature of excellence in all his labours. In his pathetic bursts, in his plaintive strains, and in his melting accents of tenderness, we think we recognize the characteristic fervour of his country.

A few words on their mere musical merit will complete the general characteristics of Mr. Sor's compositions. We will begin negatively. About three fourths of the songs which line the panes of most of our retail dealers in harmony, are of a stamp either to demonstrate intelligibly, what is meant by vulgarity of musical diction, or to cause astonishment how the mere virtue of new plates and paper can give new currency to stale and hacknied phrases, familiar even to our cook-maids; and if per chance we behold an attempt at something like sense *(rari nantes in gurgite vasto!)* we generally are compelled to bewail the premature fate of the mental offspring; the poor thing is killed in the birth. The crude limping, unfinished phrase wines a requiem worthy of the abortion. To turn to the brighter side of the picture: it would be but a poor compliment to the subject of this article, to say, that of all these negative distinctions, Mr. Sor's works offer no trace. Not to be vicious is not virtue. What we wish to convey to our readers is, that of all these failings, we behold in this gentleman's writings the opposite extremes in full force. His ideas are pure and noble; they breathe that chaste simplicity, which, in the sister art, distinguishes the works of Greece: they are, moreover, fully developed, so as to form a matured whole. His harmonies are neither trite nor extravagant; always select, frequently of the higher order as to combination, never proffered at random, but invariably chosen with reference to the expression aimed at; and whatever be the harmony, Mr. Sor is sure to exhibit it with the least possible expense of sounds, but with the utmost attention to the effect intended. We do not recollect to have seen one bar of his, which would not be materially deteriorated by the loss of a single note.

In the point of originality, too, Mr. Sor's compositions maintain a conspicuous rank. Originality in music is more often mentioned than understood. What is it? In harmony, we fear, it is not much more than a combination *not frequently* made use of. A combination of sounds *never* before put in practice makes its appearance more rarely than a comet. Its first *début* is an abomination in the eyes of the orthodox, who launch their anathema against the musical freethinker. It gains currency by time only. How many harmonic combinations, absolutely new, are there in all the works of Haydn or Mozart? — In melody, novelty is more within reach, but by no means so common as people proclaim it. To be new, the phrase must never have existed. Who has heard all, who remembers all that he has heard, to pronounce the judgment? And if the whole phrase have not appeared before, are all its component parts of virgin originality? The composer himself frequently imagines he has invented, when that invention is nothing more than a resuscitation of ideas which may have lain dormant during years.

But we must put an end to all digressions and speculation, lest our readers suspect us of the critic's habits, of wilfully lengthening the exordium, to make up for the brevity of the matter more immediately under consideration. To the arietts at once!

The following lines form the text of the first:

Ch'io mai vi posso lasciar d'amare?
Non lo credete, pupille care,
Ne men per gioco v'ingannerò.
Voi foste e siete le mie faville
E voi sarete, care pupille,
Il mio bel fuoco fin che vivrò.

After a few bars introduction, the lover, whose mistress appears to have doubted the constancy of his flame, bursts out, "That I should ever cease to love you." This exclamation, set in recitativo, is absolutely an imitation of nature. Perhaps a less decided termination, than that of a perfect cadence, would have still stronger expressed the true tone of declamation. The second line, "Non lo," &c. (p. 1,) is perfection itself. The lover drops into a strain of endearing protestation, "Do not believe it, my dearest eyes!" and the reiteration of this line, with augmented emotion, "No, no, no, non lo credete," &c. is uncommonly characteristic and emphatic. In the last line (p. 1,) the repetition of the same thought to "Ne men per gioco," and to "v'ingannerò," *Even in joke would I scorn to deceive you,* seems to us to convey an idea as if two separable phrases were in the text; but this may be an excess of critical refinement. To the subsequent recurrence of the same sentence (p. 2, 1. 1,) our remark would not apply. Here the whole line is propounded in one idea, of exquisite effect; the melody assumes greater fervour, proceeds through transient modulations into G, and is supported by a masterly contrapuntal accompaniment. "No" is once or twice more ejaculated betwixt luxuriant instrumental progress, until a pause closes the first main portion of the song. The judgment in making this full stop is conspicuous: the text now assumes a different import: "Voi foste e siete," &c. *You were and are still my fostering flame,* &c. The expression required by these words is obvious; they demanded those accents of melting melodious sweetness which have been allotted to them in a superlative degree; the passage is enchanting, and its softness is even assisted by the accompaniment; a pedal bass on C, with continued G's in the tenor.

The effect of a pedal bass, or point d'orgue, is that of blending and softening down the harmony; whereas a fundamental bass carries with it energy: its determined character often borders on harshness. Its use in old music is more frequent than in modern, which also often substitutes the inversions of the primitive chords, as being more mellow.

The remainder of the text now follows in succession, under appropriate melodies; and amplified figures of semiquavers tend to infuse spirit and animation into the winding up, which takes place p. 3, b. 4. From hence the whole of the stanza is once more gone through, with considerable additions and variations. Here the beginning, "Ch'io mai," &c. presents itself in a form both novel and highly pathetic. The exclamation in this instance is not in recitativo; it is a tempo, but eager with anxious emotion, richly and excellently accompanied. Imagination could not fancy it better. In the beginning of p. 4, the line "Ne men per gioco," &c. receives a new and interesting character from a sequence of rising fourths and ascending fifths in the bass. In the two next lines, a further novelty attracts our attention: it is a very elegant and florid accompaniment of independent instrumental melody to the words "Voi foste e siete," &c. We cannot detail the remaining parts of this page; they are all new ideas conceived in the best taste. In the 5th page (the last), the lover, as if he could not forget the painful and unmerited accusation, "I ever cease to love you?" once more bursts out with increased agitation. This line again baffles description; and the languishing, affectionate expression in the next, at "care," must be heard to be felt. The song now proceeds to a conclusion, amid passages of vivid emotion, which the author's good judgment has sparingly propped with accompaniment. The instrumental termination, or symphony as we call it, demands distinct notice: it is terse, full of precision and elegance.

But we perceive, too late, that our predilection has carried us far, far beyond our usual limits; and there are two more arietts before us. — What is to be done? — Go on, and neglect for once the other candidates for musical fame? This would be unfair indeed. We rather resort to the alternative of deferring the two arietts to our next. This liberty we take with some hesitation. Our readers will be indulgent; they will, we likewise trust, pardon us if our critique should have appeared to them too minute and tedious. The value of the subject seemed to us amply deserving of detail, and of our best endeavours to do it justice. Those of our friends who may be induced to procure these arietts, will, we have no doubt, concur in this opinion, and perhaps, too, drive some gratification from a comparison of the work with our observations upon it.

The fourth and fifth sets had been published, not by Chappell but by the newly founded Regent's (soon to become Royal) Harmonic Institution. Then back to Chappell for the sixth; and then the seventh, eighth, ninth and tenth sets, and a so-called 'first' set, all appeared from the presses of the Royal Harmonic Institution. The so-called 'first' set is something of a chronological curiosity. The plate number shows that it dates from 1821, six years after Sor's arrival; that it is not the genuine first set at all, which as we saw was published by Milhouse; and that it appeared in fact between the eighth and ninth sets. It is a kind of *8½* well before Fellini. The true first set, one supposes, must have been out of print, and so the gap was expediently, if untruthfully, filled by the publishers.[6]

At the Royal College of Music in London, MS 1111, ff. 102-106, is an autograph manuscript of the sixth set, with pencil marks indicating that this was the copy which Chappell used as printer's copy for setting up their edition of this set. The inscription 'F. Sor' in the title is in a hand corresponding to Sor's other known signatures at this time, confirming that this manuscript is indeed autograph.

The later sets of arietts, and the duets, contain some fine songs. The tenth set contains a song in Spanish style, beginning 'Lungi da te mia cara' and headed by the following note: 'Regretting that I do not find in modern Spanish Music any Melodies but such as are entirely foreign to the characteristic Style of the Airs of that Nation, and finding only in their *Canciones* the true *Cavatinas* I was desirous in this Arietta of reversing this system by Composing perfectly Spanish Music to Italian words. F.S.' The Spanish flavour is obtained by alternation of 6/8 and 3/4, and by the use of the interval of the augmented second. At this time, such interest in national characteristics was growing with the Romantic movement. The fact remains that this song is, of course, far less genuinely Spanish than the seguidillas which Sor composed within his own country and within his own native musical tradition twenty years earlier.

The eighth and tenth sets of arietts contain songs marked 'Allegretto di Polacca' and 'Tempo di Polacca'. That in the eighth set, 'La piu vezzosa e piu gentil', has a long and lively introduction, a particularly beautiful and catchy tune, and some virtuoso vocal writing at the end. The other, 'Volate piu de venti' in the tenth set, is even more acrobatic and certainly suggests writing for a professional. Songs like these raise the question: for whom exactly were they written? Were they salon pieces for amateur singers who might be expected to buy the printed editions and sing the works for their own pleasure at home? Have they anything to do with Sor's

---

[6] In some libraries, this set is catalogued, understandably, as though it were the genuine first set. However, there is no question but that the Milhouse set was the first in time and that the other, the so-called 'first' set, was in fact printed after the eighth set.

singing teaching? Or were they intended for professional and public performance? The answer in at least
some cases must be the last of these. We saw already
that the fourth set was dedicated to Mrs. Salmon; the set
of canons is dedicated to Mrs. Billington; and certain
songs demand a very agile vocal technique that seems
unlikely to have been possessed by many amateurs.
Perhaps the simpler songs were put in for amateurs; certainly most of the sets contain specimens of both easier
and more difficult music. All of them show Sor as a
composer thoroughly confident in what he was doing,
and well versed, above all, in the style of Mozart, who
had produced songs of comparable kind.

Arrangements from operas

In Spain Sor's first composition, as a small child, had
been an arrangement from an opera. In London he continued to make such arrangements: three for voice and
guitar of arias from Mozart's *Don Giovanni,* which will
be discussed later, one for voice and piano of 'Lei si
cinga d'una spada' from S. Mayer's *Le Bizzarrie
dell'Amore,* and one for two voices and piano of 'Non
piu, non piu lusinghe' from Cimarosa's *Le Astuzzie
Feminili.*

The 'Impromtu dans le genre du Boléro'

In London, as far as we know, Sor composed only
one Spanish song, the *Impromtu dans le genre du
Boléro,* for two voices and piano, published in London
in 1819. It is a version of a song which he composed in
Spain and which is found in one of the Clive manuscripts. The words begin: 'No tocarán campanas /
Quando yo muera' ('They won't ring bells when I
die . . .').

Publishing

Before Sor left Spain, two patriotic songs by him had
been published in London by Spanish patriots. From
1815 until he left London in 1823, a total of about fifty
other works by him appeared, published at first by
many different firms and later almost exclusively by the
Regent's Harmonic Institution (which on the accession
of King George IV in 1820 became known as the Royal
Harmonic Institution). Here is a chronological list of
works by Sor published in London in this period. To it
should be added certain works published in Paris in this
same period, mainly for solo guitar, which are listed
below; the Concertante for guitar and strings, which
probably existed only in manuscript and is now lost; and
the four ballets which he composed here, of which only
Cendrillon survives. For location of copies, see the
Catalogue below.

Date of entry at Stationers' Hall[7]			Publisher
—	'Vivir en cadenas' and 'Venid, vencedores', two songs in J.B. Arriaza's *Poesías Patrióticas* (London, 1810)	voice & piano	L. Lavenu
—	*A 2nd Fantasia* [op. 4] C. 1815-18[8]	guitar solo	L. Lavenu
—	*Six Divertimentos* [first set] [op. 1] 1815 or before[9]	guitar solo	Monzani & Hill
—	*Six Divertimentos,* 2nd Set [op. 2] 1815 or before? 1819 at latest[10]	guitar solo	Monzani & Hill
—	*Six Studio* [sic] (Set 1) and *Studio* [sic] (Set 2) [op. 6] C. 1815-17[11]	guitar solo	W. Milhouse, 'for the Author'

---

[7] For information about the value of entries at Stationers' Hall, see
O.W. Neighbour & Alan Tyson, *English Music Publishers' Plate
Numbers in the First Half of the Nineteenth Century* (London, 1965).

---

[8] See text above, chapter 1.

---

[9] A copy in the collection of Ingolf Olsen, Copenhagen, bears the
date 'July 1815' in an early hand.

---

[10] Probably published soon after the first set, but not simultaneously
with it because in that case the first set might be expected to bear the
words 'first set', which it does not. Before Monzani & Hill moved
from Dover Street in July 1819 (advertisement in the *Morning
Chronicle,* 20 July 1819).

---

[11] Undated, but probably near in time to the *Three Italian Ariets*
also published by Milhouse (see the following item).

Date of entry at Stationers' Hall			Publisher
—	*Three Italian Arietts* [first set] 1815-17[12]	voice & piano	W. Milhouse, 'for the Author'
—	*Three Italian Arietts,* 2nd Set C. Dec 1817[13]	voice & piano	Chappell
—	*Three Italian Arietts,* 3rd Set C. Dec 1817[14]	voice & piano	Chappell
—	*Three Canons* 1815-18[15]	3 voices & piano	Falkner's, 'for the Author'
—	*A Duett . . . Composed on Several Swedish National Airs* 1815-18[16]	piano duet	Falkner's
—	*Three Waltzes* [first set] 1815-18[17]	piano duet	?
—	*Three Waltzes,* Set 2d. 1815-18[18]	piano duet	Clementi
—	*Three Italian Arietts,* 4th Set C. Sept 1818[19]	voice & piano	Chappell
29 Jan 1819	*Six Divertimentos,* 3rd Set [op. 8] C. Nov or Dec 1818[20]	guitar solo	Rutter & McCarthy
—	*Six Waltzes,* 1st Set 1815-19[21]	piano solo	Monzani & Hill
—	*Six Waltzes,* 2nd Set[22]	piano solo	Monzani & Hill
15 June 1819	*Impromtu dans le genre du Boléro*	2 voices & piano	R.H.I.[23]
18 Dec 1819	*Three Waltzes,* 3rd Set	piano duet	R.H.I.

[12] The second and third sets were published about late 1817, and this first set was doubtless published before them.

[13] The plate numbers of this and the following item are 587 and 596, which suggest December 1817 (Neighbour & Tyson).

[14] See preceding note.

[15] The dedicatee, Mrs. Billington, died on 25 August 1818.

[16] The dedicatee, the Baroness Rehausen, was an Englishwoman, Harriet Louisa Bulkeley, married to the Swedish envoy extraordinary and minister plenipotentiary Baron Rehausen, whose appointment ended in 1818 (information from Swedish Minister in London, November 1974).

[17] The existence of this first set is hypothetical, since no copy has been found. Deduced from the words 'Set 2d' on the following item. It is just possible, though unlikely, that the missing 'first set' was in fact the first set not of three waltzes for piano duet but of six waltzes for piano solo (see below). Not the same as *Three Waltzes* published by Rutter & McCarthy (see below), which is merely a set of arrangements.

[18] This set is dedicated to 'Mlle F. Rehausen' and so, like the *Duett . . . on Several Swedish National Airs,* presumably also dates from before the termination of Baron Rehausen's appointment in England. Not the same as *A Second Set of Waltzes* (see below), which is merely a set of arrangements.

[19] The plate number is 787, which suggests September 1818 (Neighbour & Tyson).

[20] The plate number is 119, which suggests November or December 1818 (Neighbour & Tyson).

[21] Monzani & Hill's address is given as 24 Dover Street, from which they moved in 1819.

[22] The existence of this second set is hypothetical, since no copy has been found. Deduced from the words '1st Set' on the first set, implying subsequent sets. See the note to *Three Waltzes* for piano duet, Set 2d, above.

[23] Regent's (later Royal) Harmonic Institution.

Date of entry at Stationers' Hall			Publisher
18 Dec 1819	*Three Waltzes,* 6th Set	piano duet	R.H.I.
18 Dec 1819	*Six Divertimentos,* 4th Set [op. 13]	guitar solo	R.H.I.
24 Dec 1819	*Three Italian Arietts,* 5th Set	voice & piano	R.H.I.
24 Dec 1819	*Three Waltzes,* 5th Set	piano duet	R.H.I.
—	Three arrangements for voice & guitar of arias from Mozart's *Don Giovanni:* 'Vedrai carino', 'Batti, batti', and 'Deh vieni all finestra' C. Jan 1820[24]	voice & guitar	Chappell
17 Apr 1820	*Three Waltzes,* 4th Set	piano duet	Chappell
7 June 1820	*Three Italian Arietts,* 6th Set	voice & piano	Chappell
12 Sept 1820	*Three Waltzes,* 7th Set	piano duet	R.H.I.
14 Sept 1820	*Three Italian Arietts,* 7th Set	voice & piano	R.H.I.
20 Nov 1820	*Three Italian Arietts,* 8th Set	voice & piano	R.H.I.
1 Mar 1821	'Lei si cinga d'una spada', arranged from S. Mayer's opera *Le Bizzarrie dell'Amore*	voice & piano	R.H.I.
1 Mar 1821	Variations on a theme from Mozart's *Magic Flute* [op. 9]	guitar solo	R.H.I.
19 Apr 1821	*Les Cuirassiers*	piano solo	R.H.I.
9 May 1821	*Les Favorites*	piano solo	R.H.I.
2 July 1821	*Three Italian Duets* [first set]	2 voices & piano	R.H.I.
2 July 1821	*Three Italian Arietts,* 'first set' (so-called; not in fact the true first set)	voice & piano	R.H.I.
19 Jan 1822	*Three Italian Arietts,* 9th Set	voice & piano	R.H.I.
19 Jan 1822	*Three Italian Arietts,* 10th Set	voice & piano	R.H.I.
19 Jan 1822	*Les Choisies*	piano solo	R.H.I.
28 May 1822	*Three Waltzes* (not original compositions but a set of arrangements)[25]	piano duet	Rutter & McCarthy
28 May 1822	*A Second Set of Waltzes* (not original compositions but a set of arrangements)[26]	piano duet	Rutter & McCarthy

[25] The plate numbers of this and the following item, 239 and 250, suggest 1820 (Neighbour & Tyson), even though they were not entered at Stationers' Hall until 28 May 1822. They may have been issued at any time in these years. These two sets of arrangements are not part of the series of ten sets of *Three Waltzes* by Sor (see below).

[26] See preceding note.

[24] The plate numbers of 'Vedrai carino' and 'Batti batti' are 1018 and 1049, which suggest January 1820 (Neighbour & Tyson). No copy is known of 'Deh vieni alla finestra'.

Date of entry at Stationers' Hall			**Publisher**
8 June 1822	*Three Waltzes,* 8th Set	piano duet	R.H.I.
8 June 1822	*Three Italian Duets,* 2nd Set	2 voices & piano	R.H.I.
21 Aug 1822	'Farewell, for on Oviedo's towers,' a song from *Gil Blas*[27]	voice & piano	Ware & Evans
27 Aug 1822	'Should a pretty Spanish lass,' a song from *Gil Blas*[27]	voice & piano	Ware & Evans
2 Dec 1822	*Cendrillon,* piano score	piano solo	R.H.I.
—	'Non piu, non piu lusinghe,' arranged from Cimarosa's opera *Le Astuzzie Feminili*[28]	2 voices & piano	R.H.I.
—	*Three Waltzes,* 9th Set[29]	piano duet	R.H.I.
11 Aug 1823	*Three Waltzes,* 10th Set[30]	piano duet	Birchall
—	*Fantasia* [op. 7?] 1823 or before[31]	guitar solo	Clementi
—	*Duo Brillant* 1824 or before[32]	piano duet	R.H.I.

[27] The first performance of the 'Operatick Drama' *Gil Blas* was on 15 August 1822.

[28] The plate number is 1259, which suggests the spring of 1823 (Neighbour & Tyson).

[29] No copy found, but advertised in the *Harmonicon* in October 1823 as a new publication.

[30] The plate number is 1325, which suggests late 1822 or early 1823 (Neighbour & Tyson).

[31] No copy found. Listed in an 1823 Clementi catalogue (microfilm in the British Library, Mic. A.2054). Possibly merely a Paris edition of op. 7, published in Paris by Pleyel or more probably Meissonnier but sold in London by Clementi. Similarly, Sor's *Studies* op. 6 are listed in the *Giulianiad* in 1835 as published by Clementi; this may also be merely Meissonnier's Paris edition marketed in London by Clementi rather than Milhouse's original edition.

[32] No copy found. Advertised in the *Harmonicon,* March 1824, as 'new music'.

From this list it may be seen that throughout his London period Sor composed and published many different kinds of works: arietts, guitar pieces, piano solos and duets, English songs. At first it seems that he had to take the financial risk himself, but later many different publishers took on his works, and especially the Regent's Harmonic Institution.

The Regent's Harmonic Institution was 'formed by a number of professors of music with the object of publishing and selling music on a co-operative basis, and for the performance of concerts; taken over by Thomas Welsh and William Hawes, two of their number, c. 1826' (Humphries & Smith, op. cit., p. 271). Welsh was a friend of Sor's and the dedicatee of Sor's 8th Set of Italian Arietts, and it is possible that Sor was a founder member of this publishing enterprise. The Institution entered its publications conscientiously at Stationers' Hall, with the result that they can be dated fairly exactly. From their foundation in 1819, when they published Sor's *Impromtu,* until his departure from London, they published many of Sor's works; but for some reason the only guitar works among them were opp. 9 and 13.

Nearly every one of these fifty or so works has a dedicatee, either a member of fashionable society or else a professional musician or other artist or friend of Sor. Among them were the Marquis of Aylesbury, chairman of the committee which gave the King's Theatre a new lease of life in 1821 and to whom Sor dedicated the piano score of *Cendrillon;* the Duke of Sussex (the 2nd Set of Italian Arietts); Mme Ronzi de Begnis, the famous singer and 'the model of voluptuous beauty' (John Ebers, *Seven Years of the King's Theatre,* London, 1828, p. 50) (the 9th Set of Italian Arietts); Mrs. Billington, the singer (*Three Canons*); all four sisters the Ladies Paget, daughters of the Marquis of Anglesey and familiar figures at society balls (*Three Waltzes* for piano duet, 3rd and 4th Sets, and *Les Favorites* and *Les Choisies*); and the South American revolutionary Emanuel Palacio Fajardo (*Six Divertimentos,* 2nd Set). Often the dedication may have brought Sor an income.

There survives a letter written by Sor to one of these dedicatees, dated 13 February 1822.[33] Neither the work nor the dedicatee is named, but from the date it seems that the letter most probably refers to the set of quadrilles for piano solo *Les Choisies* and is addressed to Lady Jane Paget. Sor says that if the work's quality were as great as is his attachment to the lady's family, then the works of Mozart and Haydn would be forced to yield to it. The letter is reproduced below. Here is its text, together with a translation.

Mlle.

Je vous présente les premiers exemplaires du petit ouvrage que vous avez eu la bonté de permettre qu'il paraisse décoré de votre nom: Si son mérite pouvait être aussi grand que l'attachement et la reconnaissance que j'ai pour les bontés dont je suis redevable à votre famille les ouvrages de Mozart et de Haydn lui céderaient le pas; mais s'il a le bonheur de vous plaire vos suffrages lui donneront plus de valeur que celle qu'il pourrait avoir comme production de

      Votre tres humble et tres
      respectueusement dévoué
      F. Sor

Mercredi 13 Février 1822
26 Charlotte Street Fitzroy Square

('Mlle.

I am sending you the first copies of the little work which you kindly permitted to appear ornamented with your name. If its merit could be as great as are my attachment and the gratitude which I owe to your family, then the works of Mozart and Haydn would have to yield to it; but if it has the good fortune to please you, your favour will give it greater value than any it could have as the production of

      Your most humble and most
      respectfully devoted
      F. Sor

Wednesday 13 February 1822
26 Charlotte Street, Fitzroy Square.')

---

[33] The letter is in the collection of Mary Belle Swingle, Laguna Beach, California.

Mlle

Je vous présente les premiers éxemplaires du petit ouvrage que vous avez eu la bonté de permettre qu'il paraisse décoré de votre nom: Si son mérite pouvait être aussi grand que l'attachem.^t et la reconnaissance que j'ai pour les bontés dont je suis redevable à votre famille les ouvrages de Mozart et de Haydn lui céderoient le pas; mais s'il a le bonheur de vous plaire vos suffrages lui donneront plus de valeur que celle qu'il pourrait avoir comme production de

votre très humble et
très respectueusem.^t dévoué

F. Sor

Mercredi. 13 Février 1822 ———

26 Charlotte Street — Fitzroy Square ————

After Sor left London, the flood of his publications naturally slackened. Here is a list of works by him that appeared in London after his departure.

November 1830	'El amor siempre empieza' ('The Warning'), a song published in *A Musical Gem: A Souvenir for MDCCCXXXI*, Mori & Lavenu, 28 New Bond Street, November 1830. (Voice & piano.)
1830	*Twenty Four Exercises,* op. 35 (guitar solo), Johanning & Whatmore, 126 Regent Street. Advertised in the *Harmonicon* in 1830.
C. 1830–35?	*Minuets, Gallopades . . .* (guitar solo). A collection advertised by Johanning & Whatmore in a guitar publication of theirs (copy in Munich, Bayerische Staatsbibliothek, Mus. Pr. 2° 2598, no. 21). No copy found.
C. 1832	*Method for the Spanish Guitar,* translated by A. Merrick, Cocks & Co. The plate number of the music examples is 1182, which Neighbour & Tyson date at 1832.
C. 1833–34	*Andante maestoso* from op. 11 (minuet no. 5) and other selections for guitar solo published in the *Giulianiad.*
C. 1835	*Six Petites Pièces,* op. 5 (guitar solo), Cocks & Co. Plate number 2382, which Neighbour & Tyson date at 1835.
C. 1835	*Folies d'Espagne* [op. 15] (guitar solo), Cocks & Co. No copy found, but advertised on the title-page of *Six Petites Pièces* (see above), and so probably close to it in date.
C. 1835	*Six Airs Choisis de l'Opera de Mozart Il Flauto Magico,* op. 19 (guitar solo), Cocks & Co.
C. 1835–37	'Vivir en cadenas' (voice & guitar), Johanning & Co., 6 John Street, Oxford Street. According to Humphries & Smith, the firm was at this address c. 1835-37. (It should be remembered that the address on the only known copy could have been changed from an earlier one; but even so the earliest possible date is 1830, when the firm started.) This song was first published in London in 1810, and this arrangement is almost certainly not by Sor.
After c. 1838	*Six Divertimentos* [op. 8] (guitar solo), T. Swain. A re-issue of the Rutter & McCarthy edition of c. 1818.
1851	*Three Canons* (each one published separately), Leader & Cock. A new edition from the Falkner edition of 1815-18. (Three voices & piano.)
1853	'Sospiri volate' (voice & piano), Leader & Cock. Probably not an original composition by Sor but rather an arrangement from the *Three Canons.*

Meissonnier's Paris editions: opus numbers and dating

While Sor was living in London, his compositions for solo guitar (and some for piano) were being published in Paris. Only one publisher was involved: Antoine Meissonnier. He was one of two brothers who came from Marseilles and were both guitarists. He set up as a publisher in Paris at some time between about 1812 and 1817. By 1817 he was at 182 rue Montmartre; briefly in 1822 he was at 4 Boulevard Montmartre; from 1822 to 1825 he was at 15 Galerie des Panoramas; and in November 1825 he moved to 25 Boulevard Montmartre.[34] From these addresses and from his plate numbers it is possible to date his early editions.

The works of Sor which he published at this time were those now known as opp. 1-15, the *Thème Varié,* two sets of waltzes for piano solo, and two for piano duet. The earliest copies of opp. 1-12 and of the *Thème Varié* bear the words 'Journal de Guitare' (or 'Lyre') and so were presumably first published as part of that journal. Hopkinson, in his *Dictionary of Parisian Music Publishers,* p. 89, supposes that Meissonnier began his *Journal de Guitare* in about 1812, and if this is so, opp. 3 and 4 which bear the words '6e Année' and which are almost the earliest works of Sor to have been published by Meissonnier, would have appeared in 1817. This is confirmed by the *Thème Varié,* which can be dated from its plate number at 1822 or 1823 and bears the words '12e Année'.[35]

Accordingly, it seems that Meissonnier first began publishing Sor's works in 1817. By that time, Sor was living in London, but travel between London and Paris was not difficult and it is quite possible that he paid visits to Paris from time to time, or that he simply sent the music from London to Meissonnier in Paris. Originally the two men may have met in Paris in the period 1813-1815.

---

[34] C. Hopkinson, *A Dictionary of Parisian Music Publishers 1700-1950* (London, 1954), confirmed by listings in the *Bibliographie de la France.* The picturesque Galerie des Panoramas still existed in 1974, but all the other shops have either disappeared or changed greatly. From 1832 to 1839 other addresses are listed by Hopkinson, but none of these other addresses is known to have been on any issue of a work by Sor.

---

[35] The *Journal de Guitare* may have been begun not by Meissonnier but by Mme Benoist; copies of this *Journal* in the British Library, E. 1717 e. (1-7), name Meissonnier and Mme Benoist as joint publishers. This does not, of course, affect the question of dating.

Because Meissonnier published most of Sor's guitar works up to op. 33, and because those works have remained in print ever since (contrary to the later works), his editions have been widely referred to and trusted. But research has shown that as far as opp. 1-15 are concerned, a high reputation is unjustified. Meissonnier merely gathered together the fruits of other people's labours. Nearly all of his Sor editions up to op. 15 are not original editions but either reprints from other publishers or else new and inferior versions. Of the seventeen works (op. 15 consists of three separate works), eleven predate Meissonnier, two were published more or less simultaneously in London and by him, and only four seem to have been first published by him. His version of op. 9 is inferior, while his version of *Grand Solo* (op. 14) is a disgrace, reducing a fine and eloquent work to the level of an amateur's plaything. Sor himself broke with him in 1828, and surely it is on him that Sor's scorn for publishers, expressed in his *Méthode pour la Guitare* (p. 76) in 1830, must fall:

> Un guitariste très renommé me dit qu'il avait été obligé de renoncer à écrire comme moi, parceque les éditeurs lui avaient dit ouvertement: 'Une chose est l'appréciation des productions comme connaisseur, et une autre comme marchand de musique; il faut écrire des niaiseries pour le public. J'aime votre ouvrage, mais je n'en retirerais pas mes frais d'impression.' Que faire? *Il faut vivre!* et il a fait des ouvrages qui ne m'auraient jamais laissé deviner son mérite, si d'ailleurs je n'avais pas eu l'occasion de mieux le juger.

> ('A very famous guitarist told me that he had been obliged to give up composing like me, because publishers openly said to him: "Appreciation of compositions as a connaisseur is one thing, and as a music seller is another; you have to compose stupidities for the public. I like your work, but I wouldn't get back the cost of printing it." What should one do? *One must live!* and he composed works which would never have allowed me to guess how gifted he was, if I had not had other occasion to judge him.')

A distinction must be kept clear between the time of composition and the time of publication. Only after Sor's return from Russia did the two correspond, from the appearance in 1827 of his opp. 24-29. Before that time — that is to say, in the case of his guitar music, up to op. 23 — the two do not necessarily correspond, and a work may appear in print that may have been composed many years earlier, perhaps even in Spain, but never published. Up to op. 23, the history of the composition of Sor's music and the history of its publication are two different things.

Accordingly, the opus numbers should be used for convenience only. They do *not* indicate chronology of composition, nor even of publication. We know for certain, for instance, that op. 7 was composed and published before op. 6. The opus numbering derives from Meissonnier, is arbitrary, and was doubtless made for commercial purposes. Many of the earliest known copies, even of Meissonnier's editions, do not bear an opus number. It was only later that Meissonnier began numbering the works, adding opus numbers to his old publications as he reprinted them and incorporating *Folies d'Espagne*, a *Sonata* and a *Thème Varié* as op. 15 when he reached that point.

Here is a list of Sor's works published by Meissonnier in this period (c. 1817-22), arranged in order according to plate number: that is to say, they are in the order in which Meissonnier published them, which is not necessarily either the order of composition or the order of opus numbering. All are for solo guitar except two for piano solo and two for piano duet. An opus number in square brackets means that the number does not appear on the earliest known copies but only on later copies.

Plate number	Opus number	
44	[15]	*Folies d'Espagne*
47	—	Two sets of six waltzes for piano solo[36]
49[37]	[4]	*Fantaisie*
50[38]	[3]	*Thêma Varié*
51	1	*Six Divertissemens*
53	2	*Six Divertissemens*
54	[5]	*Six Petites Pièces*
63	[6]	*Douze Etudes*
100	[7]	*Fantaisie*
110	[15]	*Sonate*
118	8	*Six Divertissemens*
119	9	*Introduction et Variations sur un Thême de Mozart*
120	10	*Troisième Fantaisie*
135	11	*Deux Thêmes Variés et Douze Menuets*
144	12	*Quatrième Fantaisie*
175	13	*Quatrième Divertissement*
188	14	*Grand Solo*
219	[15]	*Thème Varié*
?	—	Two sets of six waltzes for piano duet[39]

---

[36] No copy is known of the second set.

[37] In some late copies, the plate number has been altered, on the plate itself, to 149.

[38] The only known copies have the plate number 150; but because of the work's proximity to op. 4 (both editions bear the words 'Journal de Guitare . . . 6e Année'), almost certainly the earliest copies would have borne the plate number 50, later altered to 150 in a similar fashion to the alteration carried out to op. 4.

---

[39] No copies are known.

The evidence for dating them is as follows. The *Thème Varié* can be dated 1822 or 1823 by its plate number (Meissonnier's plate numbers 208 and 213-216, on works by Piccini and Drolling, were listed in the *Bibliographie de la France* on 14 September 1822; and plate number 235, on a work by A. Miné, on 14 June 1823). This same work, the *Thème Varié,* bears the words '12e Année, 9e Liv[rais]on'; this refers to the *Journal de Guitare,* which therefore presumably started in about 1812. Opp. 3 and 4, which are near the beginning of the list, bear the words 'Journal de Guitare . . . 6e Année,' i.e., about 1817. All the works up to op. 12 were published from 182 rue Montmartre, an address which Meissonnier left in 1822 (Hopkinson); *Grand Solo* bears the address 4 Bd. Montmartre, where Meissonnier was briefly in 1822; and op. 13 bears the address 15 Galerie des Panoramas, to which Meissonnier moved in 1822. No copies are known of the two sets of waltzes for piano duet; they are listed in Meissonnier's second catalogue (in certain copies of op. 1) which goes up to op. 20, but not in the first (in certain copies of opp. 6, 7, and 11) which goes up to op. 12; accordingly the date could be anywhere between about 1820 and 1824, the date of op. 20.

The guitar music

The four sets of divertimenti, or divertimentos, as Sor calls them (opp. 1, 2, 8, and 13), each contain six pieces, varied in length, in tempo, and in key, so that it seems that they were designed as integrated sets and may be performed as such. Some of the pieces are quite short, some long, even including sets of variations. Technically the demands are not high, and the dedicatees were all apparently amateurs: Miss Davenport, Miss Smith, and Emanuel Palacio Fajardo. It is not possible to be certain, either on bibliographical or stylistic grounds, whether they were composed at this time or whether they are older works, composed in Spain before 1813 or in Paris in 1813-15.

The fourth set, op. 13, was reviewed in Ackermann's *Repository of Arts* in February 1820. The reviewer praises it highly, although most of his review is devoted to the nature of the guitar and to Sor's performance on it. Here is the review. The end is revealing, for it shows that not the guitar pieces, but the Italian arietts, were eagerly awaited.

Six Divertimentos for the Guitar,
by Sor. 4th Set. Pr. 2s. 6d.

If hitherto guitar-music has been considered by us as lying out of the sphere of our critical functions, we candidly plead in our defence, the opinion which our own experience had led us to entertain of the limited powers of the instrument; and the unimportant nature of the compositions which had come under our cognizance. It was

with this bias that we recently chanced to hear Mr. Sor touch the guitar, and our previous prejudice instantly gave way to astonishment and admiration. We will not attempt to describe the sensations which the magic of his play excited within us; but our readers may form some idea of what we felt, when we state, that this gentleman executed, with the greatest precision, and with the deepest expression, scores of five and six distinct parts, nay, played fugues of the most complicated texture. How this was done, how it can be done, remains, at this moment, a matter of wonder to us. We have seen and heard; we therefore must believe: otherwise, we own, we should have staked a round sum, that two or three guitars had been actively at work at the same time.

This unrivalled perfection we find, upon inquiry, to be the result of a system at once simple and efficient, the fruit of matured experience, and of a diligent inquiry into the nature and the capabilities of the instrument. Without this, Mr. Sor's excellence might astonish his contemporaries, like a passing meteor, whose reappearance in the horizon is a matter of chance. But, with his system, his art is in a manner perpetuated: some of his pupils already wield the lyre in a masterly manner, and its unassuming elegance daily gains ground in the higher circles. Thus the most ancient of all musical instruments, the invention of Mercury, the darling of Orpheus, seems once more reinstated in its pristine rights. Even music partakes of the spirit of legitimacy which characterizes our era.

Our readers may, in some degree, form a conception of the capabilities of the guitar, by an inspection of the six divertimentos which are the subject of the present article. They are generally written in three distinct parts, and in keys of very different kinds: the harmony is full, and modulation appears in no instance to be pressed or confined by the limits which we ourselves had erroneously considered as dictated by the nature of the instrument. Of the merit of the pieces themselves, we shall say quite enough, by stating that they are such as we were led to expect from our knowledge of Mr. Sor's vocal compositions, of which we have, on several occasions, spoken in terms of the highest commendation; and a further specimen of which is now in our portfolio, to be brought before our readers in this month's Critique, if time permits, but at all events in our next Number.

We now come to the most famous of all Sor's works, the variations on a theme of Mozart, op. 9. An English edition of this was published in London early in 1821 and is almost certainly the first edition and the one to be trusted. A French edition, published by Meissonnier, can be dated roughly in the same period. It has one variation fewer, no coda, and some differences of notes. The variation not in Meissonnier's edition is the first in the London edition; and a difference in the notes is, for example, in the theme itself, where Meissonnier reads A instead of F double sharp in the fourth bar, first note. The question is whether Meissonnier's is a simplified version of the London edition, or the London edition an elaboration of Meissonnier's. The note difference in the fourth bar of the theme strongly suggests that Meissonnier's is a simplification and that it was the London edition which came first. — Years later, in 1826 or 1827, Meissonnier brought out a so-called 'Nouvelle Edition augmentée par l'Auteur', which is exactly the same as the London edition. The work is dedicated to Sor's brother Carlos.

Mozart's *Die Zauberflöte* was first performed in Vienna in 1791, in German, and performances in Italian took place in 1794, so that Sor's piece could date from any time after that. But the first major production of the opera in England took place in May 1819,[40] and I would guess that it was this production which stimulated Sor to compose his variations.

The theme which Sor used comes towards the end of Act I of *Die Zauberflöte,* and the original German words are 'Das klinget so herrlich'.[41] There are various Italian translations, such as 'O dolce concento', 'O dolce armonia', and 'O cara armonia'. It is this last one which is named on the title-page of the English edition of Sor's variations, 'and it is also that used in, for example, the vocal score *Il Flauto Magico* published by Birchall in London in about 1813. The tune served for many arrangements and sets of variations in the nineteenth century, among others by the flautist Drouet, by Herz, and by Glinka.

The studies op. 6 were composed and first published in London, and I shall return to them later, together with the other studies. There remain a number of other works of which only the Fantasia op. 10 seems to be a new work: this has an introduction, theme, variations, and coda, like the Mozart variations. Op. 11 is called *Deux Thèmes Variés et Douze Menuets:* parts of it are certainly old, but the organization of so many separate pieces into a single publication is a product of the 1820s. The *Thème Varié* is little more than a quirk of publishing, since all of it except one section is also to be found in op. 11. *Grand Solo,* op. 14, in Meissonnier's arrangement, is a mere late version which we have already dismissed. Finally, the Fantasia op. 12 takes the theme of op. 3 and adds an introduction, coda, and three new variations. It is dedicated to Frederick Kalkbrenner, the pianist, and indeed the new work has dimensions more commonly associated with the piano music of that time than with the guitar music. In general it may be said that as time went on Sor's guitar music became less forceful and more decorated: more provided with introductions and codas, more concerned

with technical devices such as the harmonics possible on the guitar. The economy of effect of the music from his Spanish period is lost. Just as the seguidillas of eighteenth century Spain reappeared in nineteenth century Europe as boleros, dressed up and often intricate, so Sor's guitar music similarly changed its nature.

The guitar in London

In the eighteenth century, the guitar had little favour in England — only the so-called 'English guitar', which was in fact a kind of cittern. The vogue for the true guitar in England began to any considerable extent only in the early nineteenth century. The *Giulianiad* wrote in 1833:

> The successful introduction of the guitar into England has been comparatively of recent date. Till the peace of 1815, it may be assumed that few persons in this country were acquainted with its full and varied powers. From that time, however, to the present moment, no instrument can be brought in comparison with its rapid advancement in public estimation.

Sor's presence in London and his appearance in concerts such as the Philharmonic Society's in 1817, doubtless had much to do with this. The *Harmonicon* wrote in March 1824 (p. 48):

> Amongst the once favoured musical instruments, now for some time neglected, and coming into practice again, is the guitar. To the exquisite and wonderful performances of M. Sor this may be attributed, he makes the instrument "speak so sweetly, and so well," that hundreds fly to "strike the chorded shell," who never before dreamt of what it was capable of producing.

This in spite of the same writer's subsequent reservations:

> Its powers in almost every hand but his are certainly very limited, and even he, the modern Jubal, cannot give it strength enough of tone to render it useful any where but in a small room.

Sor's performances on the guitar, then, were well known in London. And he composed for the instrument, as well as for the voice and the piano; while the studies op. 6 are dedicated to his pupils, showing that he taught guitar playing as well as singing. The *Repository of Arts* in 1820 attributed the success of Sor himself and of his pupils to Sor's systematic and intelligent technique:

> But, with his system, his art is in a manner perpetuated: some of his pupils already wield the lyre in a masterly manner, and its unassuming elegance daily gains ground in the higher circles.

[40] Trevor Fawcett, 'The first undoubted "Magic Flute"?', *Royal Musical Association Research Chronicle,* 12 (1974), pp. 106-14.

[41] In the *Neue Mozart-Ausgabe,* Serie II, Werkgruppe 5, vol. 19 (Kassel, 1970), it occupies bars 293-325 of the finale to Act I.

While he was in London, the famous guitar-maker Panormo made several guitars under his direction (*Méthode pour la Guitare*, p. 7).

After he left, the guitar continued its rise to favour. More and more methods and other works were published, including a number of pieces by Sor, and in the 1830s there was even a special guitar magazine called the *Giulianiad*. In February 1831 the *Harmonicon* wrote again:

> M. Sor stands at a vast distance from all other guitarists, both as a performer and composer. He is an excellent musician, a man of taste, and his command over an instrument, which in other hands is so limited in its means, is not only astonishing, but — what is far more important — always pleasing.

Arrangements from 'Don Giovanni'

If Sor was occupied both with the voice and with the guitar during this period, we might expect to find some songs to the guitar, to set beside the seguidillas of his Spanish period. But no such original songs have been found: there are only three arrangements for voice and guitar of arias from Mozart's *Don Giovanni*, and of these I have found copies only of two, 'Vedrai carino' and 'Batti, batti'. They are idiomatically and confidently written for the guitar. Once again, they show his admiration for Mozart, as seen not only in the Mozart variations, op. 9, but also in his arrangements from the *Magic Flute* published as op. 19, as well as in his letter written from Charlotte Street which was discussed above.

Piano duets

While in London, Sor published a number of sets of three waltzes for piano duet. The first set of which a copy is known is called 'Set 2d'; its dedicatee was Mlle Rehausen, and it appeared probably in 1818 or before (see the list of publications above). It presupposes the existence of a first set, but no copy of this is known.[42] Another set, dedicated to Lady Jane and Lady Georgina Paget, is unnumbered but may be dated from its plate number at December 1819 and so is probably the third set. The next set, dedicated to Lady Augusta and Lady Agnes Paget, is numbered '4th Set', and thereafter there follows a series of sets from 5th to 10th (no copy is known of the 9th). Meissonnier in Paris published two sets of three waltzes for piano duet, but no copies are known; their existence is shown only by advertisements which give their incipits. One of them appears to be identical with the 7th London Set, and the other is new (it could correspond to the missing English 1st or 9th Set). Altogether, then, we know of ten or eleven sets of which two or perhaps three are missing.

Two other publications for piano duet, confusingly called *Three Waltzes (by different Authors)* and *A Second Set of Waltzes,* stand outside this series, for they are merely arrangements from pieces 'composed originally for a full band'.[43]

One other composition for piano duet is called *A Duett . . . Composed on Several Swedish National Airs*. Finally, a *Duo Brillant* was advertised in 1824, but no copy is known.

The waltzes are all of slight value, society divertissements which must be seen in the context of the craze for dancing at this period. On the eve of the Battle of Waterloo, for example, the Duchess of Richmond gave a ball in Brussels, which became famous in retrospect: some of the officers 'actually had not time to change their clothes, but fought in evening costume' (J.B. Priestley, *The Prince of Pleasure*, p. 141). All of Sor's sets of waltzes, without exception, are dedicated to ladies, mostly the young unmarried ones who would be the most interested in dancing, such as the four Ladies Paget.

Piano solos

Sor also composed some pieces for piano solo at this time: two sets of six waltzes and three sets of quadrilles.

Monzani & Hill published *Six Waltzes* in London in 1819 or before, marked '1st Set'. This presupposes the existence of at least one further set, but no copy of any such further set is known.[44] Conversely, Meissonnier in Paris advertised two sets of six waltzes: we have a copy of only his first set, and it is not the same as Monzani & Hill's first set. I suspect, therefore, that between Monzani & Hill and Meissonnier all of Sor's waltzes for piano solo are preserved.[45]

The sets of quadrilles, published in 1821 and 1822, each contained not only three quadrilles but also the instructions for dancing them and a concluding waltz.

---

[42] Unless it is the set of six waltzes for piano solo, which seems unlikely (see the list of publications above).

---

[43] Some libraries possessing copies of these two sets have considered them to be the first and second sets in the main series of sets of *Three Waltzes*. This is not so, because they are clearly distinguished as arrangements and not original compositions, and because the set of original waltzes dedicated to Mlle Rehausen is already called 'Set 2d'.

---

[44] Unless it is the second set of three waltzes for piano duet, which seems unlikely (see the list of publications above).

---

[45] A manuscript set of six waltzes in the Staatsbibliothek Preussischer Kulturbesitz, Berlin, contains three waltzes that are in the Monzani & Hill set and three that are in the Meissonnier.

Like the waltzes for piano duet and for piano solo, they are lightweight society dances. Once again, the dedicatees are ladies, including once more two of the beautiful Paget sisters, and Mme Buisson, who was presumably the wife of 'Monsieur Buisson, Professor of French Literature in London'.[46] The quadrille was a comparatively new dance in England: the *Morning Post* reported on 22 July 1816 that the new French dances which are called quadrilles were first seen in this country 'on Monday last'. The three sets were called *Les Cuirassiers, Les Favorites des Salons,* and *Les Choisies.* This last, dedicated to Lady Jane Paget, is almost certainly the publication referred to in the letter of 13 February 1822 which I quoted above.

Ballet music

Before his exile from Spain in 1813, Sor does not seem to have been involved with ballet, but only with opera and drama. He wrote an opera, *Telemaco;* began another, *Don Trastullo;* wrote a tonadilla, *Las Preguntas de la Morante,* and the music for a melodrama, *Elvira la Portuguesa.* He certainly knew about dance, because much later he wrote an article on the bolero incorporating very specific information about it, while his seguidillas are related to a dance tradition. But there is no indication that he was involved with formal ballet. Nor is he known to have written ballet music during his first Paris visit, 1813-15, nor in his early years in London, 1815-20.

But ballet in London at this time was very important. As we saw, the *Times* wrote that by the end of the 1816 season the ballet there had 'reached an extraordinary pitch of elegance and maturity for the meridian of London'. It was a principal entertainment of London society. The green rooms of the theatres were a favourite haunt of the nobility. The ballet-masters and above all the ballerinas were important people. And so it is not surprising that in London Sor became involved both with ballet and — with a ballerina.[47]

The ballerina was Félicité Hullin, the second of the three daughters of the ballet-master Jean-Baptiste Hullin. Virginie was the most famous of the three and often danced at the Paris Opera. Félicité was the second daughter.[48] Born in 1805 or earlier, like her sister she was an 'Elève de l'Opéra', and for eight years she

danced the roles of 'Amours' — roles which could be taken by children. In 1819 she made her first appearance in London, and on 5 February 1823 she made an official debut at the Paris Opera.[49] In the Archives Nationales in Paris is a file on the Hullins (file 0^3 1658) which includes the examiners' report on the test which was obligatory before a major debut:

> MM les Examinateurs ont reconnu à l'unanimité que Mlle Hullin seconde a les Jambes agréables, les pointes et les coude-pieds gracieux; que sa taille et l'expression de sa physionomie l'appellent au genre comique, et qu'enfin elle réunit toutes les qualités qui pourraient la rendre très-utile à l'Opéra. M. Albert déclare qu'il a dansé longtems avec cette Artiste à Londres, et qu'elle est pleine de zèle et d'intelligence.

> ('The examiners agree unanimously that the second Mlle Hullin has good legs and graceful points and insteps; that her figure and features suit the comic genre, and that all in all she has all the qualities which could make her most useful to the Opera. M. Albert declares that he has danced for a long time with this artiste in London, and that she is full of zeal and intelligence.')

But however much the examiners liked her legs, she was not taken on at the Paris Opera. From the papers in the Archives Nationales it seems that she was not in reality unanimously acclaimed — indeed, even perhaps that the debut was something of a favour to her in order that it might help her to pursue a career elsewhere.

Sor's first known ballet was *La Foire de Smyrne,* first performed at the King's Theatre, London, on 3 July 1821 (Guest). It was a 'divertissement-ballet' and received seven performances. An advertisement in the *Times* listed 'Mlle Hullin' among the performers — perhaps Félicité or possibly Virginie. The choreographer, James d'Egville, was a veteran by this time but had been very important in his day. He was an Englishman of French extraction, born about 1770 and himself originally a dancer. He choreographed many Romantic ballets. No score of *La Foire de Smyrne* is known to survive.

Le Seigneur Généreux followed very soon after, in the same month: it was first performed at the King's Theatre on 27 July 1821. On at least one occasion it was given together with *La Foire de Smyrne.* The choreographer was Deshayes, who was more important than the ageing d'Egville. He was a Frenchman who

---

[46] This gentleman composed *St. Valentin, A New French Song* (copy in Cambridge University Library, Mus. 19.23⁶).

[47] Many of the details in this section come from Ivor Guest's *The Romantic Ballet in London,* 2nd edn. (London, 1972), and from information which Mr. Guest was kind enough to communicate to me.

[48] She has often been referred to as Félicité-Virginie Hullin. This is an error (of which I also was guilty, in my article 'Fernando Sor, concert performer', *Guitar Review,* 39, 1974), as is proved by documents in the Archives Nationales.

[49] Ivor Guest, *The Romantic Ballet in Paris* (London, 1966), p. 47.

first appeared in London in 1800. He produced many ballets, among them *Kenilworth,* which the Princess Victoria (afterwards Queen Victoria) saw in 1831. After he died it was said of him that 'a more amiable or more courteous personage never existed in the realms of the fantastic toe'. He himself danced at least once in *Le Seigneur Généreux;* so did the famous ballerina Lise Noblet. Again, no score of *Le Seigneur Généreux* is known to survive.

But Sor's most successful ballet — indeed, the most successful work in its own day of any that he composed — was *Cendrillon,* first performed at the King's Theatre on 26 March 1822. Like Rossini's opera *La Cenerentola* (1817), this was a version of the Cinderella story, taken from Perrault. It fits very well into the fairytale atmosphere which was so fashionable in ballet at that time. The choreography was by the famous Albert (the pseudonym of Albert Decombe). It had three acts, and a waltz and a march which became famous. It was later put on at the Paris Opera on 3 March 1823, where it was also a success and ran for 104 performances, one of the very few works to achieve more than 100 performances at the Paris Opera. Later it was chosen for the opening of the Bolshoi Petrovsky Theatre in Moscow on 6 January 1825.

The Paris production is described by Ivor Guest in his book *The Romantic Ballet in Paris,* pp. 47-49. In terms of spectacle, the Paris production was magnificent. The sets were by the famous Pierre Ciceri.

> His first set was in the Gothic style, with a backcloth depicting a fine landscape which was revealed when the castle door opened, but the visual highlight of this scene was the emergence from the chimney of Cinderella's carriage, drawn by two white horses made up to represent unicorns. Another effective piece of stage magic in this act was the fairy Mélise's costume change, which was invented by a M. Delaistre, a former costumier who then held an administrative post at the *contrôle.* The ballroom scene in the second act was the most splendid of Ciceri's sets for this ballet, full use being made of the stage to accommodate some two hundred people . . . The costumes, which were designed by Albert himself, were praised for their elegance and lightness.

The *Allgemeine musikalische Zeitung* wrote of it: 'Schöne Tänze, herrliche Dekorationen und eine recht angenehme Musik' (September 1823) ('Beautiful dances, fine decor and extremely pleasant music'). Sir George Smart saw it in Paris on 25 November 1825, and said that 'both dancing and scenery were most exquisite', although he (or his editors?) thought that the music was by Spohr.[50]

Albert, the choreographer, was the son of a cavalry officer in the French army and a dancer who was 'unrivalled for the free and yet stately pride of his attitudes, which his uncommon strength of muscle enables him to sustain with a firmness that never trembles from the line of beauty' (*Morning Herald,* 25 April 1822). He was a man of unusual intelligence, a collector of books and paintings and a fine conversationalist.[51]

Concerning the London production, John Ebers, who was manager of the King's Theatre at the time, wrote:

> I was particularly fortunate at this time in persuading M. Albert to invent us a ballet; and I feel proud that he first brought out his beautiful 'Cendrillon' here, a ballet which he afterwards got up at the Grand Opera in Paris, with the greatest satisfaction to the Parisians. How could a ballet fail, the work of such an artist as Albert, and the music by the extraordinary Spaniard Sor, who is known to be the most perfect guitarist in the world?[52]

Cendrillon succeeded not only because of Albert and because of Sor, but also because of its star, the ballerina Maria Mercandotti, 'the Andalusian Venus', This Spanish dancer had first appeared in London when she danced the cachucha, as a child, at the King's Theatre in 1814. On her return in 1822, she first appeared in a divertissement after the first act of *Le Nozze di Figaro* in January of that year; then in a small one-acter; and in the following March she scored a great triumph in *Cendrillon.* The next year, 1823, she eloped with a Mr. Edward Hughes Ball-Hughes, an unfortunate name that gave rise to a good deal of hilarity. There circulated two verses, which Ebers quotes. One is a parody of a letter which Mercandotti wrote to Ebers excusing herself from appearing:

> Sir, being a-miss et ma santé dérangée,
> Mon médecin declares qu'il-y-a quelque chose
>   à changer;
> I suppose he means air — à la campagne je vais,
> So dispose of my rôle à quelque autre, I pray,
> But Mamma ne veut pas que je sois paresseuse,
> Bids me go to a Ball — and I cannot ref-Hughes!

And the other:

> The fair damsel is gone, and no wonder at all,
> That, bred to the dance, she is fond of a Ball.

Now, Mercandotti's London success was a carefully planned event. She was Spanish; and what more likely than that Sor was chosen to write the music for her first major appearance because he too was Spanish? I would

---

[50] *Leaves from the Journals of Sir George Smart* (London, 1907), p. 229.

[51] Guest, *The Romantic Ballet in England,* p. 35; *The Romantic Ballet in Paris,* pp. 46 and 284.

[52] John Ebers, *Seven Years of the King's Theatre* (London, 1828), pp. 162-3.

suggest that Lord Fife and Ebers had had Sor in mind for this commission for some time previously, and that he had been invited to compose *La Foire de Smyrne* and *Le Seigneur Généreux* as *essais*. The first of these two was choreographed by the old d'Egville; the second by the more popular Deshayes; now *Cendrillon* was choreographed by the star Albert, showing a gradual and deliberate progression.

After Mercandotti, the title-role was taken in London by Lise Noblet, in Paris by Bigottini, and in Moscow by Félicité Hullin. We have prints of Mercandotti, Noblet, and Hullin in the role, which are reproduced below.[53]

_____

[53] The prints of Mercandotti and Noblet are reproduced from copies in the Enthoven Collection of the Victoria and Albert Museum, London, by kind permission. The Mercandotti print was already reproduced in Guest's *The Romantic Ballet in London,* plate IIb. The print of Hullin is reproduced from a photograph kindly given to me by Mme André Verdier; its source is unknown, but perhaps it was sent by V.L. Mackevitch to the magazine *Guitare et Musique* (see chapter 4).

Painted by M.W. Sharp.   *Engraved by Robt Cooper.*

MAD.ᴸᴸᴱ MERCANDOTTI,

in Cendrillon.

Painted by M.W. Sharp.   Engraved by Robt Cooper.

MAD.^{LLE} NOBLET
in Cendrillon.

В. *Баранов. Балерина и балетмейстер*
Московского Большого театра Ф. Гюллень-Сор
Литография 1826 г.

A score and parts of *Cendrillon* are in the Bibliothèque de l'Opéra, Paris. Another manuscript score is in the New York Public Library, and a piano reduction was published in London in late 1822. Some manuscript orchestral extracts are in the Deutsche Staatsbibliothek, Berlin. The March from Act 3 apparently achieved great popularity, for Sor arranged it for guitar solo and this arrangement went through a number of editions.

According to Ledhuy, Sor wrote one more ballet in London, *L'Amant Peintre*. This was a ballet in one act, choreographed by Anatole Petit. The score does not survive. Later, in Russia, Félicité Hullin made it into three acts, and the score of this three-act version survived in the Bibliothèque de l'Opéra, Paris, called *Alphonse et Léonore ou L'Amant Peintre*. The original one-act version is very probably that listed by Guest as *Alphonse et Léonore,* first produced at the King's Theatre, London, on 19 June 1823.

During his stay in London, then, Sor was involved with the major ballet theatre in London, not merely with one of the many theatres that from time to time put on ballets. His choreographers and dancers were the stars of the day. And his *Cendrillon* was a major success in the history of the Romantic ballet of that age.

Gil Blas

In August 1822 the 'Operatick Drama' *Gil Blas* with two songs by Sor was first performed at the Theatre Royal, Strand. A copy of the playbill advertising it survives in the Enthoven Collection of the Victoria & Albert Museum, London. Most of the music was by 'Mr. Moss', with two songs by Sor called 'Should a Pretty Spanish Lass' and 'Farewell, for on Oviedo's Towers'. The songs were sung by the famous singer Miss Kelly, who at the beginning of the drama played Gil Blas at the age of seventeen, and in Acts IV and V played Antonia, 'Daughter of Gil Blas, and very like her father when he was Seventeen'. The critics thought it good but too long; one of them writes 'The bustle of scene, the style in which it was all got up, and variety of incident, interspersed with some tolerably pretty music by Mr. Moss and Mr. Sor, obtained it a favourable reception' (from a cutting in the Enthoven Collection which, however, does not name the newspaper). The two songs by Sor, which are indeed tolerably pretty, were published also in August 1822. Perhaps he was invited to write them because he, like the subject of the drama, was Spanish.

Sor and the Royal Academy of Music

The guitar is now taught in the London colleges of music; and it may amuse those who may think that its status there is too low to know that Sor appears in the list of Honorary Members at the founding of the Royal Academy of Music (*Quarterly Musical Magazine,* IV, 1822, p. 519). Honorary Members were chosen from among the most distinguished members of the musical profession in London, and Sor appears in the first list that was drawn up in 1822, the year before teaching actually began. Soon after, he had left London; but his appearance in this list·indicates not only that he was thoroughly accepted but also that he had no apparent intention of leaving. No wandering guitarist, this; but an accepted member of the London musical scene.

The end of Sor's London stay

In 1822, then, Sor achieved a triumph in a major London theatre with *Cendrillon*. His compositions were flowing steadily from the London presses. His status was high, as his inclusion in the list of honorary members of the Royal Academy shows. Ebers called him 'the most perfect guitarist in the world'. He was 44 years old. After having had to abandon his established position in Spain ten years before, now living in London presumably with his young daughter, he must have felt once more a degree of permanence. Why, then, did he leave?

The reason was Félicité Hullin. In a letter probably of December 1824 (see chapter 4) he speaks of her as 'ma Chère petite femme'. Whether they were or were not married, certainly he was very attached to her. And so, when she received an invitation to be *prima ballerina* at the Moscow Ballet, Sor went with her.

His name still appears as an Associate of the Philharmonic Society in a list which was probably printed late in 1822, but not in the corresponding list printed a year later (British Library, K.6.d.3). The Royal Academy list also dates from late 1822. He played in a concert in Paris early in February 1823, as we shall see. So he must have left London in late 1822 or early 1823, more probably the latter. Félicité Hullin danced a special examination for the Opera in Paris on 21 September 1822, and a normal official one on 8 November 1822 for her debut there, according to the file in the Archives Nationales. The debut itself was on 5 February 1823. Sor may have gone with her to Paris on any or all of these trips.

CHAPTER 4

PARIS, BERLIN, WARSAW,
MOSCOW and ST. PETERSBURG
1823-1826/7

And so Sor set out from London for Russia. On the way he passed through Paris, Berlin and Warsaw; and in Russia itself he spent three years. Ledhuy's *Encyclopédie* gives many details. But in Ledhuy, Sor omits any mention of Félicité Hullin, giving the impression that his Russian trip was exclusively on his own account as a composer and guitarist. Although it is certain that he travelled with her, and probably left London for her, by 1835 (the date of Ledhuy) he was unwilling even to mention her name.

Félicité Hullin went to Russia in her professional capacity as a ballerina, and indeed at a high level, as *prima ballerina* of the Moscow Ballet. This is confirmed, for example, by the article on her in the *Soviet Encyclopedia* (1961-7; Theatrical Encyclopedia, II, 252), and by Yuri Bakhrushin's article 'The Ballet of the Bolshoi Theatre' in *The Bolshoi Theatre* (Moscow, 1947), p. 178. She was accompanied not only by Sor and his daughter, but also by the French dancer Joseph Richard. She and Richard were the stars of the Moscow Ballet when they arrived, and they shone particularly in the grand opening of the Bolshoi Petrovsky Theatre on 6 January 1825, with the ballet *Cendrillon* with music by Sor.

Some research in Russian sources on the visit of Sor, Hullin and Richard was done by V.P. Mackevitch in the 1950s. He sent the results of his research, unfortunately, to a magazine called *Guitare et Musique,* a non-scholarly publication which appeared in Paris. In April 1958 that magazine did indeed publish an article called 'Fernando Sor en Russie', which merely summarized Mackevitch's conclusions and gave no references. This article contains a number of details, for example the following description of Hullin and Richard, apparently translated from a Russian newspaper or periodical:

Quelle alliance de la légèreté, de la force, de la rapidité, de la souplesse! Les entrechats brillent comme des éclairs; les mouvements du corps peignent des tableaux admirables! Ce sont des créatures éthérées! Ce sont une nymphe volante, un sylphe volant! Ce sont les tourbillons de Descartes sous une forme humaine! La terre n'entend pas le toucher des danseurs, les regards ne parviennent à les suivre! On imagine qu'une sorte d'étincelle électrique les soulève dans les airs, joue avec leurs membres, toujours davantage, de sorte que l'on ne peut s'empêcher de prononcer des mots d'étonnement et d'admiration! Quelles possibilités sont offertes à l'homme! Jusqu'où n'ira-t-il pas s'il en a la ferme volonté? Et où sont les limites du talent, de l'art?

('What a union of lightness, strength, rapidity, suppleness! The entrechats shine like lightning; the movements of their bodies paint wonderful pictures! They are creatures of the heavens! They are a flying nymph, a flying sylph! They are Descartes' whirlwinds in human form! The earth does not hear the dancers touch it, sight cannot follow them! One imagines that a sort of electric spark lifts them in the air, plays with their limbs, ever more and more, so that one cannot but exclaim in astonishment and admiration! What possibilities are offered to man! How far can he go if he have the firm desire? Where are the limits of talent, of art?')

According to the article in *Guitare et Musique,* Hullin was engaged for the Moscow Ballet by Prince Galitsyne (at that time governor of Moscow) at an annual salary of 17,000 roubles. Hullin was said to have been born in 1805 (though the article casts doubt on this, suggesting that it was in fact earlier); about 1829 she ceased to be a ballerina and became a teacher of ballet; and in 1838 she married a teacher of French, Hippolite Hertel, and left the theatre. Her career as a teacher of ballet is confirmed by the *Soviet Encyclopedia,* which says that she was distinguished in this capacity and trained among others the famous dancer Carpacova. In the article is reproduced a contemporary lithograph by V. Baranov of her in the role of Cinderella in *Cendrillon,* which is reproduced in the present book in chapter 3.

The editors of *Guitare et Musique,* as I said, appear to have summarized Mackevitch's findings. My own letter to Mackevitch was returned marked 'Décédé'. But in Paris, Mme André Verdier kindly gave me a page of manuscript notes, written on the reverse of a concert flyer dated 18 November 1957, which appear to have been taken by the late André Verdier from the original material gathered by Mackevitch. This page of notes adds that Hullin arrived in Moscow in November 1823, and that she danced on 9, 13 and 15 December 1823 in the ballet *Amour et Psyché.* On 31 January 1824 *Cendrillon* was given as a benefit for her, and was performed again on 4 February 1824. On 1 December 1824 *Alphonse et Léonore ou l'Amour Peintre* (music by Sor) was performed; and in January 1825 again *Cendrillon.* In Moscow, in the course of her career there, she produced more than twenty ballets, and taught at the ballet school from 1824 to 1831. She returned briefly to Paris with her pupil Carpacova and danced there on 2 May 1827 in the ballet *La Chasse de Henri IV.* Once more in Moscow, she danced in a divertissement on 7 October 1827 (Sor remaining in France). By 1829 she danced rarely, until her departure from the theatre in 1838.

It is established, then, that Hullin went to Russia from London in her professional capacity and that Sor accompanied here. Were they in fact married? If so, the ceremony probably took place in London, but I have found no record of it. Certainly Hullin in Russia called herself Hullin-Sors; and, in about December 1824, Sor called her 'ma Chère petite femme'. Yet she can have been no less than twenty years younger than he, and in 1838, according to the article in *Guitare et Musique,* she married again in Russia. The question remains open.

When they left London, they passed first of all through Paris. Ledhuy tells us that Sor arrived in Paris while *Cendrillon* was in rehearsal, and that he stayed to see its successful performance. The first performance took place on 3 March 1823. Hullin made her official debut at the Paris Opera on 5 February 1823, and probably he was already in Paris for that — perhaps even before for her two examinations on 21 September and 8 November 1822.[1]

In early February 1823 he played in a benefit concert in Paris, as we learn from the English magazine the *Harmonicon:*

> M. Sor, who so long delighted and surprised the lovers of music in London, by his performance on the Spanish guitar, is now living in Paris. Early last month he displayed his talents at the *Salle des Menus Plaisirs,* for the benefit of M. Guillou, first flute at the Grand Opera, where he charmed all the Parisian amateurs by an instrument which, says our French correspondent, might, from its appearance, have been taken for a guitar; but judging by its harmony, must have been a complete orchestra, enclosed in a small compass. He ought, continues our friend, to be called *Le Racine de la Guitare.*
>
> (*Harmonicon,* March 1823)

From Paris, he set out for Moscow, in the company of his daughter, Joseph Richard and Félicité Hullin. They passed through Berlin, and by October 1823 they were in Warsaw.

Germany

The road from Paris to Berlin passes near Bonn, and it may have been at this time that Simrock of Bonn and Cologne arranged with Sor to publish a series of his works, which he did in about 1824-5. They were the guitar works opp. 1-20 (with the exception of op. 13), the *Thème Varié,* and the March from *Cendrillon* arranged for guitar. The firm of Simrock did well by Sor, publishing more works by him in later years,[2] and keeping many of them in print for years after, some even to the present day. The relationship between Simrock and Sor seems to have been legitimate and not piratical, for when Sor published the first edition of his *Méthode pour la Guitare* in Paris in 1830, the name of Simrock appeared on the title-page as joint publisher. Sor could easily have called on him in Bonn in the course of his journey in 1823.

The plate numbers of Simrock's editions of 1824-5 show that they were published all at once (O. Deutsch, *Musikverlagsnummern,* Berlin, 1961). And at the time of Sor's journey in 1823, opp. 16-20 had not yet been published by Meissonnier. Therefore, it seems that Simrock was supplied with the music of these works not in 1823 but a year or two later, either by Sor from Russia or by Meissonnier from Paris.

Also about this time, Peters of Leipzig published a set of Italian arietts by Sor, a set of Italian duets, and his op. 9. The plate numbers show that they were published in that order but unlike the Simrock editions not all at

---

[1] Guest, *The Romantic Ballet in Paris,* p. 47; Paris, Archives Nationales, file O³ 1658.

[2] In 1830 (date established by the plate numbers) Simrock published opp. 21-33, 35 and 36 (this last called op. 34 in error), and a German/French edition of the *Méthode pour la Guitare.*

once. We know nothing of the circumstances under which they were published. Leipzig is not on the main road from Paris to Berlin. But the matter was probably arranged on this same trip, for they appeared at this time: the duets were listed in September 1823 as having just appeared, and op. 9 in 1824.[3] Peters' edition of op. 9 is Meissonnier's simplified version, not the full London one; the arietts are the same as the London Fifth Set; and the duets are the same as the London Second Set.

Ledhuy devotes two sentences to Berlin and Potsdam:

> A Berlin il composa la musique de deux pas de danse, un pour le théâtre du roi, et un autre pour celui du palais de *Sans-Souci,* à Potsdam. Spontini accueillit Sor avec distinction, et quelques circonstances particulières empêchèrent seules l'effet de ses bonnes dispositions pour lui.

> ('At Berlin he composed the music for two pas de danse, one for the king's theatre, and the other for the theatre at the palace of Sans Souci at Potsdam. Spontini received Sor cordially, but certain circumstances prevented the effect of his good disposition towards him.')

Spontini was the General Director of music at Berlin. If Sor composed two pas de danse in Berlin and Potsdam (which is about fourteen miles outside Berlin), then presumably Hullin and Richard gave performances during their stay there.[4]

Poland

From Berlin, the party travelled on to Warsaw. Józef Powroźniak has discovered some references to performances given there by the two dancers, and to a concert given by Sor and his daughter, in a Warsaw newspaper of the time, the *Kurier Warszawski (Warsaw Courier).* Here they are:[5]

---

[3] *Allgemeine musikalische Zeitung* 'Intelligenzblatt' for September 1823, and A. Hofmeister, *Handbuch der musikalischen Literatur,* 1824, respectively.

---

[4] Musical life in Berlin and Potsdam in this period is described by the English conductor Sir George Smart, who travelled there in 1825 and kept a diary, a large part of which was later published as *Leaves from the Journal of Sir George Smart* (London, 1907).

---

[5] Professor Powroźniak referred to them in his book *Gitara od A do Z* (Kraków, 1966), pp. 78-9. My thanks are due to him for providing the full texts, and to Vladimir Bobri and Martha Nelson for putting me in touch with him. The texts have been translated for this book by Stefan Themerson.

Sunday 12 October 1823:
There is now present in Warsaw Mr. Sor, a composer and a virtuoso on the guitar. He is on his way to Moscow, where he has been summoned to arrange and compose ballet music. Shortly he will be heard in our capital in the Sala Redutowa. The Parisian journal *Widowisk,* writing about a concert given for the King of France, assures us that in that concert Mr. Sor's talent drew the greatest attention and gave universal satisfaction.

Thursday 16 October 1823:
Yesterday the Parisian dancers Miss Hullin and Mr. Richard deserved an applause still greater than at their first performance, and this they duly received. At the request of the lovers of ballet, they will stay in our capital for a few more days.
Next Monday Mr. Sor, a Spaniard, a guitar virtuoso, and a composer, will give a concert in the theatre hall of the Saxon Palace. He will play the guitar and sing; and his eight-year-old daughter will also sing. Tickets can be obtained from Mr. Szowo at the Europa Hotel.

Monday 20 October 1823:
Mr. Sor's concert has been postponed until next Wednesday. — Yesterday, in the National Theatre, all seats were full to overflowing. The public honoured the Parisian dancers by encoring them. Fulfilling the wishes of the lovers of ballet, they will appear on our stage again tomorrow, and on Thursday they will definitely depart for Moscow.

Thursday 23 October 1823:
Winter is already giving signs of approaching; the day before yesterday there were two degrees of cold, and yesterday three.
A hundred and eighty persons were present yesterday at the concert of Mr. Sor. This artist is without doubt an excellent virtuoso on the guitar. When that instrument is used only to accompany the voice, it does not provide much interest for the listener; but Mr. Sor diversifies his playing so much that it gives pleasure even to the musical connoisseur. Yesterday, although the guitar pleased the audience, we were sorry that even after the expression of so many opinions against the practice, children still perform in order to show talents which only in the course of time may hope to receive a just praise and give pleasure.

These extracts raise a number of interesting points. Firstly, this is the first known reference to Sor's daughter. The *Kurier Warszawski* gives her age as eight in October 1823, and she sang in the Warsaw concert while her father played and sang.

Secondly, this is the only known occasion on which Sor did not share the concert platform with other professional performers. As far as we know, he never gave a solo concert. Here in Warsaw, he varied the programme by singing as well as playing the guitar, and by having his daughter sing.

The first extract from the *Kurier Warszawski* refers to an earlier concert of Sor's in Paris, for the King of France, a concert that was reviewed in a journal which it translated into Polish as *Widowisk.* Unfortunately this review has not been traced. *Widowisk* should mean something like *Spectacles,* but no such journal has been found. The concert may have been not actually in the presence of the French King, but at the Ecole Royale de Musique, where it seems that Sor played later, in 1826 or 1827 (see chapter 5). The Polish actually reads: 'Dziennik Paryzki *Widowisk,* piszac o Koncercie danym dla Króla Francuzkiego . . .'

The dancers, Félicité Hullin and Joseph Richard, achieved great success in Warsaw. They apparently gave no less than four performances there: the first seems to have been a few days before 15 October 1823; the second on 15 October itself; the third on 19 October; and the fourth is announced for 21 October. Sor's concert took place on Wednesday 22 October.

These performances were not isolated events, but a normal part of the life of this capital and international city, with its own numerous concerts, ballets and plays. The same issues of the *Kurier Warszawski* contain news from London, Paris and Rome, as well as musical news about fortepianos. And it is a sad footnote that also in these same issues is news that must have grieved Sor, a man of liberal sympathies and himself now in exile: an account of the French invasion of Spain under the Duke of Angoulême in 1823, called in by King Fernando VII to put down the liberal movement of Riego. Had that liberal movement succeeded, Sor and many thousands of other exiled Spaniards might well have been able to return to their country.

Russia

According to André Verdier's notes, the party arrived in Moscow in November 1823. The ballet *Amour et Psyché* was given in December; *Cendrillon* in January and February 1824; and *Alphonse et Léonore* in December 1824. This is confirmed by Ledhuy: 'Le ballet de *Cendrillon* fut joué à Moscou; bientôt après on exécuta l'*Amant Peintre,* refondu et distribué en trois actes au lieu d'un' ('*Cendrillon* was performed in Moscow, and soon afterwards l'*Amant Peintre,* revised and distributed into three acts instead of one').

Alphonse et Léonore was indeed a three-act version of *L'Amant Peintre,* which had been performed in London in one act. No score survives of the one-act version, but there is a full score of the three-act version in the Bibliothèque de l'Opéra, Paris. The title-page of that score reads as follows:

Alphonse et Léonore
ou
L'amant Peintre
Ballet pantomime en un acte par M. Anatole Petit
Sujet tireé de Molière
Refondu, augmenté, et distribué en trois actes
pour le bénéfice de Mlle Hullin,
musique de Ferdinand Sor
à Moscou l'année 1824

The words 'Ferdinand Sor' are a signature, and so the whole of this score appears to be autograph. A second title-page adds the detail that this three-act version was 'mis en Scéne par Madlle Félicité Hullin'.

The plot is taken from Molière's *Le Sicilien ou l'Amour Peintre,* and the characters are Spanish, a fact which may perhaps account for Sor's involvement with it. They include Léonore; Le comte Alphonse, amant de Léonore; Diego, valet du comte Alphonse; etc. For a full description of the ballet, see Guest's *The Romantic Ballet in Paris,* pp. 70-72. In it, the lover pretends to be an artist painting the portrait of the girl in order to be able to speak to her — hence the subtitle *L'Amant Peintre.* The score in the Bibliothèque de l'Opéra contains designs which are those of the Moscow production.

Cendrillon, which had been a success in London and Paris, was first given in Moscow in January 1824 as a benefit for Hullin, according to André Verdier's notes, and again later that year. The lithograph of Hullin in the title-role (see chapter 3) may be derived from these performances. Doubtless as a result of them, *Cendrillon* was chosen for the grand opening of the Bolshoi Petrovsky Theatre in Moscow on 6 January 1825. According to Yuri Bakhrushin, a different work was originally to have been given, but *Cendrillon* was in the end preferred, perhaps because of the opportunities which it afforded for grand spectacle. At the opening, it was preceded by a prologue called *The Triumph of the Muses* specially written by the poet M.A. Dmitriev to which Hullin danced, representing the muse Terpsichore.[6]

In the Music Department of the Bibliothèque Nationale, Paris, is a letter from Sor to the dancer and choreographer Albert Decombe, mentioning ballet performances in Moscow. It is reproduced in facsimile below. The letter bears no place or date, but judging from the references to performances of *Cendrillon* and *Alphonse et Léonore* and to the opening of the 'nouveau theatre qui est Magnifique', it must have been

---

[6] Yuri Bakhrushin, 'The Ballet of the Bolshoi Theatre', *The Bolshoi Theatre* (Moscow, 1947), p. 178.

written from Moscow in about December 1824. This is confirmed by the watermark, a Russian crowned double-headed eagle. It has several interesting features. Sor is asking Albert to forward to Félicité's father in London, J.B. Hullin, a picture of her which he sends with the letter: perhaps this was a copy of Baranov's lithograph of her in the title-role of *Cendrillon* in Moscow. The letter shows that at that time Sor was still happily with her; that he was very much concerned with ballet; that *Alphonse et Léonore* was successfully performed; and that he intended to return in a few years. It mentions that he is sending Albert a pas de deux and a pas de trois. These may have been extracted from one or other of Sor's ballets, or they may have been separate works: if the latter, no score is known to survive. Here is the text of the letter, together with a translation.

Mon cher Albert

Comptant sur votre amitié je n'hesite point a exiger de vous un service qui obligera non seulement ma Chère petite femme mais aussi son père: la boite que vous remettra le porteur de la présente renferme le portrait de Felicité; il vous sera tres facile de le lui envoyer à Londres, et j'espère que vous vous chargerez avec plaisir de cette commission.

Je vous ai ecrit par le moyen de Mr. Griffe a qui je remis la musique d'un pas de deux et d'un pas de trois. Si mes productions continuent de meriter votre approbation, ecrivez moi et je vous en enverrai d'autres, car depuis que ma Felicité s'est lancée dans la carriere de monter et de *composer des Ballets* j'ai eu l'ocasion d'en ecrire assez. Elle vient de traiter diferemment le sujet dont Anatole fit à Londres un Ballet en un acte, elle l'a distribué en trois actes, et lorsque la Direction trouve que les recettes diminuent elle a recours à son ballet, comme elle aurait recours à Cendrillon si apres l'avoir soutenue tout l'hyver dernier elle ne le reservait encore pour l'ouverture du nouveau theatre qui est Magnifique. Je n'écris pas un morceau sans penser à vous, et je ne perds point l'espoir de travailler ensemble dans quelques années d'ici.

Dites bien des choses aimables de notre part à la bonne et digne Made. Albert, embrassez pour nous vos enfants, et soyez persuadés tous, qu'il est impossible[x] de vous apprécier (et par consequence de vous aimer) mieux que

F. Sor
P.S.
mais écrivez moi donc

[x] à qui que ce soit

Je vous envoye votre Ballet en Russie et celui de Félicité.

('My dear Albert,

Counting on your friendship, I do not hesitate to ask of you a service which will be appreciated not only by my dear little wife but also by her father: the box which the bearer of this letter will give you contains the portrait of Félicité; it will be very easy for you to send it to London, and I hope that it will be a pleasure for you to undertake this.

I wrote to you through M. Griffe, to whom I sent the music of a pas de deux and a pas de trois. If my compositions continue to deserve your approval, write to me and I shall send you others, for since my Félicité began the career of putting on ballets and of choreographing them, I have had occasion to compose several. She has just rearranged the subject on which Anatole made a ballet in London in one act, and has distributed it into three acts; and when the administration finds that the takings are diminishing, she has recourse to her ballet, as she would to *Cendrillon* if, after having performed it all last winter she was not now reserving it for the opening of the new theatre which is magnificent. I don't write a single piece without thinking of you, and I hope we shall work together in a few years from now.

Give many messages on our behalf to the good and worthy Mme Albert, embrace your children for us, and please be convinced, all of you, that it is impossible[x] to appreciate you (and hence to love you) more than does

F. Sor
P.S.
But write to me!

[x] for anyone at all

I have taken your ballet, and Félicité's, to Russia.

In November 1823, when Sor arrived in Russia, Tsar Alexander was ruling. His mother was the Dowager Empress Maria Federovna; his wife, the Empress Elizabeth. On his death on 1 December 1825, he was succeeded by his younger brother Nicholas, whose wife became the Empress Alexandra Federovna. Sor seems to have impressed all three of these ladies, according to Ledhuy (from whom most of the following details are taken). In St. Petersburg he played to the Dowager Empress and the Imperial family; and a few days later, specifically to the Empress Elizabeth. She it was who showed him much favour and could have become a major patron of his until, like the Duchess of Alba many years before, she died too soon for her favour to bear fruit (May 1826).

Tsar Alexander died in mysterious circumstances; some said that he did not die at all, but disappeared on board an English yacht, and lived for many more years as a holy man in a remote part of Russia. Whether that was so or not, a funeral for him took place in St. Petersburg on 26 March 1826, at which a funeral march for military instruments by Sor was performed, 'choisie par l'empereur Nicholas'. Sor arranged the march for the Empress Alexandra, wife of the new Tsar, 'et ce fut une occasion de combler l'auteur de présens' ('and that was an occasion for giving the composer many presents'). Saldoni says (*Diccionario,* p. 265) that in Russia he was given some black pearls of fabulous value: 'en Rusia, donde le regalaron unas *perlas negras* de un valor estraordinario'. If there is any truth in this, if it is not an invention of Saldoni's, then the pearls were

3/

Mon cher Albert

Comptant Sur votre amitié je n'hesite point
a exiger de vous un Service qui obligera non
Seulement ma Chère petite femme mais aussi
Son père : La boite qui vous remettra le porteur
de la présente renferme le portrait de Felicité,
il vous Sera très facile de le lui envoyer à
Londres, et j'espère que vous vous chargerez avec
plaisir de cette commission.

Je vous ai écrit par le moyen de Mr Griffe
Griffe a qui je remis la musique d'un pas de
deux et d'un pas de trois. Si mes productions
continuent de meriter votre approbation, écrivez moi et je vous en enverrois d'autres, car
depuis que ma felicité s'est lancée dans la
carrière de monter, et de composer des Ballets
j'ai eu l'ocasion d'en écrire assez. Elle vient
de traiter diferemment le Sujet dont Anatole
fit à Londres un Ballet en un acte, elle l'a

distribué en trois actes, et lorsque la direction
trouve que les recettes diminuent elle a recours
à Son ballet, comme elle aurait recours à
Cendrillon Si après l'avoir Soutenue tout
l'hyver dernier elle ne le ~~reservait~~ reservait encore
pour l'ouverture du nouveau theatre qui est
Magnifique. Je n'écris pas un morceau Sans
penser à vous, et je ne perds point l'espoir
de travailler ensemble dans quelques années
d'ici.

    Dites bien des choses aimables de notre
part à la bonne et digne Mad.^e Albert,
embrassez pour nous vos enfants, et Soyez
~~que~~ persuadés tous, qu'il est impossible
de vous apprécier (et par consequence de
vous aimer) mieux que F. Sor

        P. S.
      mais écrivez moi donc

à qui que ce Soit   Je vous envoye votre
           Ballet en Russe et celui de
           Félicité.

probably given by the Empress Alexandra on this occasion. — Unfortunately no score of the march is known to survive.

After the funeral of Tsar Alexander in St. Petersburg, Sor returned to Moscow for the rehearsals of a new ballet of his, which was given as part of the coronation celebrations for the new Tsar Nicholas. This was *Hercule et Omphale,* 'dont la musique est, sans contredit, son meilleur ouvrage' (Ledhuy) ('of which the music is indubitably Sor's best work'). 'L'ouverture de ce ballet fit sensation en Allemagne, parce qu'elle est traitée en fugue ou imitation, et consciencieusement élaborée, sans que la correction du travail nuise à la clarté ni au charme de la musique' ('The overture of this ballet caused a sensation in Germany, because it is written in fugue or imitation, and conscientiously worked out, without the clarity or charm of the music being harmed by the correctness of the structure'). Evidently it was the ballet which gave Sor himself the most satisfaction, and when he wrote to King Fernando VII of Spain in about 1828, wishing to make the best impression possible, it was the overture to *Hercule et Omphale* which he enclosed with the letter. Here is the main theme from the overture:

The ballet was choreographed by Félicité Hullin, and she and Joseph Richard danced in it. A full score is in the Bibliothèque de l'Opéra, Paris. The 'programme', which presumably means the mythological plot of the piece, was by J.B. Hullin, Félicité's father. The queen, Omphale, is making a choice between four princely suitors. But meanwhile the infant Amour (Cupid) makes Hercules and Omphale fall in love with each other. Hercules defeats the four princes in a battle on stage; and Jupiter descends from heaven and unites the happy pair. The use of Hercules as a central character is a scarcely veiled compliment to Tsar Nicholas I.

Tsar Nicholas was crowned early in 1826, and *Hercule et Omphale* formed part of the ceremonies of the coronation. The Empress Elisabeth died in May 1826. At some time after that, Sor left Russia to return to Paris, where he arrived either late in 1826 or early in 1827. Ledhuy tells us that the overture to *Hercule et Omphale* was performed in Germany, where it caused a sensation; this may well have taken place in the course of the return journey. Félicité Hullin, too, returned to Paris; whether she travelled with Sor or not we do not know. According to André Verdier's notes she went there with her pupil Carpacova, and she danced there on 2 May 1827. Soon afterwards she returned to Russia; Sor stayed in Paris, where he was to remain for the rest of his life.

Concerts

Ledhuy tells us in general terms that Sor played the guitar with great success in Russia, and specifically mentions two performances before the Imperial family. The article in *Guitare et Musique* adds details of two concerts. One was on 3 March 1824 in the house of Stepan Stepanovitch Apaskine, in which Schultz also played, and one in the same house on an unspecified date, in which Sor played variations of his own composition and in which Field and Schultz also played. John Field (1782-1837) was the famous Irish composer and pianist who at that time was living in Russia; Schultz is presumably the same who was brother of the guitarist Leonardo Schultz, and who was later pianist to the Duke of Devonshire.[7]

The article in *Guitare et Musique* also mentions that while in Moscow Sor met the guitarist and composer M.T. Vyssotski:

> Leur première rencontre eut lieu chez un fervent de la guitare. Les deux guitaristes jouèrent beaucoup et restèrent enchantés l'un de l'autre. En souvenir de cette rencontre, Sor écrivit sur un thème de Vyssotski un duo intitulé ''Souvenir de Russie''. Les compositions de Sor firent grande impression sur les guitaristes russes et certaines furent transcrites pour la guitare russe à sept cordes par Sikhra, Vyssotski et Morkov.

> ('Their first meeting took place at the house of a guitar enthusiast. The two guitarists played a lot and were enchanted with each other. In memory of that meeting, Sor wrote a duet called ''Souvenir de Russie'' [op. 63] on a theme by Vyssotski. Sor's compositions made a great impression on the Russian guitarists, and some were transcribed for the Russian seven-course guitar by Sikhra, Vyssotski and Morkov.')

Some comments on the Russian type of guitar are in Ledhuy, and in his *Méthode pour la Guitare,* p. 7, Sor praises the guitars of the St. Petersburg maker Schroeder ('Sroeder').

---

[7] On Field, and incidentally on musical life in Russia at this time, see Patrick Piggott's *The Life and Music of John Field* (London, 1973). On Schultz, see 'The Memoirs of Makaroff', *Guitar Review,* Vol. I, no. 2, 1947.

Guitar music

Between Sor's arrival in Paris in 1823 and his return to that city from Russia in 1826 or 1827, Meissonnier published the following works by him:

Plate number	Opus number	
234	[16][8]	*Cinquième Fantaisie*
258	17	*Six Valtzes*
261	18	*Six Valtzes*
265	19	*Six Airs Choisis de l'Opera de Mozart Il Flauto Magico*
266	20	*Introduction et Thême Varié*
272	—	*Marche tirée de Cendrillon*
304	21	*Les Adieux! Sixième Fantaisie*
305	22	*Grande Sonate*
348	23	*Cinquième Divertissement*

And early in 1827 he published all at once seven more:

460	9 ('revised')	*Variations Brillantes sur un Air Favori de Mozart*
468	24	*Huit Petites Pièces*
469	25	*Deuxième Grande Sonate*
472	26	*Introduction et Variations sur l'Air: Que ne suis-je la fougère!*
473	27	*Introduction et Variations sur l'Air: Gentil Housard*
474	28	*Introduction et Variations sur l'Air: Malbroug*
475	29	*Douze Etudes*

Arguments from plate numbers and from a change of address by Meissonnier show that op. 16 was published in 1823, perhaps while Sor was still in Paris; opp. 17-20 and the March from *Cendrillon* in 1824; opp. 21 and 22 late in 1825; and op. 23 in 1826. Op. 9 ('revised') and opp. 24-29 appeared early in 1827.[9]

---

[8] The opus number does not appear on the earliest known copy.

---

[9] The plate number of op. 16, 234, is near 235 which the *Bibliographie de la France* listed on 14 June 1823. Op. 21 (plate number 304) was the last work to be published from 15 Galerie des Panoramas and op. 22 (plate number 305) was the first to be published from 25 Boulevard Montmartre, an address to which Meissonnier moved in November 1825 (Hopkinson). The intervening works, opp. 17-20 and the March from *Cendrillon*, presumably come in between, in the course of the years 1824-5. Opp. 24-29 were advertised together in the *Revue Musicale,* I (1827), in the form of a subscription closing on 1 March 1827, and the 'revised' edition of op. 9, on the evidence of its plate number, shortly preceded them. Op. 23, also on the evidence of its plate number, falls in the year 1826.

Opp. 17-23 and the March from *Cendrillon,* then, appeared during Sor's Russian period, and opp. 24-29 shortly after his return. Were all these pieces composed there? The answer is probably yes. Just as Sor sent a pas de deux and a pas de trois from Russia to Albert in Paris, so he could have sent the guitar works opp. 16-23 from Russia to Meissonnier. Opp. 24-29 appeared all at once, which suggests that he brought them back with him and gave them to Meissonnier on his return. And so it seems that this whole series of works, from op. 16 or 17 to op. 29, was composed or arranged in Russia.

However, there is a difference between the two groups. The earlier group, opp. 16-23, contains several pieces that are versions or adaptations of earlier works; the later, opp. 24-29, consists of apparently entirely new works. There is a break: at a certain point in time, Sor seems to have stopped using material from his earlier career and to have started composing exclusively entirely fresh material.

In the earlier group, op. 20 is a new set of variations on an old theme which Sor had used in a set of variations published by Castro many years before. There is some evidence that op. 21, *Les Adieux,* was composed in London in 1816 (see chapter 3). Op. 22 is the sonata which in some form was dedicated to Godoy and hence composed in Spain. And op. 23, *Cinquième Divertissement,* contains two pieces that were published by Castro many years before. The new version of op. 9 is nothing but a return to the London edition, Meissonnier's earlier edition having been a truncated one.

The later group, opp. 24-29, includes some major works. The sonata op. 25 was examined in chapter 1. Op. 24 consists of six minuets and two allegrettos, and the minuets contain many original ideas, like this one:

The studies, op. 29, we shall look at later. The three sets of variations, opp. 26, 27 and 28, contain some fine musical ideas and intricate passage-work on the guitar; however, they do not go beyond anything that was already in the Mozart variations, op. 9; they are simply more works in the same genre.

All of these compositions, of course, are thoroughly within the Western European tradition: waltzes, sonatas, sets of variations. There is no discernible Russian influence on any of them. The only known Russian influence on Sor's music is in *Souvenir de Russie,* op. 63, his last work, which according to Mackevitch is based on a theme by Vyssotski.

CHAPTER 5

PARIS
1826/7-1839

When Sor returned to Paris, he devoted himself above all to the guitar. He taught it, composed for it, played it in concerts, and published his *Méthode pour la Guitare*. Between his return in 1826 or 1827 and his death in 1839 he composed four books of studies, twelve guitar duets, and eighteen other works for guitar, and less and less in other genres: no more Italian arietts, only a very few boleros and French songs, ballet music for a short while, and a few miscellaneous instrumental works.

We know more about this period of his life than about any earlier period. It has even been possible to establish the following calendar.

Late 1826 or early 1827
Sor and Félicité Hullin travel, perhaps separately, from Moscow to Paris.

Late 1826 or early 1827
Sor plays the 'revised' version of his Mozart variations (op. 9) in a concert at the Ecole Royale de Musique.

February 1827
Opp. 24-29 are advertised together in the *Revue Musicale* in the form of a subscription closing on 1 March 1827.

11 June 1827
The ballet *Le Sicilien* is first performed at the Paris Opera.

12 January 1828
The ballet *Hassan et le Calife ou le Dormeur Eveillé* is first performed at the King's Theatre, London.

26 January 1828
Sor plays in a concert in the salon of M. Dietz the piano maker.

26 February 1828
The ballet *Le Sicilien* is first performed at the King's Theatre, London.

April 1828
Sor plays in Mme Robert's concert at the 'salle de la rue Chantereine'.

20 April 1828
Sor plays in a concert at the 'salle de la rue Clery' in which Liszt and others also played.

April/May 1828
The *Revue Musicale* mentions that op. 31, *Vingt Quatre Leçons Progressives*, has just appeared.

18 May 1828
Sor organizes a benefit concert for himself. The title-page of his op. 30, the seventh Fantasia, mentions that he played the work 'à son concert', probably this one.

24 May 1828
The prospectus of the *Méthode pour la Guitare* is out. (The work itself does not appear until 1830).

Summer 1828
Sor changes publishers, from Meissonnier to Pacini.

23 August 1828
Op. 36, *Trois Pièces de Société*, is out.

13 September 1828
Op. 35, *Vingt quatre Exercices*, is out.

9 May 1829
Op. 37, *Sérénade*, and the song 'Le Dernier Cri des Grecs', are out.

14 July (or June?) 1829
Sor (or possibly his brother Carlos) plays in a concert in the salon of M. Dietz, in which he plays some solo pieces and some duets with Aguado.

March 1830
Sor plays in a concert given by the singer Auguste Panseron and others.

24 April 1830
Three works for harpolyre are out.

24 July 1830
Despite political commotion, Sor plays in a concert in which Hummel and others also performed.

24 November 1830

The last performance of *Cendrillon* is given at the Paris Opera.

About December 1830

The *Méthode pour la Guitare* appears.

19 March 1831

Op. 44, *Vingt-quatre petites Pièces,* is out.

27 March 1831

The Spanish pianist Miró gives a concert in which Sor plays some solos and some duets with Aguado, and in which the singer García performs.

19 April 1831

Sor gives another benefit concert, in the salon of M. Dietz.

15 February 1832

Sor plays in a benefit concert of Miró.

About late 1832

Sor, who has been living in the Hotel Favart since at least May 1828, and probably in fact since his return from Russia, moves to an apartment in the Marché St. Honoré, where he lives until his death.

25 March 1833

The *Revue Musicale* reviews op. 54, *Morceau de Concert.*

23 June 1834

The ballet *The Fair Sicilian or the Conquered Coquette* is first performed at the Covent Garden Theatre, London.

1835

Sor contributes an article, 'Le Bolero', to the *Encyclopédie Pittoresque de la Musique* of A. Ledhuy and H. Bertini. The article 'Sor' in that encyclopedia is also almost certainly by him.

July 1835

La Romanesca for violin and guitar: the MS bears the inscription 'Juillet 1835'.

29 November 1835

Sor and Aguado play in a concert, which was to have been given by Legnani the guitarist, who had however broken his arm.

24 April 1836

Sor gives a benefit concert. The programme includes his *Fantaisie Villageoise* (op. 52) and a duet with Aguado, who used his *tripódison.*

8 June 1837

Sor's daughter dies.

October 1837

The *Marche Composée pour la Musique Militaire,* and op. 61, *Trois petits Divertissements* for two guitars, are out.

April or early May 1838

Napoleon Coste gives a concert, opening with a duet played by him and Sor.

June 1838

Op. 62, *Divertissement* for two guitars, is out.

24 March 1839

Sor writes to the Queen of France inviting her to take tickets for a forthcoming concert at which a Mass of his is to be performed.

June 1839

Eusebio Font y Moresco and the painter Jaime Battle visit Sor.

10 July 1839

Sor dies.

Opera

On his return to Paris, Sor wanted to write an opera, just as he had wanted to when he first came to Paris in 1813. But he found that he was not in demand:

> Vous êtes, lui disait-on, habitué aux formes sévères de la Russie et de l'Allemagne, et avec une grande connaissance de l'harmonie, vous pencherez vers le style savant: il faut être gracieux avant tout. Ces absurdités et quelques injustices le découragerent.
>
> (Ledhuy)

> ('He was told: "You are used to the strict forms of Russia and Germany, and having a profound knowledge of harmony, you would tend towards the learned style; whereas one must be graceful above all." These absurdities and some injustices discouraged him.')

Ballet music

When Sor returned to Paris, *Cendrillon* was still in repertory at the Opera: the last performance there was not given until 24 November 1830 (T. de Lajarte, *Bibliothèque Musicale du Théâtre de l'Opéra,* vol. 2, Paris, 1876, p. 104). He continued to compose ballet music. On 11 June 1827 the first performance of *Le Sicilien ou l'Amour Peintre* was given, a ballet-pantomime choreographed by Anatole Petit. The music was partly by Sor and partly by Schneitzhoeffer: the latter wrote the overture and the 'airs de danse' — though as the *Journal des Débats* pointed out (15 June 1827), since the whole thing was danced, it was hard to know what was meant by the 'airs de danse'. The score and parts survive in the Bibliothèque de l'Opéra, Paris. The plot, taken from Molière's *Le Sicilien ou l'Amour Peintre,* was the same as that of the earlier *Alphonse et Léonore ou l'Amant Peintre,* but there is no visible musical resemblance. *Le Sicilien* was a mere entertainment, was not well received, and had only six performances; but its claim to fame was that in it, on 23 July 1827, the great ballerina Taglioni made her debut.[1] In London it was given for the first time at the King's Theatre on 26 February 1828.[2]

---

[1] Guest, *The Romantic Ballet in Paris,* pp. 76-7.

---

[2] Guest, *The Romantic Ballet in England,* p. 157.

Ledhuy tells us that while Sor, in Paris, was facing difficulty in having his work performed there, London produced a three-act ballet of his called *Le Dormeur Eveillé*. This was the sub-title of *Hassan et le Calife*, first performed at the King's Theatre on 12 January 1828, again choreographed by Anatole.[3] No score is known to survive. The dancer August Bournonville appeared in it, and he described the first performance in a letter to his father:

Londres ce 22 Janvier 1828.

Mon cher & bien aimé Papa!

J'espère que vous avez recu ma dernière lettre ou je vous annonce mon arrivée a Londres & mes prochain debuts, Tout me presagoit du succès & je n'ai pas été trompé Le Kings Theatre a ouvert le 12 Janvier avec l'opera Margueritte d'Anjou de Meyerbeer & le nouveau ballet Hassan & le Calife de Mr. Anatole. — Le tout à été recu avec une bienveillance extrême notemment le ballet que tout le monde a trouvé charmant, en verité cet ouvrage se distingue par des details delicieux & possède l'avantage d'une action claire & non languissante, ainsi que des danses bien emmenées & bien distribuées. Mon pas de deux de debut etoit placé au premier acte quelques moments après celui d'Albert, A notre entrée en scène nous fumes acceuillis par des applaudissemens que etoient faits pour nous encourager, j'ai eu le bonheur de plaire a mon premier abord & n'eprouvant aucune emotion cappable de m'oter la jouissance de mes moyens, tout mon pas n'a été qu'un seul applaudissement continu, assez heureuz ou plutot assez exercé pour reussir la plupart des difficultés dont mon pas etoit rempli, ces details ont été saisis avec un toit admirable, enfin parmi tous les artistes qui en general ont été recus avec distinction, on s'est accordé a dire que moi, j'avois reçue les applaudissemens les plus unanimes.

(August Bournonville, *Lettres à la maison de son enfance*, edited by Nils Schiorring and Svend Kragh-Jacobsen, I, Copenhagen, 1969, pp. 172-3)

('London, 22 January 1828.

My dear and well-beloved Papa!

I hope you received my last letter in which I told you about my arrival in London and my forthcoming débuts. Everything foretold success for me, and I was not disappointed. The King's Theatre opened on 12 January with the opera *Marguerite d'Anjou* by Meyerbeer and the new ballet *Hassan et le Calife* by M. Anatole. — Everything was received extremely favourably, especially the ballet which everyone found charming; truly this work has many delightful details and has the advantage of a clear plot that does not drag, as well as well organized and distributed dances. My pas de deux at the beginning was placed in the first act, a few moments after Albert. When we came on we were received by applause to encourage us; I was lucky enough to please at once, and not feeling any emotion which could deprive me of any of my capabilities, all of my dance was nothing but continual

applause. I was lucky enough or rather in good enough practice to succeed in most of the difficulties in my dance. These details were admirably received; in short, among all the artistes who have in general been well received, people agree that I received the most unanimous applause.')

Apparently also in London, according to Ledhuy, a 'ballet-féerie' called *La Belle Arsène* was produced:

. . . dernièrement on vient de représenter, avec le plus grand succès, un autre ballet-féerie, *la Belle Arsène*, dont l'ouverture et les principales scènes sont composées par lui; le reste avait été soumis à sa révision.

('Recently there has just been produced with the greatest success another fairytale ballet, *La Belle Arsène*, in which he composed the overture and the principal scenes; the rest was revised by him.')

This seems to have been the ballet that was first produced in London at the Covent Garden Theatre on 23 June 1834 under the title *The Fair Sicilian or the Conquered Coquette*, with Lise Noblet and choreography by Albert. *Le Courrier des Théâtres* wrote of it on 1 July 1834:

Albert, l'ex-artiste de l'Opéra, vient de faire représenter à Covent-Garden, *La Belle Sicilienne* ou *la coquette vaincue*, dont le sujet est celui de *la Belle Arsène* du théâtre Feydeau. On a fait beaucoup de dépenses pour ce ballet dont la réussite a été complète.

('Albert, the ex-dancer at the Opera, has just put on at Covent Garden *La Belle Sicilienne ou la Coquette Vaincue*, whose plot is the same as that of *La Belle Arsène* at the Théâtre Feydeau. Much expense was devoted to this ballet, whose success was complete.')

It has been said that Sor paid a return visit to London at this time. Fétis writes: 'Pressé par le besoin, il retourna à Londres, et y composa la musique au ballet *le Dormeur éveillé*, et plus tard l'opéra féerique *la Belle Arsène*' (*Biographie universelle des musiciens*) ('Being in financial need, he returned to London, where he composed the music for the ballet *Le Dormeur Eveillé*, and later the fairytale opera *La Belle Arsène*'). This probably represents merely a misreading by Fétis of Ledhuy. Fétis is notoriously unreliable: for example, *La Belle Arsène* was not an opera but a ballet. Although it is of course always possible that Sor returned to London at this time, there is no direct evidence for it. If it occurred, the most likely time was in early 1828, when two ballets of his were performed in London.

No trace has been found of a ballet called *Arsène ou la Baguette Magique*, which according to Fétis Sor wrote in collaboration with Singelée and which Fétis says was produced in Brussels in 1845 (*Biographie universelle des musiciens*, Supplement). The performances in Brussels in 1845 at the Théâtre de la Monnoie are all listed in J. Isnardon's *Le Théâtre de la*

[3] Ibid.

Monnoie (Brussels, 1890), and they do not include *Arsène ou la Baguette Magique*.

Sor's involvement with ballet, then, began only in 1821 and ended in 1834 (except possibly for the mysterious *Arsène ou la Baguette Magique)*. He achieved two principal successes: *Cendrillon* which was the favourite in the public eye, and *Hercule et Omphale* which apart from a fair success with the public gave him the most personal satisfaction. Here is a complete list of all Sor's known ballet music.

Produced	Title	Choreographer	
London, 1821	*La Foire de Smyrne*	d'Egville	No score known to survive
London, 1821	*Le Seigneur Généreux*	Deshayes	No score known to survive
London, 1822; Paris, 1823; Moscow, 1825	*Cendrillon*	Albert	Score survives
London, 1823	*Alphonse et Léonore ou l'Amant Peintre* (in one act)	Anatole	No score known to survive
Berlin, 1823	A pas de danse		No score known to survive
Potsdam, 1823	A pas de danse		No score known to survive
Moscow, 1824	*Alphonse et Léonore ou l'Amant Peintre* (in three acts)	Félicité Hullin	Score survives
Moscow, c. 1824	A pas de deux and a pas de trois		No score known to survive
Moscow, 1826	*Hercule et Omphale*	Félicité Hullin	Score survives
Paris, 1827; London, 1828	*Le Sicilien ou l'Amour Peintre* (music partly by Sor and partly by Schneitzhoeffer)	Anatole	Score survives
London, 1828	*Hassan et le Calife ou le Dormeur Eveillé*	Anatole	No score known to survive
London, 1834	*The Fair Sicilian or the Conquered Coquette (= La Belle Arsène)*	Albert	No score known to survive
Brussels, 1845?	*Arsène ou la Baguette Magique* (music partly by Sor and partly by Singelée) (possibly a spurious reference; this ballet may never have existed)		No score known to survive

Publishing

When Sor returned to Paris from Russia, he published at first with Meissonier and then with Pacini. In 1827, as we saw in chapter 4, opp. 24-29 appeared. They were followed in 1828 by the following:

Plate number	Opus number	
497	30	*7e Fantaisie*
499	31 (livre 1)	*Vingt Quatre Leçons*
500	31 (livre 2)	*Vingt Quatre Leçons*
502	32	*Six Petites Pièces*
505	33	*Trois Pièces de Société*

Op. 31 was advertised in the *Revue Musicale* in April 1828 (or May: the exact month of the issue is not clear) as having just appeared; and to judge from their plate numbers, op. 30 appeared shortly before it, and opp. 32-33 shortly after it. They were the last works which Sor was to publish with Meissonnier before going over to Pacini. Meissonnier also published some songs by Sor at this time: three French songs, and three Spanish songs called *Tres Seguidillas Boleras*. Meissonnier also published a so-called *Collection Complète* of Sor's works for guitar. This is nothing but a number of separately printed works bound up together and provided with a new title-page. Known copies go up to op. 19 or op. 23, which suggests that it was first issued in 1824, the date of op. 19 — or in 1825, for all known copies bear the address 25 Boulevard Montmartre, to which Meissonnier moved in 1825 (Hopkinson). Meissonnier was still selling it in March 1828, when it was listed in the *Bibliographie de la France*. Thereafter, even after the break with Sor, he continued to sell his music. Many copies of works up to op. 33 are known whose title-pages bear his successive changes of address, and, from 1839, the name of Heugel, his associate and later successor.

But one of Sor's most far-reaching actions at this time was to break with Meissonnier and to form a different arrangement with the publisher Pacini. This was Antoine-François-Gaétan Pacini, who according to Fétis was born in Naples in 1778, came to Paris in about 1802, taught singing and became a music publisher.

In his *Méthode pour la Guitare,* Sor speaks not at all kindly of music publishers and their villanies. We know that Meissonnier grew richer as time went on, moving from the rue Montmartre to the Galerie des Panoramas and finally to the Boulevard Montmartre; and putting two and two together, it is a fair guess that Meissonnier managed to pay the composer little or nothing. From op. 34 on, the situation is different. All editions of Sor's music from op. 34 on bear on their title-pages the words 'propriété de l'auteur' ('property of the composer') rather than 'propriété de l'éditeur' ('property of the publisher'). Sor was now his own publisher, as he says in the preface to his op. 48, and he made some arrangement with Pacini, probably for marketing, which resulted in Pacini's name also appearing on the title-pages. Generally the title-pages bear both Pacini's and Sor's names and addresses; occasionally only Pacini's, and in two cases (op. 54 bis and his last work, op. 63) only Sor's. Op. 56 has only 'à Paris'. These differences may perhaps represent differing business arrangements between the two men; but nevertheless all the works were included in a 'Catalogue des ouvrages de Ferdinand Sor, pour la guitare, dont il est l'Editeur' which was printed with many of these later works.

The change from Meissonnier to Pacini seems to have occurred in the summer of 1828. The last Meissonnier listing of works by Sor in the *Bibliographie de la France* was on 22 March 1828, for opp. 24-29, while opp. 30-33, published also by Meissonnier, appeared later in that same year. Then on 23 August 1828 the *Bibliographie de la France* listed 'Trois pièces de société pour guitare seule, par Sor. A Paris, chez Sor, place des Italiens' [op. 36] and on 13 September his op. 35, also 'chez Sor'. This date coincides with Sor's decision not to give his *Méthode pour la Guitare* to Meissonnier but to publish it himself: the prospectus for the *Méthode* was listed in the *Bibliographie de la France* on 24 May 1828 and it announced that that the book would be published by Sor.

The change caused a slight confusion of numbering. Op. 33, the last work published by Meissonnier, was *Trois Pièces de Société*. Op. 36 is also called *Trois Pièces de Société,* although it is a different work, and it was first published without an opus number, thus leading Simrock in Germany to think that it was op. 34 and to publish it as such. Op. 37, *Sérénade,* was first published as op. 36 and only later called op. 37.

The new publishing arrangement had one unfortunate effect. It meant that after Sor's death, the later works were not kept in print, perhaps for the practical reason that the legal right in them was vested not in Pacini but in Sor. Meissonnier's successors Heugel, on the other hand, owned the legal rights in those works which Meissonnier had published (i.e. up to op. 33), and they have kept them in print up to the present day. It is true to say, therefore, that a mere accident of publishing history has meant that today, those guitar works which Sor composed before the summer of 1828 (opp. 1-33) are reasonably well known, while those which he composed after that date (opp. 34-63) are almost entirely unknown. The later group consists of no less than 32 works for guitar: twelve duets, two books of studies, and eighteen other works for solo guitar. Rafael Mitjana wrote: 'sa belle *Elégie* et son *Adieu* [presumably op. 59] sont des pages d'un sentiment profond et d'une inspiration pleine de noblesse' (A. Lavignac, *Encyclopédie de la Musique et Dictionnaire du Conservatoire,* Paris, n.d., pp. 2345-6) ('his beautiful *Elégie* and his *Adieu* are pages full of deep feeling and noble inspiration'). This late music ranges from small elegant pieces to ambitious full-scale ones. With the re-publication of all of Sor's guitar music, it should now become better known.

As well as guitar music, Pacini also published some other works by Sor: two French songs ('Le Souvenir' and 'Le Dernier Cri des Grecs'), five collections of Italian arietts (these are the same as those published in London, the 'Milhouse' set and Sets 2-5), three Spanish songs included in a collection published by Pacini called *Regalo Lirico,* and the piano duet *Marche Composée pour la Musique Militaire.* Dating is sometimes difficult, for Pacini's plate numbers are eccentric and do not help. We have the following information about the dates of Pacini's editions of Sor's music:

Work	Listing in the *Bibliographie de la France*	Other information
Collection d'Airs Italiens		Out by 1828, when it was listed in C.F. Whistling's *Handbuch der musikalischen Literatur,* Leipzig.
Op. 36	23 August 1828	
Op. 35	13 Sept. 1828	
'Le Dernier Cri des Grecs'	9 May 1829	
Op. 37 (Sérénade)	9 May 1829	
Op. 44	19 March 1831	
Regalo Lirico		Out by April 1831, a date inscribed on a known copy (in King's College, Cambridge).
Op. 54		Out by 25 March 1833, when it was reviewed in the *Revue Musicale.*
Marche Militaire		Out by October 1837, a date stamped on a known copy (in Paris, Bibliothèque Nationale)
Op. 61		— ditto —
Op. 62		Out by June 1838, a date stamped on a known copy (in Paris, Bibliothèque Nationale).

The intervening guitar works can be roughly dated from the above list.

Apart from Meissonnier and Pacini, J.F. Salomon brought out some harpolyre pieces by Sor; Savaresse Sarra a French song; Lemoine some piano duets; and Sor himself his *Méthode pour la Guitare.*

Works for solo guitar (opp. 30-60)

Soon after Sor's return to Paris, then, Meissonnier published the 'revised' edition of op. 9, and six other works. After them, Sor published with Meissonnier only four more compositions: his Seventh Fantasia, op. 30; the studies, op. 31; *Six Petites Pièces,* op. 32; and *Trois*

Pièces de Société, op. 33. The Fantasia consists of an introduction, theme with variations and coda, and an allegretto. It is an extended work, almost as long as a sonata, and indeed contains much of the same sort of writing as did the Sonata op. 25, such as melodies in the bass against steady repeated chords in the upper parts:

Sonata op. 25, fourth movement, bars 46-51:

Fantasia op. 30, first bars of coda ('Lentement'):

The studies, op. 31, we shall return to. The *Six Petites Pièces,* op. 32, belong to the divertimento form; this particular set contains a fine Mazurka and an elegant Andante. The *Trois Pièces de Société,* op. 33, are the last work which Sor published with Meissonnier. Formally they represent something new in his composition, for each of the 'Trois Pièces' is a two-movement work: Moderato cantabile and Allegretto, Andante and Valse, Siciliana and Marche. Like the other set of *Trois Pièces de Société,* op. 36, they are in effect small sonatas or sonatinas. In each case the first movement leads directly into the second. The catchy Allegretto is a kind of rondo, and the Marche has a trio entirely in harmonics.

One of the major works for solo guitar is the *Morceau de Concert,* op. 54 — the equivalent of a *Konzertstück.* Here is a contemporary review of it, from the *Revue Musicale* of 1833-4, unsigned but probably by F.J. Fétis:

> Tout le monde sait que M. Sor a étendu le domaine de la guitare, et qui'il a rendu cet instrument à sa destination naturelle en le faisant un instrument d'harmonie. Profond musicien, doué de beaucoup de goût et de la persévérance nécessaire, possédant enfin le plus beau talent d'exécution, M. Sor a écrit pour la guitare comme personne n'avait écrit avant lui et comme fort peu d'artistes pourront écrire en le prenant pour modèle; mais dans aucune de ses compositions on ne trouve peut-être de qualités aussi remarquables que dans le morceau que nous annonçons. Une introduction large, et, qu'on nous passe le terme, *vigoureuse* comme pourrait l'être un morceau écrit pour l'orchestre, sert d'entrée à un thème d'une rare élégance écrit avec autant de pureté qu'on pourrait le faire dans de la musique pour le piano. Puis viennent des variations tantôt gracieuses, tantôt brillantes et toujours remplies de ce goût d'harmonie qu'on retrouve dans toutes les compositions de M. Sor, et qu'on ne trouve que là. Il est beau d'agrandir ainsi l'objet de ses études et de ses travaux, et de se placer au-dessus de ce qu'on fait par la puissance de son talent.

('Everyone knows that M. Sor has extended the domain of the guitar, and that he has guided that instrument to its natural destination in making it an instrument of harmony. A profound musician, gifted with much taste and with the necessary perseverance, and possessing the finest talent in performance, M. Sor has written for the guitar as no-one had written before him and as very few composers will be able to write if they take him as a model; but perhaps in none of his compositions does one find such remarkable qualities as in the piece which we are discussing. An introduction, broad and, if we may so, as *vigorous* as it might be if it were written for orchestra, serves to introduce a theme of rare elegance written with as much purity as one could achieve in piano music. Then come variations, sometimes graceful, sometimes brilliant, and always filled with that taste for harmony which one finds in all M. Sor's compositions and only there. It is a beautiful thing to enlarge the object of one's studies and of one's work, and by the strength of one's talent to elevate oneself above what one is doing.')

The form of the *Morceau de Concert,* like *L'Encouragement* (op. 34) or *Les Deux Amis* (op. 41), is, once again, an introduction, theme with variations and coda, and a fast dance, here an Allegro in waltz time. Here it lends itself to a fine work, technically difficult but full of confidence and invention.

Op. 59, the *Fantaisie Elégiaque à la mort de Madame Beslay, née Levavasseur,* is a work of unrelieved grief. This is the work in which Mitjana spoke of 'une inspiration pleine de noblesse'. A funerary urn is engraved on the cover. A long introduction, andante largo, leads into a funeral march, at the end of which the dead one's name is pronounced:

The smaller-scale works are examples of the miniaturist's art. In all, seven of the later works are sets of short pieces: two called *Six Petites Pièces* (opp. 42 and 47), one *Six Valses et un Galop* (op. 57), and four with witty titles in French. Op. 43 is called *Mes Ennuis, Six Bagatelles . . . dédiées à qui les voudra.* Op. 45, *Voyons si c'est ça,* six pieces 'dont le bût est de conduire graduellement à ce que l'on est convenu d'appeler difficulté' ('whose aim is to lead gradually towards what is generally called difficulty'), is dedicated 'à celui qui aura le moins de patience' ('to whoever has the least patience'). These are simple pieces designed to present few difficulties. Still, they were too hard for some people, as appears from the preface to op. 48, *Est-ce bien ça.* In that preface, Sor ironically attacks those bad musicians who write simple music for the guitar and in so doing abandon the principles of Haydn, Mozart and Beethoven. The preface to op. 51, *A la Bonne Heure,* shows that he was himself unhappy at writing works like op. 48: 'cette musique ne ressemble du tout à la mienne' ('this music is quite different from mine'), and however easy it is, still people demand that it be made even easier. In op. 51, he says:

> J'ai taché de n'employer que des positions que je crois les plus usitées; j'ai profité des cordes à vide autant qu'il m'a été possible pour les basses: j'ai mis presque autant de numéros que de notes: enfin: j'ai fait tout ce qu'il fallait, aussi m'ont il dit que j'suis ben genti, c'est à dire: qu'un de vous en voyant mes deux premières valses s'est écrié A LA BONNE HEURE!

> ('I tried to use only those positions which I believe to be the most common; I used open strings as much as possible for the bass; I put almost as many fingerings as notes; in short: I did everything that was necessary, and so people said that that was really nice of me; to the point where one of you, seeing my first two waltzes, cried out: AT LAST!')

And so it is that in the first sets of pieces, opp. 42, 43, 45 and 47, there are some fine pieces just as there were in the Divertimenti of many years before, but scarcely in opp. 48, 51 and 57, which as Sor says suffer by their very simplicity. From one of the first sets, op. 45, a fine Andante is reproduced below.

The remaining works vary in form perhaps more than one would expect. There is only one more straightforward set of variations, the *Fantaisie sur un Air Favori Ecossais,* op. 40. The theme turns out to be 'Ye banks and braes o' bonnie Doune' — otherwise known as the fiddle tune 'The Caledonian Hunt's Delight', composed in 1780 by Neil Gow and provided with words by Robert Burns. Beethoven had written his own versions of Scottish songs, and in setting this one, Sor takes his part in the Romantic fascination with Scotland and its music. There is *Souvenir d'Amitié,* op. 46, in the familiar form

of introduction, theme with variations and coda, and an Allegretto; three more sonatina-like 'Pièces de Société', op. 36, each in two movements; *Souvenirs d'une Soirée à Berlin,* op. 56, which after an introduction consists of a single very long waltz; and the unusual *Fantaisie Villageoise,* op. 52, which has an Introduction, Appel, Danse, and Prière. Ledhuy's *Encyclopédie* contains the short *La Candeur, petite Rêverie;* and Isaias Savio prints a *Divertissement* whose source is unknown.[4] This is music that is still mostly unfamiliar, and that deserves exploration by performers.

Guitar duets

The first work which Sor published alone or with Pacini was the duet for two guitars, *L'Encouragement,* op. 34, and it was also the first guitar duet which he is known to have written. Thereafter the guitar duet became a favourite form with him. He wrote twelve of them in all, and it will be convenient to discuss them together. All were first published between 1828 and 1839. They are as follows:

Op. 34	*L'Encouragement*
Op. 38	*Divertissement*
Op. 39	*Six Valses*
Op. 41	*Les Deux Amis*
Op. 44 bis	*Six Valses*
Op. 49	*Divertissement Militaire*
Op. 53	*Le Premier Pas vers moi*
Op. 54 bis	*Fantaisie*
Op. 55	*Trois Duos*
Op. 61	*Trois Petits Divertissements*
Op. 62	*Divertissement,*
Op. 63	*Souvenir de Russie*

L'Encouragement, op. 34, consists of an introduction, theme with three variations and coda, and a waltz. No copy of the first edition has been available to me, and the earliest known is that of Böhme in Hamburg, which was out by 1841 when it was listed in Hofmeister's *Handbuch der musikalischen Literatur.* In the Böhme edition, and almost certainly in the first edition also, the two parts are entitled 'L'ELEVE' and 'LE MAITRE'; the former has a single line all the way through, with rare additional notes, and the latter has a chordal accompaniment. After Sor's death, Napoleon Coste published an arrangement of the work, in which he has split up the parts so that each has sometimes a single line and sometimes chords; this arrangement, published first by Coste himself and then by

---

[4] In *Fernando Sor, 19 Composiciones,* Buenos Aires, no date [c. 1954], no. 2. Mr. Savio does not give its source, and I did not receive a reply to an enquiry which I addressed to him.

Schonenberger, is the version generally known and played today but has absolutely no authority.

In ten of his twelve guitar duets, Sor follows this same practice of giving one guitar a high single line (with occasional additional notes) and the other an accompaniment of chords and arpeggios lower on the instrument. In eight of the twelve (opp. 34, 44 bis, 49, 53, 54 bis, 55, 61 and 62) the music is shared out in this way from beginning to end, while in two (opp. 38 and 39) the two guitars are occasionally reversed. Only in the two most advanced duets — opp. 41 and 63, dedicated to the professional guitarists Aguado and Coste respectively — do both guitars consistently have more complex music throughout.

Les Deux Amis, op. 41, has become famous, and rightly so. This most interesting of Sor's duets was dedicated to Aguado; and indeed, instead of the two parts being marked 'Première Guitare' and 'Seconde Guitare', or 'L'ELEVE' and 'LE MAITRE', they are marked 'SOR' and 'AGUADO'. The form resembles that of *L'Encouragement:* an introduction (andante largo), a theme with five variations, and this time a mazurka. After the introduction, the two parts both have the theme, one after the other; then they shine in alternate variations, Sor in variations 1 and 3, Aguado in variations 2 and 4; variation 5 is an opportunity for both; and in the mazurka they are equal in importance. This is a major work, on a level with the Mozart variations (op. 9) or the sonata op. 25.

Some of the duets, on the other hand, are on a simple level: four are even expressly didactic or dedicated to pupils. But even the simplest demonstrate Sor's gift for melodic invention. For example, op. 55 includes a short note about hand-position and so has a didactic intention to some degree, but while it looks slight on paper this is a melodically rich work.

The *Six Valses,* op. 39, are simple and a mere arrangement (four of them are arrangements of waltzes of which Sor had already published arrangements for piano duet in London). But Mlle Houzé, their dedicatee, must have made good progress, for Sor later dedicated to her a much more interesting work, the *Fantaisie* for two guitars, op. 54 bis. Here an Andante allegro is followed by theme and variations and then by an allegro marked 'Dans le genre Espagnol'. This is a lively and syncopated piece, full of Romantic atmosphere, even though it does not have the authentic Spanish flavour of, say, Sor's seguidillas of many years before. It uses the techniques of *rasgueado,* and a note says: 'Depuis cette mesure jusqu'à la fin il est impossible de bien rendre l'effet, ni même jouer simplement les notes sans être initié dans la manière espagnole de conduire la main droite dans le genre appelé *rasgueado'*

('From this bar to the end it is impossible to give the proper effect, or even simply to play the notes, without having learnt the Spanish right hand technique which is called *rasgueado').*

Souvenir de Russie, op. 63, was Sor's last work. He dedicated it to Napoleon Coste, a bad editor but presumably an able player. As in *Les Deux Amis,* in this work the two guitars both have music of a certain complexity and share the various virtuoso effects. The form, once again, is an introduction, theme, variations (this time nine of them) and coda, and an Allegretto. The theme, according to Mackevitch's article in *Guitare et Musique* (see chapter 4), is by the Russian guitarist and composer M.T. Vyssotski, whom Sor had known in Russia.

Teaching

Teaching seems to have been Sor's principal livelihood at this period. Certainly it was so by 1839, when he says as much in a letter to the Queen of France. In London we know that he taught singing as well as the guitar, but in Paris it seems to have been only the guitar. His teaching survives in the *Méthode pour la Guitare* and in the studies.

His pupils are shadowy figures who sometime emerge from the twilight. Two of his favourites were young English girls, Mary Jane Burdett and Miss Wainwright, both of whom he praises by name in the *Méthode.* Miss Burdett, the dedicatee of Sor's variations on 'Ye banks and braes', op. 40, married in later life a serving officer in the British army; but, alas, he died within the year at the Battle of Chilianwallah (Burke's *Landed Gentry,* 1894 edn., p. 249). Another surprising pupil was apparently General San Martín, the Liberator of Argentina (S.N. Contreras, *Disertaciones Musicales,* Buenos Aires, 1931, pp. 104-5).

The 'Méthode pour la Guitare' (1830)

When we speak of Sor's *Method,* let us be quite clear what we mean, for there are at least six different versions of it, of which only one is fully authoritative. They are as follows.

The first edition was published in Paris in French in 1830, under the title *Méthode pour la Guitare, par Ferdinand Sor.* It is the only version known to have Sor's direct authority, and it is this first edition to which I refer in the present book. Now extremely rare, it was never reprinted; indeed, Saldoni says (he does not state on what authority) that Sor destroyed the plates. The title-page says that the book is the 'Propriété des Editeurs', who are named as Sor in Paris and Simrock in Bonn (and there is a space for London, but it is left

Andante.

N.º 5.

blank; on one known copy, now in Madrid, Sor himself has filled in 'Johaning et Wathmore' — i.e. Johanning & Whatmore). The *Méthode,* then, was published by Sor rather than by a commercial publisher, and this at a time when guitar methods were being published in large numbers and a man of Sor's celebrity would have had little trouble in finding a publisher had he so wished.

By June 1831, when it was listed in Hofmeister's *Handbuch der musikalischen Literatur,* Simrock in Bonn had brought out a parallel French and German edition; and in 1832 (to judge from the plate number) Cocks in London published an English translation by A. Merrick, the organist of Cirencester. Both the German and the English translations are faithful to the original French, but there is no reason to suppose that Sor had any control over them.

After Sor's death, Napoleon Coste did a disservice to his friend's memory by bringing out a travesty of the original called *Méthode complète pour la Guitare par Ferdinand Sor, rédigée et augmentée de nombreux exemples et leçons . . . par N. Coste.* This bears little resemblance to the original and has little value in its own right. It was translated into Spanish. Incredibly, this travesty is still in print and still using the name of Sor; the reader should be warned against it. — Later in the century, in 1897, Frank Mott Harrison published in London a *Method for the Guitar by Ferdinando Sor,* a similar travesty of no value which says (of course wrongly) that the original was written in Spanish. Mercifully, this is at least now out of print.

We first hear of the *Méthode* in 1828. In that year John Ebers, manager of the King's Theatre in London, published his book *Seven Years of the King's Theatre,* in which he speaks of 'the extraordinary Spaniard, Sor, who is known to be the most perfect guitarist in the world . . . He is now about to publish a work in Paris, on the guitar; on the teaching of which instrument his notions are quite original' (p. 163).

Perhaps Ebers had received a copy of the printed prospectus advertising the work and inviting subscriptions. No copy of this prospectus is known to survive, but it was listed in the *Bibliographie de la France,* and from details given there we can reconstruct some of the publishing history of the book. It reveals something of a lack of business sense. The prospectus was listed in May 1828. The book was to be published by Sor; the price was to be 30 francs, or 15 francs to subscribers; and the subscription list was to be closed on 1 July 1828. Now, from the *Bibliographie de la France* we also gather that the *Méthode* itself did not appear until late in 1830, that is over two years later; and the price in the end was 36 francs. From the number of footnotes in the book, it seems that Sor rewrote a lot of it, perhaps even at proof stage, like Balzac.

When the book was at last published in 1830, Sor was 52 years old. He had had a varied life, many successes, many failures, a good deal of buffeting by fate, and a variety of amatory experience. He had composed many different kinds of music: seguidillas and patriotic songs, Italian arietts, ballet music. But throughout all this, one constant factor had been the guitar. He had played it in his childhood; the seguidillas usually had guitar accompaniments; in England his most important public appearance had been as a guitarist, at the Philharmonic Society; while from 1814 onwards the number of his guitar publications increased steadily year by year. The *Méthode pour la Guitare* shows that Sor recognized the importance of this instrument in his work, that he was prepared to devote more time to it and less to the other many and various genres that had occupied him before, that he was prepared to establish himself now as a guitar teacher and not as a would-be composer of operas and ballets. And the result is that his method is a profound work, written by a man who had spent his life in music as a whole and not merely in the limited corner of it that is the guitar.

Sor begins by pointing out that the guitar is an instrument of harmony, not merely of melody, and that as such it is capable of performing much more than a sequence of chords for accompaniment. From that point he sets out to demonstrate a serious attitude towards the guitar, and the practical methods whereby its technique can be mastered. The book is extremely detailed, always reflective and never dull. It shows a man who knew not only Haydn but also Molière, not only the guitar but also the piano and voice. Frederic V. Grunfeld has called it 'easily the most remarkable book on guitar technique ever written' *(The Art and Times of the Guitar,* New York, 1969, p. 182). Here are the headings of the sections of the work:

L'Instrument
Position de l'Instrument
Main Droite
Main Gauche
Manière d'Attaquer la Corde
Qualité du Son
Connaissance du Manche
Doigté sur la Longeur de la Corde
Emploi des Doigts de la Main droite
Doigté des Deux Mains
Du Coude
Des Tierces, de leur Nature et de leur Doigté
Des Sixtes
Appliciation de la Théorie des Tierces et des Sixtes
Doigté de la Main gauche à l'égard de la Mélodie
Doigté de la Main droite
Des Sons Harmoniques
Accompagnements
Analyse de l'Accompagnement du Fragment de
    l'Oratorio de Haydn (la Création)
Du Doigté Annulaire
Conclusion

Enthusiastic reviews of the *Méthode* appeared in the *Revue Musicale,* XI (1831-2) and in the *Allgemeine musikalische Zeitung,* 1832, both of them praising its seriousness and value.

Studies for guitar

'Ses études vivront comme celles de Cramer', we read in Ledhuy. But today Cramer has sunk into oblivion, while Sor's studies are in the repertory of every serious guitarist. He wrote five books in all, as well as one book of 'petites pièces . . . pour servir de leçons': opp. 6, 29, 31, 35, 44 and 60.

The first set, today known as op. 6, was composed and first published in London in about 1815-17. This famous work appeared without opus number, and without any introduction, comments, or fingering by Sor. We have simply the music. And this forms an entity in itself in a number of ways, just as each of the sets of divertimenti did. The keys and tempi are varied, the different techniques exercised vary from study to study. It is evidently a collection designed as an attractive whole, to be complete in itself as an aid to the study of the guitar by players of moderate attainments. Several basic techniques are exercised: separate control of different combinations of right hand thumb and fingers, slurs, arpeggios, octaves, and so on. Two of the most famous are no. 6, for agility in moving up and down the fingerboard:

and no. 8, for clarity in playing music in several parts where some parts are held while others are not:

As for the music itself, it shows above all a Schubertian or Mendelssohnian gift for melody. A fault is the excessive repetition, caused by Sor's conception of the study form, of certain rhythmic patterns; but each study is so short that even this fault scarcely has time to nag at the listener's ear.

A strange detail about this set of studies, which I confess I am quite unable to explain, is that in the original edition and indeed in all subsequent editions, study no. 10, which is a perfectly normal study in octaves, at the end suddenly breaks into a setting, with many incidental flats and chromatic passages, of 'God save the King.'

The next set of studies to appear was op. 29. This is one of the works which Meissonnier published all at once in 1827 shortly after Sor's return from Russia, strongly suggesting that they were in fact composed in Russia. Op. 29 is designed to follow op. 6 — 'pour servir de suite aux douze premières', says the title-page — and indeed the twelve studies are numbered 13-24, to follow on after the 1-12 of op. 6. This time there are a few headings to the music, such as that to no. 20: 'Cette étude doit être jouée presque piano, mais on doit attaquer les cordes à l'endroit où les vibrations sont plus prolongées' ('This study must be played almost piano, but the strings should be plucked at the point where the vibrations will last longest'). The standard of difficulty is rather higher. But there is still no fingering.

Op. 31 appeared the next year, 1828, and is a new series of twenty-four studies. The standard of difficulty is lower than in either op. 6 or op. 29; fingering is frequent; and several studies have comments added to them pointing out what their purpose is. Op. 31 shows Sor gradually taking on the role, no longer primarily of composer, but of teacher.

Yet another set of twenty-four studies appeared later in the same year, 1828: the *Vingt Quatre Exercices,* op. 35. This set resembles op. 31 in its standard of difficulty, the presence of fingering, and the musical qualities. Op. 44, the *Vingt-quatre petites Pièces Progressives pour la Guitare pour servir de Leçons aux Elèves tout à fait Commençants,* appeared in 1831 and contains extremely simple pieces; and op. 60, the *Introduction à l'Etude de la Guitare* of 1836-7, is a work of pedagogical interest and contains fine musical material.

Guitars by Lacote

One of the guitar makers whom Sor praised in his *Méthode pour la Guitare* (p. 10) was Lacote:

> M. Lacote, luthier français, le seul qui, outre son talent, m'a prouvé qu'il possède la qualité de ne point se raidir contre le raisonnement.

> ('M. Lacote, a French instrument maker, and the only one who, besides his talent, has demonstrated to me that he possesses the quality of not resisting reason.')

Many Lacote guitars are still in existence. They generally have a narrow waist, a shallow body, and relatively heavy construction, compared with the broad waist, deep body, and light construction of eighteenth century guitars. Nevertheless, they are still much smaller than the modern concert guitars of today, and represent a mid-way point in the changing shape of the guitar. One which I own, an instrument with an unusually fine sound, has 'F. Sor' written on a label inside the instrument. I understand that others bear similar labels. But it does not appear to be Sor's signature, for many genuine examples of the signature are known and the handwriting differs from that on the label. Perhaps it was Lacote who wrote the words, to advertise Sor's approval of his instruments.

Music for the harpolyre

In about 1830 Sor wrote three works for a newly invented musical instrument called the harpolyre, one of the many strange instruments that the nineteenth century produced. Essentially, it was a development from the guitar: it had 21 strings distributed on three necks. Here is what the English magazine the *Harmonicon* had to say about it (1829, p. 300):

THE HARPOLYRE, A NEW GUITAR,
INVENTED BY J.F. SALOMON,
Professor of Singing and of the Guitar at the Polytechnic School.

Many distinguished professors of the guitar had endeavoured to raise the instrument from the inferior rank which it holds in the sonorous class. But vainly has their skill conquered the difficulties of fingering, &c.: still only a thin, brief, and dry sound has proceeded from the frail machine; and while the talent of the performer is admired, we regret to see that talent wasted in conquering the defects of an unfavourable instrument.

Various efforts were also made to ameliorate the construction of the guitar, but without success. Its primitive form was changed for that of the ancient lyre about twenty-five years ago; yet the alteration was productive of no advantages as regarded the sound, which, indeed, was rendered less intense. It was necessary to revert to the old construction, with one additional chord.

Mr. Salomon's improvements on the primitive guitar are not of this slight character. The instrument is wholly re-constructed in his Harpolyre, without being materially increased in size; while its volume of sound is augmented in a tenfold degree, and its resources for execution out of all comparison with what they formerly were. The following details will render this evident:

The harpolyre is provided with twenty-one strings divided on three necks.

The central, or common neck, has six strings, like the ordinary guitar, and arranged in the same manner; that is, *mi, la, ré, sol, si, mi.* The only difference consists in the greater number of stops on that of the harpolyre. All ordinary guitar music may be executed on this neck, with the advantage of a stronger sound and more harmonious effect.

The left neck (looking at the instrument in front) is called the *chromatic,* and is furnished with seven strings in silk, covered with silver twist.

The right neck, to which Mr. Salomon has given the name of the *diatonic,* is furnished with eight strings of gut.

The power of this instrument, its sonorousness, its capabilities of varying are such, that it is scarcely possible to describe bounds to the effects which may be derived from it. For example — there are two distinct qualities of sound in the harpolyre. The central neck yield sounds full and voluminous, and the *diatonic* gives about those of the ordinary guitar. From the combination of these sounds, the most singular and delightful effects may be anticipated. Messrs. Sor and Carcassi, who have examined this novel instrument, are both sensible of its advantages, and engaged in composing music for it. With a little study, any person who plays the guitar may learn to use the two additional necks.

The inventor has prepared a method of instruction for his instrument. This will shortly be published.

The *Revue Musicale,* VIII, pp. 20-23, contains a report by a committee to the Athénée des Arts, dated 4 April 1830, recommending that the harpolyre's inventor, M. Salomon, be publicly given a medal of the '2e degré'.

Sor, a man of open mind, evidently approved of this new invention, just as a few years later he was to approve of Aguado's strange device the tripódison. For he wrote three works for it, and as far as may be discovered they are all original works and not merely arrangements from his guitar music. They are a *Marche Funèbre; Trois Pièces;* and *Six Petites Pièces Progressives.* All three were published by Salomon and were listed in the *Bibliographie de la France* for 24 April 1830, together with a method for harpolyre by Salomon. Copies of them are in the Bibliothèque Nationale in Paris. The *Six Petites Pièces* are quite simple. The *Trois Pièces* are all extended pieces: an Andante largo, an Andante cantabile, and an Andantino. They all use the new bass strings to good advantage. But it is in the *Marche Funèbre* that this rich bass register is best used, to fine melancholy effect.

Salomon, however, died in 1831, and with him died the harpolyre. Sor's pieces today remain unheard. One harpolyre made by Salomon survives in the Crosby Brown Collection in the Metropolitan Museum of Art, New York,[5] and the pieces could of course be played on this or on other surviving examples if any were found. They can scarcely be adapted to the ordinary guitar, for too many effects in the bass are lost, though the ten-string guitar would be possibility.

French songs

Six songs by Sor with words in French are known. The most interesting is 'Le Dernier Cri des Grecs', a *Marche Nocturne* for two voices and piano, which was listed in the *Bibliographie de la France* on 9 May 1829. This song is about the Greek War of Independence and once again shows Sor on the side of liberty against the

---

[5] W. Sasser, 'In search of Sor', *Guitar Review,* 26 (1962), p. 20, with a photograph of the instrument.

foreign invader. The song has a fine lithograph on the cover, and the text, by Emile de Tarade, begins as follows:

> Marchons, amis, avançons en silence,
> Et pour jamais brisons d'indignes fers.
> Voici l'instant d'une juste vengeance,
> Par nos exploits étonnons l'univers.
>
> *Entendez vous nos épouses captives,*
> *Sous nos efforts leurs cachots vont s'ouvrir.*
> *De nos enfants j'entends les voix plaintives,*
> *Marchons, marchons, il faut vaincre ou périr.*

('Let us go, friends, let us advance in silence, and break for ever these unjust bonds. This is the moment for a rightful vengeance; let us astonish the universe by our exploits. Do you hear our captive wives? By our efforts their prisons will open. I hear the plaintive voices of our children; let us go, let us go, we must conquer or die.')

The Philhellenic movement, which had gathered strength throughout the beginning of the nineteenth century, was at this time leading to action. Many individuals had gone out to Greece, among them Byron who died at Mesolonghi in April 1824; and in October 1827 the Battle of Navarino was fought and won against the Turks. A French fleet was present at that battle, and a French expeditionary force arrived in Greece in October 1828; the words of this song could refer to either (C.M. Woodhouse, *The Story of Modern Greece,* London, 1968, *passim*). The song was also published in Ledhuy's *Encyclopédie.*

Another song with words by Tarade is 'Le Souvenir', Nocturne, which exists in two versions: one for two voices and piano, published by Pacini, and one for solo voice and piano, published by Tarade after Sor's death 'comme un hommage rendu à la Mémoire de mon cher Professeur et ami' ('as a homage to the memory of my dear teacher and friend'). Then there is an arrangement, with words, of the celebrated waltz from *Cendrillon;* this was published in December 1826, and is for voice and piano or harp; an apparently later version exists for voice and guitar. The other three are all romances, 'Loin de tes yeux' (once again with words by Tarade), 'O vous que Mars rend invincible' (published in October 1827), and 'Il reviendra'. None is of great value; and one is reminded of Sor's own comment, in Ledhuy's *Encyclopédie,* on the French romances that he heard at Montserrat in the 1790s: 'Je ne pouvais concevoir que cette musique pût être trouvée bonne' ('I could not see how anyone could find that music good').

Boleros and seguidillas

In chapter 1 I discussed the seguidillas which Sor composed before he left Spain in 1813, works which form an authentic part of Spanish culture and musical history of that time. After that date, he published a number of arrangements of those earlier works, and some new ones: these later works take their place in the growing awareness of national music in Europe at that time, but they are artificial works, written in exile rather than in the main current of a living tradition. For full details on them, see my edition of Sor's *Seguidillas.* The most important of them are the three that appeared in Paris in about 1828 as *Tres Seguidillas Boleras,* dedicated to the wife of the Spanish ambassador to Paris, and the three in the *Regalo Lirico,* a collection of Spanish songs published by Pacini in Paris in 1831 or before.

Other compositions

A *Marche Composée pour la Musique Militaire* for piano duet, published probably in 1837, recalls the military fervour of earlier days, while a Mazurka for piano solo published in Ledhuy's *Encyclopédie* has a totally different lightness of touch. There are also a Romanesca for violin and guitar, and some piano duets composed for Lemoine. A mass which Sor wrote on the death of his daughter in 1837 is lost.

Concerts

During these thirteen years in Paris, one of Sor's main activities was to give concerts. And during this period we know much more about them than before, because they were reviewed in the musical periodicals, above all in the *Revue Musicale:* we know under what circumstances they were given, who played in them, and even sometimes what pieces Sor played. Altogether we know of fourteen such concerts, and doubtless there were others of which details have not come down to us.[6]

In these Paris concerts, Sor always played the guitar, and nearly always his own music. In Málaga he played the double bass, but I suspect rather as a display of virtuosity. On his arrival in London, he sang at a society soirée and even at one public concert, but nevertheless when it came to serious concerts it was always as a guitarist that he appeared. So also here in Paris.

The first concert that we know about is to be deduced from the title-page of the revised version of his Mozart variations, op. 9, 'Exécutées par l'Auteur au Concert donné à l'Ecole Royale de Musique' ('played by the composer at the concert given at the Ecole Royale de Musique'). This revised version was published most probably early in 1827, and so the concert in question

---

[6] The following section owes much to Herr Hans Radke, who found the many references to Sor in the *Revue Musicale* and published them in his article 'Sor' in the encyclopedia *Die Musik in Geschichte und Gegenwart.*

was apparently given soon after Sor's return from Russia, in late 1826 or early 1827. It was not reviewed, as far as I know.

In 1826 the *Revue Musicale* was founded by the critic F.J. Fétis. Fétis today has a bad reputation among musicologists for the many inaccuracies contained in his *Biographie Universelle des Musiciens,* yet without that work and without his *Revue Musicale* we should lack much information about this period of musical history, and there is no reason to doubt the facts in his concert reviews. He had the highest regard for Sor's musicianship, his sense of harmony and composition, and his technical achievement on the guitar, and faithfully recorded his appearances in public; but he did not like the guitar. So it is that in 1828 we find the following review:

> Le 26 janvier [1828] nous avons remarqué des variations exécutées de la manière la plus brillante par M. Woetz, et un solo de guitare joué par M. Sor. Ce dernier morceau, presque toujours écrit à quatre parties, offre une harmonie pure, élégante, et nous a paru être d'une exécution fort difficile. Mais nous avons regretté que le son de l'instrument ne fût pas plus nourri. M. Sor nous semble avoir trop négligé cette partie essentielle d'un instrument trop peu sonore par lui-même.'

> (*Revue Musicale,* III, 1828, p. 40)

> ('On 26 January [1828] we heard variations played in the most brilliant manner by M. Woetz, and a guitar solo played by M. Sor. This latter piece, almost always written in four parts, showed a pure and elegant harmony, and seemed to us to be most difficult to play. But we regretted that the sound of the instrument was not fuller. M. Sor seems to us to have neglected too much this essential aspect of an instrument which in itself is not sonorous enough.')

This concert took place in the salon of M. Dietz, the piano maker; it seems that part of the purpose of this concert and of others organized by piano makers was to show off the quality of the pianos which were played; it was a form of advertisement. And after this concert, Fétis tells us that Sor played (unspecified) solos in two more concerts in April of the same year. The first was organized by Mme Robert, and only the mere fact of Sor's appearance, playing a guitar piece, is mentioned. Details of the second, in the 'salle de la rue Clery' on 20 April 1828, are given in much greater fullness. It was a charity concert, organized, so it was said, by Mlle Amigo the singer, and on this occasion Liszt played as well as Sor and other musicians. The programme consisted of a set of variations for clarinet by Beer, played by Sabon; an air by Cimarosa, sung by the bass Levasseur; a guitar piece played by Sor; the trio from Cimarosa's *Il Matrimonio Segreto* sung by Mlles Mori, Amigo and Demeri; variations on motifs of Rossini and Auber, composed and played by Liszt; variations for

violin by Bériot played by Hauman; and the concert finished with variations played by Sor. Fétis wrote:

> M. Sor a du talent; la musique qu'il exécute, presque toujours écrites à quatre parties, est prodigieusement difficile; mais il tire un mauvais son de l'instrument.

> (*Revue Musicale,* III, 1828, pp. 302-4)

> ('M. Sor has talent; the music which he plays, almost always written in four parts, is prodigiously difficult; but he gets a poor sound from the instrument.')

He also tells us something about Sor's manner of playing, even though we have to make allowance for his dislike of the instrument itself:

> On peut lui reprocher aussi d'en changer la nature, et de le rapprocher souvent de l'effet de la mandoline, par son obstination à jouer dans les sons aigus.

> ('One might also reproach him with changing its nature, and with often making it sound like a mandolin, by his persistence in playing with a sharp sound.')

It is important, not only for these Paris concerts but also for the earlier ones in London, to remember the form of the early nineteenth century concert. The virtuoso performer's solo recital, which began with Liszt and Paganini and is still alive today, had not yet outshone the older formula of the mixed concert in which a number of artists performed: here, for example, we find the young Liszt himself appearing in the older, traditional kind of mixed concert. In such a concert, there might be half a dozen major performers, and perhaps a small orchestra. Fétis grumbles, in the 1830s, that the orchestras specially got together for these concerts seldom rehearsed enough, the sheer effort of assembling them being so huge, and he praises the violinist Baillot, on one occasion, for using only a quartet instead of such an orchestra. But that is in the 1830s; and Baillot himself, in his London concert of 1816 in which Sor also played, used an orchestra. In these Paris concerts of Sor's last years, it is the older pattern of a number of performers which prevails, and there is no evidence that Sor himself ever gave a solo recital in the modern sense.

If he did not give solo recitals, nevertheless like almost every other professional musician he did give benefit concerts, in which the general principle was that after the expenses were paid the income went to the artist. A similar arrangement was frequent in the world of ballet, and we know of a number of benefit performances for Félicité Hullin. In the concert world, it seems that the artist himself had to do the organizing; Berlioz, for example, tells us in his memoirs of the drudgery he went through in organizing concerts in Paris a few years later. The principal artist would occupy the star position in the programme, but it was normal for others, of the highest calibre possible, to be willing to appear in the course of their own career: thus,

Baillot's London concert of 1816, in which Sor appeared, was a benefit concert for Baillot.

In this Paris period, Sor's first benefit concert, as far as is known, took place on 18 May 1828. Fétis wrote:

> Nous n'avons que des éloges à lui donner pour ce qui concerne l'exécution vraiment étonnante des morceaux qu'il nous a fait entendre. Peut-être pourrait-on lui reprocher de choisir des thèmes un peu communs; mais il les varie d'une manière si heureuse qu'on oublie leur trivialité pour ne s'occuper que du charme qui les déguise.
>
> (*Revue Musicale*, III, 1828, pp. 402-3)

> ('We have nothing but praise for his truly astonishing execution of the pieces which we heard. Perhaps one might reproach him for choosing rather commonplace themes; but he varies them so felicitously that one forgets their triviality and notices only the charm which disguises them.')

We do not hear exactly what pieces Sor played, but it is possible to guess. In this same year, 1828, there appeared his Seventh Fantasia, op. 30, dedicated to Aguado, the title-page of which says that it was played by the composer 'à son concert'. The words indicate that it was a concert of Sor's own, and not merely a concert in which he happened to be playing. Of the four benefit concerts of which we know, the date of this one fits best. And if we look at the Seventh Fantasia, we find that it does indeed consist of variations upon a well-known and rather trivial air. So it is most likely that in this concert of 18 May 1828, Sor played his Seventh Fantasia, op. 30.

On 14 July 1829 (or 14 June; the month is hard to establish) another benefit concert was held, in the salon of M. Dietz; and this time, according to the *Revue Musicale* (V, 1829, p. 304), the guitarist was 'Ch. Sor'. Sor's brother Carlos was indeed a guitarist, and he did indeed live in Paris in 1817 and 1839, the only other occasions on which we hear of him, so it is possible that this was in fact his concert. But it is also at least a possibility that the name is an error for Fernando Sor. There were duets with Aguado, as well as solos; and the other performers were the singer Auguste Panseron (for whom Fernando Sor played the next year), Brod, Mlles Kunzé and Maillard, Bertini, and Fontaine. Whoever the guitarist was, in the opinion of the reviewer he played brilliantly.

When Auguste Panseron gave a benefit concert of his own in March 1830, among the performers was Fernando Sor. Fétis wrote on that occasion:

> Citer M. Sor, c'est dire qu'on a entendu jouer de la guitare avec une perfection rare. Quel dommage qu'une tête si harmonique ait employé tant de talent et de patience à vaincre un instrument ingrat!
>
> (*Revue Musicale*, VII, 1830, p. 267)

('To speak of M. Sor is to say that one has heard the guitar played with rare perfection. What a pity that someone with such a sense of harmony should have spent so much talent and patience in mastering an unrewarding

And in July 1830, despite the political commotion of the revolution which took place in that month, Sor played in a concert of Mme Farrenc, with Hummel among the other performers:

> M. Sor a fait grand plaisir dans un morceau qu'il a exécuté sur la guitare avec une rare perfection; cet artiste a le grand mérite d'avoir su tirer son instrument de l'état plus que secondaire où le retiennent ses facultés exigües.
>
> (*Revue Musicale*, VIII, 1830, p. 376)

> ('M. Sor gave much pleasure with a piece which he played on the guitar with rare perfection; this artist has the great merit of having succeeded in raising his instrument from the worse than secondary position where its slender resources keep it.')

So far Sor has played his guitar on equal terms with other players and instruments. Throughout his life the music which he composed for it was not specifically Spanish, but in the main current of European music. True, it was known as the 'Spanish guitar', and Spanish things were much in vogue throughout Europe at this time; but it was not on those nationalistic grounds that Sor succeeded. Though his country and his politics may have been Spanish, in his music he presented himself on an international footing. But now, in Paris in the last years of his life, we find him for the first time performing in a specifically Spanish gathering. The occasion was a benefit concert for the young Spanish pianist José Miró y Anoria on 27 March 1831. Most unfortunately it clashed with a concert given by Paganini, but despite this a large audience came, mostly but not exclusively Spanish. It was a wholly Spanish evening: Sor played a solo, there was a duet for two guitars played by Sor and Aguado, and the aged García sang in the trio from Rossini's *Ricciardo et Zoraïde* with 'une prodigieuse énergie' (*Revue Musicale*, XI, 1831-2, p. 71).

Miró did Sor the honour of appearing in the latter's next benefit concert, three weeks later, on 19 April 1831. Again it was in the salon of M. Dietz. Here is Fétis' review:

> Nous avons eu plusieurs fois occasion de dire ce que nous pensons du talent de M. Sor: nous n'avons donc aujourd'hui qu'à constater le nouveau succès que cet artiste a obtenu dans la soirée musicale qu'il vient de donner dans les salons de M. Dietz. M. Miro, jeune pianiste espagnol, a reçu de justes applaudissemens dans un concerto de Field qu'il a fort bien exécuté. MM. Richelmi, Domange et Mme Durand, ont chanté plusieurs morceaux italiens. Bien qu'Ebner et Mlle Dorus fussent annoncés sur le programme, ces deux artistes ne se sont pas fait entendre.
>
> (*Revue Musicale,* XI, 1831-2, p. 97)

('We have several times had occasion to say what we think of the talent of M. Sor; and so today we have only to record the new success which this artist obtained in the musical soirée which he gave in the salon of M. Dietz. M. Miró, a young Spanish pianist, received deserved applause in a concerto by Field which he played very well. MM. Richelmi and Domange, and Mme Durand, sang several Italian pieces. Although Ebner and Mlle Dorus were anounced on the programme, they were not heard.')

In the Music Department of the Bibliothèque Nationale, Paris, is a letter from Sor to 'M. Stephan' (Domange?) organizing a rehearsal, apparently for this concert.

Although he wrote about Sor for a good number of years, Fétis never changed his mind. For him, Sor was always a fine musician who played an unworthy instrument. Here he is again, putting his views forward with even more bluntness than usual, in a review of another concert by Miró in Dietz' salon on 15 February 1832, in which Sor played solos:

> M. Sor fait de très jolies choses sur la guitare; mais j'avoue que j'ai toujours regretté que cet artiste, dont l'organisation musicale est loin d'être ordinaire, n'emploie pas ses facultés sur un instrument qui offrait plus de resources à son habileté. En entendant M. Sor on reconnaît un artiste supérieur; mais, je le répète, pourquoi joue-t-il de la guitare?

(*Revue Musicale,* XII, 1832-3, p. 22)

('M. Sor does very pretty things on the guitar; but I confess that I have always regretted that this artist, whose musical intelligence is far from ordinary, does not devote himself to an instrument which would offer greater resources to his ability. On hearing M. Sor one recognizes a superior artist; but, I repeat, why does he play the guitar?')

For three years after this, we hear no more of Sor as a performer. Was he too discouraged by reviews such as Fétis'? Was he too occupied with teaching, or financially unable or unwilling to risk more benefit concerts? Or is it simply that we do not know about concerts which he may have given? However that may be, the next concert in which he is known to have played took place on 29 November 1835. Even this was unplanned: it was to have been a benefit concert by the guitarist Legnani, but it seems that Legnani suffered the misfortune of breaking an arm on getting out of a carriage. Sor and Aguado and others played instead. It took place on a Sunday afternoon in the Salle Chantereine. The *Revue Musicale* said that 'M. Sor a exécuté un solo avec une perfection qui a enlevé tous les suffrages' (XV, 1835-6, p. 403) ('M Sor played a solo with a perfection which won everybody's applause').

On 24 April 1836 took place Sor's last known benefit concert. This time the audience was largely Spanish: 'L'auditoire se composait principalement d'Espagnols accourus pour applaudir un artiste compatriote et un instrument national' ('The audience consisted principally of Spaniards come to applaud their countryman and a national instrument'), said the *Revue et Gazette Musicale de Paris* (III, 1836, p. 136). 'On a distingué une fantaisie villageoise [op. 52], composé et exécuté par le bénéficiaire, et un duo de guitare entre lui et son émule, M. Aguado' ('There was a *Fantaisie villageoise,* composed and played by the beneficiary, and a guitar duet played by him and his disciple M. Aguado'). Aguado, it seems, used his *tripódison* at this concert: 'Nous devons constater une innovation introduite par ce dernier: au lieu de tenir la guitare sur ses genoux, il l'appuie sur une espèce de piédestal, qui laisse la liberté des bras à l'exécutant et donne plus de fermeté à l'instrument lui-même' ('We must record an innovation introduced by the latter: instead of holding the guitar on his knees, he rests it on a kind of pedestal, which leaves the player's hands free and gives greater steadiness to the instrument itself').

Soon after this we know that the ageing Sor, now in his late fifties, fell ill. The last concert in which he is known to have played was in April or early May 1838, organized by Napoleon Coste as a benefit for himself. The *Revue et Gazette Musicale de Paris* (V, 1838, p. 190) reported that the concert began with a duet played by Sor and Coste. In the Bibliothèque Nationale, Paris, is a letter from Sor to the Queen of France, inviting her to take tickets for a concert which is to consist of a Mass by Sor, since he is himself now too ill to teach and has no other means of support. The letter is dated 21 March 1839. The Queen did take tickets. And the Mass is presumably that which Sor composed on the death of his daughter in June 1837. But we do not know if the concert was ever given; and Sor died in July 1839.

In these last years in Paris, then, we know of fourteen concerts in which Sor played. Four were his own benefit concerts, seven benefits for other musicians, one was a charity concert, one was organized by a piano maker, and one was at the Ecole Royale de Musique. In addition, there is the concert at which his Mass was to be performed. And we may suppose, on the analogy of other periods in his life, that he played also in private houses — possibly even for the Royal Family, since the Queen did help him and his op. 54 is dedicated to the Princesse Adelaïde, sister of Louis-Philippe.

What music did he play? As we have seen, we know definitely that he played in Paris the revised version of his op. 9, his op. 30, and his op. 52. Also, we may presume that he was the composer of the duets which he played with Aguado — and among them, surely, would have been *Les Deux Amis,* op. 41, which is dedicated to him. Sor himself tells us in his *Méthode,* p. 85, that he played 'le trio de Hummel sur *la Sentinelle*' with the violinist Lafont and the pianist Herz. This piece, for voice, violin, piano, and guitar, is an arrangement by Hummel from a French romance originally composed probably by Giuliani.[7] And — though this refers to a slightly earlier period — an anonymous reviewer in the *Allgemeine musikalische Zeitung,* September 1823, says that he has heard Sor play the overture to Méhul's *La Chasse du jeune Henri* and the closing chorus of the first part of Haydn's *Creation.*

Saldoni tells an amusing story about a concert in Paris in which Sor played, though he does not say when or exactly where. It was related to him directly by Gironella, the Spanish gentleman who was at Sor's side when he died.

> Un día en que Sors acababa de tocar un gran concierto de guitarra en una distinguida sociedad de Paris, se volvió en tono de broma al que tenía á su lado, y le dijo en dialecto catalán: *¡También lo harías tú esto, ¿eh? pedazo de alcornoque!* Y el francés, creyendo que le preguntaba qué tal le había parecido, contestó muy enthusiasmado: *¡Superbe, ravissant, magnifique!* etc., etc., etc. Replicándole Sors también en catalán: *Eso ya me lo sabía yo.*

> (*Diccionario,* pp. 265-6)

> ('One day when Sor had just finished playing in a big guitar concert in a distinguished society in Paris, he turned to the person at his side and said to him jokingly in Catalan: "You'd have done as well, wouldn't you, you old fool?" And the Frenchman, thinking that he was asking him how he had liked it, answered enthusiastically: "Superb, wonderful, magnificent!" etc., etc., etc. To which Sor replied, still in Catalan: "Yes, I know!" ')

The Hotel Favart and Dionisio Aguado

On his return to Paris from Russia, Sor lived first in the Hotel Favart in the Place des Italiens (now Place Boieldieu), and then in an apartment in the Marché St. Honoré. He was at the Hotel Favart by 24 May 1828, when the *Bibliographie de la France* listed the prospectus for his *Méthode pour la Guitare* 'A Paris, chez l'auteur, place des Italiens, hôtel Favart', and it may well be that he had lived there since his return from Russia. He moved to the Marché St. Honoré in about 1832.[8]

The Hotel Favart is still there, still a hotel, though greatly changed inside, in what is now the Place Boieldieu. It is right in the musical centre of Paris, near the Opera. It comes vividly alive in a delightful description by Saldoni, of an unexpected meeting there with Aguado in September 1838. By then Sor had moved, but it is unlikely that the hotel had changed. Clearly it was still residential, for Aguado was still living there (as he had done since at least 1826[9]), and not merely staying there for a few days. Here is Saldoni:

> Al llegar á París á eso de las cinco de la madrugada nos acostamos al momento, pues hacía tres noches que no nos desnudábamos; pero apenas habría pasado una hora de estar en cama, cuando nos despertó una música que nos pareció celestial, y estuvimos dudando qué instrumento fuera el que tanto nos entusiasmaba; tal era la dulzura y suavidad de sus sonidos y armonías, producidas por la manera con que eran heridas sus cuerdas; de modo que tuvimos que llamar al camarero y preguntarle qué instrumento era aquél que nos producía tan grata sensación, y que no nos atrevíamos á classificar. El camarero, con la sonrisa en los lábios, nos dijo: *C'est monsieur Aguado avec son ghitarre.* Calcúlese nuestro gozo y sorpresa á la vez al saber que nos hallábamos, ignorándolo completamente, y por incidencia, al lado de este gran artista, que al momento, y sin acordarnos ya más del sueño, fuimos á abrazar y á manifestarle el efecto que nos había producido el oirle á través de un tabique. Inútil es decir que todas las mañanas se repetía la misma función, pues que no dejaba pasar ninguna sin que estudiára, á pesar de contar entónces unos cincuenta y cinco años, sus dos horas diarias, con cuyo ejercicios, desde nuestra habitación, ó bien en la suya propia, gozábamos lo que no es fácil explicar, porque además de ser el Sr. Aguado el primer guitarrista en Europa en su género dulce, afectuoso y melodioso, era la persona más amable, humilde y cariñosa que hemos tratado, hasta el punto de obligarnos muchos días á tomar el chocolate que él se hacía en su cuarto en una máquina que tenía á propósito para ello. Nosotros consagramos con sumo gusto estos desaliñados renglones á la buena memoria del insigne y modesto guitarrista, á la par que al inolvidable y excelente amigo.

> (*Diccionario,* p. 253)

> ('When I arrived in Paris, about five in the morning, I went to bed without delay, for I had not undressed for three nights; but scarcely had I been there an hour, when I was awakened by music that seemed celestial; and I wondered what instrument it could be that charmed me so, such were the sweetness and softness of its sounds and harmonies, produced by the manner in which its strings were struck; so that I had to summon a servant to ask him what instrument it was that produced such a pleasant sensation and that I was unable to identify. The servant, grinning, said: "It's monsieur Aguado with his guitar." Imagine my joy and surprise to learn that completely

---

[7] Thomas F. Heck, *The Birth of the Classic Guitar* (unpublished Ph.D. dissertation, Yale University, 1970), vol. II, p. 182.

[8] The move can be dated from his works. Op. 50 bears the old address on its title-page, and op. 52 the new. Though these works bear no date, we know from other sources that they appeared in about 1832 or 1833: for op. 44 was out by 19 March 1831 (listing in the *Bibliographie de la France*) and op. 54 by 25 March 1833 (review in the *Revue Musicale,* XIII, p. 63). So it must have been in about late 1832 that Sor moved from the Hotel Favart to the Marché St. Honoré. The address "rue de Marivaux, no. 5" on the title-page of Sor's *Méthode* is that of the Hotel Favart.

[9] In 1826 the *Bibliographie de la France* listed Aguado's Method 'chez Aguado, Hotel Favart'.

unwittingly and by coincidence I was by the side of that great artist, whom immediately and without further thought of sleep, I went to embrace and to show the effect that had been produced on me by hearing him through a partition. Naturally the same thing happened every morning, for although he was 55 years old he did not allow a day to pass without practising for two hours; and I enjoyed listening to his exercises, either from my room or in his, in a way which is not easy to explain, for Sr. Aguado, as well as being the finest guitarist in Europe in his own sweet, touching and melodious style, was the most amiable, modest and charming person whom I had met, to the point of inviting me, many mornings, to take chocolate with him, which he made in his room with a machine which he kept there for the purpose. I dedicate most willingly these few untidy lines to the good memory of that distinguished and modest guitarist as well as to that unforgettable and excellent friend.')

Aguado, then, lived in the Hotel Favart from at least 1826 to 1838; Sor from at least 1828 to 1832. For some four years, then, they both lived there, presumably also with Sor's daughter.

Dionisio (or, in French, 'Denis') Aguado was born in Spain, in 1784 according to Saldoni *(Diccionario)*. He came to France in 1826, and returned to Spain in about 1839. An article on him is in Ledhuy's *Encyclopédie*. He was the inventor of a device called the *tripódison*,[10] which held the guitar firmly and thus released both hands of the player, and which Sor praised in a preface to his *Fantaisie Elégiaque,* op. 59. Sor dedicated to him his *7e Fantaisie,* op. 30 (1828), and his duet *Les Deux Amis,* op. 41 (c. 1830), in which one of the two guitar parts is marked 'SOR' and the other 'AGUADO'. Aguado played with the nails of the right hand, whereas Sor used the tips of the fingers, and Sor discusses the merits and disadvantages of the two systems in his *Méthode pour la Guitare,* pp. 21-2, where he quotes Aguado as saying that if he (Aguado) could learn the guitar again from the beginning, he would play without nails. It is evident from this same passage that Sor and Aguado had met many years earlier, perhaps in Spain. The copy of Sor's *Méthode* which he presented to Aguado is now in the Biblioteca Nacional, Madrid.

The 'Encyclopédie Pittoresque de la Musique' of A. Ledhuy and H. Bertini

In 1835 this encyclopedia was published in Paris in 52 instalments. Sor contributed to it an article, 'Le Bolero', and also it was almost certainly he who wrote the article 'Sor' devoted to himself. That article is our principal source for information about Sor's life, and I have often had occasion to refer to it.

Adolphe Ledhuy was a guitarist and composer and a friend of Sor. In instalment 47 of his encyclopedia is a study in C minor for guitar by him, dedicated 'à son ami F. Sor'. His encyclopedia shows an enquiring magpie mind: there are items on the instruments of the ancient Hebrews, on Josquin des Prez, on Cramer, Méhul and Aguado. Its 52 instalments appeared in 1835 until petty bureaucratic difficulties brought it to an end, for a note on the last page says: 'Les vexations de la Direction du Timbre ayant arrêté l'émission des feuilles de l'ENCYCLOPÉDIE, les Éditeurs ont cru devoir renoncer à publier cet ouvrage par livraisons détachées. Lorsqu'un nouveau volume sera terminé, les Journaux annonceront l'époque de la mise en vente' ('The vexations of the stamp duty office having halted the publication of the Encyclopedia's instalments, the publishers have felt obliged to give up the publication of this work by separate instalments. When a new volume is ready, the date of its publication will be announced in the newspapers.') From that moment no more is known to have been published.

Pagination is unreliable, but reference can be made by instalment numbers. The article 'Sor' is in instalments 40-43, and the article 'Le Bolero' is in instalments 11-13. The former is published in facsimile at the end of the present book, and the latter, again in facsimile, in my edition of Sor's *Seguidillas* (London, Tecla Editions, 1976).

The biographical article on Sor occupies over 24 pages, of which just over half are text and the remainder drawings and music. About eight pages are devoted to memories of his childhood at Montserrat; this part is in the first person, in quotation marks and said to be textually extracted from his Memoirs. The rest is written in the third person, but in such precise detail that it was surely Sor who wrote it. The article traces Sor's career in Barcelona, Madrid and Andalusia; through the Spanish War of Independence; through London, Paris and Russia; and finally in Paris up to the date of the encyclopedia. As well as telling us about Sor, it is one of the most important sources of information about Montserrat and about musical education in eighteenth-century Spain. I have used it in this book as the framework on which to build up a fuller picture of Sor's life from original documents and from his music.

It includes a drawing of Sor by Adam, showing him as a dignified gentleman, unlike the dashing adventurer of Goubaud's romantic picture. This drawing is included at the end of this book, as part of the facsimile of the whole article. Hippolyte-Benjamin Adam (1808-53) was a minor portrait painter of the time (E. Bénézit, *Dictionnaire . . . des Peintres,* I, 1966).

---

[10] This is the spelling used by Aguado himself in his *Nuevo Método de Guitarra* (Madrid and Paris, n.d.), which is written in Spanish. In his *Apéndice al Nuevo Método para Guitarra* (Madrid, 1849), p. 8, Aguado translates Sor's note in his *Fantaisie Elégiaque* and writes (in Spanish) *trípode*. In the article 'Aguado' in Ledhuy's *Encyclopédie*, in French, it is spelt *tripedisono*.

Spanish memories

The article in Ledhuy's *Encyclopédie* showed a growing sentimentality, a Romantic dwelling on memories such as Sor's childhood at Montserrat. As time went on, this tendency was to grow. There are, for example, the song 'Le Souvenir' and the guitar pieces *Souvenirs d'une Soirée à Berlin* and *Souvenir de Russie,* opp. 56 and 63. But above all it seems to have been Spain that held a place in his thoughts and feelings. In the last year of his life, a child's picture of a Spanish Holy Week procession, brought for him from Spain, moved him deeply.

After his return from Russia, it seems that he wanted to return to Spain. For it was then that he sent a letter to King Fernando VII of Spain, accompanied by a manuscript copy of the overture to *Hercule et Omphale.* The letter has apparently disappeared in recent years from the Madrid archive where it was kept, but its discoverer, José Subirá, saw it and published its text in his book *El Teatro del Real Palacio* (Madrid, 1950), p. 147, as follows:[11]

Señor,

La aceptación que mis producciones han merecido y el modo lisongero con que los Soberanos de los países en donde he estado han honrado mi débil talento me han hecho siempre echar de menos el honor de obtener la misma aceptación de la nación a que pertenezco, y la que debo los primeros elementos de la Ciencia Harmónica. El Jefe Supremo de la Iglesia Cathólica, a cuyos pies fué presentado un Himno de mi composición a la Santa Cruz, acaba de condecorarme con la de su Orden, y lo que más me lisongea en este acto es la idea de honrar en quanto depende de mi el nombre Español.

La obra que ofrezco a los pies de Vuestra Magestad es en mi juicio lo mejor que he compuesto; y no satisfaría los deseos de mi corazón si no la dedicase humildemente al primero a quien debo este homenage, y el Soberano cuya aceptación me honrara si la obtengo más que otra alguna.

Señor,

A.L.R.P. de V.M.

Fernando Sor.

('Your Majesty,

The approval which my compositions have merited, and the flattering way in which the Sovereigns of the countries in which I have been have honoured my feeble talent, have always made me miss and desire the honour of obtaining the same approval from the nation to which I belong, and to which I owe the first elements of the science of harmony. The Supreme Head of the Catholic Church, at whose feet was presented a hymn composed by me in honour of the Holy Cross, has just bestowed on me a decoration in his own Order, and what flatters me most in this event is the idea of honouring, as much as in me lies, the name of Spain.

The work which I offer at Your Majesty's feet is in my opinion the best which I have composed; and I would not satisfy the desires of my heart if I did not humbly dedicate it to the first person to whom I owe such homage, to the Sovereign whose approval will honour me, if I obtain it, more than any other.

Your Majesty,

At Your Majesty's royal feet,

Fernando Sor.')

Subirá gives no date. Clearly it must be after the composition of *Hercule et Omphale* (Moscow, 1826). A mere guess may be that Sor sent it from Paris to Fernando VII through the Spanish ambassador to Paris, the Duque de San Carlos, to whose wife he dedicated his *Tres Seguidillas* (Paris, Meissonnier) about this time. The duke's family name was Carvajal, and so he was presumably related to Francisco Carvajal, colonel of the Cordovan Volunteers in which Sor had once served (see chapter 1). If this hypothesis is correct, then the letter dates from before the death of the Duque de San Carlos on 17 July 1828 (*Biographie universelle*).

Spain at that time was no place for liberals such as Sor. Fernando VII had held a purge of liberals in 1814, the very year after his restoration; and a temporary liberal gain in strength under Riego in 1823 was vigorously reversed by a French army under the Duc d'Angoulême called in by Fernando himself, when a new wave of Spanish exiles joined the *afrancesados* and liberals of earlier years in exile abroad. However, Spain was still Sor's country, and it seems that now, as he grew older, he may have wished to return to it. That is the most likely reason for the letter. In it, he does not mention his patriotic songs of many years before, which would have carried little weight, but he plays the strong card of Catholicism. The Pope, he says, has just decorated him with an order.[12] Moreover, he declares his patriotism and demonstrates with the overture his musical talent. But if indeed his purpose was to return, the letter bore no fruit: no reply is known, and Sor never returned to Spain.

---

[11] According to Subirá, the letter and the accompanying music are in an archive of the Palacio Real in Madrid. But the present librarians there have been unable to locate them; they have suggested that they may be in the Biblioteca Nacional, but a search there has likewise failed to find them.

[12] Subirá suggests that the Pope was Pius VII and that Sor was named a knight of the Pontifical Order. The motet in honour of the Holy Cross, for which Sor says he received the honour, may be 'O crux, ave spes unica', composed many years earlier but published in Ledhuy's *Encyclopédie* in 1835.

As time went on, Sor mixed with Spaniards in Paris, and they came to appreciate and admire him. In 1831, as we saw, he played in a concert with the Spanish pianist Miró and with the singer García, and in 1836, at his last benefit concert, 'l'auditoire se composait principalement d'Espagnols accourus pour applaudir un artiste compatriote et un instrument national' ('The audience consisted principally of Spaniards come to applaud their countryman and a national instrument'). His great friend Aguado was of course Spanish. When Saldoni in Spain published his *Veinte y Cuatro Solfeos* (Madrid, n.d.), it seems that Sor wrote to congratulate him on it.[13] And in about 1837, he dedicated his *Marche Composée pour la Musique Militaire* (for piano duet) to General Quiroga, an ex-supporter of Riego, who had recently accepted an amnesty and had become General commanding in New Castile. In 1839 he was visited by gentlemen from Barcelona, bringing him presents.

And finally, at the end of his life, it was Spaniards who supported him. Antonio de Gironella and José de Lira were at his side when he died, and it was Lira who provided the composer's tomb. How sad, wrote Font y Moresco, one of his visitors from Barcelona, that Spain did not reward men like Sor:

> ¡Artistas españoles, que sentís en vuestras mentes la llama del genio, si llevados de un noble amor á la gloria, aspiráis á conquistar las palmas y coronas á que sois acreedores, pasad las fronteras de vuestra patria; las recompensas que esta os destina, son la indiferencia, el desaliento y quizá la miseria.

> ('Artists of Spain, who feel in your spirits the call of genius, if you are inspired by a noble love of glory and desire to conquer the laurels and crowns which you deserve, cross the frontiers of your country; for the rewards which your country destines for you are indifference, discouragement, and perhaps penury.')

Sor's daughter Caroline

On 8 June 1837 Sor's daughter died. On 10 June a mass was said over her body in the nearby Eglise Saint-Roch, and she was buried in the Cimetière Montmartre.[14] According to Eusebio Font y Moresco

(whose account is printed below), she was a gifted young woman, an accomplished harp player and painter, and her death caused her father the greatest sorrow. Font y Moresco tells how the composer played on the piano, during his visit, extracts from the Mass which he had composed on her death. Many years earlier, in 1823, she and her father had given a concert together in Warsaw, on their way to Moscow.

The sources of information conflict. All three official records give her name as Caroline Sor, and they are probably right. Thus, the register of funeral masses at the Eglise Saint-Roch was signed by Sor's friend José de Lira who must have known her true name, and there it is given as Caroline. Yet Font y Moresco gives it as Julia; unless that is a second name, it is likely that Font y Moresco, writing eleven years later, was wrong.

Her age, too, is a mystery. All three official records give it as twenty in 1837; Font y Moresco said twenty-two. In October 1823 the *Kurier Warszawski* said that she was eight years old. From these figures, it seems that she was born between November 1814 at the earliest and June 1817 at the latest — probably nearer the former, otherwise she would have been extremely young to take part in the concert in Warsaw. This being so, she was certainly born after her father's departure from Spain, probably either in Paris or in London. Her mother was not Félicité Hullin, who was herself born only in 1805, but presumably Sor's first wife.[15]

A visit to Sor in the last days of his life

In June 1839, in the last year of Sor's life, two Spanish gentlemen called on him in Paris: Eusebio Font y Moresco and the painter Jaime Battle. Font y Moresco wrote an account of the visit, which was published in 1850 in the Barcelona newspaper *La Opinión Pública*, as 'Una visita a Sors en los últimos días de su vida' ('A visit to Sor in the last days of his life'). It is the most personal and detailed account of the composer that we possess.

Felipe Pedrell discovered the article and republished it with some errors in a short-lived Barcelona periodical of which he was editor, entitled *Notas Musicales y Literarias,* in 1882. Although he was a scholar who should have known better, he did not name the source, saying only that it was 'un periódico de Barcelona en el año 1850' ('a Barcelona newspaper of the year 1850'), and it took me some research to discover that it was in fact *La Opinión Pública* for 16 and 17 January 1850.

In view of the interest of the article, here it is in its

---

[13] Saldoni, *Diccionario*, p. 265. A copy of the book is in the Biblioteca Nacional, Madrid.

[14] Paris, Archives de la Seine, register of deaths, 8 June 1837: 'Sor / Caroline / Marché St. honoré 34 / 20 ans / [date of death] 8 [June] / Célibataire / Pere et mere vivant'. Paris, Eglise Saint-Roch, register of funeral masses, 10 June 1837: 'A 9 heures le 10 a été présenté le corps de Mlle Caroline Sor decedée le 8 juin Marché St. Honoré N 34 et 36. L'on a dit la messe à laquelle ont assisté MM De Maury rue Minard N 4, et M Joseph D Lira rue de Sunyer [?] 8. Les quelles [sic] ont signé [signed:] J.M. Maury J de Lira'. Paris, Cimetière Montmartre, register of burials: Caroline Sor was buried in a temporary tomb on 10 June 1837.

[15] The register of deaths in the Archives de la Seine says 'Pere et mere vivant'. Too much reliance should not be given to this.

entirety, in facsimile.[16] It tells of Sor's grief at the death of his daughter, and how he played to his visitors, on the piano, extracts from the Mass which he had written on her death. A storm gathers over Paris; there is rain, hail and thunder; and while the composer plays, a thunderbolt crashes near the house. Highly romantic the description is, but not on that account to be disbelieved.

FOLLETIN.

UNA VISITA A SORS EN LOS ÚLTIMOS DIAS DE SU VIDA.

La *Revista Musical* de la *España* del 27 de diciembre del pasado año, firmada por don Eduardo Valaz de Madrano, publicó una breve, pero interesante reseña biográfica sobre los famosos guitarristas españoles, Sors y Aguado. El autor de la citada *Revista*, mal informado sin duda por datos inexactos, ha padecido una equivocación al afirmar que Sors murió hace veinte años. Diez y medio solo van transcurridos desde su fallecimiento; siendo prueba irrecusable de ello la siguiente anécdota. Al referirla finalmente con todas sus particularidades un testigo ocular, es su deseo sacar a la luz pública al propio tiempo un paso interesantísimo de la vida de Sors, el cual da á conocer que si aquel artista fué digno de admiracion por su grande habilidad e ingenio, no lo era menos por las esquisitas dotes de su corazon sensible y tierno.

En junio de 1839, el que suscribe estas líneas hallábase en Paris en compañía de su amigo, don Jaime Batlle, el aventajado pintor que toda Barcelona conoce. Tenia encomendada este señor una visita para el ilustre guitarrista, junto con un recado que, segun los vivos deseos manifestados por el mismo Sors, le mandaba un sugeto de Barcelona. Difícilmente atinara el lector en que consistía el tal recado; y merece mentarse este incidente, porque hay a veces en la vida de un hombre esclarecido una circunstancia, al parecer insignificante, que es la piedra de toque para conocer su corazon. Mas ¿quién creeria que el de Sors fuese tan sencillo, que este artista eminente, despues de haber recorrido varias cortes de Europa, escitando la admiracion y los aplausos con su estraordinaria habilidad en la guitarra, y visto ensalzado y galardonado su talento como compositor, inaccesible á la vanidad; cándido como un niño, anhelase poseer una de aquellas procesiones de la Semana Santa, representadas en una larga lista de papel, con que se distraen los muchachos que van á la escuela?

Tal era, sin embargo, el objeto de sus deseos; y al recibir de manos del señor Batlle la arrollada tira de papel, estrechábala con infantil alborozo entre las suyas, y descogiéndola sobre una mesa, contemplaba con lagrimas en los ojos las figuras y diferentes objetos que en ella habia estampados.

Muchos se reirán quizas del antojo de Sors: no hay porque estrañarlo. ¿Qué son para ciertos hombres los recuerdos de la infancia, los juegos de la niñez, la memoria de aquellos juveniles años, con harta rapidez trascurridos, en que todo es inocencia, candor, alegria? Sors, empero, no se parecia á aquellos? Sencillo por naturaleza, abstraido de la sociedad, viviendo con su genio en un mundo ideal, estraño á los negocios y ambiciones humanas que agostan y secan tempranamente el corazon, cuando no le corrompen y pervierten, conservaba inalterables y puros los primeros sentimientos que brotaron en su alma. ¿Qué mucho, pues, que volviendo los ojos hácia los venturosos tiempos de la infancia, los echase menos, y deseease tener en sus manos, antes de morir, uno de los juguetes predilectos que mas al vivo debian recordarle aquellos inocentes años, plácidamente pasados bajo el querido y nunca olvidado cielo de la patria?

El malogrado Sors, cuando le hicimos la visita, bien que no de muy avanzada edad, estaba ya acometido de la enfermedad funesta que debia conducirle á la huesa. Le encontramos, sin embargo, levantado, y conservaba todavia su semblante la dulzura y nobleza que eran los caractéres distintivos de su fisonomia; pero ulcerados interiormente su pecho y garganta, apenas podia hablar. Despues de un breve rato de conversacion, muy molesta y penosa para el, pues con suma dificultad acertaba á articular las palabras, manifestónos lo mucho que sentia el que hubiésemos ido á verle aquel dia, en que no era dueño de reprimir ni contener la amarga pena de que estaba penetrado; y al instante sus ojos se llenaron de lagrimas. Con efecto, aquel mismo dia (1) cumplia un año que la muerte le habia arrebatado á su idolatrada y única hija.

Llamábase esta Julia, y tenia veinte y dos años. Jóven hermosa, dotada de clarísimo entendimiento y de las mas sobresalientes disposiciones para las bellas artes, de índole apacible y afectuosa, y con un corazon, dechado de filial cariño, era la alegria y el orgullo de su padre, quien veia en ella un consuelo y un apoyo para su vejez. ¡Halagüeños cálculos y esperanzas que rustró la implacable muerte!

Privado ya de su esposa algunos años hacia, no halló Sors consuelo con la pérdida de su adorada hija; y no cabe duda que el dolor profundo que le causó aquel acontecimiento abrevió el curso de sus dias. Estábanos refiriendo esas tristes circunstancias, cuando una señora anciana que le servia le trajo una sopa, único ligero alimento con que sustentaba su cuerpo: en vano le instó para que la comiese: tomó solo dos ó tres cucharadas, y levantándose del sillon en que estaba sentado, nos acompañó á una ventana abierta que daba á unos jardines. Sostenia el antepecho de la misma una tabla cuadrada que salia fuera, sobre la cual habia un jardinito. Varias blancas y primorosas macetas, de tamaño pequeñísimo, con flores algunas y otras con hojas de ciprés, simétricamente ordenadas, rodeaban un cenotafio de mármol blanco, tambien pequeñito, de esquisita y delicada labor, el cual se elevaba en el centro. Aquel jardin, en que se veian otros fúnebres símbolos de muerte, figuraba el cementerio, donde reposaban los restos de su hija. El lo cuidaba; él lo regaba, y sin duda las lágrimas lo inundaban con mas frecuencia que el agua que caia del cielo. Encerrado en su aposento, el tierno y desventurado padre, lejos de querer mitigar el dolor, dábale constantemente pabulo. Cuantos objetos en torno tenia, recordábanle sin cesar la imágen de su querida Julia. Encima del piano, veiase colgado su magnífico retrato: la pared de enfrente estaba cubierta de cuadros al óleo y á la aguada, pintados de su mano: el arpa ocupaba el mismo sitio en que ella la tenia; y al enseñárnosla el padre, parábase silencioso ante el abandonado instrumento, cual si debiesen pulsarlo todavía las diestras y delicadas manos que en otro tiempo sacaban de sus cuerdas suaves y dulcísimas melodias. Por ultimo Sors, á cada momento mas acongojado, abriendo un armario, tomó dos ó tres cuadernos de música manuscrita, y sentándose al piano, dijo que iba á tocarnos algunos trozos de la misa que compuso para los funerales de su hija.

Jamás se borrara de nuestras memorias aquella escena patética que profundamente conmovidos, presenciabamos sintiendo las lagrimas correr a cada momento por nuestras megillas. Vestido Sors con una holgada bata, descubierta la cabeza, levantando al cielo su ancha y noble frente, con la vista fija en el retrato, difundida por su rostro la aflicion mas intensa y puestas las manos en el teclado, evocando en lugubres armonias la memoria de su hija, parecia asumir en sí solo

---

[16] Only the arrangement of the columns on the page has here been changed.

---

(1) No recordamos la fecha, solo sabemos que era del 15 al 25 de junio

el dolor de todos los corazones, que lloran sobre un sepulcro el perdido objeto de amor. Eran sus ojos dos raudales de lágrimas que no hacía ningún esfuerzo por contener. De cuando en cuando asomaba a sus labios una como ligera sonrisa, cual si viese á su hija que desde el cielo abría los brazos para recibirle. Así debe ser la sonrisa del mártir que manifiesta tranquilidad y gozo al momento de morir. Desde el principio de la visita, habíase ido acercando hacia la ciudad una ceñuda borrasca, que al sentarse Sors al piano, estalló impetuosa arrollando en la oscuridad las calles de la vasta capital. Lóbrega apareció la estancia en que estábamos. El granizo y la lluvia azotaban el cementerio simulado de la ventana. El ruido de los truenos se mezclaba con los sonidos del piano. En lo mas recio de la tempestad, un rayo con espantoso estampido cayó cerca de nuestra habitación: por un movimiento involuntario corrimos los tres circunstantes á la ventana (había con nosotros otro caballero) creyendo ver desplomarse algún edificio contiguo: Sors, inmóvil, ni siquiera volvió la cabeza, y prosiguió bañado en llanto su triste y magnífica composición. ¡Como no había de ser grande artista aquel hombre con un corazon semejante! ¡Admirable cuanto infortunado padre, mártir del mas sublime dolor!

Por fin, viendo á Sors rendido por la pena, y temiendo que nuestra presencia contribuyese aun á acrecentarla, nos despedimos de él. Estrechónos la mano con efusion y con muestras del mas vivo sentimiento como el infeliz que, condenado á muerte, abraza á sus amigos por la ultima vez. Cinco ó seis dias despues, yacia postrado en el lecho sin levantarse; y habiendo querido hacerle otra visita, debimos volvernos sin tener el consuelo de verle. Eran sus postreros momentos. A primeros de julio, habia ya ido a reunirse con su hija.

En la *Revista musical* arriba mencionada léese que Sors murió *en un estado poco menos que miserable y careciendo de lo mas indispensable*. No sabemos nosotros cual era su posicion pecuniaria al fallecer; pero si podemos decir, para satisfaccion de sus amigos y admiradores, que el aposento, que ocupaba en un tercer piso estaba muy cómodamente y hasta con cierto esmero amueblado, y que nada revelaba en él la mansion de un hombre en estado de penuria ó indigencia; ya debiese las comodidades que disfrutaba á manos de amigos y protectores caritativos; ya le permitiesen procurárselas sus propios recursos. Pero sea de ello lo que fuese, es lo cierto que aquel hombre eminente acabó sus dias, como otros artistas, paisanos suyos, en el estranjero. ¿Qué prueba esta circunstancia? Que nacieron en un pais ingrato que no premia el mérito de los artistas. España les dá el ser: otro suelo desarrolla su jenio, y lo estimula y recompensa. En estrañas naciones, los aplausos, la consideracion, los lauros: en España el desden la frialdad, el olvido. Hablen sino los artistas españoles que, en vano hacen laudables esfuerzos por dar á conocer los frutos de su ingenio, y alcanzar el renombre y la estima de que son dignos, hablen los jóvenes compositores que en esos últimos cuatro años han dado sus obras á los teatros de Barcelona, de Barcelona, la segunda Capital de España, y que con tanto engreimiento se arroga titulos que pueden disputarsele. ¿Quién pronúncia los nombres de Dominguez, de Cappa? ¿Qué estimulo han encontrado estos dos distinguidos compositores entre los que debian alentarlos? ¿Qué galardon recibieron los partos de su talento? ¡Artistas españoles, que sentis en vuestras mentes la llama del genio, si llevados de un noble amor á la gloria, aspirais á conquistar las palmas y coronas á que sois acreedores, pasad las fronteras de vuestra patria; las recompensas que esta os destina, son la indiferencia, el desaliento y quizá la miseria.

Barcelona, enero de 1850.

Eusebio Font y Moresco

('The "Revista Musical" in *España* for 27 December of last year, signed by Eduardo Valaz de Madrano, published a short but interesting biographical notice about the famous Spanish guitarists, Sor and Aguado. The author of this "Revista," doubtless ill-informed about exact dates, has made an error in saying that Sor died twenty years ago. Only ten and a half years have passed since his death, as the following anecdote irrefutably shows. This eye-witness desires, in telling it with all its details, to bring to light at the same time an interesting period in Sor's life, which shows that if that artist was worthy of admiration for his great skill and genius, he was no less so for the exquisite nature of his sensitive and tender heart.

In June 1839, he who writes these lines was in Paris in the company of his friend Sr Jaime Battle, the excellent painter whom all Barcelona knows. This gentleman had been asked to pay a visit to the famous guitarist and to give him a present which, following Sor's own fervent wishes, a resident of Barcelona was sending him. The reader will scarcely guess what this present consisted of; and this incident is worth mentioning, because sometimes in the life of an eminent man there is some circumstance, at first sight insignificant, which is in fact the touchstone to know his heart. But who would have believed that Sor's heart was so simple, that this eminent artist, after having travelled to various courts of Europe, exciting admiration and applause with his extraordinary ability on the guitar, and having seen his talent as a composer exalted and rewarded, inaccessible to vanity, and candid as a child, should long to possess one of those Holy Week processions, depicted in a long strip of paper, with which children play on their way to school?

Nevertheless that was his wish, and on receiving from Sr Battle's hands the rolled-up strip of paper, he took hold of it with childlike joy between his own hands, and stretched it out on a table, contemplating with tears in his eyes the figures and different objects which were printed on it.

Many will perhaps laugh at Sor's fancy; but there is no reason to be astonished. For certain men, what value do certain memories of infancy have, the toys of childhood, the memory of those years of youth, too rapidly passed, in which all was innocence, candour, joy? Was not Sor, then, like them? Naturally simple, apart from society, living with his genius in a world of ideals, a stranger to the business and human ambitions which prematurely parch and dry up the heart if indeed they do not corrupt and pervert it, he kept unaltered and pure the first feelings which sprang forth in his soul. What wonder, then, that turning his eyes to the happy times of his childhood, he should miss them, and should desire to hold in his hands, before dying, one of the favourite toys which would most vividly recall to him those innocent years, quietly spent under the beloved and never forgotten skies of his own country?

The unfortunate Sor, when we visited him, although not very old, was already attacked by the deadly illness which was to take him to the grave. Nevertheless we found him up, and he still had the sweetness and nobility which were the distinctive characteristics of his face; but his chest and throat had ulcers internally, and he could hardly speak. After a brief conversation, very uncomfortable and painful for him, since it was with great difficulty that he could articulate words, he told us how sorry he was that we had called to see him on that particular day, in which he was unable to restrain or contain the bitter pain which penetrated him; and immediately his eyes filled with tears. Indeed, on that day one year had passed since death took from him his adored and only daughter.

She was called Julia, and she was twenty-two years old. Beautiful and young, highly intelligent and with the most remarkable gifts for the fine arts, of a peaceful and affectionate disposition and with a heart which was a model of filial love, she was the joy and pride of her father, who saw in her a comfort and a support in his old age. What flattering thoughts and hopes, frustrated by implacable death!

His wife had died some years ago, and Sor was inconsolable at the loss of his beloved daughter; and there is no doubt that the profound sadness which it caused him shortened his own life. He was telling us these sad things, when an old woman who looked after him brought him some soup, the only light nourishment which sustained his body; in vain she insisted that he should eat it; he took only two or three spoonfuls, and getting up from the chair in which he had been sitting, he accompanied us to an open window which looked onto some gardens. The window-sill supported a rectangular board that extended outwards, on which there was a tiny garden. A number of exquisite white flower pots, of tiny proportions, some with flowers and some with cypress leaves, symmetrically arranged, surrounded a cenotaph of white marble, also tiny, and exquisitely and delicately worked, which stood in the centre. This garden, in which were also other symbols of death, represented the cemetery where his daughter lay. He looked after it, watered it, and doubtless his tears fell on it more frequently than did the rain. Confined to his apartment, the tender and unhappy father, far from wishing to mitigate his grief, constantly encouraged it. All the objects that surrounded him, incessantly reminded him of his beloved Julia. Above the piano was fixed a magnificent portrait of her; the wall opposite was covered with oil-paintings and watercolours done by her; the harp was in the same position where she had kept it; and when the father showed it to us, he stood silently before the abandoned instrument, as though once more the skilful and delicate hands should touch it which in other times had drawn from its strings soft and sweet melodies. Finally Sor, at every moment more grief-stricken, opened a cupboard, took out two or three volumes of manuscript music, and sitting at the piano said that he would play us some parts of the mass which he had composed for the funeral of his daughter.

Never shall I forget the pathetic scene which we witnessed, deeply moved and feeling the tears flowing at every moment down our cheeks. Sor, wearing a wide robe, his head uncovered, raising to heaven his wide and noble brow, his gaze fixed on the portrait, his face full of the most intense grief, his hands on the keyboard, seemed to take up into himself alone the pain of every heart that laments, at a tomb, the lost object of its love. His eyes were two torrents of tears which he made no effort to control. From time to time there appeared on his lips as it were a light smile, as though he saw his daughter open her arms from heaven to receive him. Such must be the smile of the martyr who shows tranquillity and joy at the moment of death. Since the beginning of the visit, a menacing storm had been approaching the city, and burst impetuously when Sor sat down at the piano, sweeping in the darkness through the streets of the vast capital. The room which we were in became dark and gloomy. Hail and rain lashed at the simulated cemetery in the window. The noise of thunder mixed with the sounds of the piano. At the most severe part of the tempest, a flash of lightning fell with a terrifying crash somewhere near the room; we all three rushed involuntarily to the window (a third gentleman was with us) thinking that we would see some neighbouring building collapse; but Sor, unmoving, did not even turn his head, and continued, bathed in tears, his sad and magnificent composition. How could a man with such a heart not be a great artist! How admirable was such an unhappy father, the martyr of the most sublime sadness!

Eventually, seeing that Sor was tired out by his suffering, and fearing that our presence might contribute to increase it, we took our leave of him. He shook our hands fervently, showing the most lively emotion, like an unfortunate condemned man who embraces his friends for the last time. Five or six days later he lay in bed without rising; and having wished to pay him another visit, we were obliged to return without having had the good fortune to see him. These were his last moments. In early July, he had already gone to be united with his daughter.

In the "Revista Musical" mentioned above it is stated that Sor died "in a state little removed from penury, and lacking in the most indispensable necessities." I do not know what his financial position was at his death, but I am able to state, for the satisfaction of his friends and admirers, that the third-floor apartment which he occupied was very comfortably furnished, even with a certain fastidiousness, and that nothing in it gave the appearance of the home of a man in a state of penury or indigence, whether he owed his comforts to charitable friends or protectors, or whether he was able to procure them by his own resources. However that may be, what is certain is that this eminent man ended his days, like other artists and his compatriots, in a foreign land. What does this show? It shows that they were born in an ungrateful country that does not reward the merits of its artists. Spain gives them birth; another land develops their genius, stimulates it, and rewards it. In foreign countries, applause, respect, laurels; in Spain, disdain, indifference, oblivion. Even if not those Spanish artists who have vainly made praiseworthy efforts to make known the fruits of their genius and to obtain the fame and esteem that they deserve, at least let those young composers speak who in the last four years have given their works to the theatre of Barcelona, the second capital of Spain, which with such pomposity has taken to itself titles which could be disputed. Who speaks the names of Dominguez, of Cappa? What stimulus have these two distinguished composers found among those who should encourage them? What reward did the offspring of their talent find? Artists of Spain, who feel in your spirits the call of genius, if you are inspired by a noble love of glory and desire to conquer the laurels and crowns which you deserve, cross the frontiers of your country; for the rewards which your country destines for you are indifference, discouragement, and perhaps misery.')

The apartment in the Marché St. Honoré

Font y Moresco says that Sor's apartment was on the third floor, overlooking some gardens. He describes a decent apartment with a piano, a harp, a window, a window-box that Sor tended, walls covered with his daughter's paintings, and he mentions that an old woman was looking after Sor. This is far from the widely disseminated story that Sor died in great poverty. Even in 1850 this story was current, and Font y Moresco specifically denies it, saying that nothing in the apartment gave the appearance of the home of someone in a state of poverty or indigence. The story was disseminated by Fétis, who wrote: 'après avoir langui pendant onze ans dans une situation voisine de la misère, malgré l'estime qu'on avait pour son talent, il mourut' (*Biographie Universelle des Musiciens,* 2nd edn., vol. 8, Paris, 1865, p. 66) ('after languishing for eleven years in a condition close to penury, despite the general esteem for his talent, he died'). Saldoni says, probably copying Fétis and elaborating on the theme: 'murió pobremente y sin haber dejado *ni un céntimo:* parece que todo se lo había gastado con las bailarinas, á las que profesaba entrañable cariño, y esto fue la causa que su muerte fuese horrible' (*Diccionario,* p. 265) ('he died in poverty and without leaving a single centime: it seems that he had spent it all on ballerinas, for whom he had a strong liking, and that was why his death was horrible'). But neither Fétis nor Saldoni is reliable. Even for simple facts, names and dates, they cannot be trusted and are often demonstrably wrong. We know from the letter to the Queen of France, to be sure, that Sor was in some financial difficulty at the end of his life. But the last and probably only ballerina had disappeared from his life thirteen years before, and his *Méthode pour la Guitare* and his two articles in Ledhuy's *Encyclopédie* reveal not the dissipated rake that Saldoni implies, but a man of sensitivity and regard for the truth. He seems to have spent his last years living quietly and respectably with his daughter in the Marché St. Honoré, composing, teaching and playing in concerts. The story of extreme poverty is disproved by the eye-witness Font y Moresco, and seems to be the invention of romantic biographers.

The Marché St. Honoré still exists. In Sor's day it was a pleasant square with gardens in the centre. Today, in place of those gardens, a towering concrete parking block has been erected, totally destroying the charm of the place. From plans in the Bibliothèque Historique de la Ville de Paris, it has been possible to establish that the house where Sor lived (nos. 34-36) stood on the east side, somewhere in the site now occupied by nos. 32-36. It is possible that some of the interior of the building may have survived from the 1830s, but it seems to me unlikely that the façade today bears much resemblance to the building as it must have appeared at that time.

Sor must have moved there in about late 1832, as we saw; it was from there that he wrote to the Queen of France in March 1839; and it was there that he died on 10 July 1839. Sometimes the address is given on the title-pages as Marché St. Honoré 34, sometimes 34 bis, and sometimes 36, and sometimes it appears as Marché des Jacobins, which is another name for the same square.

Illness and death

In the summer of 1838, that is one year after the death of his daughter, Sor fell ill. In March 1839, in his letter to the Queen of France, he says that he has been a victim of illness for eight months. The illness was in the throat; Font y Moresco who visited him in June 1839 wrote: 'ulcerados interiormente su pecho y garganta, apenas podia hablar' ('his chest and throat had ulcers internally, and he could hardly speak'). He was being looked after by an old woman, and fed only on soup. He was to live only a few more weeks, and he died on 10 July 1839.[17]

By his side when he died, according to Saldoni, were two Spanish gentlemen, Antonio de Gironella and José de Lira.[18] Gironella was a noted liberal politician and newspaper editor from Barcelona, living in exile in Paris (according to Alberti's *Diccionari Biogràfic,* Barcelona, 1968). Lira was a friend to whom Sor had dedicated his op. 56, *Souvenirs d'une Soirée à Berlin,* while Sor's op. 44 bis, *Six Valses* for two guitars, is dedicated to 'Mademoiselle Lira', who perhaps was his daughter. It was he who provided Sor's tomb. According to Saldoni, he took after the composer's death 'una riqueza en papeles inéditos para orquesta y para guitarra, como

---

[17] Paris, Archives de la Seine, register of deaths: 'Sor / Ferdinand / Professeur de musique / Marché St. honoré No 34 et 36 / [age] 60 / [date of death] 10 Juillet / [there follows a mark indicating that it was not known whether or not he was married or had children]'. Also in the Archives de la Seine is a copy (not the original) of the Acte de Décès. The date 10 July must be regarded as the correct one, rather than 8 July which Fétis gave in his *Biographie Universelle des Musiciens,* 2nd edn., vol. 8, p. 66, or 13 July which is given by the *Gaceta Musical,* according to Saldoni, *Diccionario,* p. 266.

[18] Saldoni writes 'Liria', but the two dedications and the signatures mentioned below all read 'Lira'.

tambien sus guitarras' ('a wealth of unpublished papers for orchestra and for guitar, as well as his guitars'), and this may be so, for a number of copies of Sor's music still extant bear Lira's signature.

Antonio de Gironella was doubtless the 'A.G.' who signed an obituary article on Sor in the *Diario de Barcelona* for 5 September 1839. Most of this article, which is largely taken straight out of Ledhuy's *Encyclopédie,* has been published by Manuel Rocamora in his *Fernando Sor,* pp. 91-101. It contains some verse. It describes how the author was at Sor's side when he died — 'Yo le hallé que moría' — and mentions that his Mass excited the greatest admiration.[19]

On 12 July 1839, a mass was said over Sor's body at the Eglise Saint-Roch, as it had been for his daughter. An invitation to the service, in the names of José de Lira and the composer's brother Carlos, survives in the collection of José Subirá, Madrid, and reads as follows:[20]

> Vous êtes prié d'assister aux Convoi, Service et Enterrement de Mr. Ferdinand Sor décédé hier 10 Juillet . . . qui se feront demain 12 . . . à 8 heures du matin en l'Eglise St. Roch. DE PROFUNDIS. De la part de Mr Ch. Sor & J. de Lira, frère & ami du défunt. On se réunira à 8 heures Marché St. Honore 36.[20]

> ('You are invited to be present at the funeral procession, service and burial of Mr Ferdinand Sor who died yesterday, 10 July . . . which will take place tomorrow, 12 July . . . at 8 a.m. in the church of St. Roch. DE PROFUNDIS. From Mr Ch. Sor and J. de Lira, brother and friend of the deceased. Meet at 8 a.m. at 36 Marché St. Honoré.')

The record of the service is preserved in the register of funeral masses of the Eglise Saint-Roch, Paris, for 12 July 1839.[21]

The tomb

Like his daughter, Sor was buried in the Cimetière Montmartre.[22] The records of the cemetery show that the burial took place on 12 July 1839, and that the tomb was provided by José de Lira. By the 1930s the tomb had almost disappeared when it was rediscovered by André Verdier (President of the society 'Les amis de la guitare'), the Danish guitarist Ostergaard, and Emilio Pujol.[23] The gravestone bore the simple inscription 'F SOR'. In 1936 a ceremony was held at the tomb to commemorate the centenary of Sor's death. The clouds that were gathering over France, Spain and the rest of Europe rightly suggested that it would be well to hold the ceremony while it was still possible rather than waiting for the true centenary in 1939. A speech was pronounced by Maestro Emilio Pujol. The gravestone was restored and renewed, and a plaque was added reading

Au génial guitariste-compositeur

FERNANDO SOR

Les amis de la guitare de Paris

---

[19] Saldoni also related an anecdote about Sor's last hours, but there is no knowing how much credence to give it:

> El día antes de morir Sors, se hallaban á su lado el espresado Sr. Liria [sic] y el Sr. D. Antonio de Gironella, á quienes pidió por señas papel y tintero, pues no podía hablar por el cáncer que tenía en la lengua, y que fue la causa de su muerte. Sors estuvo escribiendo unas dos horas, sin duda una cosa muy interesante; pero el resultado fue que, después de muerto, no pudieron entender *ni una sola palabra* de lo que el día antes de su fallecimiento había escrito, no obstante de tener una letra magnífica, cosa que sintieron muchísimo los espresados señnores.

> (*Diccionario,* p. 265)

> ('The day before Sor died, there were at his side the said Sr. Lira and Sr. D. Antonio de Gironella, whom he asked by signs for paper, pen and ink, for he could not speak because of the cancer in his tongue, which was to cause his death. Sor wrote for about two hours, doubtless something most interesting; but when he was dead, they were unable to read a single word of what he had written the day before, although his handwriting had been magnificent; and the said gentlemen regretted this very much.')

---

[20] The invitation was reprinted in facsimile in Subirá's *Historia de la Música,* 3rd edn. (Barcelona, Salvat, 1958), vol. 4, p. 1414.

---

[21] The entry in the register reads: 'A 9 heures le 12 A été présenté le Corps de Mr. Ferdinand Sore professeur de musique, décédé le 10, Marché St. Honoré N 34 et 36 agé de 60 ans, non muni des sacremens. On a dit la messe à laquelle ont assisté Mmrs Jean Maria Maury Pleville, rue St. Georges 18 et Joseph de Lira rue de Londres No. 3 et ont signé [signed:] J.M. Maury Pleville J de Lira'.

---

[22] According to 'A.G.' in the obituary in the *Diario de Barcelona,* he was buried as close as possible to his countryman the dramatist Moratín, but this must be interpreted as poetic licence, for Moratín was buried in a different Paris cemetery, that of Père-Lachaise.

---

[23] For differing accounts of the rediscovery, see M. Rocamora, *Fernando Sor* (Barcelona, 1957), pp. 106-11, and Juan Riera, *Emilio Pujol* (Lérida, 1974), pp. 46-48.

116

Contributions for the restoration and for the conces-
sion of the tomb in perpetuity were received from as far
away as Japan and Argentina.[24] Today the tomb is in
poor order but receives many visitors.[25]

Here follows the whole of the article 'Sor' from the
Encyclopédie Pittoresque de la Musique of A. Ledhuy
and H. Bertini (Paris, 1835).

[24] An account of the ceremony is in the *Boletín de la Asociación
Guitarrística Argentina,* Buenos Aires, June 1939 (a copy of this now
rare periodical is in the Appleby Collection of the Guildhall School of
Music, London). The *Boletín* prints the text of Maestro Pujol's
speech, and announces an 'acto conmemorativo' at the tomb on 2 July
1939. It has been said that a second ceremony was held at the tomb on
another day in 1936, attended by those Spaniards and others who held
different political views from those who attended the first ceremony.

[25] When I visited the tomb in October 1974, the plaque affixed in
1936 was missing. In February 1975 I was informed by the cemetery
authorities that the tomb was in such poor order that it might soon be
demolished unless it was restored. Accordingly, with official permission, I carried out certain temporary restoration work myself, including the removal of moss and rust and the repainting of the grille. It
would be desirable to carry out more thorough restoration, including
the repair of a crack in the side of the gravestone.

SOR.

Ferdinand Sor naquit à Barcelonne le 17 février 1780. La position sociale de ses parens n'annonçait pas qu'il dût un jour faire une profession de la musique, car il était destiné à l'état militaire ou à suivre la carrière administrative.

Son père ne se souciait nullement de cultiver les heureuses dispositions de son fils pour la musique. Néanmoins, à l'âge de cinq ans, il chantait déjà tout ce qu'il entendait à l'Opéra-Italien, et il imitait le style et les gestes du chanteur. Il laissait volontiers ses études élémentaires pour se livrer exclusivement à la musique ; son joujou était un violon sur lequel il essayait les airs qu'il chantait ; ou bien, debout devant le sopha où se trouvait la guitare de son père, il cherchait des accords à trois parties pour faire des accompagnemens. D'abord la guitare restait étendue sur la table de fond, et il plaçait ses deux mains sur le manche comme si c'eût été le clavier d'un piano ; par conséquent tout le doigté de la main gauche était en sens contraire. Par suite il adopta le moyen de s'asseoir à l'extrémité gauche du sopha, en mettant le corps de la guitare à sa droite appuyé sur le siége ; le manche passait devant lui, et le cheviller soutenu par le bras du sopha lui évitait la peine de la maintenir à la hauteur convenable ; alors il posait naturellement sa main gauche à la première touche, et la droite à la douzième. Il lui en coûta pour retrouver les positions à rebours, mais enfin il parvint à jouer plusieurs accompagnemens que son père faisait pour les airs qu'il chantait.

Le père de Ferdinand Sor était né bon musicien sans être notiste, et parmi les amateurs il avait acquis de la réputation. Son ami, le chevalier de Sabatea, avec le même talent, joignait le mérite de composer la plupart des morceaux de musique que le premier chantait. Il remarqua les heureuses dispositions du jeune Sor, et fit un reproche à son père de ne pas chercher à les développer : « Il ne penserait plus qu'à la musique, répondit celui-ci, et la grammaire latine y perdrait son latin. » Il disait vrai, car son fils, par une curiosité fort naturelle, aimait déjà à se rendre compte de ce qu'il faisait, et il éprouvait du dégoût à étudier la langue latine par les règles versifiées en latin par Cœlius Antonius ; la musique se mêlait déjà à toutes ses idées, et nécessairément le reste ne vint qu'en seconde ligne. Pour vaincre les premières répugnances de son père, le jeune Sor imagina de composer des chants dont les paroles étaient prises dans la grammaire latine d'Antonius. Un exercice de cette nature lui mit les règles dans la tête, parce que la musique servait de point de rappel. Son père, satisfait, prit de l'intérêt à ses études musicales, et lui donna quelques conseils pour mieux tenir sa guitare, et l'enfant laissa le violon. Quand il eut composé un certain nombre d'airs, sa mémoire les confondait, parce qu'ils étaient tous dans l'étendue de la gamme diatonique. Sans avoir aucune notion de solfége, il voulut inventer un moyen qui pût lui en tenir lieu. Il écrivit une portée fort large contenant trois lignes ; celle du milieu était plus rapprochée de la supérieure ; la plus basse servait de tonique ; sur la plus haute il posait l'octave, et la ligne intermédiaire portait la quinte : quant aux autres notes de la gamme, elles se trouvaient sur différens degrés dans les intervalles de ses lignes. Il se servait de trois mesures, nombre pair, impair et 6/8 ; par suite il faisait des phrases chromatiques en indiquant par un signe la syllabe qui devait être haussée ou baissée ; par un trait au-dessous des notes il désignait celles qui commençaient chaque mesure. Lorsqu'il vit que, dans l'écriture musicale, on séparait les mesures par des barres, rien ne put égaler son chagrin de n'avoir point trouvé cette division si simple.

Il ne voulait point adopter les principes de la notation, en disant tout haut que la méthode ordinaire ne valait pas la sienne, qui était facile à concevoir en peu de jours. Cependant des observations fort sages lui firent comprendre ce qu'il y avait de défectueux dans son système : il voulut le corriger, et il réussit si bien qu'il obtint pour la première fois des éloges de son père sur son invention, qu'il qualifia d'*obra maestra del ingenio ;* et pour témoigner à son fils toute la joie qu'il ressentait, il le conduisit régulièrement à l'Opéra-Italien.

La mémoire de Ferdinand Sor se meubla non-seulement de fragmens d'airs, mais il retenait avec une égale facilité les morceaux d'ensemble les plus compliqués. Après avoir entendu une seule fois l'opéra de *Giulio Sabino,* il nota un trio, dont il apprit une partie à sa mère, l'autre à son père, et se réserva la troisième : il trouva sur la guitare un accompagnement qui était assez en rapport avec celui de l'orchestre. Ce trio fit parler de lui ; les professeurs voulurent le connaître, et ils lui prodiguèrent des éloges. Plus on était étonné de ce qu'il faisait, plus il s'étonnait lui-même qu'on lui trouvât du talent, et qu'on ne sentît pas la musique comme lui.

Le premier violon de la cathédrale remarqua le jeune Sor ; il fit pressentir à son père l'avenir qu'il y avait dans le talent naissant de son fils, et offrit de l'instruire. Le père refusa d'abord, mais bientôt, par les instances du musicien, il consentit. Ce premier maître suivait aveuglément un système qu'il ne pouvait pas même expliquer complètement ; l'élève disputa inutilement et le professeur soutint ses idées. Sor se plaignit à son père de ces essais infructueux, mais celui-ci se souciait fort peu de toutes ces altercations ; il traita le maître de visionnaire, et enjoignit à son fils de l'écouter jusqu'à ce qu'il trouvât un moyen honnête de le remercier sans l'offenser.

Cette occasion se présenta naturellement. Sor perdit son père. Il en résulta un changement dans la direction de son éducation. La veuve ne put continuer pour lui les dépenses que son mari avait commencées, et la carrière du jeune Sor se trouva manquée. Il était trop jeune pour entrer dans un bureau du gouvernement en qualité d'aspirant (*entretenido*), et sa mère se désolait à l'idée de le laisser plusieurs années sans occupation qui eût un but. Le père D. Josef Arredondo, bénédictin, venait d'être élu abbé de Montserrat ; il entendit parler du jeune Sor, et offrit à la veuve de prendre son fils avec lui jusqu'à l'âge où il pourrait entrer dans un bureau. La mère accepta avec reconnaissance, et elle se prépara à conduire Ferdinand au collége gratuit du monastère, dans lequel l'étude de la musique était la partie principale de l'instruction.

Quelques détails sur le célèbre couvent du Montserrat ne peuvent manquer d'intéresser nos lecteurs. Nous les empruntons textuellement aux Mémoires de Sor.

A son arrivée à Montserrat, Sor témoigna le désir d'aller à l'église, où l'on chantait les complies.

« A l'audition du premier verset du psaume *Cum invocarem,* je fus frappé d'étonnement. Cette composition sublime était du père Céréols. Le chantre entonna seul le plain-chant de ce premier verset ; l'orgue donna un seul accord parfait, les basses-tailles seules recommencèrent le plain-chant avec des intonations plus prolongées ; ce plain-chant entraîna en canon toutes les voix ; les basses-tailles, les dernières, introduisaient une phrase de repos à la moitié du verset ; à l'autre moitié, des contraltos continuaient le plain-chant, sur lequel une joute s'établit entre les trois autres parties du premier chœur, et les trois parties du second exprimaient avec un grand effet le passage *in tribulatione ;* le reste était chanté par les dessus, et des accords plaqués soutenaient l'harmonie. Outre le respect dont j'étais saisi, je fus un peu humilié de voir qu'excepté les basses-tailles, toute la musique était chantée par des enfans plus ou moins âgés que moi ; je voyais bien que c'était quelque chose de plus que des chœurs d'opéra italien, que l'on devine presque toujours. En sortant de l'église, je ne songeais qu'à toute cette harmonie religieuse si grandiose. Je pris une guitare, et chantant le plain-chant avec la voix, je cherchais à trouver, moi chétif, la manière de rendre le contrepoint de Céréols.... j'échouai.... »

« Le lendemain le père abbé nous conduisit dans la sacristie pour admirer toutes les richesses qu'elle contient. L'église, vue au grand jour, me frappa d'admiration : ce pavé en mosaïque, ces murs sans ornemens ni tableaux qui tranchent l'harmonie ni les proportions de l'édifice ; ce fond blanc, qui paraît brodé d'or avec les nuances du mat et du brillant, relevé par quelques contours noirs ; tout cet ensemble, qui rappelle la destination de l'édifice, produisit un effet que je n'oublierai jamais.

« Tandis que ma mère admirait les riches étoffes et les broderies renfermées dans les tiroirs du camarin de la Vierge, le père abbé voulut me présenter à mes compagnons d'études. Il me conduisit au collège, situé au deuxième étage, où nous trouvâmes une foule d'enfans qui s'empressaient à l'envi pour approcher de *sa Paternité*, qui leur donna sa bénédiction, et à moi particulièrement, ce dont je fus très fier. Le maître parut et s'inclina ; le père abbé lui donna aussi sa bénédiction : « Je vous présente, dit-il, un nouvel élève, que votre bonté pour tous rend inutile de vous recommander ; il a bon cœur et la tête d'un petit démon (*un diablillo*). — Eh bien ! répondit le père Viola, nous nous adresserons au cœur. » Il ordonna à tous les élèves de me donner l'accolade de réception, ce qui se fit de fort bonne grâce. Le reste de la journée je le passai à profiter de toutes les heures du service d'église dans lequel il y avait de la musique. Je me rappelle encore avec quelle attention délicate on m'habitua peu à peu à revoir et à quitter ma mère, afin de nous épargner les douleurs de l'adieu, si bien qu'elle partit sans que mon chagrin fût très vif.

« On nous réveilla à quatre heures, il faisait nuit, et nous nous rendîmes à l'église avant cinq heures. Je n'avais entendu, depuis mon arrivée, que des psaumes, et autres morceaux à quatre et à huit parties accompagnées par l'orgue ; la messe était accompagnée par un petit orchestre composé de violons, violoncelles, contre-basses, bassons, cors et hautbois, et tout cela exécuté par des enfans, dont le plus âgé pouvait avoir de quinze à seize ans. A l'offertoire on joua l'introduction et l'allegro d'une des symphonies d'Haydn en *ré* ; à la communion ce fut l'andante et au dernier évangile l'allegro. Après la messe, nous passâmes quel-

que temps en récréation, puis ensuite nous nous dirigeâmes vers une chambre garnie de clavichordes. Une toile cirée en couvrait trois, et cette toile était couverte par vingt-huit petits pains ronds et plats coupés en deux, formant assiettes, sur lesquelles étaient vingt-huit petites omelettes au jambon d'égale grandeur. Bientôt après, la répétition d'orchestre commença. Les pupitres furent placés et les parties furent distribuées. L'époque de Noël est toute musicale dans le monastère du Montserrat. La solennité des matines est fort remarquable : chaque responsorio est d'une composition fort belle, et accompagnée par un orchestre et des instrumens obligés. A la fin de chaque nocturne on chanta des espèces de cantates en espagnol, dont le sujet est quelques scènes parmi les bergers qui vont à Bethléem adorer le nouveau-né. Ces sortes de composition sont appelées *villancicos*. Parmi les personnages que le poëte y introduit, il s'en trouve de rigueur un chargé du rôle comique. La musique, un peu plus correcte et plus scientifique que celle des opéras italiens, est cependant à peu près dans le genre de ceux appelés *di mezzo carattere*. On fait plusieurs répétitions d'avance, non-seulement pour s'assurer de l'exécution des parties d'ensemble, mais encore pour empêcher les élèves de concevoir cette vanité anti-musicale de jouer à livre ouvert. Le père Viola disait : « Quand on joue à première vue, on épelle plus ou moins vite ; mais si l'on veut donner le véritable sens à ce que l'on chante, il faut en avoir l'idée d'avance. »

« On commença la répétition par un responsorio du père Marti, dont le style sévère n'avait point exclu des mélodies neuves qui faisaient tressaillir : pour moi, je ne pouvais maîtriser mon émotion, et je la témoignai avec tant d'enthousiasme, que le père Viola me dit, en laissant échapper une larme : « Le père Marti fut mon seul maître, et ce fut ici, dans cette chambre, qu'il me reçut au nombre de ses écoliers comme je vous reçois aujourd'hui. » J'étais fier de ce rapprochement, et mon cœur se gonfla ; mais la musique du *Villancico* donna une autre direction à mes idées. Après l'exécution, je m'aperçus enfin que ma mère m'avait quitté ; mais une vie si nouvelle fit diversion à mes chagrins. La cloche sonna pour aller au réfectoire : n'ayant pas encore le costume requis ni les cheveux coupés, je ne pouvais faire partie de la colonne que les enfans formaient pour s'y transporter, je marchais derrière à côté du père Viola ; au réfectoire il me fit placer entre les deux plus anciens écoliers. En voyant les rations qu'on nous servait, je ne pouvais concevoir la possibilité de manger si copieusement. Le père Viola dînait seul à sa table, d'où il présidait le réfectoire. Après le dîner nous rentrâmes au collége, et immédiatement tous les écoliers endossèrent leurs surplis et descendirent à l'église, pour y réciter les vêpres et les complies du petit office. Je restai avec le père Viola, qui me questionna sur ma santé, mon instruction. Je lui avouai ma répugnance pour la langue latine (je voulais dire la méthode qu'on avait adoptée pour moi) : « Vous ne pourrez donc pas chanter le latin, car ignorant ce que vous diriez, vous vous exprimeriez mal ? — J'observerai la ponctuation, et je chanterai au moins aussi bien que les solistes que j'ai entendus ce matin. » Le père Viola sourit : « Vous ne savez pas que la plupart de ces enfans sont nés de parens pauvres, habitant les villages et la campagne, et comme il faut tout leur apprendre, ils ne peuvent arriver aussi vite à la perfection. Ainsi votre critique n'est pas absolument très juste. »

« L'heure de la récréation s'était écoulée, chacun fut prendre son instrument pour étudier. C'était un véritable charivari ; comme dans les conservatoires d'Italie, tous exécutaient en même temps. Cependant le père Viola me conduisit dans une maison où se trouva Isidore Capdevila, le sacristain, chargé de l'habillement. On me fit essayer une foule de vêtemens, jusqu'à ce que j'en trouvasse un à ma taille. On me coupa les cheveux, et je fus couvert de l'uniforme, qui consistait en une calotte courte de peau noire appelée *gamouza*, de bas violets, souliers montans à pates fermées par un bouton de cuivre, une petite veste à manches en drap noir, une chemise de toile, tout cela recouvert par une longue soutane de serge noire très large, ouverte par-devant jusqu'à la ceinture : elle était ornée d'un collet en soie bleue montant jusqu'au tiers du cou ; les manches, très larges, ont des coudes profonds servant de poches, l'un pour le mouchoir, l'autre pour le livre de l'office de la Vierge ; une courroie noire armée d'une boucle jaune nous servait de ceinture. Quand je fus ainsi équipé, je revins parmi mes camarades, qui me reçurent avec une grande démonstration de joie. Ils reprirent ensuite leurs études, et je m'assis dans la chambre du maître, où je dirigeai toute mon attention sur sa manière d'enseigner la musique.

« Il se mit à accompagner un solfége très difficile, dont la nomenclature m'étonna, parce que plusieurs intonations de la gamme étaient nommées d'une manière différente en montant qu'en descendant. Le père Viola adressa ensuite plusieurs questions théoriques que je ne compris pas davantage. Mon ignorance me faisait penser alors à cet égard comme les élèves de plus d'un conservatoire, tout en recevant un prix de solfége. Mais aussitôt la leçon terminée, je demandai à un écolier comment il nommait la gamme ? « *Ut, ré, mi, fa, sol, ré, mi, fa.* — Si elle continue ? —*Fa, ré, mi, fa, sol, ré, mi, fa.* — Et pour redescendre ? — *Fa, mi, la, sol, fa, la, sol, fa, mi, la, sol, fa, mi, ré, ut.* — Je ne pourrai jamais apprendre cela, lui dis-je. — Fais comme moi : je me suis fait chanter mes leçons par un de mes camarades, puis demandant le nom des notes à un autre, je les écrivais à part ; dès que je savais la musique par cœur, je ne les regardais plus, et au bout de sept ou huit leçons, je négligeai ce procédé. Il est vrai de dire que je n'avais rien appris quand j'arrivai ici, sans cela j'aurais été aussi embarrassé qu'un de nos camarades, qui, ayant eu l'habitude de solfier par *do, ré, mi, fa, sol, la, si, do,* ne sait que faire de son *si,* parce qu'il ne sait où le caser. Cette observation me découragea davantage, car dans les principes de musique que m'avait enseignés le violoniste de la cathédrale de Barcelonne, on employait un *si* et des noms fixes.

« Après la leçon tous les écoliers descendirent à l'église ; j'avais aussi revêtu le surplis garni de dentelles, et fermé par-dessus le collet bleu par deux cordons pareils ornés de glands. Nous entrâmes dans l'église, marchant sur deux files, qui se séparèrent, l'une à gauche et l'autre à droite, pour se retrouver devant le maître-autel.

« Ce que l'on admire le plus dans le plain-chant exécuté au Montserrat, c'est l'élégance de la mélodie et la clarté des transitions. Les PP. bénédictins du couvent n'ont pas la manie de faire crier la musique. Les voix n'ont pas cette qualité rude que l'ignorance et le mauvais goût appellent vibration. Leur plain-chant serait, à mon avis, la base d'une véritable méthode, car la prosodie est la règle qui les guide pour enseigner à augmenter ou à diminuer la liberté de l'air, pour prendre haleine, et pour savoir si telle intonation doit être produite par position ou par réponse.

« Je ne puis passer sous silence le goût délicieux avec lequel Casanova accompagnait à l'orgue. La basse qu'il employait n'était pas le plain-chant lui-même, mais une excellente basse mise sous les chants.

« Après les complies, on chanta une espèce de composition que l'on appelle *gozos* (joies) ; je ne sais pourquoi, car il y en a qui parlent des souffrances des saints auxquels ils sont adressés. Les *gozos* que les élèves chantent tous les soirs, à Montserrat, sont en l'honneur de la Vierge. Ils se composent d'une introduction à solo ou à deux voix, qui mène à un point d'orgue à la dominante ; le mouvement devient un peu plus animé, et la voix, ou les voix, établissent un sujet de refrain qui, après avoir été dit par le soliste en entier, est répété par toutes les voix en chœur. On chanta ensuite plusieurs stances de huit vers : les deux derniers sont toujours le refrain : les paroles des *gozos* sont en espagnol.

« Nous exécutâmes ensuite un cantique du père Viola : c'était une de ces compositions qu'on appelle *alla breve*, dans lesquelles aucune parole n'est répétée deux fois, et où chaque intonation ne porte qu'une syllabe, rarement deux : c'était une suite continue de solo et de tutti. D'abord l'ouvrage ne me fit point le plaisir que j'attendais ; mais le *salve* en duo avec des chœurs produisit sur moi le plus grand effet. Les deux parties principales chantaient tantôt ensemble, tantôt alternativement, et les chœurs étaient placés de manière à persuader parfois que l'on exécutait un sextuor. La plupart de ceux qui se prétendent connaisseurs en musique trouveront absurde ce que je viens de dire, car ils appellent *trio* tout ce qui est à trois voix, *quatuor* ce qui est à quatre, etc. Ils ne font point de différence entre un quatuor et un nocturne à quatre, etc. On ne trouvait pas dans la composition du père Viola de ces contre-sens sur les paroles qu'on voit fourmiller dans les œuvres de tant d'autres musiciens.

« Le lendemain nous descendîmes à l'église de grand matin. Cette église est divisée aux deux tiers de sa longueur par une grille en bronze partant du pavé jusqu'au haut de la voûte ; elle occupe toute la largeur de l'édifice ; dans le centre elle s'ouvre à deux battans, mais seulement le jour de procession. L'espace compris entre cette grille et les marches du presbytère est appelé le chœur inférieur ; on y trouve des stalles en bois d'acajou massif, dont les sculptures sont très curieuses. La seule différence qui existe entre le chœur inférieur et le chœur supérieur, c'est que dans celui-ci il y a un double rang de stalles et que le lutrin est fixe ; dans l'autre le lutrin est mobile. Les religieux n'officient dans le chœur inférieur qu'aux jours de grandes solennités. C'est là où l'on nous plaça pour chanter la messe, qui, à mon grand désappointement, n'était point accompagnée par l'orchestre. Le père Capdevila monta à l'autel, et mes collègues commencèrent l'*introït* : je n'osai pas mêler ma voix à la leur, ne sachant pas lire la musique, mais je suivais la notation, et j'étais étonné de voir ajouter et ôter des dièzes, fort à propos pour mon oreille, dans un endroit où je ne voyais aucun signe à côté des notes. J'en fis l'observation à mon voisin : « Les dièzes et les bémols, me dit-il, ne sont point ce que tu penses : dans le plainchant ils sont indiqués par la marche de la mélodie et la nature des intonations. » En voyant les notes du plainchant sans queues, et seulement de deux formes, j'avais

cru qu'il ne présentait pas plus de difficulté que la notation que j'avais inventée ; je fus détrompé. Après l'*introït*, on tourna le lutrin, qui présenta un livre dont les pages étoient divisées en deux moitiés, contenant chacune deux parties ; celles du soprano et du ténor étaient d'un côté, celles du contralto et de la basse de l'autre ; des bassons jouaient toujours la basse. On commença le *kyrie*. Je ne tardai pas à goûter ce genre de musique, dont je n'avais pas encore eu l'idée. Il y a à Montserrat une collection de messes dans ce genre, qu'il conviendrait à plus d'un compositeur de nos jours d'étudier. La science s'y montre sans ostentation, et on emploie ses ressources pour produire des effets merveilleux. On croirait qu'un canon à quatre parties, dont deux à l'unisson et deux à la quinte, ne peut offrir à l'oreille que le résultat d'un tour de force, et le mérite de la difficulté vaincue. Si l'on entendait *et incarnatus est* du *Credo* en *ré* mineur (premier mode grégorien), on serait saisi de respect, et l'on comprendrait l'admiration que causait la composition du père Cererols. Il faudrait, à la vérité, l'entendre comme on l'exécutait à Montserrat, à quatre parties seules, le basson soliste jouant la basse sans effort et d'une manière tout-à-fait chantante, dans un mouvement modéré tel que l'auteur l'indiquait ; car les élèves du père Viola n'ont jamais compris qu'on eût la prétention d'être bon musicien quand on croyait faire preuve de talent en pressant ou en altérant les mouvemens. Aussi aucun allegro et surtout aucun menuet de symphonie n'a jamais été défiguré par eux ; ils ne connaissent point l'éloge renfermé dans cette phrase : *ce morceau a été enlevé.*

« Durant les répétitions, avant la fête de Noël, j'appris par cœur toutes les parties d'un responsorio du père Viola ; je l'avais si bien retenu, que ce religieux me proposa de chanter la première partie. Fier de chanter avec accompagnement d'orchestre, je me proposai pour méthode l'actrice du théâtre italien dont la méthode m'avait plu davantage, et je commençai. Tant que je chantais des solos, tout allait à merveille, mais dans l'ensemble et les phrases à trois parties, j'arrangeai la mienne, j'en doublai une autre, le plus souvent la basse ; mais je laissai toujours un vide. Cependant le père Viola applaudit à mon coup d'essai.

« Le père abbé étant entré dans le moment.... avec le gouverneur et d'autres dignitaires, je m'aperçus qu'ils venaient pour entendre chanter le nouveau venu, ce qui me rendit très fier. Il paraît que je m'en acquittai fort bien, car le père Viola me fit des éloges qui paraissaient autre chose que des encouragemens.

« Lorsque la fête de Noël arriva, j'avais si bien exercé

ma mémoire, que j'avais retenu par cœur un responso-rio, un villancico, et une grande partie des solos de la messe de minuit, que je chantai de manière à contenter tout le monde. Depuis cette époque je devins l'objet des présens des simples religieux et de ceux qu'on nomme *paternité*. Ils se succédaient avec des plats de friandises, dont je faisais la part à mes camarades.

« Quelques jours après, le père Viola ne voulut pas me laisser au rang d'ancienneté que j'occupais depuis mon arrivée, ni suivre la règle de me placer le dernier, puisque j'étais déjà instruit : il me mit au centre.

« Après Noël, le père Viola commença à me donner de l'occupation. Il me fit donner des leçons de lecture et d'écriture aux plus jeunes : je fus nommé premier lec-teur pour le réfectoire. On lisait les sermons de Blasius, de Villegas, et le *Flos Sanctorum* de ce dernier.

« Bientôt commença mon instruction musicale. Le père Viola se mettait parfaitement à la place de celui qui n'a pas la moindre idée de la musique. Il la présentait comme science des sons. « Vous savez la musique, me dit-il, comme vous savez parler ; vous savez écrire la parole, mais vous ne savez lire ni écrire la musique. » J'expliquai au père Viola mon invention pour noter la musique. Il fut surpris : « Vous êtes harmoniste sans vous en douter. »

« La première leçon de solfége dont je fus témoin était donnée à cinq des plus jeunes ; sur leur ardoise étaient tracées quatre portées. Le père Viola ayant chanté une intonation qu'il nomma *ut*, il dit à un élève de chan-ter la gamme, ce qui fut exécuté. Le maître ayant chanté la même intonation, qu'il nomma *ré*, un autre élève chanta la gamme de *ré*, ce qui me surprit ; mais dès lors je compris dans la nomenclature du solfége quelque chose de plus lumineux que je ne le supposais. Le maître continua à donner à la même intonation tous les noms successifs de la gamme, en appelant la sixième *ré de sol*, la septième *mi de sol*, ou le *second mi*. Sur un signe, un élève partait du point indiqué jusqu'à *ut* ; car on ne lui demandait que de *finir* la gamme. Ensuite le maître fit parcourir l'octave, en donnant le point de départ de la manière précitée. Celui auquel il demanda de considérer l'intonation comme *mi*, fit entendre *mi*, *fa*, à un ton de distance, de même que d'*ut* à *ré*. Le maître l'arrêta en disant : « La gamme de *mi*, ou la gamme en *mi*, sont deux choses différentes : la première s'assemble avec celle d'*ut* ; la deuxième ne pourrait s'y unir sans blesser l'o-reille.

Quand je donne un point de départ, s'il est plus bas que *sol*, cherchez mentalement *ut* en descendant ; commencez alors la gamme (toujours mentalement) jus-

qu'à ce que vous trouviez le nom que j'ai donné. Si c'est *sol*, il a son *ré*, *mi*, *fa*, comme *ut* ; or, si le point que je donne est plus haut que *sol*, cherchez *sol* comme vous avez cherché *ut*. D'ailleurs la gamme en *mi* ne peut se décliner *mi*, *fa*, *sol*, *la*, *si*, *ut*, *ré*, *mi*, pas plus que je ne m'appellerai *fauteuil* parce que j'y suis assis. »

« Le maître ayant mis un ♯ à la deuxième ligne de la portée, et pointé le quatrième espace, il en demanda le nom à un élève, qui répondit *sol* ; une intonation fut chantée sans la nommer, et tous les élèves l'appe-lèrent *sol*. Au fur et à mesure que la baguette chan-geait de place on changeait les intonations. Après avoir parcouru les quatre parties de la musique, le maître effaça le dièze, et en mit un au troisième espace ; il pointa le second, et chanta une intonation qu'il nomma *ut* ; un élève chanta *sol* au-dessous d'*ut*, et les autres continuèrent en suivant les indications de la ba-guette.

« Cet exercice se prolongea, et en changeant d'intona-tion, de nom, de place, pour celle qui était pointée la première, ainsi que le ♯, qui occupa successivement tous les signes et les octaves de la portée, quand il le mit à la première ligne, les enfans reconnurent avoir chanté sur ce ton lorsque le dièze occupait le quatrième espace ; et quand il le posa sur le premier espace, ils reconnurent encore avoir chanté quand il était à la cinquième.

« Pour l'étude des mesures, voilà la méthode qu'on employait : une feuille de carton, sur laquelle il n'y avait point de portée, fut posée sur un chevalet. Des fi-gures dont la valeur était plus grande que la ronde for-maient la ligne supérieure. Ces valeurs se nommaient *maxime*, *longue*, *brève*. La semi-brève commençait la se-conde ligne ; une ligne verticale la séparait de deux mi-nimes (blanches), qu'une autre ligne séparait de quatre semi-minimes (noires), séparées par une ligne verticale de huit croches, et ainsi de suite : toutes ces subdivisions remplissaient une mesure à quatre temps ; en outre de la ligne verticale qui séparait chaque mesure, les quatre temps étaient divisés par des points.

« Tout ce tableau ne contenait aucune figure de valeur moindre que la croche, et elles étaient écrites en ligne droite horizontale. Le maître ayant donné une intonation, un des élèves la nomma *ut*, et il battit une mesure à quatre temps : la baguette poin-tée sur la blanche ne changea point de place à la seconde mesure, qu'un autre élève chanta *ré*, en le nommant deux fois comme avait fait le premier à la fin de la seconde mesure ; le maître plaça sa baguette sur la ronde, et le troisième élève chanta *mi*. Il changeait de position tantôt à la moitié d'une mesure, tantôt au quart, mais ces changemens devaient être suivis pendant la mesure entière par celui qui l'avait commencée, en nommant l'intonation qui lui était échue autant de fois qu'il avait de figures à indiquer.

« Comme je témoignai mon étonnement d'avoir vu chanter sans clef, le père Viola me dit qu'on avait employé la clef de dièze. Je ne connaissais que les trois clefs ordinaires, qui indiquaient seulement la place fixe sur le clavier général.

« Pour solfier musicalement, me dit ce maître, il faut un signe qui désigne le nom d'une intonation qui fait partie de la gamme du ton transporté n'importe où. Dans les morceaux où il y a plus d'un dièze, voici la règle pour s'y reconnaître : le dernier dièze, qui est le plus avancé à droite, est la septième note d'*ut*, qui est l'intonation immédiate en montant ; cela posé, on trouve facilement le reste de la gamme. Le dièze est même autre chose que le signe qui indique l'intonation, c'est l'intonation elle-même : cette intonation est le dièze de la gamme qu'on vous fait appeler *si*. Cette dénomination prouve que votre premier maître ignorait que le signe n'est qu'un avertissement pour donner à la note le caractère qui lui est propre en l'éloignant du nouveau *la*, autant que la construction de la gamme l'exige, et par conséquent en rapprochant cette note du terme de la gamme autant qu'elle doit l'être. »

« Sur un autre tableau le maître écrivit des mesures composées de toutes les figures faisant partie de la noire ; quelquefois il improvisait un chant dont il ne nommait que la première note, et donnant la baguette à un des élèves, celui-ci établissait le point de départ où bon lui semblait, en conservant toutefois une relation conséquente entre les intervalles que la voix franchissait. On ne donnait de la musique écrite aux élèves qu'après les avoir jugés suffisamment instruits dans la connaissance de l'intonation et de l'intervalle.

« Entouré de si bons exemples, je ne tardai pas à faire des progrès, et j'appris plutôt à écrire ce que je chantais qu'à chanter ce qui était écrit. Tous les instrumens étaient à ma disposition, mais l'étude de l'orgue était de rigueur ; cependant on me laissa essayer mes idées sur le clavichorde et sur le violon.

« L'époque des vacances arriva ; on nous distribua en deux moitiés, afin qu'il y eût dans chacune les voix nécessaires pour le chant journalier de la messe matinale, des *gozos*, du *Magnificat* et du *Salve*, et de quoi former, au besoin, un petit orchestre. Les dispositions faites, nous partîmes. En sortant du monastère, nous passâmes près du logement que j'avais occupé avec

ma mère ; je me rappelai ma guitare que j'y avais oubliée : je témoignai des regrets qui ne touchèrent point le père Viola, car il me parla de cet instrument avec une médiocre estime.

« Le chemin que nous suivions nous conduisit en face des croisées de notre galerie, dont nous étions séparés par un précipice de deux cents toises. Tout à coup j'entendis le menuet d'une symphonie d'Haydn, que nos compagnons exécutaient en signe d'adieu à notre apparition sur cette partie de la route. C'était un usage établi de guetter ainsi au départ et au retour les élèves qui prenaient leurs vacances. Nous arrivâmes à une petite chapelle consacrée à saint Michel, où se trouvèrent deux montures ; le maître en prit une, et on me hissa sur l'autre, qu'un valet conduisait. Nous parcourions la montagne depuis long-temps, et nous voyions de toutes parts les propriétés du monastère.

« J'ai lu en France l'ouvrage de M. Delaborde, et j'ai été fort surpris de le voir affirmer que le monastère de Montserrat ne pourrait suffire à ses dépenses et aux abondantes aumônes qu'il distribue s'il ne recevait point de dons particuliers. La vaste plaine qui se dessinait à nos regards est en partie divisée par les propriétés du couvent, ayant chacune un intendant. L'abbé de Montserrat est seigneur de plusieurs villages où il nomme les autorités principales. Le monastère a des maisons et des administrateurs dans presque toutes les villes de la Catalogne et quelques-unes de la Castille, notamment à Madrid.

« Le but de notre voyage était une ferme nommée la *Vina-Nueva*. A notre arrivée nous nous rendîmes à la chapelle, où nous exécutâmes une espèce de *gozos* à la Vierge. On chanta ensuite l'hymne *Ave Maris Stella*, à quatre parties seules. Cette composition a pour moi quelque chose de si touchant, que je ne pus retenir mes larmes lorsque je l'entendis quelques années plus tard à la cathédrale de Barcelonne (*V.* la musique.)

« Je retrouvai dans cette ferme le père abbé et trois autres religieux. Le soir, après souper, on se rendait à son appartement, et là on causait en faisant de la musique. J'y chantai avec succès un trio que j'avais entendu au théâtre : on m'applaudit beaucoup, et je m'essayai ensuite sur un autre que l'on ne connaissait point. Je proposai au père Viola de lui dicter les trois parties du chant s'il voulait écrire la basse, et ce bon moine, enchanté de pouvoir préparer une surprise à l'abbé, s'assit près de moi, et commença par me demander quel était le ton du trio. Je n'y avais jamais pensé, et je ne sus que répondre. « Je ne suis pas fâché de votre ignorance, me dit-il. Il y a des gens qui se croient musiciens parce qu'ils devinent à l'audition d'un son la touche du clavier où il correspond. Ils se trompent : leur manière de désigner les sons détruit toute idée musicale, puisqu'elle s'applique seulement au mécanisme des instrumens. Dans le bon solfége, il n'y a point de sons absolus, il n'y en a que de relatifs, et les sons n'indiquent point des touches de clavier, mais les vraies intonations de la gamme du mode. »

« A mon retour au monastère, mes études commencèrent. Le père Viola me donna un cahier sur lequel il m'écrivit le tableau suivant :

Intonations de la gamme diatonique majeure. en mont. en descendant.

			en mont.	en descendant.
8.	C sol, fa, ut	{	fa	fa.
7.	B fa, mi (DIÈZE) . . .		mi	mi.
6.	A la, mi, ré	}	ré	la.
5.	G sol, ré, ut		sol	sol.
4.	F fa, ut (BÉMOL)	{	fa	fa.
3.	E la, mi		mi	mi ou la.
2.	D la, sol, ré	}	ré	ré ou sol.
1.	C sol, fa, ut		ut	ut ou fa.

« Il écrivit ensuite une courte et large portée de musique, en mettant à la ligne inférieure la clef de *fa*, à la troisième ligne, la clef d'*ut*, et à la ligne supérieure celle de *sol*; ces trois clefs étaient précédées par ces mots : *variable de deux; variable de quatre; fixe.* Ces exemples seuls suffirent pour m'expliquer toutes les théories du solfége, et même plus tard les parties les plus essentielles de l'harmonie. Le solfége qu'on m'écrivit ne changeait pas de ton; il avait pour but d'habituer à considérer les intonations d'après leur rang, leurs mouvemens, et de familiariser l'élève avec la nomenclature qui leur était propre. Ensuite ce solfége changea le siége de la gamme au moyen des dièzes ou bémols. J'avais usé de supercherie pour apprendre les notes, le maître me fit chanter, et par une question à laquelle je ne sus répondre, il m'arrêta au premier accident, et me rappelant l'usage des clefs, il me dit : « Quand vous trouverez un dièze, ce sera le *mi* de *sol*, ou le second *mi*; ainsi songez à *mi fa* et vous trouverez le reste. N'oubliez jamais que *ut ré mi*, etc., en vrai langage musical, signifient exclusivement *des intonations* de la gamme, qui changent de *place* et jamais de caractère; il est plus naturel de les nommer plutôt d'après ce qu'elles sont, que d'après la position plus ou moins élevée qu'elles occupent. Or, si le bémol s'est transformé en dièze, tout change de place dans la gamme; en montant ou en descendant selon les dimensions de la portée, on trouve bientôt un des endroits occupés par les trois clefs du clavier général. » Je compris si bien son explication,

que je m'exerçai après la leçon à écrire au crayon sur un livre de solfége la clef qu'il fallait *supposer* à chaque changement de ton.

« Cependant je n'apportais pas assez de soin à la nomenclature, et le père Viola voyant que je chantais à livre ouvert ce qu'on me présentait, conçut ma répugnance à apprendre une chose qui, selon moi, n'avait d'autre but que de conduire l'élève au point où je me trouvais. Il prit un détour très adroit, et coupant court au solfége, me fit commencer le contre-point.

« Il m'écrivit d'abord une basse en rondes, sur laquelle je devais placer un chant en notes de même valeur, qui ne formât avec la basse, que l'octave, la quinte et la tierce; l'octave et la quinte devaient être données par mouvemens contraires, et ne jamais se rencontrer deux de suite; quant à la tierce, elle pouvait recevoir un mouvement direct ou contraire, et se présenter deux fois. J'écrivis ma leçon. Comme je n'avais rien noté qu'en chantant, je ne conçus pas une haute idée de ma composition. Je m'étonnai que la sixte ne me fût point permise, non plus que la septième quand la basse montait de quarte ou descendait de quinte, puisque mon oreille me le faisait désirer. « Vous voyez, me dit le père Viola, que le solfége vous a inculqué des préceptes d'harmonie et vous parlez déjà du mouvement de la basse sans que je vous en aie dit un mot. Quant à la sixte et à la septième, vous en saurez l'usage quand il sera nécessaire. Vous commencez à écrire dans une langue, il faut aller du connu à l'inconnu et cela par progression. Vous croyez votre leçon insipide, vous allez entendre ce qu'elle signifie.

« Le maître en écrivit la basse sur une portée, et ce que j'avais composé sur une autre portée supérieure, puis me donnant la craie : « Écrivez, me dit-il, sur la portée immédiate au soprano la clef du contralto; — bien. — En donnant l'octave à la première note de la basse, vous ne devez employer que trois consonances; il en reste deux : donnez-en une au contralto. » J'écrivis la quinte. « Que reste-t-il pour le ténor? — La tierce. — Chaque partie ayant son point de départ, occupez-vous d'une seule et écrivez-la d'après la basse, en observant les mêmes préceptes. » Ce travail fait, le père Viola appela deux élèves et à nous quatre nous chantâmes mon ouvrage qui me parut intéressant. Le maître profita de l'empressement que je montrais, pour me faire observer qu'il y avait toujours une partie à l'octave de la basse. « Ainsi, me dit-il, avec l'accord parfait seul on ne fait que de la musique à trois parties, écrite à quatre pour que les trois s'y trouvent toujours; avec l'accord de septième on fait de la musique à quatre, écrite à cinq, parce que les quatre parties doivent marcher de manière à laisser la place à une cinquième. » Puis, ajoutant l'exemple à la théorie, il écrivit une cadence parfaite qui servit d'application; il en tira encore cette règle : qu'en harmonie, dès que le nombre des parties augmente, il faut faire quelques concessions pour la facilité de leur placement; et l'octave directe est la première à tolérer dans les mouvemens de quinte.

« Le père Viola ne pouvait donner tout son temps à mon instruction, et pour hâter mes progrès il m'envoya les élèves les moins avancés en solfége. Je devais leur donner la leçon, et le bon moine n'en écrivait une autre que lorsque j'avais écrit au bas de la précédente : *Je la sais.* Par cette ruse, il sut m'engager à revenir sur le solfége, que je croyais déjà avoir abandonné.

« Une nouvelle basse me fut offerte, sur laquelle il me permit d'employer la sixte en m'expliquant son usage. Il m'enseigna ensuite à me servir de deux intonations successives pour chaque note de la basse, puis de quatre dont la marche devait suivre la progression d'une gamme ascendante ou descendante qui ne pouvait être tronquée que par un saut de quinte ou d'octave et rarement de tierce. Arrivé à ce point, on me fit apprendre la marche de chaque partie dans des suites d'accords parfaits et sur chaque mouvement de la basse. J'appris encore les retards de tierce (*ligadura de cuarta*) et celui d'octave *(ligadura de novena)*; puis enfin les accords de septième.

« Le père Viola ne les considérait pas sous le même aspect que nous aujourd'hui; mais quelque obscure que puisse paraître sa méthode à ceux qui ne sont que notistes, elle est lumineuse pour tout bon musicien. Car tous ces différens accords parlent à l'oreille et indiquent par conséquent, leur origine, leur emploi et leur résolution, sans qu'on soit obligé de l'enseigner par d'arides formules.

ACCORDS DE SEPTIÈME SUR TOUTES LES NOTES DE LA GAMME MAJEURE.

B. . . . .)	. . . .	. . . .	de *dièze.*
A.	de *ré* ou de *la*		
G.	. . . .	de *sol*	
F. . . . de *fa*			
E.	de *mi* ou de *la*		
D.	de *ré* ou de *la*		
C. . d'*ut* ou de *fa*)			

(SIMPLE.)

« Ce tableau évitait l'ennui du catéchisme machinal qui dit, que l'accord de septième majeure est composé de tierce majeure, quinte juste, et septième majeure; que la tierce majeure a deux tons; la quinte juste, trois

et demi, et la septième majeure, cinq et demi; que cet accord *se pose* (mauvaise dénomination qui laisse l'élève dans les ténèbres, si elle ne l'induit pas en erreur) sur la tonique et sur la sous-dominante. Ce bavardage était inutile; nous savions solfier les accords en musiciens et nous trouvions sans peine que la tonique et la quatrième note étaient les seules intonations de la gamme qui donnaient l'accord de septième majeure; les deuxième, troisième et sixième note, celui de septième simple; la cinquième seule, celui de septième mineure sur accord parfait majeur; et le dièze celui de septième de sensible qui dans le mode mineur devenait diminué. Notre nomenclature nous avait donné la connaissance des intervalles, *ut mi*, *fa la* ne pouvant jamais être pour nous l'expression d'une tierce mineure, ni *ré fa* et *mi sol*, une tierce mineure.

« Dès que je fus au courant sur les accords de septième, on me fit faire des exercices auxquels nous donnions plus de temps qu'il n'en fallait; mais le père Viola ne connaissait point le système des renversemens. L'habitude d'écrire à quatre parties, et les règles de notre solfége, finissaient par nous faire comprendre la nature des accords qu'on eût pu nous enseigner en une leçon.

« Il y avait quatre mois que j'étais au collége et j'étais déjà arrivé à la fugue et à l'imitation, nommée *Passo forzado.* Pour ma leçon d'orgue, j'apprenais des fugues et un accompagnement sur une basse chiffrée. On nous donnait pour sujet d'étude des sections de la gamme considérées sous toutes leurs faces. Ces exercices me firent connaître les richesses renfermées dans l'ancienne nomenclature et le système des muances.

« Après avoir travaillé mes leçons d'orgue et de contre-point, j'allais me mêler à mes camarades qui étudiaient tous ensemble dans la grande galerie. Un nommé *Sunyer*, premier violon, me donna des conseils, et je m'exerçai si bien que je devins en peu de temps en état de jouer les seconds violons, et je fus mis à leur tête. Dès lors la place de premier violon devint le but de tous mes désirs, car Sunyer devait prendre le froc, et le plus capable après lui voulait suivre la même vocation. A cette époque, un jeune garçon qui jouait bien du violon ayant été admis et placé à la partie des premiers, je redoublai de zèle et de persévérance, et dans une occasion où nous jouâmes le même morceau, je l'emportai sur lui. Sunyer était entré en noviciat, je fus nommé chef d'orchestre, après un concours dans lequel il fallait prouver son talent, dans un morceau étudié, un autre à première vue, et un troisième à plusieurs parties où il fallait rectifier, sans discontinuer, les erreurs qui étaient préparées à l'insu du concurrent.

« Au collège de Montserrat, chaque samedi, on réunit tous les élèves dans la chambre du maître ou dans celle du père sacristain major, pour être questionnés sur le catéchisme : on choisit, parmi les plus âgés, quatre censeurs *aclamadores*, qui doivent observer si la conduite de leurs condisciples ne s'écarte point des règles conventuelles. Chacun de ces censeurs accusait ceux qui avaient commis quelque faute ; l'accusé était obligé de se prosterner la face contre terre, et d'écouter l'exhortation que le maître lui adressait ; souvent au lieu d'infliger une punition, on ordonnait aux accusés d'embrasser leurs accusateurs. A la sortie de Sunyer, on me nomma censeur : et le père Viola en m'instruisant des devoirs de cet emploi, l'étendit encore à la surveillance de l'exécution musicale dans l'église. Il se plaignait des musiciens qui accordent leurs instrumens, ou qui s'amusent à les essayer, tandis que l'orchestre exécute des morceaux suivis. La satisfaction que me donna ma nouvelle dignité fut un peu tempérée par le reproche tacite qui m'était adressé ; car j'avais la mauvaise habitude de jouer des traits de concerto, des fantaisies, des sons harmoniques sur mon violon pendant que le chœur chantait le plain-chant qui précède l'entrée de l'orchestre. Je me corrigeai bien vite afin de donner l'exemple, et j'eus peu d'occasions d'accuser mes camarades.

« A l'époque de la révolution, une grande partie du clergé français émigré en Espagne, et deux moines bénédictins de Saint-Maur, furent incorporés à la communauté de Montserrat. L'un deux, le père Coste, qui aimait la musique, voulut m'apprendre quelques romances françaises, et des airs de la *Belle Arsène*. Je ne pouvais concevoir que cette musique pût être trouvée bonne. Cette première impression fut loin de se dissiper alors que le moine me montra des airs manuscrits, où les signes de dièzes et de bémols étaient placés en ligne verticale, et dans un ordre qui n'était pas le plus rationnel ; les queues des notes s'y montraient droites, fines, et les têtes étaient tournées en arrière, au lieu de regarder la direction dans laquelle on lit. Le père Viola me raccommoda avec ces musiciens français, en me jouant de magnifiques fugues composées par Charpentier et Séjan.

« Lorsque l'archevêque d'Auch, M. de la Latour-du-Pin, vint pour s'établir au monastère, je fus chargé de prononcer un discours que le père Coste m'avait appris à prononcer. Nous allions quelquefois faire de petits concerts dans les appartemens de ce prélat. Il me remarqua, et me prit en affection au point de m'enseigner le français trois fois par semaine. Depuis cette époque, je

négligeais un peu le violon. Quant à l'harmonie, le père Viola ne me la laissait point oublier. Il me faisait analyser des ouvrages classiques et chercher des mélodies dont l'ensemble fût agréable et naturel, et qui cependant, chantées séparément ne laissassent point reconnaître un vide. Il me donnait encore des règles, dont l'application me plaisait d'autant plus qu'elles avaient pour but de tromper agréablement l'oreille. Je puisais en même temps quelques connaissances de la littérature musicale dans les ouvrages de Nasarre, Kircher, Soler et Cerone.

« Lorsque ma mère entrevit la possibilité de me placer, elle écouta les conseils de quelques amis communs et elle voulut me retirer de Montserrat. Mais sa reconnaissance envers le père Viola l'engagea à s'en rapporter à lui sur l'époque de ma sortie, afin de ne point entraver le service ordinaire si l'on ne trouvait pas de suite quelqu'un qui me remplaçât.

« Cette déférence de ma mère fut appréciée, mais on lui répondit : « que d'après les statuts du monastère on ne renvoyait aucun élève sans lui procurer dans quelque chapelle une place qui fournît à tous ses besoins, à moins que ses parens le réclamassent ; et d'ailleurs puisque je ne suivais pas la carrière de la musique, il était inutile d'attendre l'époque à laquelle on eût jugé à propos de me placer. »

« L'idée de sortir du collège a d'abord de l'attrait pour tous les jeunes gens, mais la cérémonie du départ fut très imposante. Tous les élèves se rendirent dans la chambre du père Viola où ils se tinrent debout. J'étais à la porte, je me mis à genoux et récitai la formule d'usage dans laquelle l'élève demande pardon au maître et à tous ses camarades des torts qu'il a pu avoir envers eux. Le père Viola me fit un discours très touchant, puis il m'embrassa avec tendresse. Il me conduisit ensuite à la chambre du père abbé, où l'on me donna un manteau noir et un chapeau semblable à celui d'un prêtre. Dans ce costume je fus visiter les religieux qui m'avaient témoigné de la bienveillance ; puis ensuite j'allai à l'endroit où était préparée la monture qui devait me conduire. J'y trouvai le père sacristain major, qui me remit une pièce d'or de quarante francs : je la refusai d'abord, mais il me fit observer qu'on en usait ainsi envers chaque élève sortant, et que cette somme était destinée, au retour dans la famille, pour acheter un objet qui rappelât le souvenir de Montserrat. »

Lorsque Sor retourna à Barcelonne, le général Vivès le fit nommer sous-lieutenant dans le corps d'armée de Villa Franca, qui était un de ceux que la Catalogne devait fournir pour soutenir la troisième campagne. Le commandant le conduisit à Villa Franca et le presenta partout. Les membres du comité d'armement étaient les notables de la ville, et le jeune Sor, déjà fort habile sur le piano et la guitare, produisit un tel effet que lorsque le comité envoya la liste des officiers à nommer il y fut porté comme lieutenant et reçut d'avance un brevet provisiore.

A son retour à Barcelonne, Sor retrouva une excellente troupe italienne qui le rendit encore plus passionné pour la musique. Il comprenait le mérite de certains effets d'instrumentation ; mais privé de piano, il n'avait point encore songé à chercher à reproduire sur la guitare les effets qui lui plaisaient tant. A cette époque il entendit le frère du général *Solano* jouer sur cet instrument un morceau dans lequel on distinguait un chant et un accompagnement. L'auteur du morceau était Moretti, officier des gardes wallonnes, qui fut le premier à comprendre le véritable caractère de la guitare.

La musique de Moretti donna à Sor une route nouvelle, et avec un peu de travail et l'application de ses connaissances en harmonie, il parvint promptement à écrire et à exécuter la musique à plusieurs parties réelles.

Les guitaristes lui demandaient ses compositions, puis ils changeaient les valeurs des notes pour écrire, disaient-ils, dans le vrai genre de la guitare.

En parcourant la bibliothèque musicale de M. de Gispert, censeur du théâtre de Barcelonne, Sor trouva un vieux libretto : *Telemaco, opera in due atti*, musica *del Maestro Cipolla*. L'idée lui vint de s'essayer sur cet ouvrage inconnu à Barcelonne, et qui se composait de quatre personnages et des chœurs de nymphes. Il avait déjà fait la moitié de l'opéra, lorsque la réouverture de l'école militaire vint l'arrêter dans son essor. Néanmoins au bout de trois mois tout était achevé. Il montra quelques fragmens à M. de Gispert qui voulut le faire entendre à l'entrepreneur du théâtre, Tozzi. Celui-ci encouragea le jeune Sor en lui disant : « A votre âge je n'étais point capable d'en faire autant. »

Il voulut faire jouer l'ouvrage, et dit au jeune artiste d'écrire l'ouverture.—Celui-ci se trouva embarrassé. Le père Viola qui l'avait si bien instruit de la contexture, de la marche et de la conduite des morceaux classiques de musique vocale, ne pouvait porter le même esprit d'analyse sur les compositions instrumentales ; celles qu'on trouvait à Montserrat n'étaient point en partitions. Les œuvres seules du savant moine eussent pu servir de modèle, mais son extrême modestie l'empêchait de les proposer comme des sujets d'étude. Sor n'osait se proposer de faire un *allegro* dans le genre d'Haydn ; il prit une autre route, et tant bien que mal il écrivit son ouverture. Cependant, en faveur de ses dix-sept ans et de son

titre de compatriote, l'opéra de *Télémaque* eut du succès. Il est vrai de dire que n'ayant eu en vue que le sens des paroles, et ne pouvant songer à vendre sa partition, il n'avait point été forcé, comme de nos jours, d'y intercaler des contre-danses, et malgré les défauts du compositeur imberbe, on rendait justice à la vérité de son chant.

Son opéra fut joué, pendant toute l'année, avec les meilleures pièces du répertoire. Il étudia avec fruit les quatuors d'Haydn et de Pleyel, et il acquit ainsi une pratique de l'analyse musicale, qui a pour but l'appréciation des beautés d'un art, plutôt que les minuties de l'école. Après avoir passé quatre années à l'école militaire, Sor partit pour Madrid, où les anciennes relations de son père lui donnèrent accès près des grands. Sa réputation de guitariste l'avait précédé, et il reçut partout un accueil flatteur. Quelques amis voulaient lui préparer les voies pour qu'il jouât à la cour ; mais Charles IV n'écoutait d'autre avis sur la musique que celle des musiciens de sa chambre, et ceux-ci, bien loin d'encourager et d'applaudir au talent de leur compatriote, voyaient de mauvais œil qu'un amateur eût acquis des connaissances positives dans leur art. Le roi avait entendu parler de Sor, il demanda au chef de sa musique ce qu'il en pensait. « C'est, dit celui-ci, quelque chose de mieux que les *frons frons* ordinaires, mais le talent de Sor est celui de tant d'amateurs, qui jouent par instinct et d'oreille, mais sans connaître une note de musique. » Cette réponse chagrina Sor ; mais plus désireux d'obtenir de l'avancement par ses services que par la guitare, il se résigna.

A cette époque la duchesse d'Alba le prit sous sa protection et lui montra toute l'affection d'une mère. Elle ne voulait pas qu'il fît le métier de musicien, ou qu'il restât militaire en activité. Pour faciliter ses études, elle lui avait fait préparer dans son hôtel une chambre de travail, où il pouvait aller consulter des partitions italiennes et s'exercer sur le piano. Sous les prétextes les plus délicats, la duchesse trouvait moyen d'améliorer la position du jeune officier qui pouvait se livrer avec sécurité à son goût pour la musique. Il composa quelques morceaux d'un libretto *Don Trastullo*. Quelque temps après, la duchesse, qui était malade, quitta tout à coup Madrid, et laissa à son protégé une somme assez forte pour se soutenir avec honneur pendant son absence. Sor fut affligé de cette séparation, qui devait être éternelle, car la duchesse mourut presque subitement.

Le duc de Medina-Cœli voulut lui être utile ; il lui donna une commission dans l'administration générale de ses domaines, en Catalogne. L'espoir de retourner à Barcelonne le fit accepter. Sa place était une sinécure, et il continua son opéra, mais avec moins de rapidité. L'expérience l'avait rendu plus difficile. M. Quéralt, maître de chapelle de la cathédrale, ne dédaignait point de le consulter sur ses ouvrages; et celui de Sainte-Marie-del-Mar, M. Cau, le chargea de l'instrumentation de quelques morceaux de ses oratorios. Il composa alors deux symphonies, trois quatuors, un salve, cinq ou six *rosarios*, et beaucoup d'airs espagnols, qui ont peut-être contribué à faire adopter aujourd'hui comme espagnole une musique dont le caractère est tout-à-fait différent. A cette époque, Sor ne prit pas la peine de se garantir de la contagion, et les mélodies italiennes l'emportèrent sur les chants nationaux.

Ayant obtenu un congé du duc de Medina-Cœli, Sor revint à Madrid, où il composa la musique d'un mélodrame. *La Elvira Portuguese*, un motet à quatre voix, avec orchestre, pour l'église de la *Merced*, et plusieurs boleros. A cette époque on vendait déjà les copies de sa musique, qu'il donnait aux personnes pour lesquelles elle avait été faite. On tirait ainsi des fragmens de ses symphonies, des airs de *Télémaque*, et surtout de ses boleros.

Après un séjour assez long à Madrid, il fut nommé chef d'une petite administration royale, en Andalousie. Les devoirs de son emploi ne l'empêchèrent point de passer une grande partie de son temps à Malaga, où il s'occupa de musique avec succès. Il dirigeait là les concerts du consul américain, M. Kirkpatrik. Sa liaison avec l'organiste de la cathédrale lui fut utile. Ainsi s'écoulèrent quatre années qui précédèrent l'arrivée de Napoléon en Espagne. Sor demanda la permission de retourner à Madrid, où il se lia avec plusieurs Français, excellens musiciens, notamment M. d'Auberlin et M. Le Barbier de Tinand.

Après la bataille de Bailen, Madrid fut évacué par les Français, on leva des troupes pour leur résister, et ceux qui avaient été liés avec des Français étaient signalés à la fureur populaire. Sor reprit du service; son régiment, à peine formé, prit part à la résistance, et ne se dispersa qu'après l'entrée des Français à Madrid. Sor partit alors pour l'Andalousie, où il fut nommé capitaine au régiment des volontaires de Cordoue.

Mais les efforts des Espagnols n'empêchèrent point les mouvemens progressifs de l'armée ennemie, et le général Sébastiani arriva en Andalousie avant que les volontaires cordouans fussent réunis. Sor suivit l'exemple de tant d'autres; il crut le pouvoir de Joseph affermi et il prêta serment. Il occupa l'emploi de commissaire principal de police de la province de Xérez, jusqu'à la retraite des armées françaises. A Valence, le général Mazzuchelli, homme fort instruit et passionné pour la musique, le présenta à la duchesse d'Albuféra qui chantait fort bien. A sa fête, Sor composa une cantate à trois voix avec des chœurs et des accompagnemens, qui furent exécutés par les musiciens de l'orchestre du théâtre. Lorsque les josephinos quittèrent l'Espagne, Sor les suivit en France. A Paris il fut accueilli avec empressement; sa réputation grandit encore lorsqu'on l'entendit. Méhul et Chérubini lui donnèrent des témoignages de l'estime qu'ils avaient pour son talent. Berton ne fut pas le dernier à le complimenter sur la facilité avec laquelle il appliquait ses connaissances harmoniques à la musique de guitare.

Lorsque Sor eut entendu quelques opéras du théâtre Feydeau, il sentit qu'il pourrait bien écrire dans un genre qui lui permettait de s'éloigner des formes adoptées pour le grand opéra, qui ne l'avait point séduit. Il chercha un poëme; mais on lui fit observer que les poètes de renom gardaient des positions tout-à-fait différentes avec les compositeurs. Ils sont peu traitables avec le musicien qui n'a pas encore débuté à Paris, tandis qu'ils s'offrent de grand cœur au compositeur à la mode. Cela s'explique. Le poëte Marsollier entendit quelques fragmens du *Télémaque*, et il dit à Sor que sa musique était tout-à-fait italienne, qu'elle ne pouvait convenir à la scène française; il lui conseillait d'attendre, et de se mettre sous la direction de quelque homme habile, qu'alors il deviendrait peut-être en état d'écrire pour le théâtre. A cette sortie, Sor ne put contenir sa colère, et après avoir longuement énuméré toutes les platises, les fautes de prosodie et les contre-sens de certains ouvrages qu'on portait aux nues, il blâma hautement les soi-disant connaisseurs, qui entendent avec indifférence de véritables beautés musicales. Tout fut dit, et Marsollier ferma son portefeuille.

Quelque temps après l'arrivée des alliés en France, Sor partit pour Londres, où son talent de guitariste fut consciencieusement jugé. Invité dans une soirée où se trouvait le duc de Sussex, frère du prince régent, celui-ci lui parla de son séjour en Italie et de la prédilection pour Crescentini, que Sor avait connu à Madrid lorsqu'il donnait des leçons à mademoiselle Colbran (madame Rossini). Le duc commença à fredonner un des airs de ce célèbre chanteur, et Sor offrit à le chanter dans le genre de l'auteur. Il réussit si complétement, que les journaux anglais qui rendirent compte de cette soirée disaient : « Si le jeu de Sor sur la guitare annonce un grand compositeur, sa manière d'imiter Crescentini annonce un grand maître de chant. » Dès ce moment on vint à lui pour avoir des leçons de chant. Il s'occupa sérieusement à se former une méthode qui fut véritablement une suite de bons principes. Il étudia l'action des organes qui servent à former les sons, et les différences qui résultent de leur emploi.

Pendant son séjour à Londres, Sor composa la musique d'un divertissement, *la Foire de Smyrne*, trois ballets, *le Seigneur généreux*, *l'Amant peintre*, *Cendrillon*, une sonate à quatre mains pour le piano, sur des airs suédois, neuf livraisons de trois valses à quatre mains, et une livraison de six valses à deux mains; trente ariettes italiennes, avec accompagnement de piano, qui firent dire aux rédacteurs du journal *Repository of arts* : « On doit étudier dans ces productions du sentiment, soutenues par le génie et la science, la manière d'exprimer la parole tout en flattant l'oreille. » Au milieu de plusieurs autres œuvres nous citerons les douze premières études de guitare.

Sor partit de Londres pour aller en Russie. A son passage il trouva *Cendrillon* en répétition au grand opéra, et avant de continuer son voyage il put jouir du succès de sa pièce. A Berlin il composa la musique de deux pas de danse, un pour le théâtre du roi, et un autre pour celui du palais de *Sans-Souci*, à Postdam. Spontini accueillit Sor avec distinction, et quelques circonstances particulières empêchèrent seules l'effet de ses bonnes dispositions pour lui.

A Moscow, Sor fut introduit promptement dans les sociétés les plus distinguées. Dans un pays où la musique est poussée à un haut degré de perfection on apprécia son talent. Sa guitare produisit le plus grand effet. On s'étonnait de le voir jouer avec une égale facilité, dans tous les tons, avec une corde de moins que sur les guitares russes, dont les cordes à vide forment un accord parfait appuyé sur la quinte; ainsi lorsqu'on barre à une touche quelconque on trouve toujours un accord.

Le ballet de *Cendrillon* fut joué à Moscow; bientôt après on exécuta l'*Amant peintre*, refondu et distribué en trois actes au lieu d'un.

Dans un de ses voyages à Saint-Pétersbourg, Sor fut appelé chez l'impératrice mère, où se trouvait réunie toute la famille impériale. Il s'y fit entendre avec succès. Quelques jours après, il joua chez l'impératrice Élisabeth qui lui donna des marques de bienveillance telles que Sor crut son avenir assuré. Mais au moment où l'artiste allait arriver à une position digne de lui et de sa protectrice, celle-ci mourut peu de temps après l'empereur. Sor composa une marche funèbre pour la musique militaire, qui fut choisie par l'empereur Nicolas, et exécutée aux funérailles d'Alexandre par les musiciens du régiment de Preobrojenski, premier de la garde. L'impératrice Alexandrine voulut avoir cette marche arrangée pour le piano, et ce fut une occasion de combler

l'auteur de présens. A l'époque du couronnement de Nicolas, Sor retourna à Moscow pour assister aux répétitions du ballet d'*Hercule et Omphale*, dont la musique est, sans contredit, son meilleur ouvrage. L'ouverture de ce ballet fit sensation en Allemagne, parce qu'elle est traitée en fugue ou imitation, et consciencieusement élaborée, sans que la correction du travail nuise à la clarté ni au charme de la mélodie. De retour en France, Sor observa l'état de la musique au théâtre; il entendit des opéras, appelés comiques, dont les finales avaient la coupe du genre de l'opéra buffa; on y trouvait des cavatines, des airs *a cavaletta*, des duos imités de Rossini ou Generali. En songeant à proposer un ouvrage, il sentait qu'il ne serait pas obligé de calquer sur des modèles pour suivre la marche reçue, et il ne devait plus craindre qu'on lui trouvât des formes italiennes. Il échoua : cette fois-ci l'artiste qui avait fait ses preuves n'offrait point encore assez de garantie pour ceux qui exploitent le théâtre. Vous êtes, lui disait-on, habitué aux formes sévères de la Russie et de l'Allemagne, et avec une grande connaissance de l'harmonie, vous pencherez vers le style savant : il faut être gracieux avant tout. Ces absurdités et quelques injustices le découragèrent. Tandis qu'il éprouvait tant de difficultés pour être joué à Paris, on répétait à Londres un ballet de Sor, en trois actes, *le Dormeur Éveillé*, et dernièrement on vient de représenter, avec le plus grand succès, un autre ballet féerie, *la Belle Arsène*, dont l'ouverture et les principales scènes sont composées par lui; le reste avait été soumis à sa révision.

Ainsi, avec une réputation de musicien consommé, qui s'est exercé dans presque tous les genres, Sor éprouva des difficultés insurmontables à faire recevoir un opéra sur la scène française; et cependant, lorsqu'un de nos poëtes lyriques voudra chercher un digne interprète parmi les célébrités musicales de l'époque, Sor pourra offrir l'appui d'un talent original, auquel il n'a manqué que les grandes occasions d'être mieux apprécié.

Si nous cessons de considérer Sor sur un point de vue aussi élevé, nous devons nous empresser de dire que c'est lui qui a fait sortir la guitare de l'ornière où l'avait plongée le genre de musique adopté avant lui. Sor est le seul qui ait créé une langue pour exprimer les idées musicales, les plus savantes et les plus gracieuses sur cet instrument. Et tout guitariste qui voudra composer devra suivre la route qu'il a tracée, sous peine de mal faire. Ses études vivront comme celles de Cramer. Quand on voudra retrouver la tradition de la véritable musique espagnole, ce sera près de Sor qu'on devra la chercher; car il est le seul qui conserve encore le type de ces mélodies nationales, déjà

130

corrompues, en Espagne même, par les mélanges des musiques étrangères.

Le catalogue des œuvres de Sor est très nombreux, surtout pour la guitare et le chant; et le talent de cet artiste s'y montre dans toutes avec une grande supériorité. Sa méthode de guitare est un traité consciencieux qui repose sur des principes incontestables : c'est un guide sûr pour les professeurs et les élèves qui voudront tirer un grand parti des ressources de l'instrument.

SOR.

Vue du Mont Serrat du côté du Jardin.

Eleve du Mont Serrat.

AVE MARIS STELLA.

Tel qu'il était chanté à la Chapelle de la ferme nommée la Viña nueva par les enfants de chœur du Collège de Montserrat et tel qu'on le chante aussi à la Cathédrale de Barcelone pendant la huitaine de la fête de la Conception.

O CRUX.

Motet de l'hymne (Vexilla Regis)
Par FERDINAND SOR.

LE DERNIER CRI DES GRECS.

Paroles de M.̅ E: de TARADE.

Musique de FERDINAND SOR.

Marchons a _ mis avancons en si _ len_ce et pour jamais brisons d'indi_gnes fers voici l'ins _

_tant d'u _ ne jus_te ven_geance par nos ex_ploits é_ton_nons l'u_ni_vers en_ten_dez

4

vous nos é_pou_ses cap_ti_ves sous nos ef_forts leurs cachots vont sou_vrir   de nos en_

_fants j'entends les voix plain_tives marchons marchons   il faut vaincre ou pé_rir   de nos en_

_fants j'entends les voix plain_tives marchons marchons il faut vaincre ou pé _ rir

LA CANDEUR

Petite reverie sur la Guitare.

Par F. SOR.

And.te Cantabile.

GUITARE.

XLIIIe. Livon

4

4

Mazurka pour le Piano, de F. SOR.

CATALOGUE

This catalogue lists all of Fernando Sor's known works, and is arranged as follows.

The full wording of the title-pages has been reproduced except where I have indicated by dots (. . .) that something is omitted. Where there is no separate title-page but only a heading to the music, that fact is specified. Bars (/) to indicate line-division have not been considered necessary.

The format is always upright unless otherwise stated.

For the number of pages the number on the last numbered page is given.

The dates given are those of the edition or manuscript in question and not necessarily of the composition of the piece. In the case of editions, they are the dates of first publication.

All known editions up to 1850 are included, but not editions after that date.

For the location of copies, all the major music libraries of the world have been covered and their copies listed. I have personally seen and examined every copy listed except in a very few cases that are specifically marked 'not seen'. I should like to make it perfectly clear, however, that the listing of known copies does not claim to be exhaustive. There are certainly more copies, especially of the guitar music, in private hands.

To avoid unnecessary duplication, the catalogue does not repeat information already given in the main part of the book. It follows, therefore, that in order to obtain the fullest information about any given piece, it should be looked up not only in the catalogue but also in the index to the book.

The following abbreviations are used:

Hopkinson: Cecil Hopkinson, *A Dictionary of Parisian Music Publishers 1700-1950* (London, 1954).

Humphries & Smith: Charles Humphries & William C. Smith, *Music Publishing in the British Isles,* 2nd edn. (Oxford, 1970).

Neighbour & Tyson: Oliver Neighbour & Alan Tyson, *English Music Publishers' Plate Numbers in the First Half of the Nineteenth Century* (London, 1965).

References to 'Stationers' Hall' are to the manuscript registers kept at Stationers' Hall, London. For a discussion of the significance or otherwise of the entries there, see Neighbour & Tyson, Introduction.

A number of works are known or believed to have existed, but no manuscript or edition of them is known to have survived. Likewise, some early editions are known or believed to have existed but no copy of them has been found. Such works and editions are listed in this catalogue. If any reader of this book knows of the whereabouts of any of them — or indeed of any work, manuscript, or early edition which is not listed here — I should be glad to hear from him.

In the case of the guitar music, it should be noted that (as explained in the main part of this book) the opus numbers up to op. 23 are merely for publishers' convenience and do not necessarily correspond to the order of composition or even of publication. Only from op. 24 onwards — that is to say, from 1827 — do opus numbers correspond to order of composition and publication.

New editions and new issues

In a new edition, the music type is newly set up; in a new issue, the music is reprinted from the old plates. It happened frequently that Sor's music was reissued, printed from the same plates though often with some changes. Thus, on the simplest level, Monzani & Hill altered their address on the plates when they moved (see op. 1 and op. 2). Or by some business arrangement or by business succession, another publisher might use the same plates and add his own name (see op. 8). An extreme and exceptional case was when Meissonnier, the

publisher, actually altered the plate number (see op. 4). Changes in the music itself seem seldom to have been introduced in new issues.

Some notes on publishers

Meissonnier. Many of the dates given for Meissonnier's editions in the following pages are derived from his addresses. To avoid repetition, here is a list of them. They are based on Cecil Hopkinson's *A Dictionary of Parisian Music Publishers* (London, 1954), confirmed by listings in the *Bibliographie de la France*.

C. 1817-1822	Rue Montmartre, no. 182
1822	Boulevard Montmartre, no. 4
1822 to November 1825	Galerie des Panoramas, no. 15
From November 1825	Boulevard Montmartre, no. 25

From 1832 to 1839 Hopkinson lists other addresses, but none of these other addresses is known to have been used on any issue of a work by Sor. In 1839 the firm became Meissonnier & Heugel; in 1849 Meissonnier died and the firm became Heugel alone.

Simrock. The early Simrock editions of Sor's works can be dated by their plate numbers, following the data provided by O. Deutsch in his book *Musikverlagsnummern* (Berlin, 1961). These plate numbers show that Simrock published all at once in about 1824-5 Sor's opp. 1-20, including the *Folies d'Espagne* and ·the Sonata op. 15, but apparently omitting op. 13; the *Thème Varié;* and the March from *Cendrillon.* Then in 1830 he published opp. 21-33, 35, 36 (wrongly called op. 34), and the *Méthode pour la Guitare* in a German-French edition. Simrock's editions are all later than the corresponding Meissonnier ones and are very probably derived from them.

Dunst. The firm of Dunst at Frankfurt published Sor's op. 36 (wrongly numbered op. 34) and many of opp. 38-63. They were listed in Hofmeister's *Handbuch der musikalischen Literatur* in February 1841. Copies have been found of only some of them, but a list of them was published on the title-pages of these editions. See op. 38 in the catalogue.

GUITAR MUSIC WITH OPUS NUMBER

Opus 1: Six Divertimenti

FIRST EDITION:

Six Divertimentos, for the Spanish Guitar, Composed &
Dedicated to Miss Davenport, by F. Sor.   Ent. at Sta.
Hall. Price 3s. London, Published by Monzani and Hill
Music Sellers to H.R.H. the Prince Regent, 24, Dover
St. Piccadilly.

Five pages. Plate mark: 'Sor's Divtos. Set 1'. July 1815 or before. Not
earlier than 1813, when Monzani & Hill moved to 24 Dover Street
(Humphries & Smith). Note that no opus number is given.

[Copenhagen, collection of Ingolf Olsen, signed 'F. Sor' and 'Cath.
Louise Tisdall. July 1815'; London, collection of Robert Spencer,
signed 'F. Sor' and 'Puzzi'.]

Another issue:

The same, except that the address is '28 Regent St. Piccadilly' and
'H.R.H. the Prince Regent' is replaced by 'His Majesty'. Must date
from after the accession of King George IV in 1820 and before the
dissolution of Monzani & Hill in 1829.

[London, Guildhall School of Music, signed 'F. Sor'.]

FRENCH EDITION:

Six Divertissemens Pour La Guitare Composés et dédiés
à Mis [sic] Davenport Par Ferdinando Sor Oeuvre Ier.
Prix 3f. à Paris au Bureau du Journal de Guitare Chez
Meissonnier rue Montmartre No. 182 . . .

Five pages. Plate number 51. C. 1817-22.

[Brussels, Conservatoire; Copenhagen, Royal Library (two copies).]

Later issues:

i) Galerie des Panoramas No. 15. 1822-25.
[Paris, Bibliothèque Nationale (two copies).]

ii) Boulevard Montmartre No. 25. 1825-39.
[London, collection of Robert Spencer.]

iii) Meissonnier & Heugel. 1839-49.
[Barcelona, collection of Emilio Pujol; London, collection of Robert
Spencer.]

GERMAN EDITION:

Six Divertissemens . . . Bonn et Cologne chez N.
Simrock.

Seven pages. Plate number on music 2286; on title-page 2286, 2287,
2291. The same title-page serves also for op. 2 and op. 8. C. 1824-5.

[Barcelona, collection of Emilio Pujol; Copenhagen, Royal Library;
Copenhagen, Music History Museum; London, British Library;
Stockholm, Royal Music Academy (not seen).]

Opus 2: Six Divertimenti

FIRST EDITION:

Six Divertimentos for the Spanish Guitar, Composed
And Dedicated to his friend Emanuel Palacio Faxardo
Esqre. by F. Sor. Ent. at Sta. Hall Set 2d. Price 3s.
London. Published by Monzani & Hill, Music Sellers to
H.R.H. the Prince Regent, 24, Dover St. Piccadilly.

Five pages. Plate mark: 'Sor's Divertimento Set 2'. Presumably after
the first set of divertimenti, which was published between 1813 and
1815; and before Monzani & Hill left 24 Dover Street in about July
1819 (advertisement in the *Morning Chronicle,* 20 July 1819). Note
that no opus number is given.

[London, British Library, signed 'F. Sor'; London, collection of
Robert Spencer, signed 'F. Sor' and 'Puzzi'.]

Another issue:

As above, but with the address '28 Regent St. Piccadilly' and 'His
Majesty'. 1820-29.

[London, Guildhall School of Music, signed 'F. Sor'; London, collection of Robert Spencer.]

FRENCH EDITION:

Six Divertissemens Pour la Guitare Composés et dédiés
à Emanuel Palacio Faxardo Par Ferdinando Sor Oeuvre
2e. Prix 3f. à Paris au Bureau du Journal de Guitare
Chez Meissonnier, rue Montmartre No. 182 . . .

Five pages. Plate number 53. C. 1817-22.

[Brussels, Conservatoire; Copenhagen, Royal Library; Paris, Bibliothèque Nationale (two copies).]

Later issues:

i) Boulevard Montmartre No. 25. 1825-39.
[London, collection of Robert Spencer.]

ii) Meissonnier & Heugel. 1839-49.
[Barcelona, collection of Emilo Pujol.]

iii) Heugel. 1849 or after.
[Barcelona, Biblioteca Central.]

GERMAN EDITION:

Six Divertissemens . . . Bonn et Cologne chez N.
Simrock.

Seven pages. Plate number on music 2287; on title-page 2286, 2287,
2291. The same title-page serves also for op. 1 and op. 8. C. 1824-5.

[Copenhagen, Royal Library.]

Opus 3: Theme, Variations and Minuet

The theme and variations were first published by Castro in his *Journal de Musique Etrangère pour la Guitare ou Lyre,* Paris, c. 1810. Meissonnier later republished them and added a minuet, which also exists in manuscript form for piano solo. Op. 12 is another version of op. 3.

FIRST EDITION:

Air Varié pour la Guitare Par Dn. Fernando Sors.

In the *Journal de Musique Etrangère pour la Guitare ou Lyre,* edited by Castro, Paris, c. 1810.

Six pages. Plate number 3. Oblong format.

[The *Journal* is a periodical. Differing collections of various numbers of it are in Paris, Bibliothèque Nationale (two copies, not the same); London, collection of Robert Spencer; Stockholm, Royal Music Academy (not seen).]

ANOTHER EDITION:

Without a separate title-page, in the *Journal de Lyre ou Guitare,* Paris, Meissonnier, 6e. Année, 2e. Livraison (i.e., February 1817).

No copy found.

Reissued with a title-page:

Thêma Varié Pour la Guitare et un Menuet Dédié aux Amateurs composé par Ferdinando Sor. Oeuvre 3. . . . A Paris Au Bureau du Journal de Lyre, Chez Meissonnier, Rue Montmartre, No. 182 . . .

Five pages. Plate number 150 (possibly changed from an earlier plate number; see opus 4 below). At the head of the music is: 'Journal de Lyre ou Guitare Redigé par Meissonnier Thema varié Suivi d'un Menuet Composé par Ferdinando Sor . . . A Paris, au bureau du Journal de Guitare, Chez Meissonnier, Rue Montmartre, No. 182 au coin du Boulevard'. This heading suggests that the work was first issued without a separate title-page, and that issues with a title-page are later. Note that no opus number is given in the heading to the music. C. 1817-22. The theme and variations are as in Castro's edition, but with a minuet added.

[Paris, Bibliothèque Nationale (two copies).]

Later issues:

i) Boulevard Montmartre No. 25. 1825-39.
[London, collection of Robert Spencer.]

ii) Meissonnier & Heugel. 1839-49.
[Barcelona, collection of Emilio Pujol.]

GERMAN EDITION:

Thème varié suivi d'un Menuet . . . Bonn et Cologne chez N. Simrock.

Five pages. Plate Number 2288. C. 1824-5.

[Copenhagen, Royal Library; London, British Library; Stockholm, Royal Music Academy (not seen).]

A VERSION OF THE MINUET FOR PIANO SOLO:

See under 'Piano solos'.

Opus 4: Fantasia

FIRST EDITION:

A 2nd. Fantasia, for the Spanish Guitar, Composed & Respectfully Dedicated to Miss Cornewalle, by F. Sor. Pr. 1/6 London, Printed & Sold for the Author, by L. Lavenu, at his Music Warehouse, 26, New Bond Street.

Three pages. No separate title-page; the above is the heading to the music. No plate number. If the address '26, New Bond Street' is correct, then this edition dates from 1811, when Lavenu moved from no. 26 to no. 28 New Bond Street, or before (Humphries & Smith). However, the words 'Printed & Sold for the Author' strongly suggest that Sor was in London when the work was printed; and Sor did not arrive in London until 1815. Probably in fact '26, New Bond Street' is an error for '28, New Bond Street', and the edition dates from between 1815, when Sor arrived in London, and 1818, when Lavenu died.

[London, Guildhall School of Music; London, collection of Robert Spencer.]

FRENCH EDITION:

Journal de Lyre ou Guitare Redigé par Meissonnier 2me. Fantaisie Composée et dédiée à Miss Cornewalle Par Ferdinant Sor. Prix 1f.50c. A Paris, au bureau du Journal de Guitare Chez Meissonnier, rue Montmartre No. 182 . . .

No separate title-page; the above is the heading to the music. Three pages. Plate number (49-4). At the foot of the page is '6e. Année 1re. L[ivrais]on' (i.e., January 1817). Note that no opus number is given.

[Copenhagen, Royal Library.]

Reissued with a title-page:

Deuxième Fantaisie Pour la Guitare composée et dédiée à Miss Cornewalle Par Ferdinando Sor. Oeuvre 4. Prix: 2f. à Paris Au Bureau du Journal de Lyre, Chez Meissonnier, Rue Montmartre, No. 182 . . .

Three pages. The plate number has been changed in this issue, as can clearly be seen in the known copies, from the old '(49 = 4)' to '149'. Perhaps this was to make the work appear to be newly printed. A similar change may have been made with op. 3, though no known copy of that work betrays it as clearly as here. C. 1817-22.

[Brussels, Conservatoire; Copenhagen, Royal Library; Paris, Bibliothèque Nationale (two copies).]

Later issues:

i) Boulevard Montmartre No. 25. 1825-39.
[Barcelona, Biblioteca Central; London, collection of Robert Spencer.]

ii) Meissonnier & Heugel. 1839-49.
[Barcelona, collection of Emilio Pujol.]

GERMAN EDITION:

Deuxième Fantaisie . . . Bonn et Cologne chez N. Simrock.

Five pages. Plate number 2289. C. 1824-5.

[Copenhagen, Royal Library; London, British Library; Stockholm, Royal Music Academy (not seen).]

Opus 5: Six Petites Pièces

FIRST EDITION:

Six Petites Pièces Très faciles pour la Guitarre, écrites selon la méthode ordinaire. Dédiées à son Epouse Par F. Sor. Prix marqué 4f.50c. Propriété de l'Auteur. . . . A Paris A la Lyre Moderne, chez Mme. Benoist, Editeur de Musique et M[archan]de d'Instrumens, Rue de Richelieu, No. 20,

Seven pages. Oblong format. No plate number. Listed in the *Bibliographie de l'Empire Français* on 4 February 1814. Note that no opus number is given.

[Paris, Bibliothèque Nationale (two copies, both signed 'F. Sor').]

ANOTHER EDITION:

Six Petites Pièces Très faciles Pour la Guitare Ecrites selon la méthode ordinaire Dédiées à son Epouse Par F. Sor. Prix 3f. à Paris, au Bureau du Journal de Guitare Chez Meissonnier, rue Montmartre No. 182 . . .

Five pages. Plate number 54. There is no heading to the music, which shows that this work, unlike op. 3 and op. 4, was probably not first published without a separate title-page in the *Journal de Lyre ou Guitare.* C. 1817-22. Note that no opus number is given.

[Copenhagen, Royal Library.]

Later issues:

i) Galerie des Panoramas No. 15. 1822-25. 'Op. 5' is added.
[Paris, Bibliothèque Nationale (two copies).]

ii) Boulevard Montmartre No. 25. 1825-39.
[London, collection of Robert Spencer.]

iii) Heugel. 1849 or after.
[Barcelona, collection of Emilio Pujol.]

A copy of Meissonnier's edition, without title-page, is in Barcelona, Orfeó Catalá.

GERMAN EDITION:

Six Petites Pieces très faciles . . . Bonn et Cologne chez N. Simrock.

Five pages. Plate number 2303. C. 1824-5.

[Copenhagen, Royal Library; London, British Library; Stockholm, Royal Music Academy (not seen).]

ENGLISH EDITION:

Six Petites Pieces pour la Guitare . . . London . . . Cocks & Co . . .

Five pages. Plate number 2382. C. 1835 (Neighbour & Tyson).

[London, Royal College of Music.]

Opus 6: Twelve Studies

FIRST EDITION:

Two separate sets, containing studies 1-6 and 7-12. Set 1:

Six Studio [sic], for the Spanish Guitar Dedicated to His Pupils, By F. Sor. Set 1. London . . . Printed, for the Author, by W. Milhouse, Military Instrument Maker to their R.H. the Dukes of Kent, & Cumberland, 337, Oxford St. . . .

Five pages. No plate number. C. 1815-17. No opus number is given.

[London, collection of Robert Spencer, signed 'F. Sor'.]

Set 2:

Studio [sic], for the Spanish Guitar Composed & Dedicated to His Pupils, By F. Sor. Set 2. London . . . Sold at all the principal Music Shops. . . .

Pages numbered 7-12. No plate number. C. 1815-17. No opus number is given.

[London, collection of Robert Spencer, signed 'Sor'.]

FRENCH EDITION:

Douze Etudes Pour la Guitare Composées et dédiées à ses élèves Par F: Sor. Prix 6f. à Paris, au Bureau du Journal de Guitare Chez Meissonnier, rue Montmartre No. 182 . . .

Twelve pages. Plate number 63. C. 1817-22. Note that no opus number is given.

[Barcelona, Orfeó Catalá; Brussels, Conservatoire; Copenhagen, Royal Library; Paris, Bibliothèque Nationale (two copies).]

Later issues:

i) Boulevard Montmartre No. 25. With 'Oeuv. 6' added. 1825-39.
[London, collection of Robert Spencer.]

ii) Issued together with op. 29. 1825-39. See 'Collections of guitar music'.

iii) Heugel. 1849 or after.
[Barcelona, collection of Emilio Pujol.]

GERMAN EDITION:

Douze Etudes . . . Bonn et Cologne chez N. Simrock.

Twelve pages. Plate number 2295. C. 1824-5.

[Berlin, Deutsche Staatsbibliothek; Copenhagen, Royal Library; London, British Library; London, Guildhall School of Music; Vienna, Gesellschaft der Musikfreunde (not seen).]

Opus 7: Fantasia

FIRST EDITION:

Fantaisie Pour la Guitare Composée et Dédiée A son Ami Jgnace Pleyel Par F. Sor.   Prix 4fr. 50c.   Propriété de l'Auteur. . . . Chez Mr. Pleyel Auteur, Editeur et M[archan]d de Musique, Boulevard Bonne Nouvelle, No. 8   Et chez l'Auteur, Rue du Helder, No. 27.

Nine pages.   No plate number. Listed in the *Bibliographie de l'Empire Français* on 3 September 1814. The music is printed on two staves rather than one. Note that no opus number is given.

[Paris, Bibliothèque Nationale, signed 'F. Sor'.]

ANOTHER EDITION:

Fantaisie Pour la Guitare Composée et Dédiée A son Ami Jgnace Pleyel Par F. Sor.   Prix 3f. 60c. A Paris Au Bureau du Journal de Guitare, Chez Meissonnier, Rue Montmartre, No. 182 . . .

Seven pages. Plate number 100. The music is printed on one stave only. No opus number is given.   C. 1817-22.

[Brussels, Conservatoire; Copenhagen, Royal Library.]

Later issues:

i) Galerie des Panoramas No. 15. 1822-25. 'Op. 7' is added.
[Brussels, Conservatoire; Paris, Bibliothèque Nationale (two copies).]

ii) Boulevard Montmartre No. 25. 1825-39.
[London, collection of Robert Spencer.]

iii) Meissonnier & Heugel. 1839-49.
[London, collection of Robert Spencer.]

iv) Heugel. 1849 or after.
[Barcelona, collection of Emilio Pujol.]

GERMAN EDITION:

Fantaisie . . . Bonn et Cologne chez N. Simrock.

Seven pages. Plate number 2311. C. 1824-5.

[Copenhagen, Royal Library; London, British Library; Stockholm, Royal Music Academy (not seen).]

ANOTHER GERMAN EDITION:

Berlin, Lischke.

Listed in Hofmeister in 1827. No copy found.

Opus 8: Six Divertimenti

FIRST EDITION:

Six Divertimentos, for the Spanish Guitar, Composed and Respectfully Dedicated to Miss Smith by Ferdinand Sor.   Ent. at Sta. Hall.   Third Set   Pr. 2/6 London Printed by Rutter & McCarthy, Music & Musical Instrument Sellers No. 120, New Bond Street.

Five pages. Plate number 119. The plate number suggests about November or December 1819 (Neighbour & Tyson). Entered at Stationers' Hall on 29 January 1819.

[London, British Library; London, collection of Robert Spencer; Oxford, Bodleian Library; Glasgow, University Library; Laguna Beach, collection of Mary Belle Swingle, signed 'F. Sor' (not seen).]

Another issue:

The same, but printed by 'T. Swain, Music & Musical Instrument Seller 53, Upper Baker St. Regent's Park'.   C. 1838-53 (Humphries & Smith).

[London, Guildhall School of Music; Barcelona, collection of Emilio Pujol.]

FRENCH EDITION:

Six Divertissemens Pour la Guitare Composés et Dédiés à Miss Smith par Ferdinando Sor. Oeuv. 8. Prix 3 fr. A Paris Au Bureau du Journal de Guitare, Chez Meissonnier, Rue Montmartre, No. 182. . . .

Six pages.   Plate number 118.   C. 1817-22. The music is headed 'Nouvelle Collection. IIre. 12e. Livaison [sic]'.

[Brussels, Conservatoire; Copenhagen, Royal Library; Paris, Bibliothèque Nationale (two copies).]

Later issues:

i) Boulevard Montmartre No. 25. 1825-39.
[Copenhagen, Royal Library; London, collection of Robert Spencer.]

ii) Heugel. 1849 or after.
[Barcelona, Biblioteca Central.]

A copy of Meissonnier's edition, without title-page, is in Barcelona, Orfeó Catalá.

GERMAN EDITION:

Six Divertissemens . . . Bonn et Cologne chez N. Simrock.

Five pages. Plate number on music 2291; on title-page 2286, 2287, 2291. The same title-page serves also for op. 1 and op. 2. C. 1824-5.

[Barcelona, collection of Emilio Pujol; Copenhagen, Royal Library; Stockholm, Royal Music Academy (not seen).]

Opus 9: Variations on an air from The Magic Flute

ENGLISH EDITION:

The Favorite Air, "Oh Cara armonia", from Mozart's Opera Il Flauto Magico, Arranged with an Introduction and Variations for the Guitar, As Performed by the Author, at the Nobilities Concerts, Dedicated to his Brother, by F. Sor. Ent. Sta. Hall. Price 2s/6 London, Printed by the Royal Harmonic Institution . . .

Five pages. Plate number 602. Entered at Stationers' Hall on 1 March 1821.

[London, British Library (two copies); London, Guildhall School of Music; Oxford, Bodleian Library; Glasgow, University Library.]

Introduction, theme, five variations and coda.

FRENCH EDITION:

Introduction et Variations sur un Thême de Mozart Composées et Dédiées A Ch. Sor Par son Frère Ferdinando Sor. Oeuv. 9. Prix 3fr. A Paris Au Bureau du Journal de Guitare, Chez Messonnier, Rue Montmartre, No. 182 . . .

Six pages. Plate number 119.

[Brussels, Conservatoire; Copenhagen, Royal Library; Paris, Bibliothèque Nationale (two copies).]

Introduction, theme, and four variations. The first variation of the London edition and the coda are omitted, and the other four variations appear in the order: 3, 5, 2, 4. The music is headed: 'Nouvelle Collection. 9e. et 10e. Livraison'. C. 1817-22.

Another issue:

Heugel. 1849 or after.

[Barcelona, collection of Emilio Pujol.]

REVISED FRENCH EDITION:

Variations Brillantes sur un Air Favori de Mozart de l'Opera: la Flûte Enchantée O Cara Armonia Pour Guitare Seule Exécutées par l'Auteur au Concert donné à l'Ecole R[oya]le de Musique et Dédiées à son Frère par Ferdinando Sor. Op. 9. Prix: 3f. Nouvelle Edition augmentée par l'Auteur. A Paris, au Magasin de Musique de A. Meissonnier, Boulevard Montmartre, No. 25.

Five pages. Plate number 460. Late 1826 or early 1827. The same contents as the English edition.

[Copenhagen, Royal Library; London, collection of Robert Spencer.]

Another issue:

Heugel. 1849 or after.

[Barcelona, collection of Emilio Pujol.]

GERMAN EDITION:

Introduction et Variations sur un Thême de Mozart . . . Leipzig, au Bureau de Musique de Peters.

Five pages. Plate number 1807.

[Copenhagen, Royal Library; Stockholm, Royal Music Academy (not seen).]

Listed in Hofmeister in 1824. The same contents as Meissonnier's first edition.

ANOTHER GERMAN EDITION:

Introduction et Variations pour la Guitarre sur un thème de Mozart . . . Bonn et Cologne chez N. Simrock.

Five pages. Plate number 2292. C. 1824-5.

[London, British Library.]

The same contents as Meissonnier's first edition.

Opus 10: Fantasia

FIRST EDITION:

Troisième Fantaisie Composée Pour la Guitare par Ferdinando Sor. Oeuv. 10. Prix 3 fr. A Paris Au Bureau du Journal de Guitare, Chez Meissonnier, Rue Montmartre, No. 182, . . .

Seven pages. Plate number 120. C. 1817-22.

[Brussels, Conservatoire; Copenhagen, Royal Library; Paris, Bibliothèque Nationale (two copies).]

Later issues:

i) Boulevard Montmartre No. 25. 1825-39.
[London, collection of Robert Spencer.]

ii) Meissonnier & Heugel. 1839-49.
[Barcelona, collection of Emilio Pujol; London, collection of Robert Spencer.]

GERMAN EDITION:

Troisième Fantaisie . . . Bonn et Cologne chez N. Simrock.

Seven pages. Plate number 2293. C. 1824-5.

[Copenhagen, Royal Library, with a pasted sticker: 'Zu haben in August Cranz Musikhandlung in der grossen Reichenstrasse in Hamburg'; London, British Library; Stockholm, Royal Music Academy (not seen).]

Opus 11: Deux Thêmes Variés et Douze Menuets

The theme of the first set of variations is the same as that of the *Thème Varié;* see 'Guitar music without opus number'. Minuets nos. 5 and 6 date from before the publication of op. 11; also possibly no. 3 (see the main text of this book). Minuet no. 12 = op. 13, no. 4.

MINUET NO. 5:

[In a MS called 'Música pa. Guitarra' in the collection of Robert Spencer, London.]

MINUET NO. 6:

Minuetto.

One of 'Menuets Composés pour la Guitare par Dn. Fernando Sors' in the *Journal de Musique Etrangère pour la Guitare ou Lyre,* edited by Castro, Paris, c. 1810 (see op. 3). See below, 'Guitar music without opus number'.

One page. Plate number 5. Oblong format.

FIRST EDITION:

Deux Thêmes Variés et Douze Menuets Pour la Guitare Composés par Ferdinando Sor. Prix 4 f. 50 c. Oeuvre 11. à Paris Propriété de l'Editeur. Au Bureau du Journal de Guitare, Chez Meissonnier, Rue Montmartre, No. 182 . . .

Fourteen pages. Plate number 135. 1822 or shortly before.

[Copenhagen, Royal Library; Paris, Bibliothèque Nationale (two copies).]

Later issues:

i) Boulevard Montmartre No. 25. 1825-39.
[London, collection of Robert Spencer.]

ii) Heugel. 1849 or after.
[Barcelona, collection of Emilio Pujol (imperfect).]

A copy of Meissonnier's edition, without title-page, is in Barcelona, Orfeó Catalá.

GERMAN EDITION:

Deux Themes Variés et Douze Menuets . . . Bonn et Cologne chez N. Simrock.

Fourteen pages. Plate number 2295. C. 1824-5.

[Copenhagen, Royal Library; London, British Library.]

Opus 12: Quatrième Fantaisie

This work is a revised version of opus 3, omitting one variation and the minuet, and adding three new variations, an introduction, and a coda.

FIRST EDITION:

Quatrième Fantaisie Composée et Dédiée à Monsieur Frédéric Kalkbrenner par son Ami Ferdinando Sor. Op. 12. Prix 4f. 50c. à Paris Au Bureau du Journal de Guitare, Chez Meissonnier, Rue Montmartre, No. 182 . . .

Seven pages. Plate number 144. 1822 or shortly before.

[Brussels, Conservatoire; Copenhagen, Royal Library; Paris, Bibliothèque Nationale (two copies).]

Later issues:

i) Boulevard Montmartre No. 25. 1825-39.
[London, collection of Robert Spencer.]

ii) Meissonnier & Heugel. 1839-49.
[London, collection of Robert Spencer.]

GERMAN EDITION:

Quatrième Fantaisie . . . Bonn et Cologne chez N. Simrock.

Seven pages. Plate number 2297. C. 1824-5.

[Copenhagen, Royal Library; London, British Library; Stockholm, Royal Music Academy (not seen).]

Opus 13: Six Divertimenti

FIRST EDITION:

Six Divertimentos for the Guitar, By F. Sor. 4th Set. Ent. Sta. Hall. Price 2s/6 London, Published by the Regent's Harmonic Institution. . . .

Five pages. Plate number 313. Entered at Stationers' Hall on 18 December 1819. Reviewed in Ackermann's *Repository of Arts* on 1 February 1820. Note that no opus number is given. No. 4 = op. 11, minuet no. 12.

[London, British Library; London, Guildhall School of Music; London, collection of Robert Spencer; Oxford, Bodleian Library; Edinburgh, National Library of Scotland; Glasgow, University Library.]

Another issue:

As above, but 'Royal Harmonic Institution'. 1820 or after.

[London, collection of Brian Jeffery.]

FRENCH EDITION:

Quatrième Divertissement Pour la Guitare Facile et Soigneusement Doigté Composé par Ferdinando Sor. Op. 13. Prix 3f. à Paris Au Magasin de Musique de A. Meissonnier, Galerie des Panoramas, No. 15. . . .

Five pages. Plate number 175. 1822-25.

[Brussels, Conservatoire; Copenhagen, Royal Library (two copies, one signed 'A. Meissonnier'); Paris, Bibliothèque Nationale (two copies).]

Later issues:

i) Boulevard Montmartre No. 25. 1825-39.
[London, collection of Robert Spencer.]

ii) Heugel. 1849 or after.
[Copenhagen, Royal Library]

iii) Heugel. New title-page. 1849 or after.
[London, Guildhall School of Music.]

Copies of Heugel issues are in Barcelona, collection of Emilio Pujol, and in Stockholm, Royal Music Academy (not seen).

Opus 14: Grand Solo

FIRST EDITION:

Sonata Prima pour la Guitare. Par Dn. Fernando Sors.

In the *Journal de Musique Etrangère pour la Guitare ou Lyre,* edited by Castro, Paris, c. 1810. Oblong format.

Seven pages. Plate number 50.

For location of copies, see op. 3.

ANOTHER EDITION:

Grand Solo Pour La Guitare Composé et Dédié Aux Amateurs par Ferdinando Sor. Opera 14. Prix 4f. 50c. à Paris Chez Meissonnier, Boulevart Montmartre, No. 4 . . .

Nine pages. Plate number 188. 1822. A simplified version.

[Paris, Bibliothèque Nationale (two copies).]

Later issues:

i) Boulevard Montmartre No. 25. 1825-39.
[London, collection of Robert Spencer.]

ii) Heugel. 1849 or after.

[Barcelona, Biblioteca Central; Barcelona, collection of Emilio Pujol; London, collection of Robert Spencer; Stockholm, Royal Music Academy (not seen).]

GERMAN EDITION:

Grand Solo . . . Bonn et Cologne chez N. Simrock.

Nine pages. Plate number 2299. C. 1824-5.

[Copenhagen, Royal Library; London, British Library.]

AN ARRANGEMENT BY AGUADO:

Gran Solo de Sor Para Guitarra Escrito para el uso de Agustin Campo por su Maestro D. Aguado prop. del Editor . . . Madrid, Se Hallará de venta en la Guitar-rería de Campo, Ce. Angta. de Majaderitos.

Twelve pages. The dedication is dated 1849.

[Barcelona, Orfeó Catalá.]

Opus 15 (a): Folies d'Espagne and Minuet

FIRST EDITION:

Paris, Meissonnier, Rue Montmartre No. 182. Title as below. Without separate title-page and without opus number. No copy found.

Later issues:

i) Les Folies d'Espagne, variées, et un Menuet Composé pour Guitare seule, Par Ferdinando Sor. Oeuvre 15. Prix: 2 fr. 40 c. A Paris, au magasin de Musique de Meissonnier, Galerie des Panoramas, No. 15 . . .

No separate title-page; the above is the heading to the music. Three pages. Plate number 44. 1822-25.

[Brussels, Conservatoire; Copenhagen, Royal Library; London, collection of Robert Spencer; Paris, Bibliothèque Nationale (two copies).]

The plate number dates from the time when Meissonnier's address was 182 rue Montmartre, thus presupposing the existence of an earlier issue with that address of which no copy has been found. It also dates from before the opus numbering had reached 15, suggesting that that earlier issue did not bear any opus number.

ii) Heugel. 1849 or after.
[Barcelona, collection of Emilio Pujol; Vienna, Stadtbibliothek.]

GERMAN EDITION:

Les Folies d'Espagne . . . Bonn et Cologne chez N. Simrock.

No separate title-page; the above is the heading to the music. No opus number. Three pages. Plate number 2306. C. 1824-5.

[Copenhagen, Royal Library; London, British Library; Stockholm, Royal Music Academy (not seen).]

ENGLISH EDITION:

Cocks & Co., c. 1835. Advertised on the title-page of Cocks' edition of op. 5, q.v. No copy found.

Opus 15(b): Sonata

FIRST EDITION:

Sonata seconda pour la Guitare, Composée par Fernando Sors.

In the *Journal de Musique Etrangère pour la Guitare ou Lyre,* edited by Castro, Paris, c. 1810.

Four pages.   Plate number 47. Oblong format.

For location of copies, see op. 3.

ANOTHER EDITION:

Sonate, composée par Ferdinando Sor. Prix: 1f. 50c. A Paris, au Bureau du Journal de Guitare, Chez Meissonnier, rue Montmartre No. 182 . . .

No separate title-page; the above is the heading to the music. Three pages. Plate number 110.   C. 1817-22.

[Brussels, Conservatoire; Copenhagen, Royal Library; London, collection of Robert Spencer; Paris, Bibliothèque Nationale (two copies).]

No opus number is given by Castro or Meissonnier. The opus number 15 appears in Simrock's edition of c. 1824-5, and in a catalogue issued by Meissonnier. For convenience, and to distinguish it from *Folies d'Espagne,* we may call the work op. 15(b).

Later issues:

i) Meissonnier & Heugel. 1839-49.
[London, collection of Robert Spencer.]

ii) Heugel. 1849 or after.

[Barcelona, Biblioteca Central; Barcelona, Orfeó Catalá; Stockholm, Royal Music Academy (not seen).]

GERMAN EDITION:

Sonate . . . Bonn et Cologne chez N. Simrock.

No separate title-page. Three pages. Plate number 2310. C. 1824-5.

[Copenhagen, Royal Library; London, British Library; London, Guildhall School of Music; Stockholm, Royal Music Academy (not seen).]

Opus 15(c): *Thème Varié*

The opus number 15 is given to this work in a Meissonnier catalogue, although it does not appear in the music itself. For convenience, it may be called op. 15(c). The number 'op. 15(c)' has been given in at least one modern edition to the March from *Cendrillon* arranged for guitar, but there is no documentary authority for this, although copies of the March are known which are printed together with *Folies d'Espagne* or the *Thème Varié*. For the March, see 'Guitar music without opus number'.

The *Thème Varié* uses the same theme as the first set of variations in op. 11. To judge from the plate numbers, op. 11 came first. Op. 11 has the theme and six variations; the *Thème Varié* has the theme and four variations, of which three were already in op. 11 and only one is new. It seems to be merely a different and shorter version of the same set of variations.

FIRST EDITION:

Thème Varié pour la Guitare, Composé par F. Sor. Prix: 1fr. 50c. A Paris, au Magasin de Musique de A. Meissonnier, Galerie neuve des Panoramas, No. 15.

Two pages. Plate number 219. No separate title-page; the above is the heading to the music. 1822 or 1823.

[Brussels, Conservatoire, Copenhagen, Royal Library; London, collection of Robert Spencer; Paris, Bibliothèque Nationale (two copies).]

Another issue:

Heugel. 1849 or after.

[Barcelona, Biblioteca Central.]

GERMAN EDITION:

Thème Varié . . . Bonn et Cologne chez N. Simrock.

Two pages. Plate number 2302. C. 1824-5. With a title-page serving also for the March from *Cendrillon,* reading 'Diverses Pièces. . .'

[Copenhagen, Royal Library; Copenhagen, Music History Museum; London, British Library; Stockholm, Royal Music Academy (not seen).]

Opus 16: *Fantasia: Variations on Paisiello's* '*Nel cor piu non mi sento*'

FIRST EDITION:

Cinquième Fantaisie Pour la Guitare avec des Variations sur l'Air de Paisiello Nel cor piu non mi sento Composée par Ferdinand Sor. Prix: 4f. 50c. A Paris, au Magasin de Musique d'A. Meissonnier, Galerie des Panoramas, no. 15. . . .

Eleven pages. Plate number 234. 1823. Note than no opus number is given.

[Brussels, Conservatoire; Copenhagen, Royal Library.]

Later issues:

i) The same, with 'Op. 16' added. 1823-25.
[Paris, Bibliothèque Nationale (two copies).]

ii) Boulevard Montmartre No. 25. 1825-39.
[London, collection of Robert Spencer.]

iii) Heugel. 1849 or after.
[Stockholm, Royal Music Academy (not seen).]

GERMAN EDITION:

Cinquième Fantaisie . . . Bonn et Cologne chez N. Simrock.

Eleven pages. Plate number 2304. C. 1824-5. No opus number is given.

[Copenhagen, Royal Library; London, British Library.]

Opus 17: *Six Waltzes*

FIRST EDITION:

Six Valtzes pour Guitare seule Composées et Dédiées à son Ami B. Pastou par Ferdinand Sor [blank] Livre Op. 17. Prix: 3f. A Paris, au Magasin de Musique de A. Meissonnier, Galerie neuve des Panoramas, No. 15. . . .

Seven pages. Plate number 258. 1823-25.

[Brussels, Conservatoire; Copenhagen, Royal Library; Paris, Bibliothèque Nationale (two copies).]

It appears that this title-page, and perhaps also the opus number, were intended to serve also for op. 18, although in fact op. 18 has its own title-page and opus number.

Later issues:

i) Boulevard Montmartre No. 25. 1825-39.
[London, collection of Robert Spencer.]

ii) Meissonnier & Heugel. 1839-49.
[London, collection of Robert Spencer.]

iii) Heugel. 1849 or after.
[Barcelona, collection of Emilio Pujol; Stockholm, Royal Music Academy (not seen).]

GERMAN EDITION:

Six Walzes . . . Bonn et Cologne chez N. Simrock.

Seven pages. Plate number 2315 (2215 on title-page, in error). The same title-page as for op. 18. C. 1824-5.

[Copenhagen, Royal Library; London, British Library.]

ANOTHER FRENCH EDITION:

Lyon, Arnaud. A copy in the Conservatorio di Musica, Naples (not seen). Date unknown.

Opus 18: Six Waltzes

FIRST EDITION:

Six Valtzes Pour Guitare Seule Composées et Dédiées à Madame Gravier par Ferdinand Sor 2e. Livre. Op. 18. Prix: 3f. à Paris, Au Magasin de Musique de A. Meissonnier, Galerie neuve des Panoramas, No. 15.

Seven pages. Plate number 261. 1823-25.

[Brussels, Conservatoire, with the title-page of op. 17; Paris, Bibliothèque Nationale (two copies).]

Later issues:

i) Boulevard Montmartre No. 25. 1825-39.
[London, collection of Robert Spencer.]
ii) Meissonnier & Heugel. 1839-49.
[London, collection of Robert Spencer.]
iii) Heugel. 1849 or after.
[Barcelona, collection of Emilio Pujol.]

GERMAN EDITION:

Six Walzes . . . Bonn et Cologne chez N. Simrock.

Seven pages. Plate number 2305. The same title-page as for op. 17. C. 1824-5.

[Copenhagen, Royal Library; London, British Library; Stockholm, Royal Music Academy (not seen).]

Opus 19: Six Airs from The Magic Flute

FIRST EDITION:

Six airs choisis de l'Opéra de Mozart: Il Flauto Magico, arrangés pour Guitare et dédiés à Mr. Amédée par son ami Ferdinand Sor. Op. 19. Prix: 3f. A Paris, au Magasin de Musique de A. Meissonnier, Galerie neuve des Panoramas, No. 15.

Five pages. Plate number 265. 1823-25.

[Brussels, Conservatoire; Paris, Bibliothèque Nationale (two copies).]

Later issues:

i) Boulevard Montmartre No. 25. 1825-39.
[London, collection of Robert Spencer.]
ii) Heugel. 1849 or after.
[Barcelona, Biblioteca Central; Barcelona, collection of Emilio Pujol.]

GERMAN EDITION:

Six Airs Choisis de l'Opera de Mozart: La Flûte magique . . . Bonn et Cologne chez N. Simrock.

Five pages. Plate number 2301. C. 1824-5.

[Copenhagen, Royal Library; London, British Library; Stockholm, Royal Music Academy (not seen).]

ENGLISH EDITION:

Six Airs Choisis, d l'Opera de Mozart Il Flauto Magico . . . London . . . R. Cocks & Co . . .

Five pages. Plate number 2380. C. 1835 (Neighbour & Tyson).

[London, Royal College of Music.]

Opus 20: Introduction et Thême Varié

The theme is the same as that of a *Thema varié* published in the *Journal de Musique Etrangère pour la Guitare ou Lyre,* edited by Castro, Paris, c. 1810; see 'Guitar music without opus number'. Only one of the variations, however, is the same.

FIRST EDITION:

Introduction et Thême Varié pour la Guitare Composés et Dédiés à Monsieur A. Meissonnier par son Ami Ferdinand Sor Opera 20. Prix: 4f. 50. à Paris Au Magasin de Musique de A. Meissonnier, Galerie neuve des Panoramas, No. 15.

Seven pages. Plate number 266. 1823-25.

[Paris, Bibliothèque Nationale (two copies).]

Another issue:

Boulevard Montmartre No. 25. 1825-39.

[Barcelona, Biblioteca Central; London, collection of Robert Spencer.]

GERMAN EDITION:

Introduction et Thême Varié . . . Bonn et Cologne chez N. Simrock.

Nine pages. Plate number 2300. C. 1824-5.

[Copenhagen, Royal Library; London, British Library; Stockholm, Royal Music Academy (not seen).]

Opus 21: Fantasia: Les Adieux

FIRST EDITION:

Les Adieux! Sixième Fantaisie pour Guitare seule, dédiée à son Ami Fr. Vaccari, 1er Violon de la Chambre de S.M.C. par Ferdinando Sor Op. 21. Prix: 2f. 40c. A Paris au Magasin de Musique de A. Meissonnier, petite Galerie des Panoramas, No. 15. . . .

Three pages. Plate number 304. 1825.

[London, collection of Robert Spencer; Paris, Bibliothèque Nationale (two copies).]

Another issue:

Boulevard Montmartre No. 25. 1825-39.

[London, collection of Robert Spencer, inscribed 'A Dios F. Sor a su amigo F. Vaccari. Londres 28 de Julio de 1816'.]

GERMAN EDITION:

Les Adieux Sixième Fantaisie . . . Bonn chez N. Simrock.

Three pages. Plate number 2847. 1830.

[Copenhagen, Royal Library.]

SPANISH EDITION:

La Despedida Andante y Allegretto para Guitarra Sola de D. Fernando Sor dedicada a su amigo Don Francisco Vaccari Primer Violin de la Real Camara, y de la Capilla de S.M.C.

Three pages. No separate title-page; the above is the heading to the music. Plate number A.R. 2302. At the foot of the page: 'Antonio Romero, Calle de Preciados No. 1 Madrid'.

[Barcelona, Orfeó Catalá; Stockholm, Royal Music Academy (not seen).]

Opus 22: Sonata

FIRST EDITION:

Grande Sonate pour Guitare seule, Composée par F. Sor. Op. 22. Prix: 4f. 50c. A Paris au Magasin de Musique de A. Meissonnier, Boulevard Montmartre, No. 25 . . .

Eleven pages. Plate number 305. 1825. The music is headed 'Grand [sic] Sonate de Sor, qui fut dédiée au prince de la Paix'. The 'prince de la Paix' was Manuel Godoy; this dedication shows that this sonata was probably composed in some form in 1808 or before.

[Brussels, Conservatoire; London, collection of Robert Spencer; Paris, Bibliothèque Nationale (two copies).]

Later issues:

i) Meissonnier & Heugel. 1839-49.
[London, collection of Robert Spencer.]

ii) Heugel. 1849 or after.
[Barcelona, collection of Emilio Pujol.]

GERMAN EDITION:

Grande Sonate . . . Bonn chez N. Simrock.

Eleven pages. Plate number 2814. 1830.

[Berlin, Deutsche Staatbibliothek; Copenhagen, Royal Library.]

Opus 23: Six Divertimenti

Note that op. 24, on the first page of music, is incorrectly called op. 23.

FIRST EDITION OF TWO OF THE PIECES:

Nos. 4 and 2 appeared as 'Un menuet et un petit Allegro' in the *Journal de Musique Etrangère pour la Guitare ou Lyre,* edited by Castro, Paris, c. 1810. Two pages. Oblong format. For location of copies, see op. 3.

FIRST EDITION OF SIX PIECES:

Cinquième Divertissement très Facile pour la Guitare par Ferdinando Sor. Op. 23. Prix: 3f. à Paris, au Magasin de Musique de A. Meissonnier, Boulevard Montmartre, No. 25 . . .

Five pages. Plate number 348. 1826.

[Brussels, Conservatoire; London, collection of Robert Spencer; Paris, Bibliothèque Nationale (two copies).]

Another issue:

Heugel. 1849 or after.
[Barcelona, collection of Emilio Pujol.]

GERMAN EDITION:

Cinquième Divertissement . . . Bonn chez N. Simrock.

Nine pages. Plate number 2841. 1830.

[Copenhagen, Royal Library.]

Opus 24: Huit Petites Pièces

FIRST EDITION:

Huit Petites Pièces Pour Guitare Seule, Composées par Ferdinand Sor. Opéra 24. Prix: 3f. 75c. Propriété de l'Editeur. à Paris, Au Magasin de Musique de A. Meissonnier, Boulevard Montmartre, No. 25.

Six pages. Plate number 468. 1827. The music is incorrectly headed 'Op. 23'.

[Barcelona, Biblioteca Central; Brussels, Conservatoire; Copenhagen, Royal Library; London, collection of Robert Spencer; Paris, Bibliothèque Nationale.]

Another issue:

Heugel. 1849 or after.
[Barcelona, collection of Emilio Pujol.]

GERMAN EDITION:

Huit Petites Pièces . . . Bonn chez N. Simrock.

Seven pages. Plate number 2844. 1830.

[Berlin, Deutsche Staatsbibliothek; Copenhagen, Royal Library; London, British Library; London, collection of Robert Spencer, with a pasted sticker reading 'Munster, in der Instrumenten und Musikhandlung von M. Kneer'.]

Opus 25: Sonata

FIRST EDITION:

Deuxième Grande Sonate Pour Guitare Seule Composée par Ferdinand Sor. Op. 25. Prix: 7f. 50c. Propriété de l'Editeur. à Paris, Au Magasin de Musique de A. Meissonnier, Boulevard Montmartre, No. 25.

Seventeen pages. Plate number 469. 1827.

[Brussels, Conservatoire; Copenhagen, Royal Library; London, collection of Robert Spencer; Paris, Bibliothèque Nationale.]

Later issues:

i) Meissonnier & Heugel. 1839-49.
[London, collection of Robert Spencer.]

ii) Heugel. With a new title-page. 1849 or after.
[London, Guildhall School of Music.]

GERMAN EDITION:

Deuxième Grande Sonate . . . Bonn chez N. Simrock.

Seventeen pages. Plate number 2843. 1830.

[Berlin, Deutsche Staatsbibliothek; Copenhagen, Royal Library; London, British Library; London, collection of Robert Spencer, with a pasted sticker reading 'Munster, in der Instrumenten und Musikhandlung von M. Kneer'; Stockholm, Royal Music Academy (not seen).]

Opus 26: Introduction and Variations on 'Que ne suis-je la fougère!'

FIRST EDITION:

Introduction et Variations sur l'Air: Que ne suis-je la fougère! Pour Guitare Seule, par Ferdinand Sor. Opéra 26. Prix: 2f. 25c. Propriété de l'Editeur. à Paris, Au Magasin de Musique de A. Meissonnier, Boulevard Montmartre, No. 25.

Four pages. Plate number 472. 1827.

[Barcelona, Biblioteca Central; Brussels, Conservatoire; London, collection of Robert Spencer; Paris, Bibliothèque Nationale.]

GERMAN EDITION:

Introduction et Variations sur l'Air: Que ne suis-je la fougère! . . . Bonn chez N. Simrock.

Four pages. Plate number 2848. 1830.

[Copenhagen, Royal Library; Stockholm, Royal Music Academy (not seen).]

Opus 27: Introduction and Variations on 'Gentil housard'

FIRST EDITION:

Introduction et Variations sur l'Air: Gentil Housard Pour Guitare Seule par Ferdinand Sor. Opéra 27. Prix: 3f. 75c. Propriété de l'Editeur. à Paris, Au Magasin de Musique de A. Meissonnier, Boulevard Montmartre, No. 25.

Five pages. Plate number 473. 1827.

[Brussels, Conservatoire, Copenhagen, Royal Library; London, collection of Robert Spencer; Paris, Bibliothèque Nationale (two copies).]

GERMAN EDITION:

Introduction et Variations sur l'Air. Gentil housard. . . . Bonn chez N. Simrock.

Four pages. Plate number 2861. 1830.

[Copenhagen, Royal Library; Stockholm, Royal Music Academy (not seen).]

Opus 28: Introduction and Variations on 'Malbroug'

FIRST EDITION:

Introduction et variations sur l'Air: Malbroug, pour Guitare seule, par Ferdinand Sor. Op. 28. Prix: 3f. 75c. Propriété de l'Editeur à Paris, Au Magasin de Musique de A. Meissonnier, Boulevard Montmartre, No. 25.

Five pages. Plate number 474. 1827.

[Barcelona, Biblioteca Central; Brussels, Conservatoire; Copenhagen, Royal Library; London, Guildhall School of Music; London, collection of Robert Spencer; Paris, Bibliothèque Nationale.]

GERMAN EDITION:

Introduction et Variations sur l'Air Malbroug . . . Bonn chez N. Simrock.

Four pages. Plate number 2862. 1830.

[Copenhagen, Royal Library; Stockholm, Royal Music Academy (not seen).]

Opus 29: Douze Etudes

FIRST EDITION:

Douze Etudes Pour la Guitare pour servir de suite aux douze premières, Dédiées à ses Elèves par Ferdinand Sor. Opéra 29. Prix: 9f. 2e. Livre d'Etudes. Propriété de l'Editeur. A Paris, au Magasin de Musique de A. Meissonnier, Boulevard Montmartre, No. 25.

Nineteen pages. Plate number 475. 1827.

[Barcelona, Orfeó Catalá (two copies); Brussels, Conservatoire; Copenhagen, Royal Library; London, Guildhall School of Music; London, collection of Robert Spencer.]

Later issues:

i) Issued together with op. 6. 1825-39. See 'Collections of guitar music'.

ii) Heugel. With a new title-page. 1849 or after.
[Barcelona, collection of Emilio Pujol.]

GERMAN EDITION:

Douze Etudes . . . Bonn, chez N. Simrock.

Nineteen pages. Plate number 2842. 1830.

[Copenhagen, Royal Library; Vienna, Gesellschaft der Musikfreunde.]

Opus 30: Fantasia

FIRST EDITION:

7e. Fantaisie et Variations Brillantes Sur deux Airs Favoris connus Pour Guitare Seule Exécutées par l'Auteur à son Concert, donné à Paris et Dédiées à son ami Denis Aguado. Par Ferdd. Sor. Opera: 30. Propriété de l'Editeur Prix: 4f. 50c. à Paris Au Magasin de Musique de A. Meissonnier . . . Boulevard Montmartre, No. 25.

Nine pages. Plate number 497. 1828.

[Brussels, Conservatoire; Copenhagen, Royal Library; London, collection of Robert Spencer.]

GERMAN EDITION:

7e Fantaisie . . . Bonn chez N. Simrock.

Nine pages. Plate number 2845. 1830.

[Copenhagen, Royal Library.]

Opus 31: Vingt Quatre Leçons

FIRST EDITION:

Vingt Quatre leçons Progressives Pour la Guitare Doigtées avec soin Dédiées aux Elèves Commençants par Ferdinand Sor Op: 31. Prix: 4f. 50c. [blank] Livre. Propriété de l'Editeur A Paris, Au Magasin de Musique de A. Meissonnier, Boulevard Montmartre, No. 25. . . .

Published in two books. Book 1 has studies 1-12; nine pages; plate number 499. Book 2 has studies 13-24; fifteen pages; plate number 500. The same title-page, with the plate number 499, is used for both books, with a blank before the word 'Livre', to be filled in '1' or '2' by hand. 1828.

[Book 1: Barcelona, Orfeó Catalá; Brussels, Conservatoire.)

[Book 2: Barcelona, Orfeó Catalá; Barcelona, Biblioteca Central (incomplete); Brussels, Conservatoire, with a pasted sticker reading 'Bruxelles chez Mme. Nolot . . . Montagne de la Cour, No. 672'.]

Another issue:

The same, but with a new title-page beginning 'aux Jeunes Elèves'. Heugel. 1849 or after.

[Book 1: London, British Library; London, collection of Robert Spencer.]

[Book 2: London, British Library.]

GERMAN EDITION:

Vingt Quatre Leçons Progressive . . . Bonn chez N. Simrock.

Two books, of eleven and fifteen pages respectively. Plate numbers 2815 and 2846. The same title-page is used for both books. 1830.

[Book 1: Copenhagen, Royal Library (two copies, of which one has a design in red overprinted); London, Guildhall School of Music.]

[Book 2: Copenhagen, Royal Library (one copy only); London, collection of Robert Spencer.]

Opus 32: Six Petites Pièces

FIRST EDITION:

Six Petities pieces Faciles et Doigtées avec Soin Pour Guitare Seule Composées et Respectueusement Dédiées à Son Eleve Mlle. Wainewright par Ferdinand Sor. Propriété de l'Editeur Opera: 32. Prix 4f. 50. A Paris, Au Magasin de Musique de A. Meissonnier, Boulevard Montmartre, No. 25. . . .

Eight pages. Plate number 502. 1828.

[Brussels, Conservatoire, with a pasted sticker reading 'Bruxelles chez Mme Nolot . . . Montagne de la Cour, No. 672'; London, collection of Robert Spencer.]

Another issue:

Heugel. 1849 or after.

[Barcelona, Biblioteca Central.]

GERMAN EDITION:

Six Petites Pièces . . . Bonn chez N. Simrock.

Eight pages. Plate number 2819. 1830.

[Copenhagen, Royal Library; London, collection of Robert Spencer, with a pasted sticker reading 'à Amsterdam, chez la Veuve L. Hagenaar, Stil Steeg, No. 3'; Stockholm, Royal Music Academy (not seen).]

Opus 33: Trois Pièces de Société

FIRST EDITION:

Trois Pièces de Société pour Guitare Seule Composées et Dédiées à Mademoiselle Athenaïs Paulian par Ferdinand Sor Opera: 33 Prix: 4f. 50c. Propriété de l'Editeur. A Paris, Au Magasin de Musique de A. Meissonnier, Boulevard Montmartre, No. 25. . . .

Twelve pages. Plate number 505. 1828.

[Brussels, Conservatoire, with a pasted sticker reading 'Bruxelles chez Mme Nolot . . . Montagne de la Cour, No. 672'; London, collection of Robert Spencer.]

GERMAN EDITION:

Trois Pieces de Société . . . Bonn chez N. Simrock.

Twelve pages. Plate number 2816. 1830.

[Copenhagen, Royal Library: Stockholm, Royal Music Academy (not seen).]

Opus 34: L'Encouragement (guitar duet)

Note that op. 36, in Simrock's and Dunst's editions, is erroneously called op. 34.

FIRST EDITION:

L'Encouragement. Fantaisie à deux guitares . . . chez Pacini, Paris.

Plate number 2. 1828.

[Private collection (not seen).]

GERMAN EDITION:

L'Encouragement Fantaisie Pour Deux Guitarres composée par Ferdinando Sor. Oeuv. 34. Hambourg, chez Jean Aug. Böhme. . . .

Two separate guitar parts, marked '1°. [sic] Guitare. L'Eleve' and '2°. [sic] Guitare. Le Maitre'. Each part has the title-page and pages numbered 2-7. Listed in Hofmeister in 1841.

[Copenhagen, Royal Library; Copenhagen, Music History Museum.]

AN ARRANGEMENT BY NAPOLEON COSTE:

L'Encouragement de F. Sor arrangé pour deux Guitares concertantes par Nap. Coste . . . Paris, Nap. Coste, Rue du Faubg. S. Martin, 50.

Two guitar parts. Plate number N.C. 51. Paris copy received in 1879.

[Paris, Bibliothèque Nationale.]

Opus 35: Vingt Quatre Exercices

FIRST EDITION:

Vingt quatre Exercices Très Faciles & Soigneusement Doigtés pour la Guitare composés par Ferdinando Sor Livr. 35e. Prix: 4fr. 50c. Propriété de l'Auteur. A Paris, au Magasin de Musique de Pacini, Editeur des opera de Rossini Boulevard Italien, No. 11.

Published in two books. Book 1 has studies 1-12 and eleven pages. Book 2 has studies 13-24 and thirteen pages. Plate number 'Sor-2'. The same title-page is used for both books. 1828.

[Book 1: Brussels, Conservatoire, signed 'Sor'; Paris, Bibliothèque Nationale, signed 'Sor'.]

[Book 2: Brussels, Conservatoire, signed 'F. Sor'.]

Another issue:

The same, except that '35e' is deleted and replaced with, in a different position, 'Oeuvre 35'; the price is 6 fr.; and the plate number is 'Sor-3'.

[Book 1: Barcelona, Orfeó Catalá, signed 'Sor'; London, collection of Robert Spencer, signed 'J. de Lira'.]

[Book 2: Barcelona, Orfeó Catalá, signed 'Sor'; London, collection of Robert Spencer.]

GERMAN EDITION:

Vingt Quatre Exercices . . . Bonn chez N. Simrock.

Two books, of eleven and thirteen pages. Plate numbers 2768 and 2770. The same title-page is used for both volumes. 1830.

[Book 1: Copenhagen, Royal Library (two copies, of which has a design in blue overprinted); Stockholm, Royal Music Academy (not seen).]

[Book 2: Copenhagen, Royal Library (one copy only, overprinted in blue); Stockholm, Royal Music Academy (not seen).]

ENGLISH EDITION:

Twenty Four Exercises, Composed & Carefully fingered for the Spanish Guitar . . . London, Published by Johanning & Whatmore . . . 126 Regent St. . . .

Two books. The same title-page serves for both. Mentioned as 'published in the last month' in the *Harmonicon,* 1830, p. 268.

[London, Guildhall School of Music.]

Opus 36: Trois Pièces de Société

This work was first published without an opus number, thus leading Simrock and Dunst in Germany to consider it as op. 34 and to number it accordingly. Later, however, it was reissued with the opus number 36.

Note that the *Sérénade,* op. 37, was numbered op. 36 when it first appeared.

FIRST EDITION:

Trois Pièces de Société pour Guitare seule Composées et Dédiées à Mr. Pastou Par F. Sor. Prix: 4fr. 50c. À Paris, Au Magasin de Musique de Pacini, Editeur des opera de Rossini, Boulevard des Italiens, No. 11. Propriété de l'Auteur.

Ten pages. Plate mark '1 — Sor'. 1828.

[Brussels, Conservatoire, signed 'Sor'; London, collection of Robert Spencer, signed 'Sor' and with 'Op. 36' written in what appears to be Sor's hand; Paris, Bibliothèque Nationale, signed 'Sor'.]

Another issue:

The same, but with 'Oeuvre 36' added on the title-page.

[Barcelona, Biblioteca Central.]

GERMAN EDITION:

Trois Pièces de Société . . . op. 34 [sic] . . . Bonn chez N. Simrock.

Ten pages. Plate number 2817. 1830.

[Copenhagen, Royal Library; Stockholm, Royal Music Academy (not seen).]

ANOTHER GERMAN EDITION:

'Op: 34 [sic]. Trois pièces de Société', Frankfurt, Dunst.

No copy found. Listed on the title-page of the Dunst edition of op. 38 (q.v.). 1841 or before.

Opus 37: Sérénade

This work was first published as op. 36, but it appears in a later issue and in contemporary catalogues as op. 37.

FIRST EDITION:

Sérénade pour Guitare seule composée par Ferdinando Sor et dédiée à Mademoiselle S. Talbot. Oeuvre: 36 [sic]. Prix: 3f. 75. A Paris Au Magasin de Musique de Pacini, Editeur des Operas de Rossini, Boulevard des Italiens No. 11.

Eight pages. Plate number 2527. 1828 or 1829.

[Brussels, Conservatoire, signed 'Sor'; Paris, Bibliothèque Nationale, signed 'Sor'.]

Another issue:

The same, but marked 'Oeuvre: 37' and published by 'Ch. Lenglart, Editeur de Musique, Boulevart Montmartre 18'. 1838-41 (Hopkinson).

[Copenhagen, Royal Library.]

Opus 38: Divertissement (guitar duet)

FIRST EDITION:

Divertissement pour deux Guitares composé et dédié à Madame Dühring par Ferdinand Sor Propr. de l'Auteur. Op. 38. Prix: 5f. 50. à Paris, Chez Pacini, Boulevard des Italiens N. 11.

Two separate guitar parts, marked 'Première guitare' and 'Seconde guitare'. Each part has the title-page and pages numbered 2-7. Plate number 6. 1829-30.

[Copenhagen, Royal Library, the first guitar part signed 'J. de Lira'.]

GERMAN EDITION:

Published as one of a series of works by Sor, with a common title-page:

Oeuvres Pour la Guitare composées par Ferdinand Sor [List of works] Francfort s/M chez Fr: Ph: Dunst. New York chez C.F. Hoÿer.

The present work appears as 'Op: 38. Divertissement pr: deux Guitares'. 1841 or before.

[Copenhagen, Royal Library.]

AN ARRANGEMENT BY NAPOLEON COSTE:

Paris, Schonenberger.

[Copenhagen, Music History Museum.]

Opus 39: Six Waltzes (guitar duet)

FIRST EDITION:

Six Valses Composées Pour l'Orchestre Par Différens Auteurs arrangées Pour deux Guitares et dédiées à Mademoiselle Houzé Par Ferdinand Sor Oeuvre 39. Prix 6f. A Paris au Magasin de Musique de Pacini, Boulevard des Italiens No. 11. et Chez l'Auteur Hotel Favart Place des Italiens.

Two separate guitar parts, marked 'Premiere guitare' and 'Seconde guitare'. Each part has the title-page and pages numbered 2-7. Plate number 7. 1829-30.

These six waltzes are arrangements of waltzes by Mohor, Sor, Mohor, Steibelt, Mozart, and Mohor respectively. Nos. 1 and 4 correspond to *A Second Set of Waltzes, Composed for a full Band . . .,* nos. 1 and 3 respectively; nos. 5 and 6 correspond to *Three Waltzes (by different Authors) Composed originally for a Full Band,* nos. 2 and 3 respectively. See 'Piano duets'.

[Copenhagen, Royal Library.]

GERMAN EDITION:

'Op: 39. Six Valses', Frankfurt, Dunst (see op. 38). 1841 or before.

[Munich, Gitarrevereinigung (not seen).]

Opus 40: Fantasia: Introduction and Variations on 'Ye banks and braes'

FIRST EDITION:

Fantaisie Pour Guitare seule Sur un air favori Ecossais Composée et dédiée à son Elève Mary Jane Burdett par Ferdinand Sor   Oeuv: 40   Propriété de l'Auteur. Prix 5f. A Paris, Chez Pacini, Editeur de Musique, Boulevard des Italiens, no. 11.

Four pages. Plate number 8. 1829-30.

[Barcelona, Biblioteca Central; Brussels, Conservatoire, signed 'Sor'.]

GERMAN EDITION:

'Op: 40. Fant: et Variations sur un air Ecossais', Frankfurt, Dunst (see op. 38). 1841 or before.

[Copenhagen, Royal Library.)

Opus 41: Les Deux Amis (guitar duet)

FIRST EDITION:

Les Deux Amis Fantaisie pour deux Guitares, composée et dédiée à Monsieur Denis Aguado Par Ferd. Sor. Oeuv. 41. Prix 10f 50 . . . à Paris, chez l'Auteur, Place des Italiens, Hotel Favart. chez Pacini, Boulevard des Italiens . . .

Two separate guitar parts, each with the title-page and pages numbered 2-11. They are not called first and second guitar parts, but one part is headed 'SOR' and the other 'AGUADO'. Plate number 9 on Aguado's part only; Sor's part has no plate number. 1829-30.

[Copenhagen, Royal Library.]

AN ARRANGEMENT BY NAPOLEON COSTE:

Paris, Schonenberger.

[Copenhagen, Royal Library; Copenhagen, Music History Museum.]

Opus 42: Six Petites Pièces

FIRST EDITION:

Six Petites Pièces Pour Guitare Composées et dédiées à Mademoiselle Houzé par Ferdinand Sor Op: 42. Propriété de l'Auteur   Prix 4f. 50c.   à Paris Chez Pacini Boulevard des Italiens No. 11 . . .

Nine pages. No plate number. 1830-31.

[Barcelona, Orfeó Catalá, two copies. One of the copies is signed 'Sor' but over the signature is pasted a sticker reading 'Se hallará en el Almacen de Música de Dn. José Leon Calle de la Gorguera . . . Madrid'.]

GERMAN EDITION:

'Op: 42. Six petit [sic] Pièces', Frankfurt, Dunst (see op. 38). 1841 or before.

[Copenhagen, Royal Library.]

Opus 43: Mes Ennuis, Six Bagatelles

FIRST EDITION:

Mes Ennuis Six Bagatelles Pour la Guitare Composées et Dédiées à qui les voudra par Ferdinand Sor Propriété de l'Auteur. Oeuv: 45 [sic; the '5' is altered to a '3' in all copies seen]   Prix 4f. 50c.   a Paris Chez Pacini, Boulevard des Italiens, No. 11 . . .

Nine pages. No plate number. 1830-31.

[Barcelona, Orfeó Catalá, signed 'Sor' but with a sticker pasted over the signature reading 'A Bordeaux, chez A. Fillastre et Neveu, Fossés du Chapeau-Rouge, No. 2'; Laguna Beach, collection of Mary Belle Swingle (not seen); London, Guildhall School of Music; London, collection of Robert Spencer, signed 'Sor'.]

GERMAN EDITION:

'Op: 43. Mes Ennuis six Bagatelles', Frankfurt, Dunst (see op. 38). 1841 or before.

[Copenhagen, Royal Library.]

AN ARRANGEMENT BY NAPOLEON COSTE:

Paris, Schonenberger.

[Copenhagen, Royal Library; Copenhagen, Music History Museum; London, collection of Robert Spencer.]

Opus 44: Vingt-quatre Petites Pièces Progressives

Note that a German edition of op. 44 bis exists, called simply op. 44.

FIRST EDITION:

Vingt-quatre petites Pièces Progressives pour la Guitare pour servir de leçons aux Eleves tout à fait Commençants Composées et Dédiées à Mr. Rolando par Ferdinand Sor Oeuvre 44. Prix: 7f. 50c. A Paris Chez l'Auteur, Place des Italiens, Hotel Favart. Chez Pacini, Boulevard des Italiens, No. 11. . . .

Thirteen pages. No plate number. Listed in the *Bibliographie de la France* on 19 March 1831.

[Barcelona, Orfeó Catalá; Paris, Bibliothèque Nationale.]

GERMAN EDITION:

The same title, 'Hambourg, chez Jean Aug. Böhme'. Eleven pages. No plate number. C. 1841 (see op. 34).

[Copenhagen, Royal Library.]

Opus 44 bis: Six Waltzes (guitar duet)

FIRST EDITION:

Six Valses Pour deux Guitares Faciles et Progressives et Soigneusement doigtées Composées et Dediées à Mademoiselle Lira par Ferdinand Sor Oeuv. 44. bis Prix: 5f. 50c. A Paris, chez Pacini . . . Boulevard des Italiens, No. 11. et chez l'Auteur, Rue et Hotel Favart.

Two separate guitar parts, each with the title-page and pages numbered 2-5. Marked 'Premiere Guitare' and 'Seconde Guitare'. No plate number. 1831.

[Copenhagen, Royal Library.]

GERMAN EDITION:

'Op: 44 [sic]. Six Valses faciles', Frankfurt, Dunst (see op. 38). 1841 or before.

[Copenhagen, Royal Library.]

Opus 45: Voyons si c'est ça

Note that the opus number on op. 43 was wrongly printed '45'.

FIRST EDITION:

Voyons si c'est ça. Six Petites Pièces Faciles Pour la Guitare dont le bût est de conduire graduellement à ce que l'on est convenu d'appeler difficulté Composées et Dédiées à celui qui aura le moins de patience, par Ferdinand Sor Oeuvre 45. Prix: 4f. 50. à Paris, au Magasin de Musique de Pacini, Boulevard des Italiens No. 11. et chez L'Auteur, Place des Italiens, Hotel Favart, No. 5.

Ten pages. No plate number. C. 1831.

[London, Guildhall School of Music.]

GERMAN EDITION:

'Op. 45. Voyons si c'est ça, Frankfurt, Dunst (see op. 38). 1841 or before.

[Copenhagen, Royal Library.]

AN ARRANGEMENT BY NAPOLEON COSTE:

Paris, Schonenberger.

[Copenhagen, Royal Library.]

Opus 46: Souvenir d'Amitié, Fantasia

FIRST EDITION:

Souvenir d'Amitié Fantaisie Pour la Guitare Composée Pour Jules Régondi par Ferdinand Sor Oeuvre 46 Prix: 4f. 50c. à Paris, au Magasin de Musique de Pacini, Boulevard des Italiens No. 11 et chez l'Auteur Place des Italiens, Hotel Favart, No. 5. Propriété de l'Auteur . . .

Nine pages. Plate number 14. C. 1831.

[Barcelona, Biblioteca Central; Barcelona, Orfeó Catalá, signed 'Sor'.]

Another issue:

Paris, Schonenberger.

[Copenhagen, Royal Library.]

GERMAN EDITION:

'Op: 46. Souvenier [sic] d'Amitié', Frankfurt, Dunst (see op. 38). 1841 or before.

[Copenhagen, Royal Library.]

Opus 47: Six Petites Pièces

FIRST EDITION:

Paris, Pacini or Sor or both. Listed in the catalogue printed in Sor's later works. C. 1832. No copy found.

Another issue:

Six Petites Pièces progressives Pour la Guitare Composées et Dédiées à son Elève Melle. Crabouillet par Ferdinand Sor Op: 47. Prix: 5 Publié à Paris, par Ch. Lenglart, Editeur de Musique, Boulevart Montmartre 18.

Eight pages. Plate number 15. 1838-41 (Hopkinson).

[Copenhagen, Royal Library.]

GERMAN EDITION:

'Op: 47 Six petit [sic] Pieces', Frankfurt, Dunst (see op. 38). 1841 or before. No copy found.

Opus 48: Est-ce bien ça?

FIRST EDITION:

Est-ce bien ça? Six Pieces Pour la Guitare Composées et Dédiées à quelques amateurs par Ferdinand Sor Oeuvre 48. Prix: 6f. A Paris, au Magasin de Musique de Pacini, Boulevard des Italiens No. 11 et chez l'auteur, Place des Italiens, Hotel Favart No. 5. Propriété de l'Auteur . . .

Twelve pages. Plate number 16. C. 1832.

[Barcelona, Biblioteca Central; Laguna Beach, collection of Mary Belle Swingle, signed 'Sor' and sold in Spain by Carrafa (not seen).]

Another issue:

Paris, Schonenberger.

[Copenhagen, Royal Library.]

Opus 49: Divertissement Militaire (guitar duet)

FIRST EDITION:

Divertissement Militaire Pour deux guitares Composé et Dédié à Melle. Talbot par Ferdinand Sor Propriété de l'Auteur Oeuv 49 . . . Prix: 5f. 50c. à Paris au Magasin de Musique de Pacini Boulevard des Italiens No. 11 et chez l'Auteur, Place des Italiens Hotel Favart No. 3.

Two separate guitar parts. From the Schonenberger issue (see below) it seems that they both have the title-page; the first is numbered 2-6 and the second 1-5. Marked 'Première guitare' and 'Seconde guitare'. Plate number 17. C. 1832.

[Barcelona, Orfeó Catalá, second guitar part only, signed 'Sor'.]

Another issue:

Paris, Schonenberger.

[Copenhagen, Royal Library. Complete.]

GERMAN EDITION:

'Op: 49. Divertissement Militaire', Frankfurt, Dunst (see op. 38). 1841 or before. No copy found.

Opus 50: Le Calme, Caprice

FIRST EDITION:

Le Calme Caprice Pour Guitare seule Composé et Dédié à son Elève Melle. Crabouillet par Ferdinand Sor Prix: 4f. 50c. Oeuv. 50. à Paris, au Magasin de Musique de Pacini, Boulevard des Italiens No. 11 et chez l'Auteur Rue Favart, No. 5.

Seven pages. Plate number 18. C. 1832.

[Barcelona, Orfeó Catalá, two copies, of which one incomplete; Barcelona, collection of Emilio Pujol, two copies, one signed 'Sor' and the other signed 'J. de Lira'; Brussels, Conservatoire, signed 'Sor'; Copenhagen, Royal Library.]

GERMAN EDITION:

'Op: 50. Le Calme Caprice', Frankfurt, Dunst (see op. 38). 1841 or before. No copy found.

Opus 51: A la bonne heure, Six Waltzes

FIRST EDITION:

À la bonne heure six valses Pour la Guitare Composées Selon le desir de quelques Amateurs par Ferdinand Sor Prix: 4f. 50c. Oeuv. 51 . . . [in the Barcelona copy, it is possible to read that this was published by Pacini, under a pasted sticker reading 'Se hallará en el gran Almacen de música de Carrafa, sito en la calle del Príncipe, número 15 nuevo . . .']

Seven pages. Plate number 19. C. 1832.

[Barcelona, Orfeó Catalá; Brussels, Conservatoire, signed 'Sor'.]

Another issue:

Paris, Schonenberger.

[Copenhagen, Royal Library.]

Opus 52: Fantaisie Villageoise

FIRST EDITION:

Fantaisie Villageoise pour guitare seule Composée et dédiée à Mr. Denis Aguado par son ami Ferdinand Sor. Propriété de l'Auteur. Oeuvre 52 Prix 5f. Paris Chez l'Auteur, Marché St. Honoré No. 34. et chez Pacini, Boulevard des Italiens No. 11.

Nine pages. Plate number 20. C. 1832.

[Barcelona, Biblioteca Central; Barcelona, Orfeó Catalá, signed 'Sor' and with a pasted sticker reading 'A Bordeaux, chez Raver Md. de Musique et d'instrumens Rue du Chateau trompette No. 5'; Copenhagen, Royal Library, signed 'Sor' and 'H: Rung'.]

Another issue:

Paris, Schonenberger.

[Copenhagen, Royal Library.]

Opus 53: Le premier pas vers moi (guitar duet)

FIRST EDITION:

Le premier pas vers moi. Petit duo Pour deux Guitares composé Et Dédié à ceux qui ayant appris à jouer de cet instrument, voyent de grandes difficultés ou il n'y a que de la correction. Par Ferdinand Sor. Oeuvre 53. Prix 4f. 50c. Propriété de l'Auteur. A Paris, Chez l'Auteur, Marché St. Honoré No. 34. et chez Pacini, Boulevard des Italiens No. 11.

Two separate guitar parts, each with the title-page and pages numbered 2-4. Marked '1re. guitare' and '2e guitare'. Plate number 21. 1832-3.

[Barcelona, Orfeó Catalá. both title-pages signed 'Sor'.]

Another issue:

Paris, Ch. Lenglart. 1838-49 (Hopkinson).

[Copenhagen, Royal Library.]

GERMAN EDITION:

Title as above. Hamburg, J.A. Böhme. C. 1841 (see op. 34).

[Copenhagen, Royal Library; Copenhagen, Music History Museum, with an extra copy of the second guitar part.]

ANOTHER GERMAN EDITION:

'Op: 53. Le premier pas vers moi', Frankfurt, Dunst (see op. 38). 1841 or before.

[Copenhagen, Royal Library.]

AN ARRANGEMENT BY NAPOLEON COSTE:

Paris, Schonenberger.

(Copenhagen, Music History Museum.]

Opus 54: Morceau de Concert

Note that a German edition of op. 54 bis exists, called simply op. 54.

FIRST EDITION:

Morceau de Concert Pour Guitare Seule Composé et très humblement Dédié a Son Altesse Royale Madame la Princesse Adelaide Soeur du Roi Par Ferdinand Sor Op: 54. Prix: 4f. 50c. Prop. de l'Editeur. . . . à Paris, Chez Pacini. Editeur des Operas de Rossini, Boulevard des Italiens, No. 11.

Nine pages. Plate number 780. Reviewed in the *Revue Musicale* in March 1833.

[Barcelona, collection of Emilio Pujol; Brussels, Conservatoire.]

AN ARRANGEMENT BY NAPOLEON COSTE:

Paris, Schonenberger.

[Copenhagen, Royal Library; Copenhagen, Music History Museum.]

Opus 54 bis: Fantasia (guitar duet)

FIRST EDITION:

Fantaisie Pour deux Guitares, Composée expressement pour Mlle. Houzé, par Ferdinand Sor. Prix 10 Fcs. 50 Ces. Oeuvre 54 (bis.) A Paris, chez Sor, Marché St. Honoré, No. 34.

Two separate guitar parts, each with the title-page and pages numbered 2-7. Marked '1re. guitare' and '2de. guitare'. No plate number. C. 1833.

[Copenhagen, Royal Library, both title-pages signed 'Sor'.]

GERMAN EDITION:

'Op: 54 [sic], Fantaisie', Frankfurt, Dunst (see op. 38). 1841 or before.

[Copenhagen, Royal Library.]

Opus 55: Trois duos (guitar duet)

FIRST EDITION:

Trois Duos Faciles et progressifs Pour deux Guitares Composés Et soigneusement Doigtés par Ferdinand Sor. Oeuvre 55. Prix 1er. 4f 2e. 4 3e. 5 Ensembles [sic] 10 50 A Paris Chez l'auteur, Marché St. Honoré No. 34. Et chez Pacini Boulevard des Italiens No. 11.

The three duos were issued separately, in each case with two separate guitar parts marked '1re. guitare' and '2me. guitare'. In each case, each guitar part has the title-page and pages numbered up to 5. All title-pages have the plate number 22. The music of the first duo has the plate number '22.1.L', the second '22.2.L', and the third '22.3.L'. 1833-4.

[Copenhagen, Royal Library; Copenhagen, Music History Museum, the second duo only, signed 'J. de Lira'.]

GERMAN EDITION:

Title as above. Hamburg, J.A. Böhme. C. 1841 (see op. 34).

[Copenhagen, Royal Library; Copenhagen, Music History Museum, first and third duos only.]

ANOTHER GERMAN EDITION:

'Op: 55. Trois Duos faciles et progressifs', Frankfurt, Dunst (see op. 38). 1841 or before.

[Copenhagen, Royal Library.]

Opus 56: Souvenirs d'une Soirée à Berlin

FIRST EDITION:

Souvenirs d'une Soirée à Berlin. Fantaisie pour guitare seule, Composée et dédiée à son Ami Mr. de Lira par Ferdinand Sor. Oeuv. 56. Prix: [blank]. A Paris. [No name of publisher].

Eleven pages. No plate number. 1833-5.

[Copenhagen, Royal Library.]

GERMAN EDITION:

'Op: 56. Souvenirs d'une Soirée à Berlin', Frankfurt, Dunst (see op. 38). 1841 or before.

[Stockholm, Royal Music Academy (not seen).]

Opus 57: *Six Valses et un Galop*

FIRST EDITION:

No copy found. Doubtless published in Paris by Pacini or Sor or both. C. 1834-5.

Another issue:

Six Valses et un Galop, pour guitare seule Composés et dédiés à son Elève Mademoiselle Larivée par Ferdinand Sor. Oeuvre. 57. Prix 4f. 50. Propriété de l'Auteur Paris, Schonenberger . . . Boulevart Poissonnière, 28 . . .

Nine pages. Plate number 14. 1843 or later (Hopkinson).

[Copenhagen, Royal Library.]

GERMAN EDITION:

'Op: 57. Six Valses et un Galop', Frankfurt, Dunst (see op. 38). 1841 or before.

[Stockholm, Royal Music Academy (not seen).]

Opus 58: *Fantasia*

FIRST EDITION:

Fantaisie pour Guitare Seule, expressement composée et dédiée à son Elève Madame Boischevalier, née Mertian par Ferdinand Sor. Oeuvre 58. Prix. 4f. 50. A Paris, chez l'auteur, Marché St. Honoré, 36. et chez Pacini, Boulev[ar]t Italien, 11.

Eight pages. No plate number. C. 1835.

[Barcelona, Biblioteca Central; Copenhagen, Royal Library.]

GERMAN EDITION:

'Op: 58. Fantaisie facile', Frankfurt, Dunst (see op. 38). 1841 or before. No copy found.

Opus 59: *Fantaisie Elégiaque*

FIRST EDITION:

Fantaisie Elégiaque, pour Guitare seule à la mort de Madame Beslay, née Levavasseur, Composée par Ferdinand Sor. Oeuvre 59 Prix 4f. 50 A Paris, Chez l'Auteur, Rue du Marché St. Honoré, 34. et chez Pacini, Boulevart des Italiens, 11.

Eight pages. No plate number. C. 1836.

[Barcelona, collection of Emilio Pujol (lacking title-page); Copenhagen, Royal Library, signed 'Sor' and 'H. Rung'; London, collection of Robert Spencer, signed 'Sor'.]

SPANISH EDITION:

Fantaisie elégiaque. pour guitare à la mort de Madame Beslay née Levavasseur composé par Ferdinand Sor. Op. 59 Pr: 10RS.

No separate title-page; the above is the heading to the music. At the foot of the page is: 'Madrid. Se hallará en el almacen de música de Carrafa calle del Principe No. 15.' Six pages. Plate number B.C. (134).

[Barcelona, Biblioteca Central.]

GERMAN EDITION:

'Op: 59. Fantaisie Elégiaque', Frankfurt, Dunst (see op. 38). 1841 or before. No copy found.

Opus 60: *Introduction á l'Etude de la Guitare*

FIRST EDITION:

Introduction à l'Etude de la Guitare en vingt cinq leçons progressives composées et Soigneusement Doigtées par Ferdinand Sor Oeuvre 60. Prix. 12fr. Propriété de l'Auteur A Paris Chez l'Auteur, Rue du Marché St. Honoré, 34. et Chez Pacini, Boulevard des Italiens, No. 11.

Nineteen pages. No plate number. C. 1836-7.

[Barcelona, Orfeó Catalá; London, collection of Robert Spencer, signed 'L'auteur á son ami J. de Lira' and 'Sor'.]

GERMAN EDITION:

'Op: 60. Introduction à l'Etude de la Guitare', Frankfurt, Dunst (see op. 38). 1841 or before.

[Copenhagen, Royal Library.]

Opus 61: *Trois petits Divertissements (guitar duet)*

FIRST EDITION:

Trois petits Divertissements Pour deux Guitares Composées et Dédiés á Madame Hamilton par Ferdinand Sor Op: 61. Prix [blank] Paris, chez l'Auteur, Marché des Jacobins, No. 54. et chez Pacini, Boulevard Italien No. 11.

Two separate guitar parts, with pages numbered up to 7 and 9. Marked '1re. guitare' and '2e. guitare'. In the Copenhagen copy, both parts have the title-page; in the Paris copies, only the first guitar part. No plate number. Not later than October 1837, a date stamped on one of the Paris copies.

[Copenhagen, Royal Library; Paris, Bibliothèque Nationale, two copies, both signed 'Sor'.]

GERMAN EDITION:

'Op: 61. Trois petit [sic] Divertissements', Frankfurt, Dunst (see op. 38). 1841 or before.

[Copenhagen, Royal Library.]

Opus 62: Divertissement (guitar duet)

FIRST EDITION:

Divertissement pour deux Guitares Composé et Dédié à son Elève Madame Fondard par Ferdinand Sor Oeuv. 62. Prix: 6f. 50c. à Paris, chez l'Auteur, Marché des Jacobins, No. 34. bis. et chez Pacini, Boulevard des Italiens, No. 11.

Two separate guitar parts, each with seven pages. Marked '1e. guitare' and '2e. guitare'. In the Copenhagen copy, both parts have the title-page; in the Paris copies, only the first guitar part. No plate number. Not later than June 1838, a date stamped on one of the Paris copies.

[Barcelona, collection of Emilio Pujol (first guitar part only); Copenhagen, Royal Library, both parts signed 'Sor' and the first guitar part also inscribed in Sor's hand 'L'auteur à Son ami N. Coste;' Paris, Bibliothèque Nationale, complete (two copies).]

GERMAN EDITION:

'Op: 62. Divertissement', Frankfurt, Dunst (see op. 38). 1841 or before.

[Copenhagen, Royal Library; Copenhagen, Music History Museum.]

Opus 63: Souvenir de Russie (guitar duet)

FIRST EDITION:

Souvenir de Russie Fantaisie pour deux Guitares Composée et Dédiée à son Ami N. Coste par Ferdinand Sor Op: 63 Prix: 10f. à Paris, chez l'auteur Marché St. Honoré 36.

Two separate guitar parts, each with the title-page and seven and nine pages respectively. Marked '1re. guitare' and '2de. guitare'. No plate number. 1838-9.

[Barcelona, Orfeó Català, first guitar part only, signed 'J. de Lira' and 'Lira á su buen am[ig]o el Sr. Marques de Benaben'; Copenhagen, Royal Library, complete.]

AN ARRANGEMENT BY NAPOLEON COSTE:

Paris, Schonenberger.

[Copenhagen, Music History Museum.]

GERMAN EDITION:

'Op: 63. Souvenir de Russie', Frankfurt, Dunst (see op. 38). 1841 or before.

[Copenhagen, Royal Library.]

GUITAR MUSIC WITHOUT OPUS NUMBER

Air Varié

Air Varié pour la Guitare Par Fernando Sors.

In the *Journal de Musique Etrangère pour la Guitare ou Lyre,* edited by Castro, Paris, c. 1810.

Six pages. Plate number 2.

For location of copies, see op. 3.

Thema Varié

Thema varié pour la Guitare ou Lyre Par Dn. Fernando Sors.

In the *Journal de Musique Etrangère pour la Guitare ou Lyre,* edited by Castro, Paris, c. 1810.

Six pages. Plate number 1.

For location of copies, see opus 3.

Opus 20 is based on the same theme, but only one of the variations is the same.

Four minuets

Four minuets, each of them headed 'Minuetto', were published together as 'Menuets Composés pour la Guitare' in the *Journal de Musique Etrangère pour la Guitare ou Lyre,* edited by Castro, Paris, c. 1810. The second of them is the same as op. 11, no. 6.

Four pages. Plate number 5.

For location of copies, see op. 3.

Arrangement of the March from 'Cendrillon'

FIRST EDITION:

Marche du ballet de Cendrillon Pour Guitare par F. Sor. Prix 1f. 50c. A Paris, au Magasin de Musique de Meissonnier, Galerie du Passage des Panoramas No. 15 . . .

No separate title-page; the above is the heading to the music. Two pages. Plate number 272. 1823-25.

[Barcelona, Biblioteca Central; Brussels, Conservatoire; London, Guildhall School of Music; London, collection of Robert Spencer; Paris, Bibliothèque Nationale (two copies).]

GERMAN EDITION:

Marche tirée du Ballet de Cendrillon . . . Bonn et Cologne chez N. Simrock.

Two pages. Plate number 2309. C. 1824-5. With a title-page serving also for the *Thème Varié,* reading 'Diverses Pièces . . .'

[London, British Library.]

ANOTHER GERMAN EDITION:

Marche du ballet de Cendrillon Pour Guitare par F. Sor . . . Bonn chez N. Simrock.

Two pages. Plate number 2845. 1830.

[Copenhagen, Royal Library.]

An arrangement of the overture to Méhul's 'La Chasse du jeune Henri'

In the *Allgemeine musikalische Zeitung* for September 1823, an anonymous reviewer says that he has heard Sor play on the guitar an arrangement of the overture to Méhul's 'La Chasse du jeune Henri'. No score has been found.

Pieces in the 'Méthode pour la Guitare'

Sor's *Méthode pour la Guitare* incorporates a number of pieces for solo guitar, as well as some for guitar and voice or voices.

La Candeur

La Candeur Petite reverie sur la Guitare. par F. Sor.

Published in Ledhuy's *Encyclopédie* (Paris, 1835). No separate title-page; the above is the heading to the music. Two pages.

COLLECTIONS OF GUITAR MUSIC

Collection Complète

In the mid-1820s, Meissonnier began binding together Sor's works for guitar and issuing them with a new title-page headed 'Collection complète . . .' Copies are known going up to op. 19 or op. 23.

Op. 6 and op. 29

Vingt Quatre Etudes Pour Guitare Composés par F. Sor . . . à Paris Au Magasin de Musique de A. Meissonnier, Boulevard Montmartre, No. 25.

Op. 6 and op. 29 bound together with a new title-page. 1825-39.

[London, collection of Robert Spencer.]

Minuets, Gallopades . . .

Minuets, Gallopades, Marches, Waltzes, and Marlboro.

No copy found. Advertised by Johanning, London, in a catalogue in 'A Spanish Seguidilla Gitana' by del Busto (copy in Munich, Bayerische Staatsbibliothek).

PIANO SOLOS

Arrangements from 'Telemaco'

1) The overture. Montserrat, Arxiú de Música, MS 1562, pp. 36-40. Headed 'Sigue Sinfonia del Signore Ferdinando Sor'.

2) Largo and part of a minuet. Barcelona, Biblioteca Central, MS M 791/19. Headed 'Sinfonia para Fortepiano, del Sr. Fernando Sors dell'Opera Telemaco nell Isla de Calipso'. Three folios.

Minuets

A manuscript containing minuets for piano solo was in the Arxiú de Música at Montserrat but now appears to be missing.

Six Waltzes, 1st Set

ENGLISH EDITION:

Six Waltzes, for The Piano Forte, Composed and Dedicated to the Countess of St. Antonio, by Ferdinand Sor. Ent. at Sta. Hall Price 3s./ London, Published by Monzani & Hill, Music Sellers to H.R.H. the Prince Regent, 24, Dover St. Piccadilly.

Six pages. Plate mark: 'Sor's Waltzes. 1st Set'. Published before July 1819 and probably after 1815.

[London, British Library, signed 'F Sor'.]

FRENCH EDITION:

Six Valses pour le Piano, 2e Liv[raison].

No copy has been found. Listed in an advertisement issued by Meissonnier on the verso of the title-page of Sor's op. 1 in the *Collection Complète* (copy of the Bibliothèque Nationale, Paris). The incipit given in that advertisement is that of the first waltz in the English 1st Set; there is no way of telling whether the other five waltzes were the same or not. Published c. 1817-20.

Six Waltzes, 2nd Set

No copy has been found. But the words '1st Set' on the surviving set of Six Waltzes published by Monzani & Hill presuppose the existence of a '2nd Set' probably also published by Monzani & Hill. The set may have contained the same pieces as the following item.

Six Waltzes Pour le Piano Forte

Six Waltzes Pour le Piano Forte Composées et Dédiées à Madame la Comtesse de Jersey, par Ferdinando Sor. Prix: 3f. A Paris Au Bureau du Journal de Guitare Chez Meissonnier, Rue Môntmartre No. 182 au coin du Boulevard Chez Boieldieu Jeune, Mn. de Musique, Rue de Richelieu No. 80 et Chez Bochsa Père, Rue Vivienne, No. 18. [On the only known copy, the words from 'Au Bureau' onwards are covered by a pasted slip reading 'Chez Frere, Fils, Md. de Musique, Rue de Richelieu No. 69 vis-à-vis la porte de la Bibliothèque du Roi' but can be read with the aid of a lamp. I am indebted to Dr. Heinz Ramge for sending me this information.]

Six pages. Plate number 47.

[Berlin, Staatsbibliothek Preussischer Kulturbesitz.]

This set is listed as 'Six Valses pour le Piano, 1er Liv[raison]' in an advertisement issued by Meissonnier on the verso of the title-page of Sor's op. 1 in the *Collection Complète* (copy of the Bibliothèque Nationale, Paris). The incipit given in that advertisement is that of the first waltz in this printed edition. Published c. 1817-20. The third waltz resembles the celebrated waltz from *Cendrillon* (see 'Ballet music').

A manuscript collection of waltzes

A manuscript collection of six waltzes by Sor for piano solo, possibly autograph, is in Berlin, Staatsbibliothek Preussischer Kulturbesitz, Mus. ms. 20,898. It is headed 'Six Walzes for the Pianoforte Composed and dedicated to the Countess of Jersey by F. Sor'.

Ten pages. Oblong format. The six waltzes are all in one or other of the two surviving printed collections listed above:

> No. 1 = Meissonnier, no. 2.
> No. 2 = Monzani & Hill, no. 1.
> No. 3 = Monzani & Hill, no. 2
> No. 4 = Monzani & Hill, no. 6
> No. 5 = Meissonnier, no. 3
> No. 6 = Meissonnier, no. 1

Les Cuirassiers

Les Cuirassiers, A First Set of New Quadrilles, and a Waltz for the Piano Forte, with their Respective Figures. Composed & Respectfully Dedicated to Mrs. Buisson, By Ferdinand Sor. Ent. Sta. Hall. Price 3/- London, Printed by the Royal Harmonic Institution. . . .

Seven pages. Plate number 700. Entered at Stationers' Hall on 19 April 1821.

[London, British Library; Cambridge, University Library; Glasgow, University Library.]

Les Favorites des Salons

Les Favorites des Salons. A Second Set of Original Quadrilles, and a Waltz, for the Piano Forte, with their Proper Figures as Danced at Almacks, Bath & New Argyll Rooms, and at the Nobilities Assemblies, Respectfully Dedicated to Lady Georgina Paget, Composed by Ferdinand Sor. Ent. Sta. Hall. Price 3/- London, Printed by the Royal Harmonic Institution. . . .

Seven pages. Plate number 746. Entered at Stationers' Hall on 9 May 1821.

[London, British Library; Cambridge, University Library; Glasgow, University Library.]

Les Choisies

Les Choisies, a Third Set of New Quadrilles, and a Waltz, with their Respective Figures for the Piano Forte, Composed and Respectfully Dedicated to Lady Jane Paget, by Ferd. Sor. Ent. Sta. Hall Price 3s/- London, Published by the Royal Harmonic Institution. . . .

Five pages. Plate number 885. Entered at Stationers' Hall on 19 January 1822.

[London, British Library; Oxford, Bodlelian Library; Cambridge, University Library; Glasgow, University Library.]

Minuet

A minuet for piano solo by Sor is in Paris, Bibliothèque de l'Arsenal, MS Musique 955, f. 78. It is a version of the minuet for solo guitar which appears at the end of op. 3. It is headed 'Menuet — Composé par Sor'.

Funeral March

In Russia, according to Ledhuy's *Encyclopédie,* Sor arranged for piano solo the march which he composed for the funeral of Tsar Alexander. No score is known to survive.

Mazurka

A Mazurka for piano solo by Sor is printed in Ledhuy's *Encyclopédie* (Paris, 1835).

PIANO DUETS

Three Waltzes, 1st Set

No copy has been found. However, the Three Waltzes, 2nd Set (see below) presuppose the existence of a 1st Set.

Possibly the same as *Trois Valses à quatre mains dédiées à Mme. Albert,* 4e Liv[raison] (see below), of which likewise no copy has been found.

The publication called *Three Waltzes (by different Authors)* is a set of arrangements and stands outside the main series of ten sets of waltzes for piano duet. See below.

Three Waltzes, 2nd Set

Three Waltzes for Two Performers on one Piano Forte, Composed & Dedicated to Mlle. F. Rehausen, By Ferdinand Sor. Ent. Sta. Hall. Set 2d. Price 3/- London, Printed for the Author by Clementi & Co. 26, Cheapside. & Sold at the Principal Music Shops.

Seven pages. No plate number. 1815-18.

[Stockholm, Royal Music Academy, signed 'F. Sor'.]

Three Waltzes, 3rd Set

Three Waltzes, for Two Performers on one Piano Forte, Composed & Dedicated to Lady Jane & Lady Georgina Paget, by F. Sor. Ent. Sta. Hall. Price 2s/ [altered by hand to 3/- in all copies seen] London, Published by The Regent's Harmonic Institution . . .

Seven pages. Plate number 295. Entered at Stationers' Hall on 18 December 1819.

[London, British Library; Oxford, Bodleian Library; Cambridge, University Library; Bath, Municipal Library (not seen); Glasgow, University Library.]

Three Waltzes, 4th Set

Three Waltzes, for Two Performers on the Piano Forte, Composed & respectfully Dedicated to Lady Augusta & Lady Agnes Paget, by F. Sor. 4th. Set. Price 2/6 London, Printed & Sold by Chappell & Co. . . . 50, New Bond Street.

Seven pages. Plate number 1427. Entered at Stationers' Hall on 17 April 1820.

[London, British Library; Oxford, Bodleian Library; Cambridge, University Library; Glasgow, University Library.]

Three Waltzes, 5th Set

Three Waltzes for Two Performers on one Piano Forte, Composed & respectfully dedicated to Miss B. Bollman, by F. Sor. 5th. Set. Ent. Sta. Hall. Price 3s/- London, Printed by the Regent's Harmonic Institution. . . .

Seven pages. Plate number 361. Entered at Stationers' Hall on 24 December 1819.

[London, British Library; Oxford, Bodleian Library; Cambridge, University Library; Bath, Municipal Library (not seen); Glasgow, University Library.]

Three Waltzes, 6th Set

Three Waltzes, for two Performers on one Piano Forte, Composed, & Respectfully Dedicated to Miss A. Macdougall, by F. Sor. Ent. Sta. Hall. 6th. Set. Price 3s/- London, Printed by the Regent's Harmonic Institution. . . .

Seven pages. Plate number 312. Entered at Stationers' Hall on 18 December 1819.

[London, British Library; Oxford, Bodleian Library; Cambridge, University Library; Bath, Municipal Library (not seen); Glasgow, University Library.]

Three Waltzes, 7th Set

ENGLISH EDITION:

Three Waltzes, for two Performers on the Piano Forte. Composed and Dedicated to Mrs. Ellis Heaton, by F. Sor. Ent. Sta. Hall. 7th. Set. Price 3s/- London, Printed by the Royal Harmonic Institution. . . .

Seven pages. Plate number 506. Entered at Stationers' Hall on 12 September 1820.

[London, British Library; Oxford, Bodleian Library; Cambridge, University Library; Bath, Municipal Library (not seen); Glasgow, University Library.]

FRENCH EDITION:

Trois Valses à quatre mains 3e Liv[raison].

No copy has been found. Advertised by Meissonnier in a catalogue printed in some copies of Sor's op. 1. Published within the period c. 1820-24. The incipit given by Meissonnier is the beginning of the first waltz in the English 7th Set. Advertised as '3e Liv[raison]'; the first and second livraisons were for piano solo. For the '4e Liv[raison]', see below.

Three Waltzes, 8th Set

Three Waltzes for two Performers on the Piano Forte Composed and respectfully Dedicated to Miss Adolphus, By Ferd. Sor. Ent. Sta. Hall 8th. Set. Price 3s/ London Published by the Royal Harmonic Institution . . .

Seven pages. Plate number 1044. Entered at Stationers' Hall on 8 June 1822.

[London, British Library; Cambridge, University Library.]

Three Waltzes, 9th Set

No copy has been found. This set was advertised by the Royal Harmonic Institution in the *Harmonicon,* vol. I, 1823, in an advertisement dated October 1823 for new music, as 'Three Waltzes, 9th Set'. It was not entered at Stationers' Hall. Perhaps Sor's departure from London in 1823 caused it not to be published, unlike the following item. Ledhuy's *Encyclopédie* mentions only nine sets and not ten, which supports the theory that this set was never published.

Three Waltzes, 10th Set

Three Waltzes, for Two Performers on One Piano Forte, Composed & Dedicated to The Honorable Miss

Waldegraves, by Ferdinand Sor. Entd. at Sta. Hall. 10th. Set. Price 3s./ London, Printed & Sold by Birchall & Co. 133 New Bond Street.

Seven pages. Plate number 1325. Entered at Stationers' Hall on 11 August 1823.

[London, British Library; Cambridge, University Library.]

Trois Valses à quatre mains . . . 4e Liv[raison]

Trois Valses à quatre mains dédiées à Mme. Albert 4e Liv[raison].

No copy has been found. Advertised by Meissonnier in a catalogue printed in some copies of Sor's op. 1. Published within the period c. 1820-24. The incipit given by Meissonnier does not correspond to any of the English series of waltzes; it could correspond, however, to the missing English 1st or 9th Sets. Advertised as '4e Liv[raison]'; the first and second livraisons were for piano solo, and the third livraison was for piano duet and its incipit corresponds to that of the English 7th Set (see above).

Three Waltzes (arrangements), 1st Set

Three Waltzes. (by different Authors) Composed originally for a Full Band. Arranged for two Performers on the Piano Forte, by Ferdinand Sor. Ent. Sta. Hall. Price 2/6. London Printed by Rutter & McCarthy . . . 120, New Bond St.

Seven pages. Plate number 239. Entered at Stationers' Hall on 28 May 1822, though perhaps printed earlier.

[London, British Library; Oxford, Bodleian Library; Cambridge, University Library; Edinburgh, National Library of Scotland.]

The three waltzes are by Sor, Mozart, and Mohor.

Three Waltzes (arrangements), 2nd Set

A Second Set of Waltzes, Composed for a full Band, by Mohor, Mozart & Steibelt. Arranged for Two Performers on the Piano Forte, by Ferdinand Sor. Ent. Sta. Hall. Price 2/6. London, Printed by Rutter & McCarthy . . . 120, New Bond St.

Seven pages. Plate number 250. Entered at Stationers' Hall on 28 May 1822, though perhaps printed earlier.

[London, British Library; Oxford, Bodleian Library; Cambridge, University Library.]

Duet on Swedish National Airs

AUTOGRAPH MANUSCRIPT:

Duett for the Piano forte Composed on several Swedish National airs and respectfully Dedicated to the Baroness De Rehausen by F. Sor.

This manuscript is in Stockholm, in the Royal Music Academy, shelf-mark I 4779. It consists of ten pages. The words 'F. Sor' correspond to Sor's known signature at this time, thus suggesting that the whole of this manuscript is autograph. Pencil marks show that this is the copy used by the printer to set up the following item.

FIRST EDITION:

A Duett, For two Performers on the Piano Forte, Composed on Several Swedish National Airs, & Respectfully Dedicated by Permission to The Baroness Rehausen, by F. Sor. Ent. Sta. Hall. Price 8s/- London, Publish'd at Falkner's Opera Music Warehouse, 3, Old Bond St. where may be had all Mr. Sor's Publications.

Thirty-three pages. No plate number. 1815-18.

[London, British Library, signed 'F. Sor' and inscribed 'A M. Bird de la part de l'auteur'; Stockholm, Royal Music Academy, signed 'F. Sor'.]

Duo Brillant

No copy has been found. This was advertised by the Royal Harmonic Institution in the *Harmonicon,* vol. II, 1824, in an advertisement dated March 1824 for new music. It was not entered at Stationers' Hall and possibly was never published.

Marche Composée Pour la Musique Militaire

Marche Composée Pour la Musique Militaire et dédiée à son Excellence le Général Quiroga Commandant genral. de la nouvelle Castille Par Ferdinand Sor arrangée par l'Auteur pour le Piano à Quatre mains Prix: 5fr. à Paris, chez l'Auteur, Marché des Jacobins, No. 34. bis. et chez Pacini, Boulevard des Italiens, No. 11.

Eleven pages. No plate number. 1837 or before.

[Paris, Bibliothèque Nationale, two copies, both signed 'Sor'.]

Pieces in the 'Ecole de la Mesure'

Twenty-two short pieces attributed to Sor are in a printed book entitled *Ecole de la Mesure et de la Ponctuation Musicale,* 2nd edition, no date (the copy in the British Library was received in 1877), by H. Lemoine.

MUSIC FOR HARPOLYRE

Trois Pièces

Trois Pièces pour la Harpolyre Composées et dédiées à Mr. J.F. Salomon Inventeur de cet Instrument, Par Ferdinand Sor   Propriété de l'Editeur.   Prix: 4f. 50.   A Paris Chez Salomon, Rue Colbert, No. 2, à l'angle de la Rue Vivienne. . . .

Nine pages. Plate number S.4. Listed in the *Bibliographie de la France* on 24 April 1830.

[Paris, Bibliothèque Nationale.]

Six Petites Pièces Progressives

Six Petites Pièces Progressives servant de Leçons pour la connaissance des manches de la Harpolyre à ceux qui connaissent déjà celui de la Guitare par Ferdinand Sor Oeuvre 3.   Prix: 2f. 50.   A Paris Chez Salomon, Rue Colbert, No. 2, à l'angle de la Rue Vivienne. Propriété de l'Editeur. . . .

Five pages. Plate number 5.S. Listed in the *Bibliographie de la France* on 24 April 1830.

[Paris, Bibliothèque Nationale.]

Marche Funèbre

Marche Funèbre pour Harpolyre composée à la mort d'une bonne épouse et Dédiée à son Epoux par son ami Ferdinand Sor   Prix: 2fr.   A Paris Chez Salomon, Inventeur de la Harpolyre, Editeur et Professeur de Musique, Rue Colbert, No. 2, à l'angle de la Rue Vivienne. Propriété de l'Editeur. . . .

Three pages. No plate number. Listed in the *Bibliographie de la France* on 24 April 1830.

[Paris, Bibliothèque Nationale.]

Danse de Requejo

This arrangement for flute and piano of a tune associated with the Spanish dancer Requejo was published in Ledhuy's *Encyclopédie* in 1835; facsimile in my edition of Sor's *Seguidillas*.

La Romanesca

A short piece for violin and guitar. Paris, Bibliothèque Nationale, MS 12992. One folded leaf headed 'Juillet 1835' and 'Manuscrit de la main de Mr. F. Sor célèbre Guitariste'.

MUSIC FOR ORCHESTRA
(other than ballet music)

Two symphonies

According to Ledhuy's *Encyclopédie,* Sor composed two symphonies in Barcelona, c. 1802-4. No score is known to survive.

Violin concerto

Mr Abel Nagytothy-Toth, of Montreal, owns the manuscript of a concerto by Sor, apparently for violin and orchestra. Not seen.

Waltz

In *Three Waltzes (by different Authors)* for piano duet (q.v.), it is stated that the waltzes were originally composed for 'a Full Band' (which means an orchestra, not a band in the modern sense). One of the three waltzes is by Sor. Its original version has not been found.

CHAMBER MUSIC

Three string quartets

According to Ledhuy's *Encyclopédie,* Sor composed three string quartets in Barcelona, c. 1802-4. No score is known to survive.

Concertante for Spanish guitar and strings

This is the title of a work by Sor, in which he performed the guitar part at a concert of the Philharmonic Society in London on 24 March 1817. It was for guitar, violin, viola, and cello. It probably existed only in manuscript and no score is known to survive.

MUSIC FOR MILITARY BAND

March

Sor's March for piano duet (q.v.) is said to have been originally for 'la musique militaire', that is to say presumably a military band. The original version has not been found.

Funeral March

According to Ledhuy's *Encyclopédie,* while Sor was in Russia he composed a march for the funeral of Tsar Alexander in 1826. It was performed at the funeral by the musicians of the regiment of Preobrojenski. No score is known to survive.

BALLET MUSIC

La Foire de Smyrne

First produced in London in 1821. No score is known to survive.

Le Seigneur Généreux

First produced in London in 1821. No score is known to survive.

Cendrillon

First produced in London in 1822; Paris, 1823; Moscow, 1825.

MANUSCRIPT ORCHESTRAL SCORES:

1) Paris, Bibliothèque de l'Opéra. Score and parts. Shelf-mark A 469. 312 pages.

2) New York Public Library. 527 pages.

AUTOGRAPH MANUSCRIPT EXTRACTS:

Berlin, Deutsche Staatsbibliothek. No shelf-mark. Sixteen folios. Contains two quadrilles, the waltz, and a pas de deux from *Cendrillon*.

PIANO SCORE:

Cendrillon, A favorite Ballet in three Acts, as performed with unprecedented success at the King's Theatre; Composed & Arranged for the Piano Forte, and dedicated to The Most Honble. The Marquiss of Ailesbury, by Ferd: Sor. Ent. at Sta: Hall. Price 15s. London Published by the Royal Harmonic Institution. . . .

86 pages. Plate number 1120. Entered at Stationers' Hall on 2 December 1822.

[London, British Library; Oxford, Bodleian Library; Edinburgh, National Library of Scotland; Glasgow, University Library.]

ARRANGEMENT OF THE MARCH FOR GUITAR:

Marche du ballet de Cendrillon . . .

See above under 'Guitar music without opus number'.

VOCAL ARRANGEMENT OF THE WALTZ:

Valse du Ballet de Cendrillon . . . ('En ce moment parlez vous même').

See below under 'French songs'.

SELECTIONS FROM 'CENDRILLON':

1) Bochsa, *Selection of favourite Airs from Sor's celebrated Ballet of "Cendrillon."* Advertised in the *Harmonicon* in May 1823 as new music.

2) W. Etherington, *La Cendrillon, a Set of Quadrilles from the celebrated Ballet Arranged by W. Etherington.* Advertised in the *Harmonicon* in May 1824 as new music.

Alphonse et Léonore ou l'Amant Peintre (in one act)

First produced in London in 1823. No score is known to survive.

Two 'pas de danse'

Composed in Germany in 1823. No score is known to survive.

Alphonse et Léonore ou l'Amant Peintre (in three acts)

First produced in Moscow in 1824. A manuscript score bearing Sor's signature and possibly autograph is in Paris, Bibliothèque de l'Opéra, shelf-mark A 485a. 176 pages.

A pas de deux and a pas de trois

Composed in Russia, c. 1824. No score is known to survive.

Hercule et Omphale

First produced in Moscow in 1826.

FULL SCORE:

Paris, Bibliothèque de l'Opéra, shelf-mark 1011. Signed by Sor and possibly autograph. 468 pages.

OVERTURE:

A manuscript copy of the overture is missing from the Palacio Real, Madrid. It accompanied a letter which Sor wrote to Fernando VII, King of Spain. See 'Poetry and prose'.

Le Sicilien ou l'Amour Peintre

First produced in Paris in 1827; London, 1828. Music partly by Sor and partly by Schneitzhoeffer. Manuscript score and parts in Paris, Bibliothèque de l'Opéra, A.485.b. 516 pages.

Hassan et le Calife ou le Dormeur Eveillé

First produced in London in 1828. No score is known to survive.

The Fair Sicilian or the Conquered Coquette (= La belle Arsène)

First produced in London in 1834. No score is known to survive.

Arsène ou la Baguette Magique

Possibly a spurious work. No score is known to survive.

SACRED VOCAL MUSIC

Motet: 'O crux, ave spes unica'

O crux. Motet de l'hymne (Vexilla Regis) Par Ferdinand Sor.

For four unaccompanied voices. Published in Ledhuy's *Encyclopédie*.

Probably the same as 'un motet à quatre voix, avec orchestre' which, according to Ledhuy's *Encyclopédie,* Sor composed in Madrid c. 1804 for the church of La Merced, even though no orchestral parts are given in Ledhuy. Probably also the same as a motet in honour of the Holy Cross which is referred to in Sor's letter of c. 1828 to Fernando VII, King of Spain, and for which Sor received a Papal decoration.

Ave Maris Stella

Ave Maris Stella Tel qu'il était chanté à la Chapelle de la ferme nommée la Viña nueva par les enfants de choeur du Collège de Montserrat et tel qu'on le chante aussi à la Cathédrale de Barcelone pendant la huitaine de la fête de la Conception.

For four unaccompanied voices with sections for two voices. Published in Ledhuy's *Encyclopédie*.

Rosarios

According to Ledhuy's *Encyclopédie*, Sor composed four or five 'rosarios' in Barcelona, c. 1802-4. No score is known to survive.

Salve

According to Ledhuy's *Encyclopédie*, Sor composed a 'salve' in Barcelona, c. 1802-4. No score is known to survive.

Mass

According to Eusebio Font y Moresco, Sor composed a mass on the death of his daughter in 1837. In March 1839, according to a letter to the Queen of France, it was to be performed in a sacred concert. In June 1839 Sor played extracts from it on the piano to Font y Moresco and his companions. It is not known to survive.

OPERAS

Telemaco

FULL SCORE:

Montserrat, Arxiú de Música, MSS 659-60. 72 and 63 pages respectively. Both MSS are inscribed 'Copia de Magi Bosch'; I am told that Magi Bosch was a monk of Montserrat who made copies of manuscripts there before the destruction of Napoleon's time.

EXTRACTS:

Barcelona, Orfeó Catalá, II/305. 13 folios. Headed 'Telemaco Recit i Aria de Mentor — Aria Cavatina Ferran Sor.' Contains Cavatina 'Mia dolce speranza', Recitativo 'Qual terra é questa mai', and Aria 'Figlio, oh Dio!'.

ARRANGEMENTS FOR PIANO

See under 'Piano solos'.

Don Trastullo

According to Ledhuy's *Encyclopédie*, Sor began the composition of this opera in Madrid, c. 1800-1802, and worked on it further in Barcelona, c. 1802-1804. It was probably never finished and no score is known to survive.

TONADILLA

Las Preguntas de la Morante

This tonadilla was announced in the *Diario de Barcelona* on 2 February 1799. No score is known to survivie.

MELODRAMA

La Elvira Portuguesa

According to Ledhuy's *Encyclopédie*, Sor composed the music for this melodrama in Madrid in about 1804. No score is known to survive.

CATALAN SONG

'Draps i Ferro Vell'

FOR FOUR VOICES AND STRING ORCHESTRA:

Crits del carrer. Draps i Ferro Vell Cuarteto par F. Sors.

Barcelona, Orfeó Catalá, II/305. Manuscript full score and parts (3 violin I, 3 violin II, 2 viola, 3 cello and bass).

FOR FOUR VOICES AND PIANO:

Crits del Carrer. F. Sors.

Barcelona, Orfeó Catalá, II/305. Manuscript score.

FOR FOUR VOICES AND PIANO:

Draps y ferru vell. Cuarteto del S. Sors. arreglado para forte-piano. Canto. El S. D. José Sastre y Castells lo regala a la Escolanía de Montserrat. . . .

Montserrat, Arxiú de Música, MS 1786. Manuscript score and four voices parts. The above is the heading to the piano part; the other parts also have their own headings.

AN ARRANGEMENT FOR THREE VOICES AND ORCHESTRA:

Draps y ferro vell. El autor de esta pieza, el Sr. Sors célebre guitarrista. Arreglada a 3 veus i Orquesta per Blanch.

Montserrat, Arxiú de Música, MS 1786. Manuscript full score, three voice parts, and six instrumental parts (violin I, violin II, flute I, flute II, trombone, bass). The bass has its own title-page, which reads: Draps y ferro vell. Pieza propiamente llamada el cuarteto del S. Sors. Arreglada a tres voces y coro por D.B. Blanch en 1861.

'Serrafoll de Barcelona'

This is probably another name for 'Draps i Ferro Vell'.

SPANISH PATRIOTIC SONGS

Himno de la Victoria: 'Venid, vencedores'

FIRST EDITION:

Poesias Patrioticas de Dn. J.B. de Arriaza. "Unanimi densete catervas, et Regem vobis pugnâ defendite raptum." Virgilius. Reimpresas á solicitud de algunos Patriotas Españoles residentes en Londres. Londres. En la imprenta de T. Bensley, Bolt-Court, Fleet-Street. 1810.

[London, British Library; Madrid, Biblioteca Nacional (two copies).]

This printed book contains at the end a section of music with three songs for solo voice and piano, of which two are by Sor and one by B. Pérez. The first one by Sor is 'Venid, vencedores'. The music section bears at the bottom of the first page: 'London Printed by L. Lavenu No. 26 New Bond Street.' C. 8 cm. x 14 cm.

ANOTHER EDITION:

Poesias [as above] . . . en Londres. . . . México. En la imprenta de Don Manuel Antonio Valdes, Impresor de Cámara de S.M.

[Madrid, Biblioteca Nacional.]

A new edition of the preceding item, including the music section, which has been faithfully copied by hand even down to the words 'London Printed by L. Lavenu No. 26 New Bond Street.' No date.

MANUSCRIPT:

Paris, Bibliothèque Nationale, 4° Y 146 (no foliation). Five pages. Headed 'Segadilha Patriotica'. For two voices and piano, in duple time.

MANUSCRIPT:

Paris, Bibliothèque Nationale, Vm^7 4284, inscribed '1838 Malaga'. Headed 'Himno Patriotico. Los Versos de Arriaza y la Música de Sor'. Pp. 103-5. For three voices and piano. In triple time.

MANUSCRIPT:

London, collection of Robert Spencer, 'Clive' MS, two versions:
1) for voice and guitar, pp. 174-6. In duple time.
2) for voice and piano, pp. 277-80. In duple time.

Canción Cívica: Los Defensores de la Patria: 'Vivir en cadenas'

FIRST EDITION:

Poesias [as in preceding item] . . .

ANOTHER EDITION:

Poesias [as in preceding item) . . .

A VERSION FOR VOICE AND PIANO OR GUITAR:

No. 3 in:

Tres Canciones patrioticas Españolas Drey Original-Spanische Vaterlands Gesaenge mit Begleitung des Piano-Forte oder Guitarre. Wien, im Verlage der k: k: priv: chem: Druckerey am Graben no. 612.

One page. Plate number 2164. 1814? The title of the song is: 'Cancion de los Defensores de la Patria compuesta por Dno. F. Sor.' The voice and piano parts are in B flat, the guitar part in A. Triple time.

[London, collection of Robert Spencer.]

A VERSION FOR VOICE AND GUITAR:

"Vivir en cadenas quan triste es vivir" Spanish Song of the Defenders of their Fatherland with an accompaniment for The Guitar, Composed by Ferdinand Sor Ent. Sta. Hall. Price 1/6 London Published by Johanning & Co. . . . 6 John Street, Oxford Street.

Three pages. No plate number. The guitar part is the same as in the preceding item.

[Munich, Bayerische Staatsbibliothek, Mus. pr. 2° 2598.]

Published c. 1835?

MANUSCRIPT:

Paris, Bibliothèque Nationale, 4° Y 146 (no foliation). Five pages. Headed 'Segadilha Patriotica'. For two voices and piano, in triple time.

MANUSCRIPT:

Paris, Bibliothèque Nationale, Vm^7 4284, inscribed '1838 Malaga'. Headed 'Cancion Civica Compuesta el año de 1808 pr. Dn. Juan Bta. Arriaza y puesta en musica pr. D. Fdo. Sor'. Pp. 101-2. For three voices and piano. In triple time.

MANUSCRIPT:

Madrid, Biblioteca Musical del Ayuntamiento, MS 12 (no foliation). Two versions:
1) for three voices and piano. In duple time.
2) for three voices and piano. In triple time.

MANUSCRIPT:

London, collection of Robert Spencer, 'Clive' MS, two versions:
1) for voice and guitar, pp 182-3. In triple time.
2) for three voices and piano, pp. 322-4. In triple time.

Marche Patriotique Espagnole: 'Marchemos, marchemos'

Marche Patriotique Espagnole avec Accompagnement de Piano Paroles de M. N. . . . Musique de Mr. F. Sor. faite en 1809. N.B. cette Chanson doit être chanté [sic] par deux Ténors pour en entendre le véritable effet. A Paris A la Lyre Moderne Chez Mme. Benoist Editeurs [sic] de Musique et Mde. d'Instrumens Rue de Richelieu No. 20 Prix 1f. 50c.

Three pages. No plate number. Listed in the *Bibliographie de la France* on 20 August 1814. For two voices and piano.

[Paris, Bibliothèque Nationale, Vm^7 101190 (two copies, both signed 'F. Sor').]

Chanson relative aux événements d'Espagne: 'Adonde vas, Fernando incauto'

Chanson relative aux événements d'Espagne depuis le départ du Roi Ferdinand 7. jusqu'à la fin de l'an 1811 Paroles et Musique de Mr. Ferd. Sor l'an 1812. Imitation Française par Made. xxx Prix 1f. 50c. A Paris A la Lyre Moderne Chez Mme. Benoist Editeur Mde. de Musique et d'Instrumens Rue de Richelieu No. 20.

Three pages. No plate number. Published probably in 1814. For voice and piano or guitar.

[Paris, Bibliothèque Nationale, Vm^7 101188 (two copies, both signed 'F. Sor').]

'Fuentes son de llanto'

Probably spurious. See text for details.

SEGUIDILLAS AND BOLEROS

All Sor's known seguidillas and boleros are listed in full detail in my edition of the earliest of them: F. Sor, *Seguidillas* (London, Tecla Editions, 1976). The following list is therefore given in abbreviated form. Those marked * are in my edition.

*'Acuérdate, bien mío'

London, British Library, MS Egerton 3289, ff. 108 verso-109.

'Al mediator jugando'

London, collection of Robert Spencer, 'Clive' MS, pp. 101-3.

*'Cesa de atormentarme'

London, British Library, MS Egerton 3289, ff. 106 verso-107.

*'Cómo ha de resolverse'

London, British Library, MS Egerton 3289, ff. 110 verso-111.

'Cuantas naves se han visto'

Copenhagen, Royal Library, Rung Collection, MS 1065.

*'De amor en las prisiones'

London, British Library, MS Egerton 3289, ff. 107 verso-108.

'El amor siempre empieza'

A Musical Gem, ed. N. Mori and W. Batt, London, 1830, pp. 31-3. Copy: London, British Library. The English version is called 'The Warning' and begins 'Love that from flower to flower'.

*'El que quisiera amando'

London, collection of Robert Spencer, 'Clive' MS, pp. 93-5.

*'Las mujeres y cuerdas'

London, collection of Robert Spencer, 'Clive' MS, pp. 109-11.

'Lo que no quieras darme'

No. 3 in *Tres Seguidillas Boleras,* Paris, Meissonnier, c. 1828. Copy: London, British Library.

'Los canónigos, madre'

*1) London, collection of Robert Spencer, 'Clive' MS, pp. 89-91.
2) *Bolero à Société par Mr. Sor,* Paris (?), c. 1830 (?). Copy: Milan, Conservatorio di Musica.

'Me pregunta un amigo'

No. 2 in *Tres Seguidillas Boleras,* Paris, Meissonnier, c. 1828.

*'Mis descuidados ojos'

Bolero de Société, Paris, Mme Benoist, 1814.

'Morena de mis ojos'

London, collection of Robert Spencer, 'Clive' MS, pp. 105-7.

'Muchacha, y la vergüenza'

London, British Library, MS Egerton 3289, ff. 111 verso-112.

'No doblarán campanas'

London, collection of Robert Spencer, MS entitled 'Songs with Accompaniments for the Spanish Guitar': 'Boleras de Sor'.

'No quiero, no, que vengo'

Regalo Lirico, Paris, Pacini, c. 1830, p. 19. Copy: Cambridge, King's College Library.

'No tocarán campanas'

1) *Impromtu, dans le genre du Boléro,* London, Regent's Harmonic Institution, 1819. Copy: London, British Library.

2) *Bolero à Société par Mr. Sor,* Paris (?), c. 1830 (?). As second stanza of 'Los canonigos, madre' (q.v.).

'Pajarillo amoroso'

Cantos Españoles, ed. E. Ocón, Málaga, 1874, pp. 38-43. Copy: Madrid, Biblioteca Nacional.

'Prepárame la tumba'

London, British Library, MS Egerton 3289, ff. 109 verso-110.

'Puede una buena moza'

No. 1 in *Tres Seguidillas Boleras,* Paris, Meissonnier, c. 1828.

'Si a otro cuando me quieres'

London, collection of Robert Spencer, 'Clive' MS, pp. 97-99.

'Si dices que mis ojos'

London, British Library, MS Egerton 3288, ff. 88 verso-89.

'Si mis ojos te dicen'

Printed in Sor's article 'Le Bolero' in Ledhuy's *Encyclopédie* (Paris, 1835). Facsimile in my edition of Sor's *Seguidillas.*

'Sin duda que tus ojos'

Regalo Lirico, Paris, Pacini, c. 1830, pp. 52-3.

'Yo no sé lo que tiene'

Printed in Sor's article 'Le Bolero' in Ledhuy's *Encyclopédie* (Paris, 1835). Facsimile in my edition of Sor's *Seguidillas.*

'Yo sembré una mirada'

Cantos Españoles, ed. E. Ocón, Málaga, 1874, pp. 25-9.

'Yo soy el cocinero'

Regalo Lirico, Paris, Pacini, c. 1830, pp. 26-7.

OTHER SPANISH SONGS

'Las quejas de Maruja'

MANUSCRIPT:

Las Quejas de Maruja Cancion con acompañamiento de Piano y Guitarra Por D. Fernando Sor.

Five folios.

[Copenhagen, Royal Library, CI, 529.]

PRINTED EDITION:

Las quejas de Maruja. Cancion Con acompañamiento de Piano y Guitarra. Por D. Fernando Sor. Madrid. [Music follows.] Se hallara en el almacen de musica de Carrafa calle del Principe No. 5.

Plate number B. (1002) C. No separate title-page.

No copy has been found. The above details are taken from an illustration in J. Subirá's *Historia de la Música Española e Hispano-americana,* Barcelona, 1953, p. 670.

ANOTHER EDITION:

Las quejas de Maruja Cancion con acompañamiento de piano forte y guitarra por D.F. Sor. No. 6. Madrid. . . .

Three pages. Plate number A.R. [Antonio Romero, Madrid] 2243.

[London, collection of Robert Spencer, stamped 'Casa Dotesio Sociedad Anonima Bilbao'.]

'La Sal de España'

This is the title not of a song, but of a collection of six songs of which only one, 'Las quejas de Maruja', is by Sor.

CANTATA

Cantata

Cantata à S.E. la Signora Duchessa [at this point a part has been physically cut out; a modern hand has added 'd'Albufera'].

The above is the inscription on the outside of a bound manuscript in Barcelona, in the collection of M. Rocamora. The spine reads 'Cantata de Sor'. 58 unnumbered folios. The score is for soloists, four-part chorus, strings, and wind. If this is indeed the cantata that Sor wrote in Valencia, it dates from 1812 or 1813.

ITALIAN SONGS

Three Italian Arietts, 1st Set

FIRST EDITION:

Three Italian Ariets, with an Accompaniment for the Piano Forte, Composed & Dedicated to Miss C. Naldi, by F. Sor. [in an early hand is written on the Royal College of Music copy '1rst Set'] Ent. Sta. Hall [in the same hand: 4s.] London, Printed for the Author, by W. Milhouse, Military Instrument Maker to their R.H.s the Dukes of Kent & Cumberland, 337, Oxford Street.

Nine pages. No plate number. 1815-17.

[London, British Library, signed 'F. Sor'; London, Royal College of Music, signed 'F. Sor' and 'Elizabeth Windsor'.]

FRENCH EDITION:

'5e. Recueil. Dédié à Mme. [sic] Naldi' in the *Collection d'Airs Italiens* (see Three Italian Arietts, 3rd Set, below). Paris, Pacini, 1828 or before.

Three Italian Arietts: the wrongly so-called 'First' Set

Three Italian Arietts with an Accompaniment for the Piano Forte. Composed and Respectfully Dedicated to Miss A. Mori. by Ferdinand Sor. Ent. Sta. Hall First Set Price 5s/- London, Printed by the Royal Harmonic Institution . . .

Eleven pages. Plate number 802. Entered at Stationers' Hall on 2 July 1821. Not the genuine first set (for which see above), but in fact a later set published between the eighth and ninth sets of arietts.

[London, British Library; London, Royal College of Music; Oxford, Bodleian Library; Cambridge, University Library; Glasgow, University Library.]

Three Italian Arietts, 2nd Set

FIRST EDITION:

Three Italian Arietts, with an Accompaniment for the Piano Forte, Composed & Dedicated (with permission) To His Royal Highness The Duke of Sussex, by F. Sor. [in an early hand on the Royal College of Music copy is written '2 Set'] Entd. at Sta. Hall. Price 5s. London. Printed & Sold by Chappell & Co. . . . 124, New Bond Street.

Thirteen pages. Plate number 587. The plate number suggests late 1817 (Neighbour & Tyson). Reviewed in Ackermann's *Repository of Arts* on 1 January 1819.

[London, Royal College of Music, signed 'Elizabeth Windsor'; Brussels, Conservatoire, signed 'F. Sor'.]

FRENCH EDITION:

'3e. Recueil. Dédié à S.A.R. le Duc de Sussex' in the *Collection d'Airs Italiens* (see Three Italian Arietts, 3rd Set, below). Paris, Pacini, 1828 or before.

Three Italian Arietts, 3rd Set

FIRST EDITION:

Three Italian Arietts, with an Accompaniment for the Piano Forte, Composed & Dedicated to The Rt. Honble. The Lady Burghersh, by F. Sor. 3rd. Set. Entd. at Sta. Hall. Price 5s London, Printed & Sold by Chappell & Co. . . . 124, New Bond Street.

Seventeen pages. Plate number 596. The plate number suggests late 1817 (Neighbour & Tyson). Reviewed in Ackermann's *Repository of Arts* on 1 September 1818.

[London, Royal College of Music, signed 'Elizabeth Windsor'; Manchester, Henry Watson Music Library (not seen); title-page only in Barcelona, collection of M. Rocamora, inscribed 'To Mrs. Salmon with the author's best Compliments F. Sor'.]

FRENCH EDITION:

'1r. Recueil. Dédié à Lady Burgherst [sic]' in the *Collection d'Airs Italiens*, Paris, Pacini, 1828 or before. The title-page of this collection, designed to go with any one of the five sets, reads:

Collection d'Airs Italiens, Composés par Ferdinando Sor . . . A Paris, au Magasin de Musique de Pacini, Boulevard des Italiens, No. 11 . . .

Plate numbers 671-5.

[Paris, Bibliothèque Nationale, a set lacking pp. 7-8 of the 5e Recueil; Dublin, National Library of Ireland, Ariett 2 only of the 2e Recueil.]

Three Italian Arietts, 4th Set

FIRST EDITION:

Three Italian Arietts, with an Accompaniment for the Piano Forte, Composed & Dedicated to Mrs. Salmon, by F. Sor. 4th Set. Ent. at Sta. Hall. Price 5/- London, Printed & Sold by Chappell & Co. . . . 124 New Bond Street.

Thirteen pages. Plate number 787. The plate number suggests about September 1818 (Neighbour & Tyson). Reviewed in Ackermann's *Repository of Arts* on 1 April 1819.

[London, Royal College of Music, signed 'Elizabeth Windsor'.]

The second ariett (perhaps in the version of the MS listed below) may be that sung by Mrs. Salmon at the Philharmonic Society's concert on 11 May 1818.

FRENCH EDITION:

'4e Recueil. Dédié à Mr. [sic] Salmon' in the *Collection d'Airs Italiens* (see Three Italian Arietts, 3rd Set, above). Paris, Pacini, 1828 or before.

MANUSCRIPT:

The second ariett, with an added recitative beginning 'Oh stella', is in London, British Library, MS Add. 48,348, ff. 35-40 verso.

Three Italian Arietts, 5th Set

FIRST EDITION:

Three Italian Arietts, with an Accompaniment for the Piano Forte, Composed, & dedicated to his Friend J.B. Cramer, by F. Sor. Ent. Sta. Hall. Set. 5th. Price 5s/- London, Printed by the Regent's Harmonic Institution . . .

Twelve pages. Plate number 314. Entered at Stationers' Hall on 24 December 1819. Reviewed in Ackermann's *Repository of Arts* on 1 March and 1 April 1820.

[London, British Library; Oxford, Bodleian Library; Cambridge, University Library; Glasgow, University Library.]

A version of 'Un fanciullin tiranno' for three voices and piano is in *Three Canons* (see below).

Another issue:

The same title, except that the word 'Regent's' is replaced by 'Royal', showing that it must have been printed after the accession of George IV in 1820. Some errors are corrected.

[London, Royal College of Music, signed 'Elizabeth Windsor'; Manchester, Henry Watson Music Library (not seen).]

FRENCH EDITION:

'2e. Recueil. Dédié à son ami J.B. Cramer' in the *Collection d'Airs Italiens* (see Three Italian Arietts, 3rd Set, above). Paris, Pacini, 1828 or before.

GERMAN EDITION:

Ariette italiane coll accompagnamento di Piano-Forte composte da F. Sor. Lipsia, Presso C.F. Peters. Pr. 12gr.

Eleven pages. Oblong format. Plate number 1620. Listed in C.F. Whistling, *Handbuch der musikalischen Literatur*, Leipzig, 1828, p. 1098.

[Vienna, Gesellschaft der Musikfreunde.]

Three Italian Arietts, 6th Set

AUTOGRAPH MANUSCRIPT:

Three Italian Ariets with an acompaniement for the Pianoforte Composed and respectfully dedicated to Mrs. Leshmere Russell by F. Sor 6th. Set.

[London, Royal College of Music, MS 1111, ff. 102-6.]

The words 'F. Sor' in the title resemble Sor's known signature from this period and so suggest that the whole of this manuscript is autograph. Pencil marks on the manuscript show that this is the copy used by the printer (Chappell) for setting up the printed edition.

FIRST EDITION:

Three Italian Arietts, With an Accompaniment for the Piano Forte. Composed and Respectfully Dedicated to Mrs. Leshmere Russell, by F. Sor. Ent. at Sta. Hall. 6th. Set. Price 5/- London, Printed by Chappell & Co., 50 New Bond Street.

Eleven pages. Plate number 1522. Entered at Stationers' Hall on 7 June 1820. Reviewed in Ackermann's *Repository of Arts* on 1 December 1820.

[London, British Library; London, Royal College of Music, signed 'Elizabeth Windsor'; Oxford, Bodleian Library; Cambridge, University Library; Glasgow, University Library.]

The first part of the second ariett, 'Lagrime mie d'affanno', was published in a different setting, for voice and guitar, in Sor's *Méthode pour la Guitare*, ex. 83.

Three Italian Arietts, 7th Set

Three Italian Ariets, with an Accompaniment for the Piano Forte, Composed and Respectfully dedicated to The Right Honorable Marchioness of Anglesea, By F. Sor. 7th. Set. Ent. Sta. Hall. Price 5s/- London, Printed by the Royal Harmonic Institution . . .

Thirteen pages. Plate number 507. Entered at Stationers' Hall on 14 September 1820. Reviewed in Ackermann's *Repository of Arts* on 1 January 1821.

[London, British Library; London, Royal College of Music, signed 'Elizabeth Windsor'; Oxford, Bodleian Library; Cambridge, University Library; Glasgow, University Library.]

Three Italian Arietts, 8th Set

Three Italian Arietts with an Accompaniment, for the Piano Forte, Composed and Dedicated to His Friend, Mr. T. Welsh, by F. Sor. Ent. Sta. Hall. 8th. Set. Price 5s/- London, Printed by the Royal Harmonic Institution . . .

Thirteen pages. Plate number 536. Entered at Stationers' Hall on 20 November 1820.

[London, British Library; London, Royal College of Music, signed 'Elizabeth Windsor'; London, collection of Brian Jeffery; Oxford, Bodleian Library; Cambridge, University Library; Glasgow, University Library.]

Three Italian Arietts, 9th Set

Three Italian Arietts, with an Accompaniment, for the Piano Forte, Composed & Respectfully Dedicated to Madame Ronzi de Begnis, by Ferdinand Sor. Ent. Sta. Hall 9th. Set Price 5s/- London, Published by the Royal Harmonic Institution. . . .

Fifteen pages. Plate number 876. Entered at Stationers' Hall on 19th January 1822.

[London, British Library; London, Royal College of Music, lacking the last page; Oxford, Bodleian Library; Cambridge, University Library; Glasgow, University Library.]

Three Italian Arietts, 10th Set

Three Italian Arietts with an Accompaniment for the Piano Forte Composed and Dedicated to his Friend B. Livius Esqr. by Ferd. Sor. Ent Stat Hall. 10 Set Price 5s/- London Published by the Royal Harmonic Institution . . .

Fifteen pages. Plate number 901. Entered at Stationers' Hall on 19 January 1822.

[London, British Library, London, Royal College of Music; Oxford, Bodleian Library; Cambridge, University Library; Glasgow, University Library.]

Three Italian Duets [1st Set]

Three Italian Duetts, with an Accompaniment for the Piano Forte, Composed and Respectfully Dedicated to Her Excellence the Duchess of Frias, By Ferdinand Sor. Ent. Sta. Hall. Price 5/- London, Printed by the Royal Harmonic Institution . . .

Sixteen pages. Plate number 772. Entered at Stationers' Hall on 2 July 1821.

[London, British Library; London, Royal College of Music; Oxford, Bodleian Library; Cambridge, University Library; Glasgow, University Library.]

Three Italian Duets, 2nd Set

FIRST EDITION:

Three Italian Duetts, with an Accompaniment for the Piano Forte, Composed and Respectfully Dedicated to The Countess St. Antonio, By Ferd. Sor. Ent. Sta. Hall. 2nd. Set. Price 5/- London, Published by the Royal Harmonic Institution . . .

Twenty-one pages. Plate number 1051. Entered at Stationers' Hall on 8 June 1822.

[London, British Library; London, Royal College of Music; Oxford, Bodleian Library; Cambridge, University Library; Glasgow, University Library.]

GERMAN EDITION:

Tre Duetti coll accompagnamento di Piano-Forte composti da F. Sor. Lipsia, Presso C.F. Peters. Pr 20gr.

Twenty-three pages. Oblong format. Plate number 1737. Listed in the Intelligenzblatt of the *Allgemeine musikalische Zeitung*, Leipzig, 1823, as just published in September 1823.

[Berlin, Deutsche Staatsbibliothek; Copenhagen, Royal Library; Vienna, Gesellschaft der Musikfreunde.]

Three Canons

FIRST EDITION:

Three Canons, for Three Voices, With an Accompaniment for the Piano Forte, Composed & Dedd. to Mrs. Billington, by F. Sor. Ent. Sta. Hall Price 5s/- London, Pubd. for the Author, at Falkner's, Opera Music Warehouse, 3, Old Bond Str.

Fifteen pages. No plate number. 1815-18.

[London, British Library; London, Royal College of Music, signed 'F. Sor'; London, collection of Brian Jeffery, inscribed 'à Mlle. Bird de la part de l'auteur F. Sor']

The third canon, 'Un fanciullin tiranno', was published in a version for solo voice and piano in Three Italian Arietts, 5th Set.

ANOTHER EDITION:

The three canons were later published separately by Leader & Cock:

Piacer d'amore, Canone, a tre voci, Composto da F. Sor. Ent. Sta. Hall. Price 2s/- London, Published by Leader & Cock, 63, New Bond Street.

Seven pages. Plate number L & C 1280.

[London, British Library.]

The British Library copies of this and the next two items were received in 1851, and so they probably date from that year.

Sospiri volate . . . [as above]

Seven pages. Plate number L & C 1281.
[London, British Library.]

Un fanciullin tiranno . . . [as above]

Seven pages. Plate number L & C 1282.
[London, British Library.]

AN ARRANGEMENT OF 'SOSPIRI VOLATE':

Sospiri volate, Aria, Composta Da F. Sor. Ent. Sta. Hall. Price 1/6 London, Published by Leader & Cock, 63, New Bond Street.

Five pages. Plate number L & C 1816.

[London, British Library.]

Received by the British Library in 1853.

A version for solo voice and piano of the second of the Three Canons. Most probably merely a mid-century arrangement from that work, but just possibly an original version by Sor from some manuscript or publication now disappeared.

AN ARRANGEMENT OF 'PIACER D'AMORE':

Fair Summer Morning. Canon for three voices. 'Piacer d'Amore', transposed to the key of F, and set to English words by M.A. Sidebotham. Composed by F. Sor. London, Novello [1907]. Novello's School Songs, no. 860.

[London, British Library.]

'Lei si cinga d'una spada'

"Lei si cinga d'una spada", from the Opera of Le

Bizzarria [sic] dell amore, Composed by S. Mayer, Written from Memory, with an Accompaniment for the Piano Forte, Dedicated to The Honble. Miss Greville, by Ferdinand Sor. Ent. Sta. Hall. Price 5s/- London, Printed by the Royal Harmonic Institution . . .

Twenty-two pages. Plate number 592. Entered at Stationers' Hall on 1 March 1821.

[Cambridge, University Library; Glasgow, University Library.]

An arrangement from S. Mayer's opera. For three voices and piano.

'Non piu, non piu lusinghe'

"Non piu, non piu lusinghe", A Duett, from the Opera of Le Astuzzie Feminili, Composed by D. Cimarosa, Written from Memory, with an Accompaniment for the Piano Forte, by Ferdinand Sor. Ent. Sta. Hall. Price 3/6 London, Published by the Royal Harmonic Institution . . .

Thirteen pages. Plate number 1259. The plate number suggests early 1823 (Neighbour & Tyson).

[Glasgow, University Library.]

An arrangement from Cimarosa's opera. For two voices and piano.

'Vedrai carino'

Mozart's favorite Air Vedrai Carino, with an Accompaniment for the Guitar, Arranged & Dedicated to The Honble. Miss Upton, by F. Sor. Ent. at Sta. Hall. Price 1/6. London, Printed & Sold by Chappell & Co. . . . 50, New Bond Street.

Three pages. Plate number 1018. No separate title-page; the above is the heading to the music. The plate number suggests January 1820 (Neighbour & Tyson).

[London, collection of Robert Spencer.]

This is one of three arias from Mozart's *Don Giovanni* which Sor arranged for voice and guitar. All three are advertised in a catalogue printed on the back of a copy of P. Verini's 'On yonder rock reclining' in the National Library of Scotland, Edinburgh, Mus. Vol. 28.2. The other two are:

'Batti, batti'

Mozart's favorite Air, Batti, batti O, bel Masetto, with an Accompaniment for the Guitar, Arranged & Dedicated to Mrs. George Edwards, by F. Sor. Ent. at Sta. Hall. Price 1/6. London, Printed & Sold by Chappell & Co. . . . 50, New Bond Street.

Four pages. Plate number 1049. No separate title-page; the above is the heading to the music. The plate number suggests January 1820 (Neighbour & Tyson).

[London, Guildhall School of Music.]

'Deh vieni alla finestra'

No copy found.

ENGLISH SONGS

'Farewell, for on Oviedo's towers'

Farewell [for on] Oviedo's Towers, Sung by Miss Kelly, at the Theatre Royal English Opera House in the new Operatic Drama of Gil Blas, Composed & arranged for the Piano Forte, by F. Sor. Ent. Sta. Hall. Price 2s/- London, Printed for Ware & Evans, 146, Strand.

Five pages. No plate number. Entered at Stationers' Hall on 21 August 1822.

[London, British Library; Oxford, Bodleian Library; Cambridge, University Library; Glasgow, University Library.]

The title-page omits the words 'for on', present in the first line of the song itself.

'Should a pretty Spanish lass'

Should a pretty Spanish Lass, A much Admired Spanish Air, Sung by Miss Kelly, In the New Operatic Drama of Gil Blas, at the Theatre Royal, English Opera House, Composed & Arranged for the Piano Forte, By F. Sor. Ent. Sta. Hall. Price 1/6 London, Published by Ware & Evans, 146, Strand.

Four pages. No plate number. Entered at Stationers' Hall on 27 August 1822.

[London, British Library; Oxford, Bodleian Library; Cambridge, University Library; Glasgow, University Library.]

'Love that from flower to flower'

This is a parallel English translation to Sor's Spanish song 'El amor siempre empieza' (q.v.).

FRENCH SONGS

'Marchons comme à la fête de l'immortalité'

This is a parallel French translation to Sor's Spanish song 'Marchemos, marchemos' (q.v.).

'Las, où vas tu, crédule Ferdinand'

This is a parallel French translation to Sor's Spanish patriotic song 'Adonde vas, Fernando incauto' (q.v.).

'En ce moment parlez vous même'

EDITION FOR VOICE AND PIANO OR HARP:

Valse du Ballet de Cendrillon, Avec Accompagnement de Piano ou Harpe, Musique de F. Sor. Prix: 1f. 50c. A Paris, Au Magasin de Musique de A. Meissonnier, Boulevard Montmartre, No. 25.

Two pages. No plate number.

[Paris, Bibliothèque Nationale.]

At the bottom of the first page is 'Troubadour des Salons, 12e. Liv[rais]on', and this is the IIIe Année. According to the *Bibliographie de la France,* the third year of the *Troubadour des Salons* was 1826, so this edition may be dated December 1826.

A vocal arrangement of the waltz from Sor's ballet *Cendrillon.*

EDITION FOR VOICE AND GUITAR:

Valse du ballet de Cendrillon. Musique de F. Sor.

Two pages. No plate number. C. 1830?

[No. 36 in a volume of miscellaneous pieces bound together in the collection of Robert Spencer, London.]

'O vous que Mars rend invincible'

EDITION FOR VOICE AND PIANO:

O vous que Mars rend invincible. Romance chantée dans Les Trois Sultanes, Par Melle. Nadeje Fusil, Orpheline de Wilna. Mise en Musique avec Accompt. de Piano, Par F: Sor. Prix: 1f. 50c. A Paris, Au Magasin de Musique de A. Meissonnier, Boulevard Montmartre No. 25.

Three pages. No plate number.

[Paris, Bibliothèque Nationale.]

At the bottom of the first page is 'Troubadour des Salons, 10e. Liv[rais]on', and this is the IVe Année. According to the *Bibliographie de la France,* the fourth year of the *Troubadour des Salons* was 1827, so this edition may be dated October 1827.

EDITION FOR VOICE AND GUITAR:

O vous que Mars rend invincible. Romance, Chantée dans les Trois Sultanes, Par Melle. Nadeje Fusil. Orpheline de Wilna. Mise en Musique avec Accompt. de Guitare, Par F: Sor. Prix: 75c. A Paris, Au Magasin de Musique de A. Meissonnier, Boulevard Montmartre No. 25.

Two pages. No plate number.

[London, collection of Robert Spencer.]

Bears the same indication as the edition for voice and piano, and so may also be dated October 1827.

ANOTHER EDITION FOR VOICE AND GUITAR:

O vous que Mars rend invincible, Romance, Chantée dans les trois Sultanes, mise en musique avec accompt. pr. F. Sor.

Two pages. No plate number. C. 1830?

[No. 28 in a volume of miscellaneous pieces bound together in the collection of Robert Spencer, London.]

'Il reviendra'

Il reviendra Romance Paroles de Mr. Aristide Tarry Mises en Musique avec Accompagnement de Guitare, par F. Sor. Prix: 1f. A Paris, Au Magasin de Musique de A. Meissonnier, Boulevard Montmartre No. 25. No. 470.

Two pages. No plate number. Not before 1825, when Meissonnier moved to 25 Boulevard Montmartre, and probably not after 1828, when Sor changed from Meissonnier to Pacini.

[Barcelona, collection of M. Rocamora.]

Le Dernier Cri des Grecs:
'Marchons, amis, avançons en silence'

FIRST EDITION:

Le Dernier Cri des Grecs Marche nocturne avec accompagnement de Piano, Paroles de M.E. de Tarade Musique de Ferdinand Sor Propriété de l'Auteur. Prix 2f. 50c. A Paris, Chez l'Auteur, Place des Italiens, Hôtel Favart Et chez Pacini, Boulevard des Italiens . . .

Five pages. No plate number. Published within the period 1827-29.

[Paris, Bibliothèque Nationale (two copies).]

ANOTHER EDITION:

Le Dernier Cri des Grecs. Paroles de Mr. E. de Tarade. Musique de Ferdinand Sor.

Published in Ledhuy's *Encyclopédie* (Paris, 1835). First stanza only.

'Le Souvenir'

FIRST EDITION: FOR TWO VOICES AND PIANO

Le Souvenir. Nocturne à deux voix. avec accompagnement de Piano. Paroles de M.E. de Tarade. Musique de Ferdinand Sor. Propriété de l'auteur. Prix 3f. A Paris au Magasin de Musique de Pacini Editeur des Opéra de Rossini Boulevard des Italiens No. 11.

Five pages. Plate number 2677. About 1830.

[Milan, Conservatorio, signed 'Sor'.]

ANOTHER EDITION: FOR SOLO VOICE AND PIANO

Le Souvenir. Paroles d'Emile de Tarade. Musique de Ferdinand Sor.

[Paris, Bibliothèque Nationale.]

No. 3 in an untitled printed collection of six songs, the other five being by Tarade. The Bibliothèque Nationale copy is stamped '1871', which late though it is it may still be the date of publication. The song bears the heading 'Je [i.e., Tarade] fais graver cette pièce comme un hommage rendu à la Mémoire de mon cher Professeur et ami'.

'Loin de tes yeux'

Loin de tes yeux Romance avec accompagnement de Piano Paroles de M. E. de Tarade, Musique de Ferdinand Sor Prix 2Fs. à Paris, chez Savaresse Sarra, Editeur de Musique, Galerie du Perron, No. 96.

Three pages. No plate number. Before 1835, by which time Savaresse Sarra had been taken over by Meissonnier (Hopkinson).

[Brussels, Conservatoire.]

POETRY AND PROSE

'Adonde vas, Fernando incauto'

A poem written by Sor and set to music by him in 1812. See 'Spanish patriotic songs'.

A letter to the Duc de Fleury

Paris, 14 January 1815.

[Missing from the Bibliothèque Nationale, Paris.]

A manuscript treatise on singing

Not found. According to P.J. Bone, *The Guitar and Mandolin,* London, 1954, p. 342, this was at one time in the collection of Madame Sidney Pratten in London. If it existed, it was written in French and was probably written in London.

A letter to an unnamed dedicatee

London, 26 Charlotte Street, 13 February 1822.

[Laguna Beach, California, collection of Mary Belle Swingle.]

A letter to Albert Decombe

No address or date, but evidently from Moscow, about December 1824.

[Paris, Bibliothèque Nationale.]

A letter to Fernando VII, King of Spain

No address or date, but evidently from Paris, c. 1828.

[Missing from the Palacio Real, Madrid.]

Méthode pour la Guitare

PROSPECTUS:

No copy found, but listed in the *Bibliographie de la France* on 24 May 1828 as follows:

Nouvelle Méthode de Guitare. Par Ferdinand Sor. (Prospectus.) In-4° d'un quart de feuille. Imprim. de Conian, à Paris. — A Paris, chez l'auteur, place des Italiens, hôtel Favart.

L'ouvrage paraîtra en une seule livraison de deux cahiers, l'un de texte, l'autre de lithographies et musique. Le prix sera de 30-0. Pour les souscripteurs 15-0. La souscription sera fermée le premier juillet.

METHOD:

Méthode pour la Guitare, par Ferdinand Sor. Prix: 36 francs. Propriété des Editeurs, A Paris, l'Auteur, rue de Marivaux, no. 5; A Bonn, N. Simrok; A Londres [here is a blank, filled in in the Madrid copy 'Johaning et Wathmore' (sic)]. On la trouve aussi à Paris chez les principaux marchands de musique. 1830. . . .

88 pages of text and 50 pages of music and diagrams.

[Madrid, Biblioteca Nacional, inscribed 'Présenté par l'auteur à son Excellent ami D. Aguado'; Barcelona, Orfeó Catalá; Paris, Bibliothèque Nationale, lacking the music and diagrams.]

PARALLEL FRENCH AND GERMAN EDITION:

Méthode pour la Guitare Guitarre-Schule von Ferdind. Sor. . . . Bonn bei N. Simrock. Paris bei dem Verfasser. Eigenthum der Verleger.

Plate number 2810. Out by June 1831.

[Copenhagen, Royal Library.]

ENGLISH TRANSLATION:

Method for the Spanish Guitar, by Ferdinand Sor. Translated from the original by A. Merrick. London: R. Cocks & Co., 20, Princes-Street, Hanover-Square.

Plate number 1182. Published in 1832.

[Madrid, Biblioteca Nacional; London, collection of Robert Spencer; London, Guildhall School of Music (music pages only).]

A modern facsimile edition of this translation has been published by Da Capo, New York.

NAPOLEON COSTE'S VERSION:

Méthode complète pour la Guitare par Ferdinand Sor, rédigée et augmentée de nombreux exemples et leçons, suivis d'une notice sur la 7e corde par N. Coste. . . . Publiée à Paris, par Schonenberger, Boulevt. Poissonnière, 28 . . .

Published about 1845. Plate number 1726.

[London, British Library; London, collection of Robert Spencer; Copenhagen, Royal Library (two copies).]

A SPANISH TRANSLATION OF NAPOLEON COSTE'S VERSION:

Metodo completo para guitarra por Ferdinand Sor Redactado y aumentado . . . por N. Coste Traducido por Tamaris. Paris, Schonenberger . . .

[Barcelona, Biblioteca Central.]

There exist at least two modern editions of this Spanish translation.

FRANK MOTT HARRISON'S VERSION:

Method for the Guitar by Ferdinando Sor (Originally translated from the Spanish by A. Merrick). Condensed, Re-written, and Edited, by Frank Mott Harrison. London, Cocks & Co.

[London, British Library; Cambridge, University Library.]

Received by the British Library in 1896.

Merrick's translation was, of course, made from the French, not from the Spanish.

A treatise entitled 'De l'harmonie appliquée à la Guitare'

Mentioned as a project on page 62 of Sor's *Méthode*. There is no evidence that it was ever written.

A letter to 'M. Stephan'

No address or date, but evidently written in Paris, and the contents refer to a concert which may be that of April 1831.

[Paris, Bibliothèque Nationale.]

The article 'Sor' in Ledhuy's 'Encyclopédie', Paris, 1835

Although written in the third person, it is most likely that Sor wrote this. Published in facsimile at the end of the present book.

The article 'Le Bolero' in Ledhuy's 'Encyclopédie', Paris, 1835

Published in facsimile in my edition of Sor's *Seguidillas,* London, Tecla Editions, 1976.

Memoirs

The article 'Sor' in Ledhuy's *Encyclopédie* contains a long passage, written in the first person and printed in quotation marks, which is there said to be an extract from Sor's memoirs. No more than this one extract is known to exist.

A letter to the Queen of France

Paris, 36 Marché St. Honoré 21 March 1839.

[Paris, Bibliothèque Nationale.]

Sor invites the Queen to take tickets for a concert performance of his Mass. The Queen did take five tickets, and the Bibliothèque Nationale also owns a receipt for the sum paid by her.

DOUBTFUL AND SPURIOUS WORKS

Divertissement

Published in Fernando Sor: *19 Composiciones,* edited by Isaias Savio, Buenos Aires, n.d. [c. 1954], no. 2. No source is given and I have not found this piece elsewhere. For solo guitar.

Prelude and Sarabande; and Seventeenth-Century Suite

Two publications issued by Clifford Essex in London in 1956. For solo guitar. The Prelude is in fact by Coste; the Sarabanda by de Visée; and there is no evidence to connect the suite with Sor.

'Bolero a duo'

Listed by Domingo Prat in his *Diccionario de Guitarristas* (Buenos Aires, no date [c. 1936], p. 302. Probably authentic, to judge from the quotation which Prat gives from his copy: 'se hallará en el despacho de música de la calle del Turco, con un completo surtido de música vocal e instrumental Nacional y Extranjera'. Perhaps for two voices and guitar or piano.

Tema con variaciones

For solo guitar. Published by Union Musical Española, Madrid, no date [c. 1920]. Plate number A.R. 2329. Dedicated to 'Don Manuel Ibargoitia'.

Andante con variaciones

For solo guitar. Published by Union Musical Española, Madrid, no date [c. 1920]. Plate number A.R. 2328.

Guitar concerto

This name has been applied to two separate works:

a) Concertante for Spanish guitar and strings. This work, of which no copy has been found, was not a concerto but a chamber work. See under 'Chamber Music' above.

b) A concerto of which Mr Abel Nagytothy-Toth of Montreal, Canada, owns a manuscript. This appears to be a violin concerto and not a guitar concerto. See 'Music for Orchestra' above.

PORTRAITS

A painting or drawing by Innocent-Louis Goubaud

The two lithographs listed below bear the words 'Goubeau pinxit' and 'Drawn by J. Goubaud' respectively. An original painting or drawing by Goubaud, on which these two lithographs were based, presumably once existed but has not been found.

A lithograph

This lithograph in an oval frame shows Sor with a guitar with six separate strings. It bears the words 'Goubeau pinxit. Lith. de Engelmann. Lithoé par Bordes.' It is reproduced in the present book.

[Paris, Bibliothèque Nationale, Cabinet des Estampes; London, British Library, Department of Prints and Drawings; London, collection of Brian Jeffery (by the generous gift of Mme André Verdier, Paris).]

Another lithograph

Again in an oval frame, this once more shows Sor with a guitar, but here the strings of the guitar are not separate but schematized. It bears the words 'Drawn by J. Goubaud Engraved by M.N. Bate.' Reproduced in the present book.

[Paris, Bibliothèque Nationale, Cabinet des Estampes.]

A drawing by Hippolyte-Benjamin Adam

Published in Ledhuy's *Encyclopédie* (Paris, 1835) and reproduced at the end of the present book.

Another portrait (?)

A picture said to be of Sor is reproduced in the *Enciclopedia Universal Ilustrada Europeo-Americana* (Madrid, Espasa-Calpe, 1927), article 'Sor', and in *El Mundo de la Música* (Madrid, Espasa-Calpe, 1962). This picture, for which no authority is known, is of doubtful authenticity.

Bochsa's selection from 'Cendrillon'

See under 'Ballet music'.

W. Etherington's selection from 'Cendrillon'

See under 'Ballet music'.

Adolphe Ledhuy's 'Etude'

Etude pour la Guitare (à son ami F. Sor)

Printed in Ledhuy's *Encyclopédie*, 47th Livraison.

Caroline Molique's 'Melody'

Melody on a study by F. Sor

For violin and piano. One of *Twelve Pieces*, London, Novello, c. 1910. The piano part = Sor's op. 6, no. 1; the violin part is new.

Miguel Llobet's 'Variaciones'

Variaciones sobre un tema de Sor Op. 15

Madrid, Union Musical Española, c. 1964. Plate number 20379.

Based on Sor's *Folies d'Espagne*, op. 15. Llobet's work begins with Sor's theme and the first two variations; then Llobet adds four more variations, an intermezzo, followed by four more variations.

Daniel Fortea's 'Homenaje a Sor'

Homenaje a Sor Op. 46

Madrid, Biblioteca Fortea, 1945. Plate number 595.

Composed in 1939. With a preface by Emilio Pujol.

WORKS DEDICATED TO OR INSPIRED BY SOR

P. Verini's 'Rudiments'

Rudiments for the Spanish Guitar Composed and Respectfully Dedicated to Mr. F. Sor.

[London, Guildhall School of Music; London, collection of Robert Spencer.]

INDEX

WORKS OF FERNANDO SOR

GUITAR MUSIC WITH OPUS NUMBER:

Opus 1, 62, 68-70, 80, 148
Opus 2, 45, 62, 66, 68-70, 80, 148
Opus 3, 36, 38, 68-71, 80, 149
Opus 4, 36-38, 41, 62, 68-70, 80, 149
Opus 5, 36, 41, 44, 68-70, 80, 150
Opus 6, 49, 62, 68-71, 80, 101, 150, 168
Opus 7, 36-38, 41, 44, 65, 68-70, 80, 151
Opus 8, 63, 68-70, 80, 151
Opus 9, 41, 45, 53, 64, 66, 68, 69-72, 80-81, 87, 89, 94, 103, 106, 152
Opus 10, 68-71, 80, 152
Opus 11, 36-37, 41, 68-71, 80, 152-153
Opus 12, 36, 38, 50, 68-71, 80, 153
Opus 13, 64, 66, 68-70, 80, 153
Opus 14, 36-38, 68-69, 71, 80, 154
Opus 15 (a) (Folies d'Espagne and Minuet), 36-37, 41, 68-69, 80, 154, 185
Opus 15 (b) (Sonata), 36-38, 68-69, 80, 154-155
Opus 15 (c) (Thème Varié), 68-71, 80, 155
Opus 16, 41, 80, 87, 155
Opus 17, 80, 87, 155-156
Opus 18, 80, 87, 156
Opus 19, 68, 72, 80, 87, 93, 156
Opus 20, 36, 38, 70, 80, 87, 156
Opus 21, 52, 80, 87, 157
Opus 22, 18, 21, 36-38, 80, 87, 157
Opus 23, 36-37, 69, 80, 87, 93, 157
Opus 24, 69, 80, 87, 89, 157-158
Opus 25, 38, 69, 80, 87, 89, 95, 158
Opus 26, 69, 80, 87, 89, 158
Opus 27, 69, 80, 87, 89, 158
Opus 28, 69, 80, 87, 89, 158-159
Opus 29, 69, 80, 87, 89, 101, 159, 168
Opus 30, 80, 89, 93-95, 105-106, 108, 159

Opus 31, 80, 89, 93-95, 101, 159
Opus 32, 80, 93-95, 159-160
Opus 33, 69, 80, 93, 95, 160
Opus 34, 95-97, 160
Opus 35, 68, 80, 89, 93-94, 101, 160
Opus 36, 80, 89, 93-96, 161
Opus 37, 89, 93-94, 161
Opus 38, 96-97, 161
Opus 39, 96-97, 161-162
Opus 40, 96-97, 161-162
Opus 41, 95, 97, 106, 108, 162
Opus 42, 96, 162
Opus 43, 96, 162
Opus 44, 90, 94, 101, 162-163
Opus 44 bis, 96-97, 163
Opus 45, 96, 163
Opus 46, 96, 163
Opus 47, 96, 163-164
Opus 48, 93, 96, 164
Opus 49, 96-97, 164
Opus 50, 164
Opus 51, 96, 164
Opus 52, 90, 96, 106, 164
Opus 53, 96-97, 165
Opus 54, 90, 94-95, 165
Opus 54 bis, 93, 96-96, 165
Opus 55, 96-97, 165
Opus 56, 93, 96, 109, 165-166
Opus 57, 96, 166
Opus 58, 166
Opus 59, 94-95, 108, 166
Opus 60, 101, 166
Opus 61, 90, 94, 96-97, 166-167
Opus 62, 90, 94, 96-97, 167
Opus 63, 86-87, 93, 96-97, 109, 167

Street sign, Barcelona